Introduction to the Counseling Profession

Second Edition

Introduction to the Counseling Profession

Duane Brown
University of North Carolina at Chapel Hill

David J. Srebalus
West Virginia University

Allyn and Bacon
Boston • London • Toronto • Sydney • Tokyo • Singapore

To Cassandra, Kindra, Jeffrey, and Tamara Brown
John and Cathy Srebalus

Series Editor: Ray Short
Editorial Assistant: Christine Shaw
Senior Marketing Manager: Kathy Hunter
Editorial-Production Administrator: Donna Simons
Editorial-Production Service: Shepherd, Inc.
Composition and Prepress Buyer: Linda Cox
Manufacturing Buyer: Megan Cochran
Cover Administrator: Suzanne Harbison

Copyright © 1996, 1988 by Allyn & Bacon
A Simon & Schuster Company
Needham Heights, MA 02194

Library of Congress Cataloging-in-Publication Data

Brown, Duane.
  Introduction to the counseling profession / Duane Brown, David J.
Srebalus.—2nd ed.
      p.   cm.
  Includes bibliographical references and index.
  ISBN 0–205–16204–5
  1. Counseling.   2. Counseling—Practice.   I. Srebalus, David J.
II. Title.
BF637.C6B745   1996
158'.3—dc20   95–33253
                                                                   CIP

Printed in the United States of America

10 9 8 7 6 5 4 3 2 1   00 99 98 97 96 95

Contents

Preface

This edition, like the first, is aimed at introducing students to the largest of the mental health groups, the counseling profession. Since the publication of the first edition, the rapid movement of counselors toward professionalization has continued unabated. For example, forty-one states now have some form of credentialing legislation for counselors and that number may increase before this volume wends its way through the publication process. The increase in credentialing legislation and other exciting events that are shaping the counseling profession are chronicled in this edition.

Many features of the first edition have been updated and retained in this edition. The history of the counseling profession as well as current legal, professional, and ethical issues are all discussed in detail, as they were in the first edition. The section on counseling program accreditation has also been retained and has been updated to reflect current practice in this area. Every effort has been made to show how credentialing and program accreditation in particular are pivotal in the professionalization process. The chapters on normal development, counseling theory and process, career counseling, cross-cultural counseling, assessment, consultation, and counseling in educational and mental health settings have all been retained and updated. Important changes in chapters that were in the first edition include a discussion of transpersonal and cognitive counseling theory in Chapter 3, and a discussion of the new certification specialities offered by the National Board of Certified Counselors in Chapter 13.

However, there are some important changes in this edition. For example, an entire chapter on group counseling and group interventions has been included in this volume (Chapter 5). This chapter looks beyond the traditional small group emphasis to large group interventions, and provides the reader with insights into both large and small group interventions. Another chapter that has been added deals with three counseling specialities: couples and family counseling, gerontological counseling, and substance abuse counseling (Chapter 8). The reader will be provided with interesting insights into what makes these specialities unique, as well as the reasons why there is a demand for counselors in these areas.

The final chapter (Chapter 18), as did the first chapter, addresses the issues confronting counselors. Some of these issues have remained the same, some old issues have been resolved, and some new issues have arisen since the publication of the first edition. The result of the changes in this edition is a cutting edge publication that will inform and excite readers who have committed to becoming counselors and those considering it.

D.B.
D.J.S.

Chapter 1

Counseling and Counselors: An Overview

Goals of the Chapter

The primary goal of this chapter is to present a historical as well as a current view of how the counseling profession strives to serve society. A secondary goal of the chapter is to prognosticate about the future of the profession.

Chapter Preview

- The history of the counseling profession will be presented.
- The mental health needs of our society will be discussed.
- Counselors' roles in meeting current mental health problems will be identified.
- An assessment of the current status of the profession will be made.

Introduction

This book is about the counseling profession. The discussions herein will range broadly, focusing variously upon the history, future, strengths, limitations, theories, and techniques of the profession. For the most part, the theories and techniques are shared with other professions, namely psychology and social work. To some degree, counseling is historically linked to psychology as well.

In this first chapter the history of the profession will be outlined. This will be followed by a discussion of the mental health needs of our society and how counselors are particularly well positioned to address many of these needs. Finally, the current status of the counseling profession will be addressed, with attention given to both its strengths and its limitations.

History of the Counseling Profession

Pre-Twentieth Century

Because of the diversity within the counseling profession, it is impossible to identify a definite historical point at which the profession began. Some (e.g., Gibson & Mitchell, 1995) attempt to link the work of Plato and Aristotle to the origins of the profession because of their early insights regarding the functioning of the individual. Earlier Belkin (1975) placed the origins of the profession in this period, drawing specifically from the work of Plato. It is unquestionably the case that Plato, Aristotle, and a number of other early Western philosophers addressed the matter of how individuals learn and develop and, in some instances, attempted to generalize their thinking to practical processes such as teaching and counseling. Their philosophy can still be found in the fabric of the profession.

While the roots of counseling can be tenuously tied to philosophers in early Greece, a more definite historical linkage can be made to Europe and the middle ages. Zytowski (1972) identified a number of books devoted to specific occupations aimed at helping people make career choices. The earliest of these seems to have been *The Mirror of Men's Lives*, authored by a bishop of the Roman Catholic Church, Rodrigo Sanches, which describes occupations within the church and crafts careers in fifteenthth-century Europe. This book, according to Zytowski, appeared in illustrated form in 1472 and had German, French, and Spanish editions over its 125-year life span. During the decades that followed, a number of other books were published that were the forerunners of much of today's thinking. Included among these are Juan Huartis' *The Examination of Men's Wits* (1575), which expounded upon Plato's beliefs that people differ in their abilities; and Powell's *Tom of All Trades* (1631) and Pathway to Preferment (1631), which are analogous to current books that detail occupational information. Ten such books were published during the 1700s, including an anonymously authored work called *A General Description of all Trades* (1747). Zytowski (1972) reports that this trend of publishing books regarding careers accelerated in the nineteenth century, when at least 65 were published. A number of these volumes were published in the United States.

The early American guides to occupations, including *A Treatise of the Vocations* by William Perkins (1603), and *The Parents and Guardians Directory* and the *Youth's Guide in the Choice of a Profession or Trade* by Joseph Collyer (1761), emphasize the work ethic and the importance of moral training. Also, in keeping with the Puritan emphasis of the time, the uniqueness of the individual was emphasized in these early works (Picchioni & Bonk, 1983). Picchioni and Bonk trace how this emphasis upon the individual plus the Puritan belief in self-discipline through work and education combined with laissez-faire economics (individual enterprise) to form a philosophy of individualism—a philosophy that still pervades the counseling profession.

The nineteenth century was particularly influential in the historical development of the profession, partly because of the growing emphasis on career guidance. However, there were forces outside the field that were to have great impact later. Wilhelm Wundt established the first psychological laboratory in Germany in 1879. In 1883 G. Stanley Hall started the first psychology laboratory devoted to the study of children. These two laboratories would provide the impetus for scientific psychology in the United States. Also, in 1890 a little-known physician, Sigmund Freud, began the treatment of mental patients with an unknown technique, psychoanalysis, which along with Pavlovian psychology in Russia and Gestalt psychology in Germany would provide the impetus for many current theories of human behavior.

The pre–Civil War period in America was characterized by rapid industrial expansion in the North and a flourishing agriculturally based economy in the South. The Civil War accelerated the industrial movement, specialization in the work force, and awareness of the need for vocational education and guidance (Picchioni & Bonk, 1983). In 1881 Salmon Richards published what may have been the first true call for counselors. In his book *Vocophy,* he called for vocophers who could provide vocational assistance to those in need to be located in every town. Brewer (1942) stopped short of giving credit to Richards for founding the vocational guidance movement. However, Picchioni and Bonk recognize him as the first individual to call for a counseling profession.

The Early Twentieth Century

Not surprisingly, given the rapid industrialization at the turn of the century, programs aimed at providing career guidance were springing to life, primarily in public school settings. Brewer (1942) reports that the first vocational guidance program began in Cogswell High School, San Francisco, in 1888. This program included vocational exploration through work samples, counseling for vocational choice, vocational training, and job placement. In 1897 Jessie B. Davis began a program of moral and vocational guidance in Detroit, where he served as 11th-grade counselor until 1907, when he became principal of Grand Rapids High School. Davis (1904) was later to publish a book detailing his approaches, *Vocational and Moral Guidance.* Eli Weaver in New York and Anna Reed in Seattle also established school-based guidance programs in the early 1900s.

Two things should be clear at this point. There was no single starting point for the counseling profession, and a number of individuals made contributions to its inception. In spite of this, one man, Frank Parsons, is generally identified as the founder of the guidance movement in the United States (Aubrey, 1977; Brewer, 1942; Picchioni & Bonk, 1983; Whitely, 1984). In order to understand why, the man and his contributions must be fully explored.

Parsons was born in Mount Holly, New Jersey, in 1854. Early on, he demonstrated high academic ability and entered Cornell at age fifteen, graduating three years later with a degree in civil engineering. During the subsequent years he served as a railroad engineer, common laborer, high school teacher, lawyer, and politician. However, his most salient characteristic lay not in the traits associated with any of these jobs, but in his penchant for social reform. He rejected Social Darwinism, the belief that social evolution was based on the survival of the fittest, and developed his own philosophy of Mutualism (Miller, 1961; Picchioni & Bonk, 1983). Mutualism held that the common good of society was based to a large extent on cooperative efforts to ensure benefits for all. Parsons advocated urban renewal projects, educational reform, women's suffrage, uniform divorce laws, and a host of other social changes.

In 1905 Parsons was asked to establish what became known as the Breadwinner's College in the famous Civic Service House in Boston. The Civic Service House had been created in 1901 as a continuing education center for immigrant and native youth. Parsons' Breadwinner's Institute, as it was renamed, thrived, and in 1907 he asked Mrs. Quincy Adams Shaw, benefactor of the Civic Service House, to underwrite what was to become the Vocational Bureau of Boston in 1908. Parsons died a few months later. Soon after his death, his book *Choosing a Vocation* (Parsons, 1909) was published. In this volume he set forth a tripartite model of career counseling: (1) self-analysis, (2) analysis of occupations, and (3) choosing a career using true reasoning.

In 1905 Alfred Binet and Theodore Simon, working with the Paris schools, published the first standardized intelligence tests, which were to provide the impetus for the testing movement. A scientific basis for self-analysis, unavailable to Parsons, was beginning to evolve. During World War I and into the 1920s, the production of tests to measure human traits would reach a peak unparalleled since. The Great Depression would result in the publication of the forerunners of the *Occupational Outlook Handbook* and, in 1939, the *Dictionary of Occupational Titles*. These provided a device by which counselors could help students conduct an analysis of occupations.

Parsons' work and that of the other pioneers spawned numerous guidance programs throughout the United States. Much of this early effort was directed at improving vocational guidance. In 1910 the First National Conference on Vocational Guidance was convened in Boston. Three years later the National Vocational Guidance Association was formed as the first professional organization for counselors. In 1915 it published the first journal, the *Vocational Guidance Bulletin*, which was the forerunner of today's *Career Development Quarterly*.

In another movement that focused to some degree on vocationally related services, the National Civilian Rehabilitation Conference was formed in 1924. The purpose of this organization, now titled the National Rehabilitation Association, was to enhance services to the handicapped through counseling, vocational assessment, and placement.

Early developments in the counseling profession were not restricted to schools or community agencies, nor were they limited to vocational concerns. Student personnel programs variously emphasizing guidance, counseling, and discipline were being formed across the United States. Generally, these programs were headed by deans, a title later widely copied by high schools. Northwestern University was the first to establish an extensive student personnel program, while Teachers College at Columbia University pioneered the training of student personnel workers (Picchioni & Bonk, 1983).

It is probably clear that much of the activity detailed to this point focused on guidance programs and services rather than other forms of counseling. To be sure, counseling as an activity was being talked and written about, particularly by E. G. Williamson (1939) in *How to Counsel Students* and others at the University of Minnesota. In a parallel movement, Freud and neo-Freudians were having a tremendous impact on psychiatry and the fledgling psychology profession. However, counselors were largely unaffected by this influence.

From Guidance to Counseling: The 1940s, 1950s, and 1960s

In 1942 Carl Rogers published *Counseling and Psychotherapy*. This was followed nearly a decade later by *Client-Centered Therapy* (Rogers, 1951) and nineteen years later by *On Becoming a Person* (Rogers, 1961). While it is difficult to pinpoint any single turning point in the development of any profession, Carl Rogers and his publications probably contributed more than any other phenomenon to the transition of the counseling profession from a focus on group-delivered guidance services, such as classroom units on choosing a career, to a group that provided counseling services (Aubrey, 1977; Bradley, 1978; Picchioni & Bonk, 1983), His emphasis on humanism and his nondirective approach to counseling captured the imagination of counselors because of its positive nature and its departure from the medical model that characterized people with problems as medically ill. Counseling, not testing or guidance, became the central thrust of a young profession (Aubrey, 1977).

The fifties and sixties were characterized by many significant developments. In 1949 Eli Ginzburg was the first to present a theory on why people choose occupations over the life span (Ginzberg, 1984), a theory he published in 1951 (Ginzberg, Ginsburg, Axelrod, & Herma, 1951). In 1953 Super published what remains one of the dominant career development theories. It was and is the major competitor to the trait-and-factor theory initiated by Parsons and popularized by E. G. Williamson and others.

However, theorizing did not dominate the growth of the profession in the forties, fifties, and sixties. The development of professional structures did. In 1951, after nearly 20 years of collaborative efforts, the National Vocational Guidance Association and the American College Personnel Association voted to merge under an umbrella organization, the American Personnel and Guidance Association (APGA). A third organization, the National Association of Deans of Women, long a collaborator, declined to join. At the first meeting of the APGA in Los Angeles in 1952, two additional associations had become chartered members: National Association of Guidance Supervisors and Trainers, and Student Personnel Association for Teacher Education. Robert Shaffer became the first president of the association and Donald Super its first president-elect.

Following the formation of APGA, the growth of a fledgling profession took a predictable path. Scholarly journals were added (e.g., *The Personnel and Guidance Journal*, 1958), standards for counselor preparation were promulgated (1958), a proposed code of ethics was published in *The Personnel and Guidance Journal* in 1959, and the profession began to support legislation that corresponded to its goals (Picchioni & Bonk, 1983).

Just as Carl Rogers' publications propelled the counseling profession toward counseling, the launching of a Russian satellite in 1957 and the nation's response in the form of the National Defense Education Act (NDEA) in 1958 provided a springboard for the development of the profession. Title V-A of NDEA provided monies to support school counseling programs and V-B established funds to support the training of counselors. The result was a rapid expansion of secondary school counseling programs and a parallel increase in both the number and size of training programs.

In 1964 the limited focus of NDEA was expanded to include elementary schools, junior colleges, and technical schools. The major impact of this amendment was to legitimize elementary school counseling and, as Faust (1968) noted, provide a major impetus for this movement.

A period that had been initiated by the development of the theories of Rogers and Super was to be characterized by the presentation of a variety of theories that would underpin the work of many counselors. Rational-Emotive Therapy was developed by Albert Ellis (1978) during the 1950s, as was Reality Therapy (Glasser & Zunin, 1978). Behavioral counseling also surfaced during this period, introduced first by Wolpe (Chambliss & Goldstein, 1979), but probably brought most forcefully to the attention of counselors by John D. Krumboltz (1966) in works such as *Revolution in Counseling.* A professional group dedicated in the practice of counseling had a whole new set of theoretical constructs to consider.

Career choice and career development also received much attention from theorists in the fifties and sixties: Anne Roe published the first comprehensive view of the career choice and development process in 1956, John Holland presented his theory of occupational choice in 1959, and Tiedemann and O'Hara put forth their framework for career decision making in 1963. These theories, along with Super's framework, would dominate the field into the 1980s (Brown & Brooks, 1996).

The Professionalization Era

The roots of the profession can be traced to 1913 and beyond. However, during the last twenty years, those roots have borne fruit. In 1978 APGA established an independent training program accreditation body, now known as the *Council for the Accreditation of Counseling and Related Educational Programs* (CACREP). While efforts to establish standards for training counselors had been underway for more than thirty years, much of that time under the leadership of Robert Stripling, this was a public affirmation of the importance of preparation standards. APGA also provided vigorous leadership in the area of individual credentialing and established a Licensure Commission chaired by Thomas Sweeney in 1974. In 1976 Virginia became the first state to pass a licensure law for professional counselors, a move followed by seventeen other states in the next twelve years. Currently, almost all states have active legislative programs aimed at securing licensing for counselors.

Credentialing of another sort also reflects the rapid professionalization of the early 1980s. The American Mental Health Counselors Association, the American Rehabilitation Counselors Association, and the National Vocational Guidance Association (now National Career Development Association) embarked on programs to certify counselors in the counseling specialties they represented. The American Association for Counseling and Development also established the National Board for Certified Counselors as a certifying agency for all counselors. The basic purpose of all of the councils and commissions established by these organizations is to recognize counselors who have met certain criteria, including certain training requirements (e.g., supervised practicums in the area of specialty), and who possess a knowledge base as reflected by successfully passing an examination. A second purpose of certification is to encourage maintenance of skills and knowledge by requiring continuing education for maintenance of the certification.

During the 1980s a number of associations, including the parent organization, the American Personnel and Guidance Association, changed their names, partly because some of the names no longer adequately reflected the purposes of the organizations, and partly to reflect the organizations' emphasis on counseling. APGA became the American Association for Counseling and Development (AACD), the Association for Non-White Concerns became the Association for Multicultural Counseling and Development (AMCD), the National

Vocational Guidance Association became the National Career Development Association, and the Association for Measurement and Evaluation in Guidance became the Association for Measurement and Evaluation in Counseling and Development.

The decade of the nineties continued to bring significant changes in the counseling profession. In 1990 the International Association of Marriage and Family Counselors and Therapists became a division of AACD reflecting a growing interest in this area and increased efforts by counselor education programs to prepare practitioners for this specialty. In 1992 the American Association of Counseling and Development officially became the American Counseling Association (ACA) and the American College Personnel Association dissolved its relationship with ACA. It was subsequently replaced within ACA by the American College Counseling Association. The Association of Measurement and Evaluation in Counseling and Development also changed its name to the Association for Assessment in Counseling to reflect ACA's emphasis on counseling and the Public Offenders Counselor Association became the Addiction and Offenders Counselor Association to highlight that organization's focus on treating substance abusers. Perhaps more importantly, the recognition of counseling as a profession has increased, as shown by the passage of numerous new credentialing laws and significant changes in others—changes that recognize the ability of counselors to diagnose and treat mental health problems in most instances. Given the need for mental health services that will be discussed in the following section, the changes that have occurred by mid-decade can be expected to accelerate until the year 2000 and beyond.

The Need for Counseling Services

A decade ago it was conventional wisdom that one in ten persons in the general population was in need of mental health services at any given time. Currently that estimate has been revised to one in five. Of the approximately 45 million people who are in need of services, no more than 2.5 million can be classified as chronically mentally ill (Bates, 1985). The remainder, some 40 million people, have problems ranging from a temporary need for support to ones requiring long-term psychotherapy. This section will be devoted to identifying the scope of the mental health problem confronting our society and a brief discussion of the need for development and preventive services. This discussion will be followed by one that illustrates how members of the counseling profession are positioned to deal with these problems.

At the outset, it may be useful to note that the mental health problems in our society are not restricted to a single age group. Children, adolescents, adults, and the elderly all have problems that vary in type to a considerable degree. To illustrate this point, let us consider some of the recent factual reports that have surfaced for these groups.

Children

The major problems confronting children in our society can be directly related to poverty and instability in the family. In 1991 four million children lived in families who had incomes below the poverty line (GAO, 1992). The Children's Defense Fund (1985) reports that black children in particular are victims of these forces, and the results are alarming: Black children are twice as likely as white children to die before age one, three times as likely as their white counterparts to live in poverty, only one-quarter as likely to live with either parent, five times more likely to be on welfare, and twelve times as likely to live with an unmarried parent. Hispanic children are also likely to find themselves living in poverty: More than 70 percent live in this condition (Children's Defense Fund, 1985).

Divorce has also had a dramatic impact on children. Approximately sixteen million children live in single parent homes (Hodgkinson, 1990). Divorce, coupled with the dispersion of the extended family, has caused social support networks for children to evaporate in many instances. Predictably, mental health problems among children have skyrocketed.

Physical, sexual, and psychological abuse of children has also received increasing attention with more than a million cases being reported each year (Bureau of the Census, 1991). The result is that all states have enacted legislation that requires that abuse be reported by individuals who care for children, including physicians, teachers, and counselors. The gradual lessening of taboos regarding the discussion of incest has also contributed to the identification and reporting of sexual abuse.

Without question, child abuse is related to a number of other problems. For example, 36 percent of 10–18-year-old runaways reported that they had either been sexually or physically abused (National Network of Runaway and Youth Services, 1985). Abuse, along with poverty and other family problems, also contributes to other mental health problems manifested by children and to problems that surface later in life, including suicide and depression.

Adolescents

The mental health needs of adolescents are among those most often studied, perhaps because they can easily be surveyed through the public schools. The result is that there is a vast amount of data suggesting that adolescents have a variety of serious mental health concerns. For example, a study conducted by the University of Michigan Institute for Social Research (Johnston, 1985) indicated that drug abuse was once again on the upswing among young people after half a decade of decline. Alcohol abuse continued to lead the list of abused substances, with 37 percent of the responding students reporting an occasion of heavy drinking—defined as consuming five or more drinks in a row—during the two weeks prior to the study. Five percent of the respondents in the study reported daily use of alcohol.

The University of Michigan study reported a continued decline in the use of such illegal substances as amphetamines, methaqualine, and LSD. However, this was offset to some degree by an upswing in the use of cocaine: 17 percent of the respondents reported that they had tried cocaine. A total of 61 percent of those surveyed reported experimenting with an illegal drug at some time, of which 40 percent indicated that it was a substance other than marijuana.

Sargent (1984) reports that substance abuse, along with medical and psychological illnesses and family problems, distinguished an increasing number of adolescents who attempt and succeed at suicide. The suicide rate among white adolescent males in 1978 was 138 per million, white adolescent females 34 per million, black adolescent males 75 per million, and black adolescent females 16 per million (Lipsitz, 1985). There is every reason to believe that these numbers are increasing rapidly, although the increase may be accounted for by more accurate reporting procedures (Sargent, 1984).

Just as it is difficult to get an accurate estimate of the number of adolescents involved in either successful or unsuccessful suicide attempts, accurate figures regarding mental health problems of adolescents are difficult to obtain. However, Lipsitz (1985) reports, after a survey of the literature in this area, that about one-fifth of the individuals treated for depression are under age eighteen, and that approximately 15 to 16 percent of adolescents need some form of mental health services, although many are not receiving the assistance they need.

Teenage pregnancy cannot be interpreted as a mental health problem, although it is an area in which adolescents need assistance. There are approximately five million sexually active adolescents in this country. The result is 1.15 million pregnancies annually, of which approximately 460,000 are terminated by abortion and 153,000 by miscarriage. Of the 537,000 births that occur among adolescents, 268,000 are to unmarried mothers. The media have often dramatized this problem as children having children. The results of teenage pregnancy can be dramatic: Adolescent mothers attempt suicide seven times as often as their peers, 72 percent of all teen marriages end in divorce, and over 70 percent of teen mothers will be on welfare for one to five years (The Crier, 1985).

Pregnant girls often leave school prematurely, and they represent a substantial portion of the nearly 25 percent who fail to complete high school. Among certain groups (e.g., Hispanics in large cities and Native Americans), the drop-out rate may range from 50 percent to 85 percent (NCES, 1991). Reasons given for leaving school prematurely vary widely, including financial needs (had to support family), expulsion, poor academic performance, low motivation, inability to get along with other students or teachers, and so forth. The consequences are much more predictable: lower chances of gaining and keeping jobs and lowered lifetime earnings (NCES, 1991). The unemployment rate among adolescents is generally two to three times that of their adult counterparts, although it is likely to be twice that for black 16–19 year olds. Unemployment, drug abuse, and other problems already mentioned are related to the adolescent crime rate and the number of runaways. Adolescents commit 20 percent of all crimes reported (FBI, 1993). These facts, in turn, can be tied to many of the problems facing our society generally, such as poverty and discrimination, and to the problems of the parents of adolescents.

Adults

As we have seen in the two preceding sections, the problems of children and adolescents are, to a large degree, tied to adults. While it would be impossible to pinpoint a predominant causal force, divorce would have to be one of the leaders. For the past twenty-five years there have been slightly more than two million marriages each year in this country. In 1970 about one-third of first marriages ended in divorce. Currently about one in two, or more than one million, marriages end in divorce or annulment each year (Bureau of Census, 1993). The mental health consequences of divorce on adults can be severe. Depression and suicide attempts are often the most dramatic result. Even those adults who manage to escape psychologically debilitating symptoms are often beset by stress resulting from role changes, such as entering or reentering the job market, becoming a single parent, and/or reentering the "dating scene."

Alcoholism and drug abuse are widespread maladies among adults, although their exact dimensions arc not fully known. One estimate is that 10 percent of all employees in this country are impaired by psychological or substance abuse problems (Turkington, 1985), costing businesses untold millions of dollars in profits. Substance abuse is also a prime contributor to marital breakup, child and spouse abuse, and a variety of health problems.

The unemployment rate during the 1990s has been approximately six to seven percent of the work force. In real terms, this means that probably six to eight million people are out of work at any given time. Some of these job losses are the result of seasonal fluctuations (e.g., farm workers), economic downturns, and occupational structural changes (e.g., manufacturing to information processing). Those changes that occur precipitously and have the potential for being long-term in nature produce the greatest stress and hence are more likely to have a deleterious effect on the mental health of the individuals concerned. It is not uncommon to see depression, substance abuse, and child and spouse abuse rise soon after job loss, although some workers seem to rebound psychologically quite quickly (Herr & Cramer, 1991).

Dealing with families and work are two of the major problems confronting adults, and it appears that nearly ten million individuals could benefit from assistance in these areas alone. Other aspects of adulthood that may be related to mental health concerns are accepting one's mortality, adjusting to declining physical prowess, health problems (particularly those that are life threatening), and loss of parents. These stressors precipitate a variety of difficulties, including anxiety, depression, and psychosomatic illnesses (e.g., lower back pain).

There is also an increasing possibility that adults and others will become the victims of crime. In 1993 over 100,000 cases of rape, one million cases of aggravated assault, three million burglaries, and 24,700 murders were reported in this country (FBI, 1993). Victims of crime often suffer symptoms ranging from anxiety due to fear of vulnerability to post traumatic stress disorder.

The Elderly

In 1900 only 4 percent of the population in the United States was over age 65. The latest report places this percentage at 12.5, and it is increasing (U.S. Committee on Aging, 1985–86). This same report notes that the fastest growing age group is the over-85 group. These figures dramatize not only what has been termed the graying of America, but the increasing longevity of older people. By 2050 one-third of our population will be over fifty-five and one-fifth over sixty-five (U.S. Committee on Aging, 1985–86). With these figures comes the sobering reality that counselors and other mental health professionals must prepare to assist the elderly to cope with mental health concerns.

In the previous section it was observed that many Americans will need assistance because they will be victims of violent crimes. The elderly are disproportionately represented in this group, since they are viewed as vulnerable by many criminals. However, retirement, marital relationships, widow(er)hood, grandparenting, institutionalization, and coming to grips with one's mortality represent the major developmental crises of the elderly.

The retirement period is characterized by greatly reduced incomes. Families headed by persons over age sixty-five have average incomes less than two-thirds of the average for families headed by persons between twenty-five and sixty-four. There is also evidence that minorities and white women who are older fare considerably less well than older white males with regard to income (U.S. Committee on Aging, 1985–86). The financial situations of most groups of older persons is greatly exacerbated by the need for increasing expenditures for health care.

Adjusting to chronic health problems such as arthritis, hypertension, hearing loss, heart conditions, orthopedic impairment, sinusitis, and visual impairment are also major concerns of the elderly. Heart disease, cancer, and stroke, which are the leading causes of death among the elderly, often result in serious adjustment problems for the patients and their families.

Older people appear to have fewer mental problems than other age groups. However, cognitive impairment was a problem for about 14 percent of the elderly. Although National Institute of Mental Health studies found that persons sixty-five years of age and older had the lowest incidence of eight common disorders, suicides among the group were the highest for any age group, varying from nineteen per 100,000 for sixty-five–seventy-four-year-olds to about fifteen per 100,000 for persons eighty-five and older (U.S. Committee on Aging, 1985–86).

In addition to the so-called common crises and to the other problems discussed above, the elderly also experience many of the problems of the other age groups, including physical, psychological, and sexual abuse (Fisher, 1985), alcohol and substance abuse, and psychosomatic complaints.

Counselors and Mental Health Problems

The result of the historically unprecedented demand for mental health services has been a veritable explosion in the numbers of mental health practitioners, including psychologists, psychiatrists, psychiatric nurses, social workers, and counselors. The latter group, counselors, are in a very real sense newcomers, although, as we saw, the roots of the counseling profession go back at least three-quarters of a century. As newcomers, counselors have assumed fewer of the trappings of an established profession, such as extended training programs, certification boards, and aggressive enforcement of ethical codes, although these are rapidly being put into place. However, no group is better situated to address the mental health problems confronting members of our society.

Any of the aforementioned groups may take at least three approaches to dealing with mental health problems. One of these, the *developmental–primary prevention approach,* focuses upon programs and techniques that will keep mental health problems from arising. Drug education programs are an example of this approach to mental health problems. *Secondary prevention approaches* attempt to control mental health problems that have already surfaced, such as keeping mild substance abuse from becoming chronic. In the *tertiary approach,* mental health practitioners work to prevent serious mental health problems from becoming chronic or life threatening. Counselors primarily work with primary and secondary mental health prevention programs and techniques.

There are approximately 125,000 to 150,000 counselors in the United States, of whom about 55,000 belong to the American Counseling Association. Of these, large numbers are situated in public schools, colleges and universities, churches, rehabilitation agencies, employment offices, and mental health agencies. Additionally, a growing number of counselors offer counseling services as a part of business and industry, and as practitioners in consulting firms.

The number of counselors and the far-ranging nature of their placement are impressive in terms of their potential to meet the growing mental health problems. The general orientation of counselors to health and wellness, as opposed to psychopathology and mental illness, also enables counselors to deal with the burgeoning mental health concerns of our society. Some counselors are prepared to design and implement educational programs aimed at preventing mental health problems, to deal with short-term developmental crises such as divorce or death of a loved one, and to assist people to cope with developmental difficulties. These counselors may work in such areas as interpersonal relationships, career choice and development issues, time and stress management, developing decision-making skills, making education decisions, coping with authority figures, anger management, achievement motivation, adjusting to or coping with disabilities, and so on. Others are prepared to deliver long-term psychotherapy to those more seriously impaired. Among mental health practitioners, only counselors and counseling psychologists share this orientation, although there is some movement by other groups in this direction.

Not only does the orientation of counselors make them ideally suited to meet the mental health needs of our society, their placement in public agencies provides them with an opportunity to provide the needed services as well.

Current Status of the Profession

As can be discerned from the foregoing sections, the counseling profession has made giant strides toward assuming the trappings of a profession and is well positioned to assume a major role in the delivery of mental health services. Training standards are in place, a code of ethics has been adopted, certification programs have been established for a number of counseling specialties, and, in a number of states, legislatures have legally recognized counselors by passing licensure laws that regulate the use of the title *counselor* in the private sector. Another form of recognition has been accorded counselors in some states, such as Alabama and Florida, in the form of third-party payments by insurance companies for the provision of mental health services. School counseling has also been increasingly recognized as central to the process of schooling.

However, there are still issues to be addressed. The training standards for counselors are not uniform and are still somewhat lower than those for social workers, among whom the two-year Masters in Social Work (MSW) is the accepted norm (although some social workers practice with a bachelor's degree). For psychologists, of course, the doctoral degree is expected in most states. The Association for Mental Health Counselors is now pressing for a training standard that would be equivalent to the MSW and the two-year training program required for entering school psychology, in terms of both coursework and clinical experience.

Little consideration is being given to the doctorate as a training standard for counselors, although many institutions offer the degree.

Because the counseling profession has not adopted the doctorate as a training standard, interest in the training programs at this level has waned at many institutions. As a result, many major counselor preparation institutions have converted their counselor education doctorates to counseling psychology training programs. One result of this has been to exacerbate the job hunting problem for individuals with a doctorate in counseling, since most of these institutions now require degrees in counseling psychology for employment. A second result is that individuals from major research institutions do not participate to the same degree in the affairs of the counseling profession, and thus a source of leadership has been lost. Finally, the move from counselor education to counseling psychology has in some instances focused research efforts on issues more related to psychology than to counseling, with the result that the empirical bases for certain aspects of the counseling profession have not grown as one would expect. To be sure, much of the research relating to counseling psychology pertains to counselors because of their common interests and focus.

Recognition of the counseling profession by governmental groups such as CHAMPUS (U.S. Office of Civilian Health and Medical Programs of the Uniformed Services) and by insurance companies has been slow in coming, but progress had been steady. However, in some instances, counselors have to be supervised by psychiatrists or psychologists in order to be eligible for payment. One counselor (Covin, undated) has even developed a guide for collecting third-party payments from insurance carriers. States such as Florida, where freedom-of-choice legislation requires insurance companies to recognize counselors along with psychiatrists and psychologists, appear to be the most successful in this domain.

The enforcement of ethical behavior is one of the true hallmarks of a professional group. Until the last decade, national and state level ethics committees have not been active, but this is gradually changing.

A companion problem to enforcing ethical behavior is legislative recognition of privileged communication between counselors and clients, which protects counselors from disclosing information gained in counseling. Subsectors of all licensing and certification laws deal with this problem and grant counselors immunity from disclosure. In other instances counselors have lobbied for, and been granted, privileged communication by legislatures independent of licensing laws. The fact remains that in a few states, counselors have not been accorded privileged communication. Efforts to correct this problem are under way.

Finally, counselors have, at times, either not been included in the state mental health system, or found themselves supervised by psychologists or psychiatrists. To be sure, in some states, counselors are accorded the same status as other mental health professionals. These problems and the others mentioned are being aggressively addressed by the profession and will be resolved. Just how this is being done will be covered in later chapters.

Summary

At the outset of the chapter, a brief history of the counseling profession was presented. An important part of the heritage of the profession is its ties to career decision making, a part that remains a central focus of the profession. However, more recently, the profession has increased its focus on dealing with the myriad of personal problems confronting our society. Counselors, because of their placement and training, are well suited to deal with both sets of problems.

The current status of the profession was also addressed, and will continue to be addressed throughout the book. The counseling profession is in a state of dynamic growth and development at this time.

Review Questions

1. Identify the key developmental periods in the development of the counseling profession. What did each contribute to the current status of the profession?

2. Given the vast number of problems confronting our society, can we justify a mental health strategy that concentrates on remediation? Provide a rationale for your answer.

3. Discuss the pros and cons of adopting a master's level training standard for the counseling profession.

4. What does the counseling profession have to offer to our society that other mental health professions such as social work and psychology do not?

5. Write a prescription for the future development of the counseling profession.

References

American Association for Counseling and Development. (1985–86). *AACD today.* Washington, DC: American Association for Counseling and Development.

American Journal of Public Health. (1984). Editorial, 75, p. 1.

Aubrey, R. F. (1977). Historical developments of guidance and counseling and implications for the future. *Personnel and Guidance Journal, 55*(6), 288–295.

Bates, J. (1985). Families could aid mentally ill. *APA Monitor, 16*(7), 14.

Beers, C. (1908). *A mind that found itself.* New York: Longmans, Green, & Co.

Belkin, G. S. (1975). *Practical counseling in the schools.* Dubuque, IA: Wm. C. Brown Publishers.

Bradley, M. K. (1978). Counseling past and present: Is there a future? *Personnel and Guidance Journal, 57*(1), 42–45.

Brewer, J. M. (1942). *History of vocational guidance: Origins of early developments.* New York: Harper and Brothers.

Brown, D., & Brooks, L. (Eds.). (1996). *Career choice and development.* (3rd ed.) San Francisco: Jossey-Bass.

Bureau of the Census (1991). *Statistical abstracts of the United States 1990.* Washington, DC: Bureau of the Census.

Chambliss, D. L., & Goldstein, A. J. (1979). Behavioral psychotherapy. In R. J. Corsini (Ed.), *Current psychotherapies* (pp. 230–272). Itasca, IL: F. E. Peacock.

Children's Defense Fund (1985). News release cited in *Washington Post,* Tuesday, June 4, 1985.

Covin, T. M. (undated). *How to collect third-party payments: The professional counselor's guide to third-party reimbursement.* Ozark, AL: Center for Counseling and Human Development, Inc.

Crier, The (1985). Research on teenage pregnancy. Charlotte, NC: The Junior League.

Davis, J. B. (1904). *Moral and vocational development.* Boston: Ginn and Company.

Ellis A. (1978). Rational-emotive therapy. In R. J. Corsini (Ed.), *Current psychotherapies* (pp. 185–229). Itasca, IL: F. E. Peacock.

Faust, V. (1968). *History of elementary school counseling.* Boston: Houghton Mifflin.

FBI (1993). *Crimes in the United States.* Washington DC: Dept. of Justice.

Fisher, K. (1985). Experts probe who, what, whys of elderly abuse. *APA Monitor, 16*(12), 24–26.

GAO (1992). *Educational Issues.* Washington, DC: General Accounting Office.

Gibson, R. L., & Mitchell, M. H. (1995). *Introduction to guidance.* (3rd ed.) New York: Macmillan.

Ginzberg, E. (1984). Career development. In D. Brown & L. Brooks (Eds.), *Career choice and development* (pp. 169–191). San Francisco: Jossey-Bass.

Ginzberg, E., Ginsburg, S. W., Axelrad, S., & Herma, J. (1951). *Occupational choice: An approach to a general theory.* New York: Columbia University Press.

Glaser, W., & Funin, L. M. (1978). Reality therapy. In R. J. Corsini (Ed.), *Current psychotherapies* (pp. 302–339). Itasca, IL: F. E. Peacock.

Herr, E. L., & Cramer, S. H. (1991). *Career guidance and counseling through the life span: Systematic approaches.* (4th ed.) Boston: Little, Brown & Co.

Hodgkinson, H. L. (1990). *The demographics of school reform: A look at the children.* Center for Demographics Policy Newsletter, 1 (pp. 1–3).

Johnston, L. D. (1985). News release. Ann Arbor, MI: News and Information Services, The University of Michigan Institute for Social Research.

Krumboltz, J. D. (Ed.). (1966). *Revolution in counseling.* Boston: Houghton Mifflin.

Lipsitz, J. (1985). A statistical portrait of American adolescents. *Common Focus, 6*(1), 1–5.

Miller, C. H. (1961). *Foundations of guidance.* New York: Harper & Row.

National Network of Runaway Youth Services (1985). News release. Washington, DC: National Network of Runaway Youth Services.

NCHS (1985a). Births, marriages, divorces, and deaths for September 1985. *NCHS Monthly Vital Statistics Report, 34*(9), 1–3.

NCHS (1985b). Advance report of final divorce statistics, 1983. *NCHS Monthly Vital Statistics Report, 34*(8) (Supplement), 1–13.

NCES (1991). *Digest of Education Statistics.* Washington, DC: National Center for Educational Statistics.

Parsons, F. (1909). *Choosing a vocation.* Boston: Houghton Mifflin.

Picchioni, A. P., & Bonk, E. C. (1983). *A comprehensive history of guidance in the United States.* Austin, TX: Texas Personnel and Guidance Association.

Rogers, C. R. (1942). *Counseling and psychotherapy.* Boston: Houghton Mifflin.

Rogers, C. R. (1951). *Client-centered therapy.* Boston: Houghton Mifflin.

Rogers, C. R. (1961). *On becoming a person.* Boston: Houghton Mifflin.

Sargent, M. (1984). Adolescent suicide: Studies reported. *APA MHA News, 10*(7), 8.

Siegel, M. (1985). Executive summary. Final report of the APA task force on victims of crime and violence. *American Psychologist, 40*(1), 107–112.

Super, D. E. (1953). A theory of vocational development. *American Psychologist, 8*(2), 185–190.

Turkington, C. (1985). EAPS: Healthier employees, lower cost spur growth of programs. *APA Monitor, 16*(8), 22–23.

U.S. Committee on Aging (1985–86). *Aging America: Trends and projections.* Washington, DC: U.S. Senate Special Committee on Aging.

Whitely, J. M. (1984). Counseling psychology: A historical perspective. *The Counseling Psychologist, 12*(1), 7–95.

Williamson, E. G. (1939). *How to counsel students.* New York: McGraw-Hill.

Zytowski, D. G. (1972). Four hundred years before Parsons. *Personnel and Guidance Journal, 50*(6), 443–450.

Chapter 2

Normal Development and Adjustment

Goals of the Chapter

The aim of this chapter is to provide an overview of social and emotional development, factors that must be considered when one is planning counseling interventions. This chapter also can serve as a review of important developmental theories appearing on counselor licensing examinations.

Chapter Preview

- Development and adjustment will be defined.
- Historic influences in the counseling profession that have promoted a developmental perspective toward clients will be presented.
- Developmental theories that have influenced the counseling profession will be discussed.
- A composite picture of developmental issues affecting clients will be drawn.

Introduction

Understanding human development and using it as a basis for helping clients is a major emphasis in counseling. At one time developmental change was a concept most often applied to the young; it is now used to understand persons of all ages. Its prominence in current thinking has altered views about delivery of human services. This chapter will provide an overview of the use of developmental theory in the counseling profession. Important developmental concepts and theories will be abstracted, and a sketch of developmental issues at each important period in a person's life will be presented. This treatment will become a basis for many of the ideas developed in later chapters.

Defining Development

Development can be defined simply as change over time. Observation of a person's behavior from birth to death would reveal numerous behavior changes. Lefrancois (1984) notes that development involves growth, maturation, and learning, with each term having its own meaning. Growth refers to physical changes; maturation, to changes relatively independent of the environment; learning, to lasting changes attributable not to maturation but to experiences in the environment. Development is the composite outcome in terms of adaptability for the person; it represents not short-term learning but gradual adaptation over many years. Thus, adults have a better chance for survival than infants simply because they are better developed. In light of this, the counseling profession promotes human development as a way of helping clients adapt.

Promoting Development Through
Counseling and Consultation

The counseling profession has a rich tradition with regard to promoting development. This had been particularly true in school counseling. Reference to developmental issues appears very early in the history of counseling and guidance (Little & Chapman, 1955). Mathewson (1962) was a pioneer in attempting to articulate the role of the school counselor. He drew a continuum, with the practice of intense psychotherapy at one end and the practice of casework at the other; between these extremes he placed school counseling and guidance. Counselors were seen as utilizing to a degree the intense, personal relationship found in psychotherapy while also intervening broadly in the client's social environment. Thus, the early view of a counselor's role was somewhere between psychotherapist and case-oriented social worker.

Later Peters (1966) and Dinkmeyer (1966) elaborated on this view. They emphasized counselor effort at team-building, that is, working with other professional service-providers such as teachers, school administrators, and other social service professionals to promote the acquisition of adaptive behavior on the part of young clients. Fundamental to this position was the realization that many individuals and forces contribute to adjustment. At first the articulation of developmental counseling was general in nature. As increased effort was made to provide counseling and consultation services to elementary school-age children, the need for more precise developmental theories and concepts became evident (Dink-meyer, 1966; Dinkmeyer & Caldwell, 1970).

Counselors over the last decade and a half took this beginning, did their home-work in developmental psychology, and evolved what now is an elaborate devel-opmental framework. Reliance on developmental concepts in counseling now goes far beyond school counseling and efforts with children to include work with clients of all ages. For example, Ivey has proposed a therapy that integrates de-velopmental processes into clinical practice (Ivey & Ivey, 1990; Ivey, 1986; Ivey & Goncalves, 1988). He argues for the importance of beginning with the client's men-tal construction of real events rather than one of the traditional therapies (e.g., humanistic, behavioral, psychodynamic). To Ivey, Jean Piaget's structural devel-opmental theory, more than any other, helps counselors understand how clients think and act. Using Piaget's cognitive-developmental levels, Ivey has matched counseling methods with those levels. Through this he argues that counseling and therapy can be intentionally used to produce movement within and across several levels of development.

STUDENT LEARNING EXERCISE

Read the following descriptions of incidents and indicate whether what the counselor is doing utilizes positive developmental forces. Circle Y for yes or N for no.

1. A school counselor pressures a mental health center to have its therapists see student clients at school so the children will not miss classes while being transported to the mental health center.   Y   N

2. A counselor in a group home for adolescents encourages residents to join other intramural teams instead of forming their own.   Y   N

3. A family counselor refuses to mediate a dispute between a teenager and her parents.   Y   N

Important Developmental Concepts and Theories

Several developmental theories appear repeatedly in the counseling literature, and form the basis for interventions aimed at promoting client growth and maturation. Some developmental theories attempt to explain human change over time by di-viding all or part of the lifespan into steps or stages through which people evolve; the stages usually are connected to chronological age. Other theories describe the kinds of changes that occur in persons as they develop. According to such theo-ries, developmental stages begin and end when some significant change takes place; chronological age may or may not predict the change. This chapter will refer to some of the developmental theories as *stage-progression theories* and others as *stage-hierarchy theories.* These labels are used because they are descriptive of the essential nature of the theories classified.

The first group of theories in effect divides all or part of the lifespan into stages that signal different challenges, which ideally prompt new and different strategies in coping. No one stage is "better" than another; stages are simply different; they are more relevant to one age group than another. For example, adolescence can be viewed as a different developmental stage from childhood, but not necessarily a better one. Stage-hierarchy theories attempt to describe qualitative changes that occur in some dimension of human functioning. Later stages are clearly viewed as more advanced, "superior" levels of human existence.

The qualitative changes in human performance described by these theories are generally based on the notion that some structural development has occurred "inside" the individual. The person has a new implement or structure to use in dealing with the world. Such structures are not directly observable; their presence is based on the observation of response changes. For example, up to a certain age a child thinks a ribbon of clay becomes smaller when it is rolled into a tight ball. When a specific structure is formed in the intellect (called the Principle of the Conservation of Matter—by Piaget), a further developed child will recognize that both the ribbon of clay and the ball of clay contain the same amount of clay.

Moral development provides another example. Altruism, a selfless form of love, is not part of a person in the early stages of moral development. Rather, self-oriented pleasure-seeking is more representative of people at these stages (Kohlberg, 1969). Thus, self-sacrifice for the welfare of another would be unimaginable as a worthwhile and meaningful activity. This is so because the structure containing the idea of altruism has yet to be developed.

Stage-hierarchy theories provide us with an architectural view of self-development, whether the theory applies to cognition, the making of moral decisions, or ego development. Study of these theories can enhance one's ability to conceptualize how adaptive resources build in an individual. Such theories are mostly descriptive; that is, they describe different levels of development without saying much about what it is that influences the advance to the next developmental level.

Both progression and the hierarchy theories, popular among counselors, are epigenetic in nature, which means that the theories see earlier stages of development as the basis for later stages (Lidz, 1976). Development in later stages utilizes as a foundation that which was achieved in previous stages. In stage-progression theories, if an individual does not achieve at least baseline objectives in an earlier stage, the person will have a poor basis for gaining the full benefit of developmental experiences at later stages. This deficit will be carried through the entire balance of that person's developmental history. However, the individual will progress on to later developmental stages. At a later stage the person with earlier developmental problems will not meet the challenges of that period as well as others who did not suffer the earlier difficulty. For example, identity formation is the key issue in adolescence, according to Erikson (1968). In early adulthood the principal developmental objective is the formation of intimate relationships. If identity formation does not progress well for the adolescent, adult intimacy is also in jeopardy, since it is best built on a stable self-image.

In stage-hierarchy theories, if a person gets "hung up" or stopped at a particular developmental stage, there can occur no further development in the particular area of functioning the theory is describing. If the issue is moral development, for example, a person may reach a certain stage of moral decision making and not advance to higher levels (Kohlberg, 1969). Individuals of the same chronological age will respond differently to the same moral dilemmas depending on the different stages of moral development each has attained.

The counseling profession has drawn on many of the developmental approaches that fit into this category. The most popular is Erik Erikson's eight ages of man (1963). More recently adult development has been the dominant focus of attention in the literature. Counselors have enriched their therapeutic practice by incorporating key concepts concerning adult life changes. In the counseling literature, Daniel Levinson and his colleagues (Levinson, Darrow, Klein, Levinson, & McKee, 1978) are the most frequently quoted contributors to understanding adult development. Gail Sheehy's best-selling *Passages* (1974) was based on Levinson's principal concepts.

Erik Erikson's Developmental Theory

Erik Erikson is a fascinating author. Among his many works are his general theory of development (1963), numerous comments on social issues (e.g., nuclear war, racial tensions, changing sex roles, etc.), and several biographies of great men. One of these biographies, *Gandhi's Truth* (1969), won a Pulitzer Prize.

Erikson's theory of development is considered to be neo-Freudian; it is an expansion on Freud's psychosexual stages. Erikson looks at both psychological and social development over the lifespan, mapping development by means of eight psychosocial stages (see Table 2.1). Each stage is differentiated from the other by means of the separate issues or "crises" a person must face at a particular stage. For example, in Stage 2 a child struggles for increased independence and resistance to control by parents, yet maintains a lingering awareness of vulnerability and the need for protection. A clash of wills, symbolized by toilet training, represents this particular stage.

In coping with the crises at each stage of development, according to Erikson, people risk both positive and negative outcomes, such as autonomy versus shame and guilt. Obviously, favorable development strives for more of the positive; at least it is hoped that positive outcomes will predominate over negative ones. Since Erikson's theory is epigenetic in nature, each stage builds on earlier ones, mandating stage-related successes as the foundation for later development.

TABLE 2.1 Worksheet Summarizing the Eight Stages of Development

Stage	A Psychosocial Crises	B Radius of Significant Relations	C Related Elements of Social Order	D Psychosocial Modalities	E Psychosexual Stages
1	Trust versus mistrust	Maternal person	Cosmic order	To get To give in return	Oral-respiratory, sensory-kinesthetic (incorporative modes)
2	Autonomy versus shame, doubt	Parental persons	"Law and order"	To hold (on) To let (go)	Anal-urethral, muscular (retentive-eliminative)
3	Initiative versus guilt	Basic family	Ideal prototypes	To make (= going after) To "make like" (= playing)	Infantile-genital, loco-motor (intrusive, inclusive)
4	Industry versus inferiority	"Neighborhood," school	Technological elements	To make things (= completing) To make things together	"Latency"
5	Identity and repudiation versus identity diffusion	Peer groups and out-groups; models of leadership	Ideological perspectives	To be oneself (or not to be) To share being oneself	Puberty
6	Intimacy and solidarity versus isolation	Partners in friendship, sex, competition, cooperation	Patterns of cooperation and competition	To lose and find oneself in another	Genitality
7	Generativity versus self-absorption	Divided labor and shared household	Currents of education and tradition	To make be To take care of	
8	Integrity versus despair	"Mankind" "My kind"	Wisdom	To be, through having been To face not being	

Source: From Identity and the Life Cycle by Erik J. Erikson, by permission of W. W. Norton & Company, Inc. Copyright © 1980 by W. W. Norton & Company, Inc. Copyright © 1959 by International Universities Press, Inc. Reprinted by permission.

Hamachek (1990, 1988) has suggested criteria for each of Erikson's psychosocial stages that may be helpful in evaluating self-concept and ego development. This may be helpful to counselors in identifying areas of strengths and weaknesses. More reliable assessment of development also is possible via a more detailed description of characteristics of people at each developmental stage.

Social involvement is integral to Erikson's theory. As a person matures, social contact expands. During the first three stages parents and the family are central; broader involvements follow. The peer group is central to Stage 5. Partners and lasting friendships follow in Stage 6. Finally, in Stage 8 union with the brotherhood of humankind becomes the ultimate social issue.

Throughout Erikson's theory, but especially during adolescence, identity formation is a chief point of emphasis. People at all ages are asking themselves who they are. Again, this points out the potential value of Hamachek's work cited earlier. Just as synthesis is considered one of the highest mental functions, a synthesized view of self (identity) is a life-long goal. At adolescence the struggle for identity reaches a crisis (Erikson, 1968). This is not surprising in light of the fact that adolescents have just developed a new body with new urges. New pressures develop, especially around education and career. Erikson (1968) notes that adolescents will experiment with many identities through participation in different peer groups, clubs, and political movements. Affluent youth may find they have too many choices; disadvantaged youth may succumb to the negative identity repeatedly pressed upon them.

Levinson's Theory of Adult Development

Levinson's theory originated in his early study of men's lives (1977, 1978), with an emphasis on mid-life, the years between forty and forty-five. His theory represents a pioneering attempt to chart changes adults experience.

Besides developing a theory that at present describes nine developmental periods in adulthood, Levinson introduces a series of global concepts to capture the chain of events in people's lives. One such concept is *life course*. Levinson (1986) believes that life needs to be studied as it unfolds over the years in order to account for stability and change, continuity and discontinuity, orderly progression as well as stasis and chaotic fluctuation. In studying life course, one must look at life in all its complexity at a given time to include all its components and their evolution. Beyond life course is *life cycle*, which is divided into various segments or seasons, just as the year is divided into seasons. *Eras* are broad segments of the life cycle; preadulthood, early adulthood, middle adulthood, and late adulthood are the eras of Levinson's theory.

Within each era there are stable periods and periods of flux or change. The work done on what Levinson calls the *life structure* determines stability or flux. As people go through life they work on forming an underlying pattern or design that is called the life structure. Relationships are the primary determiner of a person's life structure at any given time. The relationships can be with people, self, groups, institutions, culture, or a particular object or place. Most important are relationships with marriage and family and with occupation.

At different times a person will follow a given life structure for five to seven years, but will eventually recognize that the life structure is not satisfying all needs. Momentum will build to question that life structure, to evaluate it with the intent to change or rebuild it in some way. As this happens the person begins another five-to-seven–year period of transition between one structure and another. Half of a person's life is spent in transition (Levinson, 1986). A particularly negative and intense transition is called a crisis.

Like many other developmental theories, Levinson's assigns special tasks to be worked on at different periods (see Figure 2.1). The developmental tasks are like questions asked of everyone. Answers to the questions can vary infinitely. How a given person answers these questions relates to the work done on forming a life structure. Overall, if one looks at the life course as an order shaped by eras and by periods of life structure development, the underlying order to human life becomes apparent. Stage-progression theories make sense out of experiences that as single events lose meaning.

Piaget's Theory of Cognitive Development

Piaget's description of development is more than a statement of cognitive growth; it is a narrative on adaptation (Piaget, 1954, 1955, 1965, 1985). Children begin life without the knowledge or skills to cope with the world. At first their responses are limited to simple reflexes; they cannot symbolize their world; they cannot problem solve. Increased adaptation results from the formation of mental or cognitive representations which Piaget calls schema or schemata. The individual uses the process of assimilation to take in experiences and fit them to already present schemas. Some experiences do not fit already present mental structures, so accommodation is necessary, i.e., current structures must be changed to fit with experience.

Through the adaptive process just described, the person passes through a series of stages in which the perception of the world is very different. The sensorimotor period (zero to two years) precedes the acquisition of language; the child can understand the world for the most part through sensations and immediate actions. Between ages two and seven, the period of preoperational thought, the individual draws conclusions largely on perception. Their thought does not permit the use of logic. Operational thought that follows in the next period, called concrete operations (seven to twelve years) does allow for the use of logic. The individuals can formulate classes and relations; they can understand number, but their thinking still remains concrete. With the development of formal operations in the early teens the person is free of the concrete world and can now deal with the

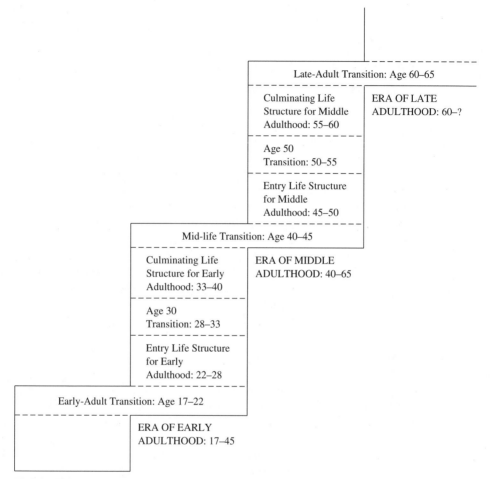

Late-Adult Transition: Age 60–65

Culminating Life
Structure for Middle
Adulthood: 55–60

ERA OF LATE
ADULTHOOD: 60–?

Age 50
Transition: 50–55

Entry Life Structure
for Middle
Adulthood: 45–50

Mid-life Transition: Age 40–45

Culminating Life
Structure for Early
Adulthood: 33–40

ERA OF MIDDLE
ADULTHOOD: 40–65

Age 30
Transition: 28–33

Entry Life Structure
for Early
Adulthood: 22–28

Early-Adult Transition: Age 17–22

ERA OF EARLY
ADULTHOOD: 17–45

ERA OF PREADULTHOOD: 0–22

**FIGURE 2.1   Developmental Periods in the Eras of Early
and Middle Adulthood**

Source: "Developmental Periods in the Eras of Early and Middle Adulthood from a Conception of Adult Development," by Daniel J. Levinson, 1986, *American Psychologist*, 41(1), p. 3. An earlier version appeared in Daniel J. Levinson with C. N. Darrow, E. B. Klein, M. H. Levinson, and B. McKee, *The Seasons of a Man's Life*, Copyright © 1978 by Alfred A. Knopf, Inc. Reprinted by permission.

hypothetical. Thought can become quite abstract; propositional thinking also supports the development of strong idealism.

To these four stages of Piaget, Ivey (Ivey & Goncalves, 1988) adds a dialectic stage. Based on Plato's epistemology, this stage permits even more integrated thinking. The search for truth can weigh seemingly opposing views at one time.

Thinking can be more flexible, allowing for both greater change and greater commitment to a position.

Kohlberg's Theory of Moral Development

As portrayed in Table 2.2, Lawrence Kohlberg (1969) offers a useful stage-hierarchy theory of moral development. In it he proposes the progressive acquisition of three levels of moral judgment. The earliest level is based on reward and punishment, followed by a conventional morality based on rules, and finally a stage of relativistic values based on universal principles. Within the levels are stages of moral development that further define how individuals make moral decisions. Since clients often seek counselors when an important decision must be made, Kohlberg's theory can help in understanding the decision-making process and some of its outcomes. Hayes (1994) discusses Kohlberg's basic assumptions and demonstrates how they are applicable to counseling.

Like many theories, Kohlberg's sequence of development has not always been verified by research findings (Holstein, 1976). Of considerable interest in such stage-hierarchy theories is the description of the process by which one can achieve the highest level. For Kohlberg this is altruism. This is especially relevant to counselors, who have devoted themselves to caring for others.

Loevinger's Theory of Ego Development

Jane Loevinger (1976) has attempted an integrative theory of ego development in which moral judgment, character formation, socialization, and intellectual development are treated. As represented in Table 2.3, the student of human development, through Loevinger, can examine and integrate concepts from Erikson, Piaget, Kohlberg, and others. See Table 2.3 for a comparison of developmental stages across these developmental theorists.

TABLE 2.2   Kohlberg's Stages of Moral Development

Level	Stage	Description of Stage
Preconventional	Punishment/obedience	Decisions based on physical consequences
	Instrumental hedonism	Seek pleasure and avoid pain
Conventional		Seek approval of others
	Good-boy, nice-girl	Uncritical following of authority
	Law and order	
Autonomous		Obey contract arrived at democratically, will of the people
	Social contract	
	Individual conscience	Ethics self-chosen based on universal principles

STUDENT LEARNING EXERCISE

Read the following statements and indicate whether the counselor's action is consistent with the developmental theories just reviewed. Circle Y for yes or N for no.

1. A high school counselor spends considerable time training students to be peer counselors.   Y   N
2. A mental health counselor believes that depression is more likely at certain ages than at others because of predictable life changes.   Y   N
3. A child counselor rarely works with the parents of his child clients.   Y   N

Merging Theories of Development

The composite picture of human growth and development resulting from theory-building and related research helps the counselor to monitor the progress and problems of clients. This section provides a synopsis of selected but important challenges facing clients at different periods in their lifespan, hopefully introducing ideas that help with decisions regarding what a counselor can do to wisely assist clients. The discussion treats three broad life periods: childhood, adolescence, and adulthood. Social and emotional development are emphasized.

Developmental Issues During Childhood

Much of the developmental literature associated with early childhood emphasizes the importance of the parenting received by the infant and toddler. If the persons caring for the child are comfortable with their role and nurturing to the child, it is

TABLE 2.3   A Comparison of Developmental Stages Across Important Developmental Theorists

Piaget	Kohlberg	Loevinger
Sensori-Motor		Presocial
Preoperational	Preconventional (Law and Order)	Self-Protective
Concrete Operations	Conventional (Approval-Seeking)	Conformist Conscientious Conformist
Formal Operations	Postconventional	Individualistic
	Autonomous	Autonomous
Dialectical (Ivey)	Social Contract Moral Principle	Integrated

likely that the child's future relationships will be positive. In these early relationships the basis for bonding with others is established. Attachment and loss are relationship issues of enormous magnitude in human life; they appear repeatedly regardless of the age of a client. Early separations from the primary-care adult can have a major impact on the long-term emotional health of a person (Bowlby, 1969).

While some parent-child relationship factors may be subtle with regard to their long-range impact, issues of abuse and neglect are not. Each year thousands of children in the United States are sufficiently abused that intervention from social agencies is required. Regrettably the most seriously injured are usually the very young. Counselors who work exclusively with adults will likely deal with clients who portray in later years the crippling effects of early abuse (Leehan & Wilson, 1985). Armsworth and Holaday (1993) underscore the importance of helping the victim resolve and integrate the traumatic event as quickly as possible to avoid the development of later difficulties.

Another paramount issue in rearing children is their socialization in the family. This includes the important topic of discipline. Ideally parents help a child learn respect for the rights of others and how to conform to arrangements that lead to harmonious social relationships while concurrently maintaining and enhancing personal autonomy.

An important landmark in development is the first time a youngster says "no" (Spitz, 1957); this event marks the development of one of those internal structures by which it can be ascertained that the child has differentiated self from important others. From that point on there exists the potential for a conflict of will. Effective parenting does not defeat the child's effort to exercise the will and at the same time provides experience in the beneficial nature of cooperative relationships. A breakdown in the resolution of this important developmental issue can lead to the extremes of either an overly compliant individual or one obsessed with power and control. Later, as such a child enters school, repercussions from this unresolved developmental struggle can result in problems of both discipline and achievement (Dreikurs, Grunwald, & Pepper, 1982).

Schooling constitutes much of the developmental mainstream in middle childhood. During these years peer relationships and personal achievement replace dependence on caretakers as central challenges. Sullivan (1953) associates childhood friendships with meaningful and lasting relationships in adulthood. For this reason the ability to assess peer acceptance and rejection (utilize such techniques as sociometry) is an important competency for both teachers and counselors. Through relationships with peers, youngsters manufacture much of their self-esteem. In turn self-esteem constitutes much of the raw energy used to fuel academic achievement.

The ease or difficulty that a child has in meeting academic requirements warrants careful attention. Although there are some negative consequences associated with giftedness (e.g., feeling different), the repeated experience of failure in the classroom eventually wears down adaptive resources. Contemporary counselors, with the help of other professionals, can more fully understand such difficulties. Minimal brain dysfunction and specific learning disabilities, important contributors to school failure, have been better understood in recent years. However, these and other factors that contribute to developmental delays are not easily diagnosed. Estimates are that 2–4 percent of U.S. students have identifiable learning disabilities (Johnson & Morasky, 1980). Learning disabled individuals are of normal intelligence but have difficulty in one or more subject areas. Some learning disabled individuals can be identified through visual, motor, or speech/hearing problems; others are less obvious, appearing restless or inattentive.

From this brief overview of childhood development several critical features stand out as worthy of monitoring by the counselor. These include parental nurturing and discipline, a child's over-compliance or oppositional behavior, emotional energy and self-esteem, peer relations/social withdrawal, and school failure or uneven achievement. Important but not discussed in this abbreviated summary are both language and physical development.

Developmental Issues During Adolescence

Physical development and its primary psychological counterpart, body image, achieve major significance in adolescence. Since pubescence marks the beginning of this period, sexual self-image is an essential part of the teenager's effort to form an acceptable identity. Adolescents are extremely self-conscious about their bodies and their behavior. Elkind (1980) describes this self-consciousness as a feeling of being perpetually "on stage"; adolescents unconsciously sense that everyone is watching them, waiting for them to make a mistake so they can be ridiculed.

Coleman (1981) lists the following as important issues that arise in counseling adolescent males: changing relationships, masturbation, premarital sex, unwanted pregnancy of a sexual partner, sexually transmitted diseases, and drug problems. Sexual orientation and considerable uneasiness regarding homosexuality combine with initial attempts at personal intimacy to dominate the teenager's view of sexuality.

Adolescence is certainly one of the most intense periods of social development. Dunphy (1963) describes the evolution of adolescent social relationships. This process begins with isolated same-sex groups, the higher status members of which begin to form heterosexual cliques. The formation of heterosexual cliques spreads to others with considerable interaction among the various cliques, leading to what is often referred to as "the crowd." However, in late adolescence "the crowd" begins to disintegrate into a loose network of couples. Of major concern developmentally are those individuals who do not achieve membership in heterosexual groups; they remain on the periphery of the adolescent social world.

Late adolescence is the most common time for an individual to come to grips with questions of sexual orientation. A consistent pattern of "childhood gender nonconformity" (Bell, Weinberg, & Hammersmith, 1981) and an increasing awareness of feeling "different" begin to engender very difficult questions. Most people who eventually develop a gay or lesbian identity begin dating as heterosexuals (Bell & Weinburg, 1978), but they experience closeness with members of the opposite sex as lacking in physical attraction. Concurrently they begin to experience undeniable awareness of their strong sexual attraction toward members of the same sex. During late adolescence or early twenties most begin to acknowledge, often with difficulty, and eventually come to accept their different sexual orientation. With this acceptance begins an evolution toward a workable lifestyle.

Adolescents are frequently accused of being moody. They do frequently become depressed, and in fact suicide has been found to be the leading cause of adolescent death (Klagsbrun, 1976).

A major factor that contributes to the unevenness of mood and behavior among adolescents is the still-developing sense of identity (Erikson, 1968). As the self-image becomes more secure, behavior becomes more stable. Unfortunately self-concept development is the basis for career decision making (Super, 1957), and often teenagers are pushed to make extremely important initial career decisions while their self-concepts are still somewhat unstable. This sometimes forces impulsive choices, ones much less appropriate than choices made later when a better developed self-image acts as a guide. Planning for the future is a paramount concern at this time of life, and it generates within the young person considerable anxiety.

Going to college or becoming employed has great symbolic meaning in connection with the adolescent's struggle to separate from parents. Counselors know full well how common tensions are among teenagers and their parents. In fact authority figures in general often do not interpret the rebelliousness of youth as an effort on their part to gain a sense of control over the various roles they must play. The relationship between dependence on others and independence in adolescence is ultimately solved by developing adaptive forms of connectedness, while avoiding maladaptive forms of separateness. College students with low distress often have supportive relationships with their parents without being so enmeshed that their own identity suffers (Quintana & Kerr, 1993).

Developmental Issues During Adulthood

Levinson and his associates (1978) identify the real beginning of adulthood as that day in a person's life when he leaves his parents' home realizing that it will never again be his home. Adult development differs from that of childhood and adolescence in that it is less closely linked with chronological age. It begins with the challenges of economic independence and intimate relationships.

In contrast to earlier generations, where heterosexual marriage and children were seemingly the only acceptable courses, contemporary adulthood has many more lifestyle options. Remaining single, choosing a gay or lesbian lifestyle, and living with another person of the opposite sex without getting married have become more acceptable than they were earlier. Regardless of chosen lifestyle, the questions facing adults remain the same; people simply execute a greater variety of answers. Will I marry? Will I have children? Will I attempt to use my employment as a major source of gratification? These and others are common questions for the adult.

Early Adulthood

If leaving home, both physically and psychologically, marks the beginning of adulthood, the developmental challenge is to reach out to others without the security of knowing that they are part of one's family. Most views of adult development portray the twenties as a time to further complete a sense of personal identity by making commitments to relationships, a career, and possibly a community. Making such choices provides a concrete representation of who we are trying to become. In addition to including spouses/living partners and young children, early adulthood involves other important relationships. One such relationship can be with a mentor. This individual, according to Levinson and associates (1978), is a person one-half a generation older who promotes especially one's career development through sponsorship and teaching of the subtle, success-related maneuvers. Relationships with mentors, while beneficial, require additional energy, which further complicates this life period.

The difficulty of combining the themes just mentioned with learning to manage finances and household, and possibly beginning a family, taxes the adaptive resources of the person. Early adulthood ends with a period of transition from the late twenties to the mid-thirties during which relationships and values are reappraised. Pressure intensifies to make significant career gains during just the period when one's challenge at home may be to adjust to growing children. It is a time to reevaluate a marriage that is likely different from how it began. For the unmarried who would like to be married it is a time to reconcile with a single lifestyle.

Middle Adulthood

The last half of the thirties can be a fulfilling period marked with career success and improved psychological autonomy. This only precedes the much-publicized "midlife crisis" or transition. At approximately age forty people go through a stage that is second only to adolescence for being explosive and unstable. Neugarten (1976) provides the key indicator of midlife: Prior to it people think of how old they are; after it they think of how many years they have left.

Midlife is a time for intense reevaluation. It is a time when many compare achievements to goals, with the former never quite matching the latter. It is common for an individual to experience at this time what in retrospect will be viewed as the peak of his or her career; most people also become very aware of the magnitude of what they have sacrificed for their career achievements. The questions often faced during this period are fundamental to the search for meaning. What makes it all the more difficult for many people are the challenges to deal also with teenage children, the recognition of clear signs of personal aging, and possibly the need to care for aged parents.

This self-examination, while at times painful, has the value of enabling individuals to balance out their personalities, fulfill neglected needs, and possibly repair damaged relationships with important others. As in earlier transitional periods it helps launch the person into a new level of maturity. A significant outcome of this growth often is more genuine and complete self-acceptance.

Such a transition in life is described by many as a mellowing of the individual. If successful in dealing with the changes of adulthood to this point, an individual can broaden her or his involvements and become less driven by a handful of life goals. Certainly health problems can become more significant, and financial pressures continue even for the middle-class with the need to finance college for children.

The themes developed following the midlife evaluation continue as middle adulthood enters its last phase. At this point such issues as preparing for retirement or adjusting to the loss of a mate become more important.

Late Adulthood

Some caution needs to be mentioned regarding generalizations that can be made about persons in their sixties and beyond. A major investigation conducted by the Social Security Administration (Irelan, Motley, Schwab, Sherman, & Murray, 1976) presents evidence that suggests major differences among groups of retirees at six-year intervals. This suggests a new generation of retirees at approximately each half decade. As the proportion of our population becomes older, better educated, better prepared for the last era of life, we are strongly encouraged to reevaluate and revise our theories of old age (Sarason, Sarason, & Cowden, 1975). In summary, the verdict about what it means to be elderly in the twenty-first century is as yet not available.

Counseling Applications

From the study of human growth and development can be drawn some specific principles to guide counselor practice. First, it is evident that clients at different developmental levels possess differing capacities to cognitively process events, to accomplish moral reasoning, and to make decisions. Both Elkind (1980) from a Piagetian position, and Swensen (1980) from a Loevinger-based ego development point of view, argue for the selection of counseling strategy with developmental level as a major criterion. For example, Swensen suggests that certain clients might benefit more from a behavioral approach than from one of the "actualizing" therapies because these clients remain at a developmental stage in which their behavior is influenced by external consequences and they are not yet at a level at which an evolving autonomy can be fostered so as to strengthen their ability to transcend such external controls.

Counselors would be wise to integrate into their practice another of Swensen's (1980) recommendations: to be cognizant of the fact that within each counseling dyad the ego development of the counselor may need to be more advanced than that of the client in order for the latter to benefit optimally from the relationship. The self-development of the counselor may determine the ceiling for client self-development as a result of that treatment, provided Swensen is correct. If the profession is to treat all persons, including well-functioning individuals in search of additional personal growth, the above implies two powerful mandates: (1) careful selection of candidates for the profession and (2) the continued self-development of counselors and other helpers.

The developmental literature uses the concept of readiness to describe optimal periods during which it is possible for an individual to make a significant advance in development. To prompt the development of a particular capability prior to that time, though not impossible, requires more effort than it is ultimately worth. Any gain achieved, beyond what another individual at the same developmental level could accomplish without special effort, would be lost at a later date. Hopefully the recognition of this phenomenon encourages among members of the counseling profession a deep respect for "nature" and the order that has evolved over time.

Probably the most impelling impression a counselor would experience on reviewing normal developmental histories is of the intensity of the struggle that is inherent in growing up. It is no simple task to take advantage of all the opportunities for becoming more mature. Many developmentalists describe the process involved in progressive and positive development as the "stretching" of a person. If a challenge lies too far beyond the capability of an individual, it provides an opportunity for failure, discouragement, and defeat. If a challenge is too easy, it does not help the individual build further on his or her repertoire of adaptive capabilities. Ideally, from a developmental point of view, a life challenge should be just a little beyond what is comfortable for a person to attain (McCoy, Ryan, & Lichtenberg, 1978). The individual must "reach" or "stretch" in order to succeed in the effort. This optimal distance promotes progressive, positive development by providing the incentive for enlarging one's repertoire of adaptive responses.

Beginning counselors have difficulty achieving this ideal balance; they vacillate between being overly protective and overly confrontive. At times they encourage their clients to escape from some of the pain necessary to overcome important problems and conflicts. In other situations beginning counselors get impatient and tend to hurry a client through the careful deliberation of changes at a transitional stage in life. With experience comes a greater capacity to set reasonable expectations during the initial phase of work with a client, and also the self-confidence and security to adjust or change treatment plans in accord with what will promote client growth.

Finally, one might reflect again on the fact that an understanding of normal development certifies the frequent anxieties and uncertainties people experience as they live out the human experience. As Moreland (1979) points out, confusion, feeling out-of-control, and being depressed are common to individuals going through predictable life transitions. Yet such feelings are often diagnosed by counselors as clear indicators of psychopathology. Familiarity with normal development assists the counselor in both avoiding the misdiagnosis of problems and in timing appropriate treatments. A thorough understanding of human development is certainly one of the most important factors in the knowledge foundation of a competent counselor.

Summary

This chapter reviewed the respect for and the utilization of normal developmental forces in the work of counselors. Maturation was described as a life-long process that helps build adaptive skills in people. In part the building process results from being forced to meet predictable challenges at regular intervals in life. Counselors attempt to understand these challenges to help their clients increase the benefit achieved from these experiences. In this way natural forces instead of artificial ones are used to enhance the development of clients.

Review Questions

1. Compare the period in the history of the counseling profession when developmental concepts began to influence practice with other historic influences of the same period (see Chapter 1).

2. List developmental theories other than the ones treated in this chapter that also can be classified as "stage-progression" or "stage-hierarchy."

3. List the key concepts in this chapter. Look up those concepts in the index at the back of the text to note other places where they are discussed.

4. List the issues one can expect to meet when counseling adolescent clients.

5. What is the explanation for the developmental changes adults experience?

6. What are some developmental explanations for anxiety?

7. What sexual issues are likely to arise during different developmental periods?

8. How do interpersonal relationships change as one matures? What relationships are likely to cause problems for clients at different life stages?

References

Armsworth, M. W., & Holaday, M. (1993). The effects of psychological trauma on children and adolescents. *Journal of Counseling and Development, 72,*(1), 49–56.

Bell, A. P., & Weinberg, M. S. (1978). *Homosexualities: A study of diversity among men and women.* New York: Simon and Schuster.

Bell, A. P., & Weinberg, M. S., & Hammersmith, S. K. (1981). *Sexual preference: Its development in men and women.* Bloomington, IN: Indiana University Press.

Bowlby, J. (1969). *Attachment and loss.* New York: Basic Books.

Clark, F. V. (1977). Transpersonal perspectives in psychotherapy. *Journal of Humanistic Psychology. 17*(1), 69–81.

Coleman, E. (1981). Counseling adolescent males. *Personnel and Guidance Journal, 60*(4), 215–218.

Dinkmeyer, D. (1966). Developmental counseling in the elementary school. *Personnel and Guidance Journal, 45*(3), 262–266.

Dinkmeyer, D., & Caldwell, E. (1970). *Developmental counseling and guidance. A comprehensive school approach.* New York: McGraw-Hill.

Dreikurs, R., Grunwald, B. R., & Pepper, F. C. (1982). *Maintaining sanity in the classroom: Illustrated teaching techniques.* (2nd ed.) New York: Harper and Row.

Dunphy, D. C. (1963). The social structure of urban adolescent peer groups. *Sociometry, 26*(3), 230–246.

Elkind, D. (1980). Child development and counseling. *Personnel and Guidance Journal, 58*(5), 353–357.

Erikson, E. H. (1963). *Childhood and society* (2nd ed.). New York: W. W. Norton.

Erikson, E. H. (1968). *Identity: Youth in crisis.* New York: W. W. Norton.

Erikson, E. H. (1969). *Gandhi's truth: On the origins of militant nonviolence.* New York: W. W. Norton.

Freidman, M. (1976). Aiming at the self: The paradox of encounter and the human potential movement. *Journal of Humanistic Psychology, 16*(1), 5–34.

Hamachek, D. (1990). Evaluating self-concept and ego status in Erikson's last three psychosocial stages. *Journal of Counseling and Development, 68*(6), 677–683.

Hamachek, D. E. (1988). Evaluating self-concept and ego development within Erikson's psychosocial framework: A formulation. *Journal of Counseling and Development, 66*(8), 354–360.

Hayes, R. L. (1994). The legacy of Lawrence Kohlberg: Implications for counseling and human development. *Journal of Counseling and Development, 72*(3), 261–267.

Holstein, C. B. (1976). Irreversible stepwise sequence in the development of moral judgment: A longitudinal study of males and females. *Child Development, 47*(1), 51–61.

Irelan, L. M., Motley, D. K., Schwab, K., Sherman, S. R., & Murray, J. (1976). *Almost 65: Baseline data from the retirement history study.* Washington, DC: U.S. Government Printing Office.

Ivey, A., & Ivey, M. B. (1990). Assessing and facilitating children's cognitive development: Developmental counseling and therapy in a case of child abuse. *Journal of Counseling and Development, 68*(3), 299–305.

Ivey, A. E. (1986). *Developmental therapy: Theory into practice.* San Francisco: Jossey-Bass.

Ivey, A. E., & Goncalves, O. F. (1988). Developmental therapy: Integrating developmental processes into the clinical practice. *Journal of Counseling and Development, 66*(9), 406–413.

Johnson, W. W., & Morasky, R. L. (1980). *Learning disabilities* (2nd ed.). Boston: Allyn & Bacon.

Klagsbrun, F. (1976). *Youth and suicide.* Boston: Houghton Mifflin.

Kohlberg, L. (1969). Stage and sequence: The cognitive developmental approach to socialization. In D. A. Goslin (ed.), *Handbook of socialization theory and research*. Chicago: Rand McNally.

Leehan, J., & Wilson, L. P. (1985). *Grown-up abused children*. Springfield, IL: Charles C. Thomas Publisher.

Lefrancois, G. R. (1984). *The lifespan*. Belmont, CA: Wadsworth Publishing Company.

Levinson, D. J. (1977). The mid-life transition. *Psychiatry, 40*(1), 99–112.

Levinson, D. J. (1986). A conception of adult development. *American Psychologist, 41*(1), 3–13.

Levinson, D. J., Darrow, C. N., Klein, E. B., Levinson, M. H., & McKee, B. (1978). *The seasons of a man's life*. New York: Ballantine Books.

Lidz, T. (1976). *The person: His and her development throughout the life cycle* (revised ed.). New York: Basic Books.

Little, W., & Chapman, A. L. (1955). *Developmental guidance in the secondary school*. New York: McGraw-Hill.

Loevinger, J. (1976). *Ego development*. San Francisco: Jossey-Bass.

Maslow, A. H. (1954). *Motivation and personality*. New York: Harper & Row.

Mathewson, R. H. (1962). *Guidance policy and practice*. New York: Harper & Row.

McCoy, V. R., Ryan, C., & Lichtenberg, J. W. (1978). *The adult life cycle: Training manual and reader*. Lawrence, KS: Adult Life Resource Center.

Moreland, J. R. (1979). Some implications of lifespan development for counseling psychol-ogy. *Personnel and Guidance Journal, 57,*(3), 299–304.

Peters, H. J. (1966). Developmental counseling. *Clearing House, 41,*(1), 111–117.

Piaget, J. (1954). *The construction of reality in the child*. New York: Basic Books.

Piaget, J. (1955). *The language and thought of the child*. New York: New American Library.

Piaget, J. (1965). *The moral judgement of the child*. New York: Macmillan.

Piaget, J. (1985). *The equilibration of cognitive structures*. Chicago: University of Chicago Press.

Quintana, S. M., & Kerr, J. (1993). Relational needs in late adolescent separation-individuation. *Journal of Counseling and Development, 71*(3), 349–354.

Sarason, D. B., Sarason, E. K., & Cowden, P. (1975). Aging and the nature of work. *American Psychologist, 30*(5), 584–592.

Sheehy, G. (1974). *Passages: Predictable crises of adult life*. New York: E. P. Dutton and Company.

Spitz, R. A. (1957). *No and yes*. New York: International Universities Press.

Stensrud, R., & Stensrud, K. (1984). Holistic health through holistic counseling: Toward a unified theory. *The Personnel and Guidance Journal, 62*(7), 421–424.

Sullivan, H. S. (1953). *The interpersonal theory of psychiatry*. New York: W. W. Norton.

Super, D. E. (1957). *The psychology of careers*. New York: Harper & Row.

Swensen, C. H. (1980). Ego development and a general model for counseling and psychotherapy. *Personnel and Guidance Journal, 58,*(4), 382–388.

Chapter 3

Counseling: Theory and Practice

Goal of the Chapter

The purpose of this chapter is to survey popular counseling theories and how they are developed and used.

Chapter Preview

- The historic development of the practice of counseling as distinct from psychotherapy will be explored.
- An overview of the characteristics and components of counseling theories will be presented.
- Major counseling approaches will be summarized.

Introduction

This is the first of two chapters designed to acquaint readers with the theory and practice of counseling. Counseling will be defined. The similarities and differences between counseling and psychotherapy will be reviewed, with emphasis on the search for effective, short-term therapies. Following a brief historical review, short-term treatment will be explored. Ways of classifying counseling approaches will be discussed; components of theoretical systems in counseling will be examined. Several popular approaches to counseling will be outlined. In Chapter 4 the discussion begun here will be completed with a discussion of some general aspects of the counseling process.

Helping People Change

Helping people change has always been a concern of advancing cultures. For centuries western civilization has sanctioned some of its members as helpers for others in this change process. For a little less than a century one general way to help has been through talk, persuasion, and caring. Individuals trained to do this well have been called either counselors or psychotherapists. Both work in similar ways; they are trained healers who help suffering people primarily through words, acts, and rituals (Frank, 1973). While differences between these two disciplines exist (to be discussed later), the need to help people change is a common reason for the existence of each.

Most texts identify Freud and psychoanalysis as the beginning of modern psychotherapy. In its classical form, psychoanalysis was an expensive, long-term treatment. In addition, it was not useful in treating all clients.

Clients seek assistance for a number of reasons. First, some people are in need of remedial help. They not only lack means to adapt to life challenges, but also have other characteristics or behaviors that are troublesome and best abandoned. Other individuals, by societal standards are considered functional, maybe even successful. However, they desire to live more fully, to actualize themselves, to grow. The changes they seek are additive to what they already are capable of doing. They do not seek remediation.

A second distinction, related to those in need of remedial help, separates those unable to function independently in society from others who can get through difficult life challenges, but suffer emotional pain. The former, if left alone, could be dangerous to themselves or others; the latter would not. For the latter group a third distinction emerges. Some of them struggle because of acute circumstances; others have lasting characteristics that make their emotional pain cyclical or chronic.

Classical psychoanalysis did not treat all these different kinds of clients; it was intended to serve the functionally capable but emotionally troubled. Left untreated via psychotherapy were the severely mentally ill, the client seeking growth, and the people in crisis. While psychiatry made advances in treating the more severe conditions, an alliance of many helping professions worked on finding more brief treatments for less disabled clientele.

The impetus for brief treatments (less than one year) gained strength during the last four to five decades. Through the work of Carl Rogers (1942, 1951) therapists learned how to establish effective working relationships with clients in a short time. The behavior therapies, developed during the last four decades, helped to streamline treatment by encouraging work toward more modest objectives, instead of the more global personality changes posed by early therapies. Many of the cognitive therapies, also developed in the last four decades, quickened the pace of treatment through emphasis on more direct confrontation of problems. These and many other innovations streamlined the talking therapies.

Counseling versus Psychotherapy

Many different therapy approaches have developed during the last forty years. Nisenholz (1983) lists more than one hundred different approaches. No doubt the variety of clients seeking help has influenced the proliferation of approaches. To date no one has taken all these therapies and divided them between counseling and psychotherapy. Belkin (1984), as have others, concludes that many similarities and differences exist between counseling and psychotherapy. They both rely on verbal interaction within a trusting interpersonal relationship to help clients understand problems, plan, and enact changes. However, the setting in which the treatment occurs and the severity of client problems in part distinguish the two treatments. Counseling signifies a more brief treatment for less severely disturbed clients who seek assistance in educational and community settings. Psychotherapy usually signifies a more long-term treatment for more chronic and severe problems conducted in a medical setting. A number of professions such as psychiatry, clinical psychology, and social work label their treatment psychotherapy.

However, it is not uncommon, for example, for someone to work for several years at a school and to be thought of as doing counseling. This same person may become employed at a residential treatment setting for youth of the same age as those in the educational setting. But since the clients at the residential center are considered more disturbed than those at the school, the counselor now becomes viewed as a therapist who performs psychotherapy. The same person may do many of the same things in trying to help. Some things will change. If nothing else, the latter treatment probably will be of longer duration. Because the client may be more troubled, more at risk, other help-givers may be involved with the client (e.g., a consulting psychiatrist). In this setting psychotherapy may be the traditional label for interactions between client and therapist that in another setting would be called counseling.

The counseling profession shows a preference for brief therapies with particular application to a broad spectrum of clients. Counselors are not deterred from using an approach to helping if it is called psychotherapy as long as it has that broad application and is more or less a short-term treatment. In line with Wolberg's (1980) view of short-term therapy, counselors often select treatment strategies with the following in mind:

1. Those strategies that fit in a time period not to exceed one year.
2. Strategies that assume the client to be an active and willing participant in treatment. While clients may be resistant at times, such resistances can be treated directly and resolved. The client will be able to form a relationship with the counselor.
3. Strategies that emphasize client strengths and allow for the minimization of deficits. The focus is on learning new ways to solve problems along with how this learning generalizes to other situations.

4. Strategies that assume clients will be able to endure periods in treatment when their anxiety will be raised as a result of the direct confrontation of problems.
5. Strategies that apply to outpatient treatment, that is, with clients who "walk in" for weekly treatment and can cope with life stresses between sessions.
6. Strategies that can be learned within the framework of a master's degree program. While these strategies are further developed over a lifetime of actual practice, the recent master's counseling graduate can be certified as competent to practice those strategies.

In general, it is very difficult (probably impossible) to distinguish between counseling and short-term psychotherapy, especially if both offer a supportive relationship and are educational in nature. In mental health settings in which a client in crisis may require medication (antidepressants or tranquilizers), the accompanying talk therapy very often is labeled counseling even though the client would be considered at much greater risk without the medication. At least over a brief period the condition of the client is serious. Thus, the more versus less severely troubled client often does not distinguish counseling from psychotherapy.

There are some advantages to using the label counseling. This label has less stigma attached to it and is more palatable to more people. Also, less liability is incurred as a counselor than as a psychotherapist. Some may prefer the label of counseling over the more generic label therapy, since the latter is understood as a treatment for some disorder. As mentioned earlier, counselors have the opportunity to treat nondisordered clients, those already functioning well but in search of further growth. Counseling is useful in more efficiently coping with predictable life changes and challenges. Thus, counseling deserves its own title, one that historically has come to represent a broad set of short-term strategies aimed at helping a wide variety of people.

STUDENT LEARNING EXERCISE
Read the statements below and indicate whether they represent the nature of counseling or not. Circle T for true and F for false.

1. Counseling and other forms of short-term therapy were developed to serve clients not served by the early forms of psychotherapy.   T   F

2. Seeking greater self-actualization is a valid reason for a client to pursue counseling.   T   F

3. The differences between counseling and psychotherapy are clear and straightforward.   T   F

Characteristics of Counseling Approaches

Counseling theories are specialized theories of behavior change. Most of them emerge from broader views of human behavior. Theorizing about human behavior could begin with very broad philosophical concepts regarding being and how one comes to know about that which exists. This is a branch of philosophy called metaphysics. Usually it is more practical to see theories of counseling as emerging from theories of personality. These theories speculate on how humans adjust or adapt to the many challenges of life. Special attention is paid to those characteristics allowing humans to survive and possibly evolve the species to an even higher form.

A subset of personality theory is the study of psychopathology (problem behavior), that is, a description and explanation of what happens when individuals are not able to cope well with life's challenges. Also part of the study of personality is speculation on how human behavior changes. When such principles of behavior change are applied to a situation in which one person tries to influence another primarily through verbal communication, a theory of counseling or psychotherapy emerges. Thus, many major theories of personality have spawned theories of counseling.

Theories of counseling or psychotherapy can begin as more or less pure speculation. They are nothing more than ideas or concepts linked together to form hypotheses. Several hypotheses linked together form the theory. A few counseling theories are well structured into hypotheses called postulates, theorems, and corollaries—much like the euclidean geometry studied in high school. Other theories are rambling narratives about a theorist's experiences as a therapist. When one reads most of the original sources written on a particular counseling theory, it is like sitting down with an experienced practitioner to "talk" counseling. Most theory books have sections in which concepts are defined and discussed. These references frequently make the ideas live through case illustrations and examples. Thus, reading counseling theory is exposure to real life; the emphasis is on helping people solve problems in living.

It is important to recognize that a theory is first and foremost a set of ideas used as a convenience in explaining what happens when the counselor and client work together. An idea is an abstraction that only exists in the mind. They are not able to exist by themselves, i.e., outside of human minds. In many instances one idea can explain reality (possibly several different realities) just as well as another idea. Pure speculation eventually is shown to be useful or not useful through the experience of those who use the ideas. Since two different ideas can be equally useful in explaining the same aspect of our experience, it is difficult to determine one set of ideas as being better than another set.

For some sets of ideas (theories), there is more experience or evidence verifying (or proving) the ideas to be useful. A theory is proved by gathering evidence in favor of the explanations provided. Different disciplines and schools of thought within a discipline argue about what constitutes valid evidence in support of theories. For example, in counseling some practitioners will accept as evidence only tightly controlled empirical research. Others argue that the "court" hearing a case for a counseling approach should admit more evidence than empirical data. For example, subjective experience of participants that is carefully analyzed and recorded may be just as valid evidence as simulations (analogues) of counseling, empirically studied in the human relations laboratory. The most productive method for advancing the practice of counseling is to develop counseling theories as a consequence of the research and experience of its practitioners. Admitting evidence too restrictively or too liberally can negatively affect this development. In the former, knowledge is lost through narrow bias; in the latter, knowledge is buried in nonsense.

Generally, theories tend to mature over time. In the beginning a theoretical approach may be identified with one person as its founder but later becomes associated with many different persons as the approach expands and is verified. However, as time passes some approaches seem to lose popularity, even though they are still useful. Transactional Analysis is an example of this process. People in the field seem to tire of the concepts, replacing it with a more recent or more novel approach.

The better counseling/psychotherapy theories tend to have application for a wider variety of clientele. They are parsimonious; they neither over or under explain the issues. Their explanations are believable.

Making a believable explanation is not easy. A theorist will begin to explain something new by relying on familiar ideas. The theorist then draws an analogy from the old to the new. For example, scientists had the idea of the solar system before a scheme existed for the atom. They used the solar system as a conceptual model for the structure of the atom.

Theorists use metaphors; that is, they denote one idea by relating it to another. For example, someone familiar with auto mechanics might explain counseling as "like [analogous to] overhauling an internal combustion engine." We would learn about counseling through the engine overhaul metaphor. Theories can be judged according to the quality of the metaphors used. One metaphor can "grab" us, while another stimulates little involvement.

The point should be made again that counseling theories are meant to be convenient ways of explaining what goes on when one counsels. It is better to say that a theoretical approach is useful rather than that it is *the* truth. There are many truths when it comes to finding ways to explain how counseling works, just as there are many stories or parables that can portray a belief.

For the reasons stated, it would seem useful for a student of counseling to view the process of helping others as a task with such dimensions that a full depiction of its breadth would take a long time to develop. Over the last ninety or so years numerous individuals have contributed to our evolving understanding of helping. There has been a great deal of collaboration among many individuals to advance our understanding of how counseling works. This understanding will continue to grow.

Reading about theorists and their contributions is truly a saga; there are real heroes who have tended to attract followers. Adopting a theoretical orientation, however, is not an exercise in finding a hero to follow. One approach may bind together ideas and metaphors that are particularly resonant with one's own values and experience. A theoretical approach may pay special attention to the population of clients one expects most to serve. The integration found in such an approach may make it particularly attractive. One may identify with the approach and publicly proclaim that identification. On the other hand, any one of the current counseling approaches may not explain everything needed for a particular practitioner. Several systems may need to be integrated in order for the practitioner to have all the explanatory power necessary. The pros and cons of integrating theoretical concepts of different origins will be treated when eclectic counseling is discussed.

Classifying Counseling Approaches

As various approaches develop, their similarities and differences are noted. With the extensive number of counseling/psychotherapy approaches in existence, the need to find ways of classifying them has arisen. Baruth and Huber (1985) divide treatment approaches into those that are primarily affectively oriented, behaviorally oriented, or cognitively oriented. Depending on the classification, feelings, observable behavior, or thoughts have primacy in relation to understanding why clients seek the assistance of the counselor, what changes are likely to occur, and how the counselor eventually helps the client. At issue among different approaches is not that affect, cognition, and behavior are connected and mutually influence one another. Rather, what is often argued (Zajonc, 1984; Lazarus, 1984) is whether one precedes the others in a chain of reactions, whether changes in one is the most effective way to achieve positive changes in the others.

A more popular way of classifying approaches divides them into psychoanalytic, humanistic, and behavioral categories (Lichtenstein, 1980; Morse & Watson, 1977). To these three classes Belkin (1980) adds what he calls a "cognitive-dynamic" category.

The psychoanalytic or psychodynamic class of therapies can be traced back to Sigmund Freud. According to Tremblay, Herron, and Schultz (1986), therapists with these orientations emphasize in treatment inner subjective states, unconscious motivation, appropriate expression of feeling, and childhood experience. These factors are traditional to the Freudian and neo-Freudian approaches.

Humanistic therapies are associated with what has been called the "third force" in psychology, the force other than psychoanalysis and behaviorism. Actualizing potential is the key emphasis in these therapies. Tremblay, Herron, and Schultz (1986) suggest that humanistic therapists favor spontaneous expression of feelings and behavior, flexibility, self-disclosure, and personal relationships as the major vehicles for personality change.

Behavior therapies are closely tied to academic psychology. They apply the principles studied in the laboratory to behavior problems of people in real life. Tremblay, Herron, and Schultz (1986) suggest that behavior therapists stress objectivity, external events, detachment, planning, control, and a focus on the present.

Table 3.1 attempts to classify selected counseling approaches. Other texts portray some of these approaches differently. For example, Adlerian (individual) psychology is often classified as a psychodynamic approach. Since the variety of concepts present in many of these approaches do not conveniently fit the categories, differences in interpretation of the basic thrust of the approach will result.

Components of a Counseling Theory

When counselors-in-training enroll in a counseling theories course, they usually learn more than counseling theory. Usually they also study the personality theory out of which the treatment theory evolved. Some parts of the theory of psychopathology within the parent personality theory might also be treated. This is necessary in order for counselors to understand human behavior more completely in accordance with the view presented. The following are the principal components of counseling theory.

Preconditions for Treatment
A mature counseling theory will not purport to help everyone under all conditions. Most important to be discussed are any client characteristics necessary for effective outcome. For example, many approaches may stipulate some of the following as necessary for treatment to be effective: minimal age, client motivation as a result of emotional pain, absence of thought disorders (psychosis), and so forth.

TABLE 3.1   Selecting Approaches to Counseling and Psychotherapy

Behavioral	Cognitive	Humanistic	Analytic
Behavior therapy Reality therapy	Rational-emotive Transactional (TA) Trait and factor	Client-centered Existential Gestalt therapy Adlerian	Psychoanalysis Psychoanalytic therapy Jungian

Counselor Characteristics
A very important part of any counseling theory is the description of the attitudes and behavior of the counselor. Mention may be made of the training required.

Relationship between Counselor and Client
Historically, the relationship between the counselor and the client in counseling and psychotherapy has been viewed as one of the most important elements in achieving favorable outcome. However, differences in the type of relationship developed produce sharp distinctions among different approaches.

Diagnosis of Client Problems
The type and importance of diagnosis is another differentiating factor among approaches, with significant implications regarding necessary training for the counselor. Diagnosis is usually tied to the theory's view of problem behavior (psychopathology) and how it is manifested by the client.

Counseling Goals
Treatment objectives can be divided into terminal and process goals. The former refer to final outcomes on completion of the process; the latter are accomplishments arrived at during the process of treatment. Goals are usually connected to the diagnosis of client difficulties; often they are the antitheses of the problems. Some counseling approaches utilize broad goals applicable to every client; others are more specific, with particular goals applied to individual clients depending on their circumstances and needs.

Techniques
Techniques are the methods used by the counselor to explore, define, and attain treatment objectives. They include ways of saying things, special procedures enacted during an interview, and tactics used by both counselor and client between (outside of) interviews.

The Process
A well-developed counseling theory will describe shifts and changes that occur during the treatment. From early in the process, to the middle, and finally to the end, the movement to be observed may be noted, possibly through the identification of stages in the process. The theory may note that a certain condition must precede another. Critical periods may be noted, such as times when attrition is most probable or when setbacks usually occur.

How to Evaluate Outcome
A counseling theory should identify the type of evidence it views as valid in determining progress or the lack of it. Criteria should be offered to assist the counselor in determining when the process can be terminated, when outcomes have been achieved.

Major Counseling Approaches

Client-Centered Therapy

If one recognizes that prior to Carl Rogers very little was written regarding how
one actually does counseling and psychotherapy, the importance of his contributions becomes even more significant. Some of his earliest writings (Rogers, 1942)
demonstrate his keen interest in the actual practice of counseling and psychotherapy.

The central emphasis in client-centered therapy is the relationship between
counselor and client (Raskin & Rogers, 1989). The primary goal of treatment, to
free the actualizing tendency of the client, is best achieved by creating an interpersonal environment full of warmth and understanding and free of constraint.
This is achieved by having the counselor offer the conditions of empathy, uncon-
ditional positive regard, and congruence. If the client is able to perceive these conditions, in part by being physically present to the counselor, and is motivated to
change because the difficulties make the client feel anxious or vulnerable, Rogers
(1957) argued that positive personality change would result. This constitutes the
essence of Rogers' theory; nothing else is needed.

The goal of counseling, to make the client more fully functioning, is represented during the process of therapy by increasing levels of self-acceptance. As
counseling continues, the client's actual self-image becomes more congruent with
his or her ideal self-image. When a counselor enters the subjective world of a client,
understanding it and communicating that understanding (empathy) to the client,
the counselor lowers the client's defenses to more honestly evaluate experiences.

Feeling safe in the relationship as a result of the warmth and caring (uncon-
ditional positive regard) of the therapist, the client reflects this greater openness
in deeper levels of self-disclosure. As the counselor remains genuine (congruent),

showing no pretense or phoniness, the client also becomes congruent; his self-concept begins to coincide more with the ideal he has for himself.

During his long career Rogers applied his approach to many different types of individuals, to groups, and to married and other committed couples. In addition, his ideas have been applied to educational, interracial, and international problems. Rogers (1977) suggested that his approach be called the *person-centered approach,* since its emphasis ultimately is to return power and control to the individual.

Client-centered therapy has stood the test of time; its ability to achieve its stated treatment goals has been documented repeatedly. Its position on the necessity of offering the conditions described earlier has been accepted by the majority of professional help-givers. As will be described in Chapter 8, training procedures have been carefully refined to teach counselors-in-training how to communicate empathy, positive regard, and congruence. Few helping professionals will be unaffected in their career by the teachings of Carl Rogers. He died in 1987 of heart disease.

Adlerian Counseling

Adlerian or individual psychology has come to practitioners in this country primarily from the work of Rudolf Driekurs (1953), a follower and careful interpreter of Alfred Adler's ideas. Ansbacher and Ansbacher (1956) have been responsible for collecting the writings of Adler, while Don Dinkmeyer and coworkers (Dinkmeyer, Pew, & Dinkmeyer, 1979) have applied Adlerian psychology to elementary school counseling. Adlerian concepts have been directed extensively toward parenting and child rearing (Driekurs & Soltz, 1964).

Adlerian counseling seeks to correct mistakes in perception and logic that people make in their effort to fit into social relationships and to overcome feelings of inferiority. According to this view, people are born with feelings of inferiority. Certainly the need to rely on caretakers so long reinforces those feelings in the young child.

As a result of conclusions drawn about early experiences in the extended family, clients adopt "mistaken goals." Rather than pursuing social interest, they strive for attention, power, revenge, or the showing of inadequacy. Depending on the mistaken goal, the client will formulate other supportive misconceptions. The complex of this faulty logic leads to a particular lifestyle or way of acting consistent with the logic.

The counselor attempts to develop a positive relationship with the client in order to discover the mistaken goals of faulty logic. In other words, if the counselor can find out what the client is up to (goals), all the rest of his or her behavior will be understandable. Once discovered, the logic is interpreted to the client. Dreams and early recollections reveal the logic clearly. Recollections are vivid memories of very early experiences retained out of the millions of brief life episodes.

They are remembered because they support (defend) the faulty (private) logic of the client. To simplify the use of dreams, early recollections, and beliefs regarding the client's role in the family (family constellation), the Adlerians have developed a structured way to inventory them, called a lifestyle questionnaire (Mosak, 1972). Once discovered and interpreted, the client's faulty logic is repeatedly confronted and challenged in an effort to demonstrate its flaws. Persuasion and paradoxical intention (wish for unwanted consequences) are also used. In addition, Adlerian counselors encourage clients to try behaviors between sessions that they would ordinarily not use because of their faulty beliefs. Such practice, followed by favorable consequences, may help clients change their minds about themselves and what they might be able to achieve.

The Adlerian approach, while not well researched, utilizes common techniques (e.g., interpretation) favored by many other approaches. In this respect it is a "mainstream" form of intervention.

Reality Therapy

William Glasser, the founder of reality therapy, is one of many contemporary therapists who have tried to demystify the process of helping. Glasser has had a particular interest in developing a common sense approach that can be used by parents, teachers, and all kinds of professional help-givers besides those with extensive training and experience.

Reality therapy is a very optimistic, highly involved way of helping people confront the problems of modern society. To achieve, and in particular to learn to accept oneself, individuals must develop a success identity (Glasser & Zunin, 1979). While being loved and accepted by others helps develop a success identity, those without it can only develop one through actions that lead to accomplishments. Such accomplishments then lead to self-acceptance.

According to Glasser and Zunin (1979), people who are unhappy, who get into trouble, and who develop many different emotional problems are persons with a failure identity. This identity leads to loneliness, poor contact with reality, and the giving up of responsibility. Responsibility is a key word in reality therapy (Glasser, 1965); by it Glasser means learning how to fulfill one's own needs so that the needs of others are not violated.

During the process of helping change a client's failure identity and subsequent irresponsible behavior, acting or doing is emphasized. Glasser believes it is easier to change behavior than to change feelings and cognitions (Glasser & Zunin, 1979). The counselor works hard to develop a strong, warm, but confrontive relationship with the client; to emphasize what can be done in the present; to encourage the client to forget the past; and to seek alternatives to ineffectual client actions of the past, never giving up, and never accepting excuses for not trying to be different. Special effort is made to avoid punishing the client for past failures; the emphasis in sessions is on the planning of responsible actions.

Wubbolding (1988, 1991) provides a good synthesis of reality therapy as developed by Glasser. In addition, he enlarges reality therapy practice by introducing the use of paradoxical techniques. His metaphors clarify many reality therapy concepts.

Rational-Emotive Therapy

Albert Ellis, the founder of rational-emotive therapy (RET), has been one of the most prolific and energetic messengers of a therapeutic approach. He has maintained that the root source of human problems is irrational thoughts (mistaken ideas) learned by people early in life and maintained by a continual process of reindoctrination, willingly undertaken by those same people (Ellis, 1973). A counselor can help such clients by vigorously disputing those irrational thoughts and offering as a substitute a different set of ideas, based primarily on the tolerance of self and others.

RET epitomizes the view that sound thinking leads to emotional well-being; people feel bad because intervening between an unpleasant situation and strong negative feelings are thoughts that amplify the negative feelings. Two such thoughts have to do with believing that one must be loved and appreciated by everyone and that one must try to be perfect.

RET therapists teach clients how to intervene in this process by substituting more healthy thoughts for those that create strong negative feelings. When this substitution occurs, clients develop thought processes more consistent with the scientific method. Their mental health improves as a result of greater self-direction and acceptance of uncertainty. Their behavior changes; it becomes more flexible, and more risks are taken (Ellis, 1973). Behavior is not ignored in RET. Strong emphasis is placed on "homework" between sessions in order for the client to develop the skills needed to cope with life's situations, especially those of a social nature. Semantics also plays an important role in the teaching provided by the RET practitioner (Ellis & Abrahms, 1978). Words such as "terrible," "must," and "should" are replaced by words such as "unpleasant," "preferable," and "desirable." Such a vocabulary reminds the client of thought processes that are equally tolerant and flexible.

Behavior Therapy

Behavior therapy is a diverse and ever-expanding approach to behavior change that has its origins in academic psychology. In particular, it emphasizes the learning and unlearning of behaviors and associations between feelings and environmental stimuli. The principles governing this learning strive for scientific precision. At first behavior therapy was promoted as more or less an alternative to traditional therapy. While it directed attention to the treatment of anxiety and other common client complaints, it was developed as a specialized treatment for more select human problems (e.g., phobias). As it has matured, behavior therapy in actual practice has begun to resemble the more traditional therapies, with increased attention being paid to client variables other than observable behavior. In part this may be explained by looking at some of the historical developments within this approach.

Wolpe (1958) was one of the earliest to apply behavioral principles to the treatment of anxiety and other affective problems. Basic to his approach was the process of classical conditioning in which autonomic responses such as anxiety or fear became associated with the wrong stimuli. His approach, called reciprocal inhibition, was an attempt to reconnect more appropriate responses to those environmental stimuli.

Anxious clients were most often put in a peaceful state through progressive relaxation techniques. Anxiety-producing stimuli were then paired with this state. Important to the process was the building of hierarchy of anxiety-producing stimuli. The client was exposed to the least anxiety-producing ones first. For Wolpe this was mostly done in the interviewing room through client imagery. Other behavior therapists used "in vivo" techniques where clients were exposed to stimuli in their actual environment. This process of systematic desensitization is still an important part of behavior therapy.

Behavior modification, based on operant conditioning principles promoted by B. F. Skinner, emerged as the primary thrust behind the practice of behavioral counseling (Krumboltz & Thoresen, 1976). The 1960s were a time of much growth in behavioral treatments (Ullmann & Krasner, 1965). Emphasis was on control of environmental factors influencing client behavior. In particular, the management of reinforcers, especially positive ones, was viewed as the way to change not only motor responses but verbal behavior as well. Together these behaviors were defined and categorized with particular relevance to social situations (social skills), a common area of concern for clients seeking counseling.

Learning such complex behaviors as those necessary to succeed in social situations expanded the repertoire of the behavior therapist through the use of modeling, a process in which one person learns complex responses by observing others and then imitating the actions that become reinforced (Bandura, 1977). When combined with sufficient practice, even that resulting from role playing (behavior rehearsal), the acquisition of a larger behavior repertoire is possible. Extended practice is also important in order for the client to be able to discriminate when one set of responses might or might not be appropriate. Depending on the situation, one set could be reinforced and another not.

Of all the different reinforcement strategies used in behavior therapy, self-management approaches have appealed to many counselors. They essentially share their knowledge of learning principles with the client so the client can begin to use reinforcement, behavioral observation, and monitoring on their own (Thoresen & Mahoney, 1974). It is a "power to the people" approach that sets a high standard for informed consent in the counseling profession. The counselor educates the client in these behavior principles, but the client has control of their use. Self-management places considerable emphasis on between-session practice and recording of behaviors.

Common among the diverse strategies used in behavior therapy is an emphasis on specificity and the treatment of problem behavior as is, instead of as a "symptom" of some other problem. Specific behaviors become targeted first for observation, in order to specify the conditions under which the behaviors occur and the frequency in which they are emitted. The treatment goals are carefully set forth in light of the data gathered.

Treatment goals often have to do with both unlearning some behaviors and learning new ones. Reinforcement contingencies are at the core of most learning activities, whether they be observing a model, role playing, or real life practice.

Unlike other approaches, behavior therapy has paid special attention to consolidating gains by applying learning principles to prevention of relapse. Often clients make significant gains in counseling, only to see these gains disappear over time. It is like losing ten pounds on a diet only to gradually regain the weight over a period of several months. The weight gain is a result of returning to old habits. Relapse prevention strategies strengthen new, more healthy habits, making return to old ones less probable.

Cognitive Behavior Therapy

As such learning principles were demonstrated as effective with observable behavior, greater attention was directed toward applying those same principles to unobservable behavior, especially to thoughts or cognitions (Mahoney, 1974; Michenbaum, 1977). This evolution was reasonable for the practice of counseling or psychotherapy, in spite of some of the rigid emphasis in academic psychology on only observable behavior. One will recall the early emphasis in behavior therapy (Wolpe, 1958) on the use of cognitive imagery to inhibit inappropriate emotional responses.

The defining element in cognitive behavior therapy is a process called cognitive restructuring (Meichenbaum, 1972). It is similar in some ways to rational-emotive-therapy (RET) in that the ultimate goal is to replace self-defeating thoughts with adaptive ones. However, where RET theory prescribes rational and irrational thinking, cognitive behavior therapy teaches the client how to use self-observation to empirically identify their own self-defeating cognitions. Where RET counselors actively dispute irrational thinking in their dialogue with clients, cognitive behavioral counselors help clients assess the data they have collected on the consequences of their thoughts.

Cormier and Cormier (1991) see cognitive restructuring as a six-step process. First, counselors present a rationale that contrasts self-defeating and self-enhancing thoughts with an emphasis on how they affect performance. Problem situations are then reviewed in order to identify client thoughts that accompany them. The third step introduces thoughts that might help the client cope better. Practice of those coping thoughts is encouraged. In the next step the counselor demonstrates the shift from self-defeating to coping thoughts. The fifth step involves the use of positive reinforcement to strengthen the bond between the coping thoughts and the problem situations. Finally, the counselor and client map out a strategy for additional practice and evaluation, mostly in the form of homework.

While cognitive restructuring is central to cognitive behavioral therapy (CBT), the approach is flexible in its technique. It will use any number of strategies that have good data to support their effectiveness. For example, CBT might add social skills training as part of the treatment plan. The client might observe a live or symbolic (e.g., videotaped) model in order to learn social skills. That might be followed by homework in which the client imagines someone performing behaviors (covert modeling). In another instance the counselor may instruct clients in what to say to themselves while they are taking an exam in order to reduce test anxiety. This is called cognitive modeling.

Cognitive behavior therapy accepts the linkages among thoughts, emotions, and behaviors. A change in one often leads to changes in the others. Thus, one can be eclectic in approach. At one time the counselor can work at changing behavior directly through self-reward strategies. At another time changing a person's beliefs or thoughts may be the path to the client feeling better and performing more effectively.

Gestalt Therapy

Gestalt therapy is one of the earliest modern therapies (Perls, Hefferline, & Goodman, 1951) that remained largely unknown until the 1960s, when Frederick (Fritz) Perls' work at the Esalen Institute in California became well known. This approach is an imaginative marriage of concepts from existential philosophy and techniques from psychodrama (Moreno, 1946). Passons (1975) has taken elements of the approach, one best conducted in a controlled environment (e.g., a retreat-like, growth center), and reframed the procedures for application to a broader range of clientele seeking treatment at a variety of agencies. Earlier versions of Gestalt therapy often led to an intense expression of emotions that benefited from a more total integration into the client's personality, not efficiently achieved via once-a-week outpatient treatment.

According to Gestalt therapy, people strive for balance (homeostasis) in their interactions with the world and themselves (Perls, 1973). As one lives, one contacts the environment, deals with it for a time, then moves on to new experiences once old ones are complete. Unfinished situations inhibit the flow of experience, restricting the person, blurring boundaries, producing negative feelings of detachment and engulfment, creating rigidity in the person, and in general upsetting equilibrium. Awareness of self as an evolving entity with a unique identity with unique involvements becomes stalled.

To treat such problems, Gestalt counselors emphasize the expansion of awareness by focusing on the here-and-now experiences of the client. As unfinished experiences emerge, they are brought into the present, treated, and finished. To recapture meaning in life the client is continually challenged to assume responsibility for what is going on. The emphasis is extended even to language in which a statement like "I am sad" is changed to "I choose to be sad." The objective is to help the client assume greater self-responsibility and control over life.

The Gestalt-oriented counselor often uses a variety of confrontive strategies to help the client remove barriers to here-and-now experience. For example, the counselor may ask the client to live a fantasy, exaggerate a posture that represents something of meaning, stay in a feeling that the client often tries to flee, or act out a dream. Many of these strategies are quite dramatic.

Gestalt techniques are not applicable to the entire spectrum of clients seeking assistance (Shepherd, 1970). For this reason only a small percentage of practitioners are likely to identify with this approach (Smith, 1982). Gestalt therapy often is studied in counselor preparation programs as a means of enrichment and for its major contributions to treating client resistances.

Other Important Approaches

In addition to learning about the approaches briefly described above, counselors-in-training often are exposed to other therapy systems that will be discussed only briefly in this text. These include psychoanalytic therapy, transactional analysis, and trait and factor counseling.

Psychoanalytic theory, besides being the oldest conceptual framework, is one of the richest and most rapidly expanding of the dominant systems in use today. Its elegance and depth make it an approach best learned after considerable postdoctoral treatment experience and supervision.

In a master's degree program, at best one can expect to review principal concepts developed by Freud and some of his contemporaries. Contemporary psychoanalytic theory is called by a number of titles. They include ego psychology, object relations theory, psychoanalytic developmental psychology, and possibly a few others. After Freud's death, psychoanalytic theory began to move away from an emphasis on instincts (primitive human impulses) to careful consideration of adaptive functions, called ego functions. While Freud contributed to such concepts to a degree, his daughter, Anna, and Hans Hartmann are considered to be the initial driving forces in the development of ego psychology (Blanck & Blanck, 1974).

With important contributions from Margaret Mahler (1979), Edith Jacobson (1971), Otto Kernberg (1984), Althea Horner (1991), and many others, ego psychology has made important advances in the treatment of depression, narcissism, and borderline conditions. The latter disorders are quite complicated to understand and treat, but worthy of study for the experienced practitioner or advanced student with prior counseling experience.

Transactional analysis (TA) is often studied in counselor preparation. It appears to have attracted few practitioners coming from graduate training programs (Smith, 1982), but is still used extensively by paraprofessionals, clergy, and other groups of help-givers.

Developed in the 1950s by Eric Berne, TA began as a system with primary use in groups, but has expanded to individual treatment as well. The unique contribution of TA has to do with understanding social interactions and how they influence mental health. Through his theory of interpersonal games, Berne (1964) offered the helping professions and the public as well a way of understanding subtle manipulations people use to both avoid intimacy and to control others.

At first TA relied on concepts represented by a vocabulary of terms intended to be easily understood by almost anyone entering a therapy group as a client. Today that vocabulary has expanded to include a complex array of terms to represent subtle features of personality and social interaction (Woollams & Brown, 1979). The essence of TA as a treatment approach is to do a lot of explaining of behavior using its vocabulary; then the goal becomes to help clients decide to redirect their lives. Once this decision is made, called a redecision (Goulding & Goulding, 1979), a process of reversing behavior or relearning takes place.

Trait and factor counseling is one of the few approaches that has it roots in differential psychology rather than psychiatry or clinical psychology. This approach is used extensively as a basis for career counseling and is discussed in Chapter 7.

Eclectic Approaches

Earlier in this chapter it was mentioned that Nisenholz (1983) has listed more than one hundred different treatment approaches. The point was made that some approaches do not purport to be effective with all clients; rather, they have been developed with particular populations in mind. In addition, the reader was reminded that counseling theories are merely ideas developed to explain what happens in treatment. Rychlak (1985) describes his experiences in graduate school where he was supervised by three different, but equally renowned, professors, each of whom had developed therapy theories. At times he would have to discuss the same clients in a different way, depending on who was supervising him at that time. Of course, he noted that this was possible—the same client with the same behavior and problems was conceptualized to the satisfaction of each renowned professor and theoretician. Again the point is that there are many ways of understanding human situations, empirical data or "facts." In an earlier work Rychlak (1968) noted several forms of reasoning. Demonstrative reasoning essentially posits that there is only one correct answer to a question; however, dialectical reasoning proves that there is more than one correct answer. Rychlak (1968) argues that dialectics is more appropriate to conceptualizing issues in counseling and psychotherapy than demonstrative reasoning. If this is true, counseling practitioners may have to examine the utility of sticking firmly to only one theoretical system to explain what happens to clients.

Apparently this is precisely what people who practice counseling and psychotherapy have done. Surveys of theoretical preference among practicing psychologists (Jensen, Bergin, & Greaves, 1990; Smith, 1982; Garfield & Kurtz, 1976) show that the majority of those questioned identify themselves as eclectic, that is, not subscribing to only one theoretical approach. Rather, when faced with everyday treatment issues, practitioners seem to draw on several of the established systems.

There are pros and cons of eclecticism (Brabeck & Welfel, 1985; Hutchins, 1984; Ward, 1983). Eclecticism can be positive if it is simply drawing the largest variety of explanations and treatment techniques to become equipped to deal with the broadest range of issues. This position makes eclecticism seem an open and flexible way of both helping clients and advancing the profession. It does not seem so positive if it is viewed as a "shotgun" technique of amassing concepts and techniques without much consideration of how they fit together and how they can be justified. In fact, using an approach to treat a client without a sound rationale for doing so is not only a hodgepodge way of doing things, but is also unethical.

To avoid some of the problems noted, Hutchins (1984) and Brabeck and Welfel (1985) argue for the development of broader, more comprehensive models to synthesize current theories; such systems would provide the concepts to unify elements frequently combined in eclectic approaches. Rychlak (1985) cautions practitioners, reminding them that choosing a number of explanatory systems is more realistic than naively thinking that "facts" can eventually be explained by one "true" system.

Ward (1983) helps resolve some of the controversy by contending that the development of new theories is on the decline. Greater interest seems to exist in more fully developing current ones into more comprehensive systems. This brings attention to the fact that approaches to counseling and psychotherapy for the most part can be considered as still in their infancy. If the last twenty years is any indication of the momentum behind the development of counseling approaches, by the time today's counselors-in-training reach the midpoint in their careers, there will be major additions and revisions to the ways in which we understand how clients are helped.

Targeted Therapies

Mental health, like the rest of the health care system, is being pressured to contain costs of its services. Insurance companies and managed care organizations need to anticipate expenditures. They do not like to pay for counseling that does not clearly define what it is treating, the specific procedures and personnel to be used, and the number of sessions it will take to complete the treatment. Beyond insisting on carefully written treatment plans, this health care climate has endorsed the development of specific treatments for diagnosable conditions. Often they are called focal treatments because they target specific problems. In the future, general approaches to counseling may give way to a menu of focal therapies. The latter will have been carefully researched. Data favoring the efficacy of a particular treatment may be used by third party payers to determine which treatments they will and will not cover. In this way treatment of diagnosable conditions may become standardized. The following are examples of focal treatments.

Focal Treatments for Depression

Most of the popular therapy approaches have been applied to clients with depression. However, by virtue of the extent to which people suffer from depression, and its cost to our society, focal treatments for depression were developed in the late 1960s. They were intended to be brief, time-limited therapies for the treatment of nonbipolar, nonpsychotic, depressed adult outpatients. Over the years these therapies have been extensively researched and modified for application to other similar populations, including adolescents.

Two such approaches will be discussed in this chapter. They are: Cognitive Behavior Therapy for Depression (CBT) and Interpersonal Psychotherapy for Depressed Adolescents (IPT-A). Extensive research has shown each to be effective. Extensive research by NIMH comparing these therapies has shown them to be equally effective (Elkin, Shea, Watkins, Imber, Sotsky, Collins, et al., 1989).

Cognitive Behavior Therapy for Depression (CBT)

CBT as modified for the treatment of depression is a structured, directive, often time-limited approach that encourages the development of problem-solving skills, and the changing of thoughts associated with behavior. Aaron Beck's general concepts about depression are the basis for this intervention. David Burn's book, *Feeling Good*, also portrays this approach.

Beck and his associates (Beck, 1967; Beck, Rush, Shaw, & Emery, 1979) proposed a model of depression that is based on the client's negative view of self, the world, and the future. The client reacts to stress by activating these overly negative beliefs. Attached to the beliefs are also faulty thought processes. They include: dichotomous thinking, overgeneralization, personalization, and selective abstraction. The thought processes and beliefs combine in the client's life to minimize the positive and accentuate the negative. Depressive cognitions, called "depressogenic cognitions," result.

For Beck, therapy attempts to correct misperceptions and misattributions by means of structured tasks, both during therapy sessions and between. The goals of cognitive therapy are to relieve symptoms while uncovering beliefs that lead to depression. Therapy reality tests the beliefs by helping clients to make associations between cognitions, affect, and behavior. It is a form of "guided discovery" between the therapist and client. It is also called "collaborative empiricism," because the consequences of thought patterns are so closely observed. Clients learn to monitor negative beliefs, fantasies, dreams, and images, and see the consequences of them in their lives. The approach is eclectic in technique, utilizing many behavioral and thought control procedures. In particular, language is taken seriously; meanings of words are investigated carefully.

As a treatment for depression, CBT is intended to be short-term with mild- to moderately-depressed clients. Anecdotal evidence suggests that low self-esteem, perfectionistic clients are especially good candidates. To work best, clients need to be able to tolerate activity and homework; be motivated to change, and of average intelligence. Usually, twenty-five sessions is seen as the maximum treatment.

Interpersonal Psychotherapy for Depression (IPT)
Interpersonal psychotherapy is another short-term treatment that has been specifically developed for the treatment of depression. Klerman and associates (Klerman, Weissman, Rounsaville, & Chevron, 1984) have developed specific treatment protocols with a special adaptation for adolescents (Mufson, Moreau, Weissman, & Klerman, 1993; Mufson, Moreau, Weissman, & Klerman, 1993). The latter (IPT-A) will be described.

IPT-A has been designed for use with twelve to eighteen year olds who have experienced an acute onset of major depression. The main goals of the treatment are to decrease depressive symptoms, while improving the interpersonal problems associated with the depressive episode. The therapy is planned for twelve sessions as follows.

The first session is used to explore the reasons for seeking treatment, and getting a history of the depression and its symptoms. Besides assessing suicide potential, the adolescent is examined for both drug abuse and antisocial behavior. By the end of the second session the assessment should be complete and determination made regarding the treatability of the client with IPT-A. The next two sessions (three and four) review the client's present and past social relationships in order to determine how the client functions interpersonally. Significant people the client is asked about include family, friends, and teachers. Often one or more of these relationships has become even more difficult as a result of the depression. Together, these first four sessions help establish the sequence of events that may have precipitated the depression. The therapist helps the client to connect symptoms with problem areas. With the symptom review complete, the therapist by the fourth session attempts to educate the adolescent and parents about depression, and how it can be placed in an interpersonal context. The treatment contract is made, defining the goals of improved relationships and symptom reduction, and steps toward that recovery are described. A positive expectancy is developed by forecasting feeling better as the treatment continues.

The middle phase of treatment lasts between the fifth and eighth sessions. The therapist now becomes less active, less questioning, and directive. The client is encouraged to discuss topics relevant to the identified problem areas. These may include discussing some loss, maybe a death of a parent. It may involve exploration of some interpersonal role disputes, such as an adolescent going to the senior high school, wanting more freedom to stay out late, but being carefully controlled by parents. It could be a case that the parent may be overcontrolling, and the adolescent has not come to terms with how to deal with it.

The therapist would help the adolescent find ways to deal with these types of disputes. The interpersonal problems explored in the middle phase often deal with role-transition problems. For example, the client may have entered puberty and is having difficulty dealing with sexual feelings and ways to respond effectively to members of the opposite sex. Therapy in this situation may review social role expectations, educate parents about the transition, and help the adolescent to assess and develop social skills. While attending to these issues, the therapist also will pay attention to the availability of support for the client during the transition.

Also in the middle phase the therapist may help the adolescent client work on interpersonal deficits, i.e., the lack of social and communication skills that impairs the development and maintenance of interpersonal relationships. As such skills are practiced during and between sessions, the client will likely experience an increase in self-confidence. That may allow more appropriate risk-taking, including initiating relationships, something the client may have been hesitant to do. Depending on how many of these problems may exist determines if the middle phase may be extended several more weeks. It is not uncommon for the original plan of twelve sessions to be lengthened to sixteen.

By the ninth or tenth session in the twelve-week process the therapist will remind the client that treatment is drawing to a close. In the late sessions the possibility of the depression returning is explored. Clients are helped to better recognize their competence in dealing with the problems. Accomplishments during treatment are noted. Throughout this review the therapist shows how treatment was oriented toward improving relationships. Repeated reference is made regarding improved communication, being able to see another's point of view, and being able to negotiate a dispute.

With adolescents there is also a need to have a final termination session with the family. The goals for this session are similar to those with the adolescent alone. Management of future episodes of depression are discussed along with the accomplishments of the treatment.

Summary

This chapter offered a brief overview of counseling theory, to be followed in the next chapter by a more detailed look at common elements in the counseling process. Counseling was compared to psychotherapy. A mental set was offered concerning how theoretical approaches to counseling might be used most effectively. The components of a counseling theory were identified, as were ways of classifying different theories. Finally, some of the dominant counseling/psychotherapy approaches were described briefly.

Review Questions

1. Briefly describe some of the similarities and differences between counseling and psychotherapy.

2. Describe how the personality of the counselor might influence the selection and use of a counseling theory.

3. List and discuss the components of a counseling theory.

4. List two approaches that emphasize the importance of early childhood experience. How are these experiences explored during an interview?

5. List three approaches that emphasize here-and-now experience. How do they differ in the ways these experiences are utilized?

6. Explain why rational or cognitive approaches to counseling are so popular.

References

Ansbacher, H. L., & Ansbacher, R. R. (ed.). (1956). *The individual psychology of Alfred Adler: A systematic presentation in selections front his writings.* New York: Harper & Row.

Bandura, A. (1977). *Social learning theory.* Englewood Cliffs, NJ: Prentice-Hall.

Baruth, L. G., & Huber, C. H. (1985). *Counseling and psychotherapy: Theoretical analyses and skills applications.* Columbus, OH: Charles E. Merrill Publishing Co.

Beck, A. T. (1967). *Depression: Clinical, experimental and theoretical aspects.* New York: Harper & Row.

Beck, A. T., Rush, A. J., Shaw, B. F., & Emery, G. (1979). *Cognitive therapy of depression.* New York: Guilford Press.

Belkin, G. S. (1984). *Introduction to counseling* (2nd ed.). Dubuque, IA: Wm. C. Brown.

Berne, E. (1964). *Games people play.* New York: Grove Press.

Blanck, R., & Blanck, G. (1974). *Ego psychology: Theory and practice.* New York: Columbia University Press.

Brabeck, M. M., & Welfel, E. R. (1985). Counseling theory: Understanding the trend toward eclecticism from a developmental perspective. *Journal of Counseling and Development, 63*(6), 343–348.

Cormier, W. H., & Cormier, L. S. (1991). *Interviewing strategies for helpers: Fundamental skills and cognitive behavioral interventions* (3rd ed.). Pacific Grove, CA: Brooks/Cole Publishing Company.

Dinkmeyer, D. C., Pew, W. L., & Dinkmeyer, D. C., Jr. (1979). *Adlerian counseling and therapy.* Monterey, CA: Brooks/Cole.

Dreikurs, R. (1953). *Fundamentals of Adlerian psychology.* Chicago: Alfred Adler Institute.

Dreikurs, R., & Soltz, V. (1964). *Children: The challenge.* New York: Hawthorn.

Elkin, I., Shea, M. T., Watkins, J. T., Imber, S. D., Sotsky, S. M., Collins, J. F., Glass, D. R., Pilkonis, P. A., Leber, W. R., Docherty, J. P., Feister, S. F., & Parloff, M. B. (1989). National Institute of Mental Health treatment of depression collaborative research program: General effectiveness of treatment. *Archives of General Psychiatry, 46*, 971–983.

Ellis, A. (1973). *Humanistic psychotherapy: The rational-emotive approach.* New York: McGraw-Hill.

Ellis, A. (1989). Rational-emotive therapy. In R. J. Corsini & D. Wedding (eds.). *Current psychotherapies* (pp. 197–240). Itasca, IL: F. E. Peacock.

Ellis, A., & Abrahms, E. (1978). *Brief psychotherapy in medical and health practice.* New York: Springer.

Ellis, A., & Dryden, W. (1987). *The practice of rational-emotive therapy.* New York: Springer.

Frank, J. D. (1973). *Persuasion and healing. A comparative study of psychotherapy* (2nd ed.). Baltimore: Johns Hopkins University Press.

Garfield, S. L., & Kurtz, R. (1976). Clinical psychologists in the 1970s. *American Psychologist, 31*(1), 1–9.

Glasser, W. (1965). *Reality therapy.* New York: Harper & Row.

Glasser, W., & Zunin, L. M. (1979). Reality therapy. In R. J. Corsini (ed.), *Current psychotherapies.* Itasca, IL: F. E. Peacock.

Goulding, M., & Goulding, R. (1979). *Changing lives through redecision therapy.* New York: Brunner/Mazel.

Horner, A. J. (1991). *Psychoanalytic object relations therapy.* Northvale, NJ: Jason Aronson Inc.

Hutchins, D. E. (1984). Improving the counseling relationship. *Personnel and Guidance Journal, 62*(10), 572–575.

Jacobson, E. (1971). *Depression.* New York: International Universities Press.

Jensen, J. P., Bergin, A. E., & Greaves, D. W. (1990). The meaning of eclecticism: New survey and analysis of components. *Professional psychology: Research and Practice, 21*(2), 124–130.

Kernberg, O. F. (1984). *Severe personality disorders: Psychotherapeutic strategies.* New Haven: Yale University Press.

Klerman, G. L., Weissman, M. M., Rounsaville, B. J., & Chevron, E. S. (1984). *Interpersonal psychotherapy of depression.* New York: Basic Books.

Krumboltz, J. D., & Thoresen, C. E. (ed.). (1976). *Counseling methods.* New York: Holt, Rinehart and Winston.

Lazarus, R. S. (1984). On the primacy of cognition. *American Psychologist, 39*(2),124–129.

Lichtenstein, E. (1980). *Psychotherapy: Approaches and applications.* Monterey, CA: Brooks/Cole.

Mahler, M. S. (1979). *The selected papers of Margaret S. Mahler.* New York: Jason Aronson.

Mahoney, M. J. (1974). *Cognition and behavior modification.* Cambridge, MA: Ballinger.

Meichenbaum, D. (1977). *Cognitive-behavior modification: An integrative approach.* New York: Plenum.

Moreno, J. L. (1946). *Psychodrama.* Beacon, NY: Beacon House.

Morse, S. J., & Watson, W. I., Jr. (1977). *Psychotherapies: A comparative casebook.* New York: Holt, Rinehart and Winston.

Mosak, H. H. (1972). Life style assessment: A demonstration based on family constellation. *Journal of Individual Psychology, 28*, 232–237.

Mufson, L., Moreau, D., Weissman, M. M., & Klerman, G. L. (1993). *Interpersonal psychotherapy for depressed adolescents.* New York: Guilford Press.

Nisenholz, B. (1983). Solving the psychotherapy glut. *Personnel and Guidance Journal, 61*(9), 535–536.

Passons, W. R. (1975). *Gestalt approaches in counseling.* New York: Holt, Rinehart and Winston.

Perls, F. (1973). *The Gestalt approach and eyewitness to therapy.* New York: Bantam.

Perls, F., Hefferline, R., & Goodman, P. (1951). *Gestalt therapy: Excitement and growth in the human personality.* New York: Dell.

Raskin, N. J., & Rogers, C. R. (1989). Person-centered therapy. In R. J. Corsini & D. Wedding (eds.), *Current psychotherapies* (pp. 155–196). Itasca, IL: F. E. Peacock.

Rogers, C. R. (1942). *Counseling and psychotherapy.* Boston: Houghton Mifflin.

Rogers, C. R. (1951). *Client-centered therapy.* Boston: Houghton Mifflin.

Rogers, C. R. (1957). The necessary and sufficient conditions of therapeutic personality change. *Journal of Consulting Psychology, 21,* 95–103.

Rogers, C. R. (1977). *Carl Rogers on personal power: Inner strength and its revolutionary impact.* New York: Delacorte.

Rychlak, J. F. (1968). *A philosophy of science for personality theory.* Boston: Houghton Mifflin.

Rychlak, J. F. (1985). Eclecticism in psychological theorizing: Good and bad. *Journal of Counseling and Development, 63*(6), 351–353.

Shepherd, I. (1970). Limitations and cautions in the Gestalt approach. In J. Fagan & I. Shepherd (eds.), *Gestalt therapy now.* New York: Harper & Row.

Smith, D. (1982). Trends in counseling and psychotherapy. *American Psychologist, 37*(7), 802–809.

Tremblay, J. M., Herron, W. G., & Schultz, C. L. (1986). Relationship between therapeutic orientation and personality in psychotherapists. *Professional Psychology: Research and Practice, 17*(2), 111–114.

Ullmann, L. P., & Krasner, L. (1965). *Case studies in behavior modification.* New York: Holt, Rinehart and Winston.

Ward, D. E. (1983). The trend toward eclecticism and the development of comprehensive models to guide counseling and psychotherapy. *Personnel and Guidance Journal, 62*(3), 154–157.

Wolberg, L. R. (1980). *Handbook of short-term psychotherapy.* New York: Thieme-Stratton.

Wolpe, J. (1958). *Psychotherapy by reciprocal inhibition.* Stanford: Stanford University Press.

Woollams, S., & Brown, M. (1979). *TA: The total handbook of transactional analysis.* Englewood Cliffs, NJ: Prentice-Hall.

Wubbolding, R. E. (1988). *Using reality therapy.* New York: Harper & Row.

Wubbolding, R. E. (1991). *Understanding reality therapy: A metaphorical approach.* New York: Harper & Row.

Zajonc, R. B. (1984). On the primacy of affect. *American Psychologist, 39*(2), 117–123.

$$Chapter \quad 4$$

The Counseling Process

Goal of the Chapter

The purpose of this chapter is to provide an overview of elements of the counseling process.

Chapter Preview

- The characteristics of clients will be explored.
- The characteristics of effective counselors will be treated in detail.
- The relationship between the counselor and client during counseling will be examined.
- Stages in the counseling process will be summarized.

Introduction

The purpose of this chapter is to provide a synthesis of the diverse approaches to counseling surveyed in Chapter 3. The general motives of clients seeking counseling will be discussed, along with the characteristic ways effective counselors respond to clients. The relationship between the counselor and client will receive particular emphasis. Common goals established for the relationship will be discussed, as will how material and events tend to change as counseling continues.

Characteristics of Clients

Counseling works best when clients enter it voluntarily. At some point even the most reticent clients gain more if they affirm the relevance of counseling and willingly participate in its process. At times this is difficult for the client to do, since the matter treated is often of a sensitive nature. Much of the technology underlying counseling has evolved to help clients join together with counselors in mutual problem-solving.

Whether a client was self-referred or referred by a third party, to remain motivated throughout counseling, the client must sense some improvement at least at various intervals during the process. Most often this means that clients have emotional pain upon entering counseling and begin to hurt less as it continues. Anxiety, depression and lesser forms of grief, and difficult-to-control hostility constitute types of emotional pain behind the client's quest for help.

In addition, clients may feel a loss of cognitive control over their behavior and the life events they must face. They are often confused and feel disorganized in their attempt to cope. Very seldom are clients so in control that they begin the first interview with a statement like this: "I have come to you with three issues in mind. The first is . . . ; the second is . . . ; finally, the third is. . . ." Rather, they will struggle to make sense out of their concerns, even if they have rehearsed what they planned to say. Certainly, this will vary across clients, but negative feelings and cognitive confusion are common client characteristics at the beginning of counseling.

Negative feelings and confusion reduce normal problem-solving ability. The resultant decline in problem solving can lead to reduced self-esteem and the confidence necessary to persist at alternative solutions. If what has been described portrays short-term adjustment, the difficulty in helping the client will be less. On the other hand, if the client has a long history of struggling to cope with everyday challenges, the prospect of helping may be more long-term.

While most clients have difficult decisions to make, see a need to change themselves in some way, or find themselves not coping as well as they might with life, these and other problems are insufficient to prompt prospective clients to select counseling. Clients must be interested in understanding why these problems exist, their own personal responsibility for those problems, and how they can change to cope better with the same problems in the future. Heilbrun (1982) calls this set of attitudes "psychological-mindedness"; it becomes essential in order to complete the process of counseling. If one does not have it, other ways to solve problems are sought. For example, it is not unusual for someone to suggest that a friend seek counseling for some problem only to have the friend respond in disbelief, viewing the suggestion as inappropriate, perhaps preposterous. The friend would acknowledge the problem but not the proposed way to solve it.

Other desirable characteristics for clients include intelligence, flexibility, trustfulness and trustworthiness, and the ability to assume responsibility for personal actions. Goldstein (1971), in a classic description of preferred clients, proposed the acronym YAVIS (young, attractive, verbal, intelligent, and successful) to portray them. Such characteristics have importance, not because they are absolutely essential, but because they make the process more pleasant for the counselor. If a client can contact reality, attend appointed sessions, comprehend verbal communication, and minimally bond with another human being, some benefit from counseling is possible.

Characteristics of Effective Counselors

While the use of counseling techniques influences positive outcomes in counseling (Brammer & Shostrom, 1982), there is widespread agreement that the personal characteristics of the counselor are largely responsible for the ultimate success or failure of counseling (Cormier & Hackney, 1993). Kurpius (1986) suggests that caring is the key ingredient in counseling and indicated that the source of caring is within the individual. Nearly twenty years earlier Combs (1969) put the same idea in somewhat different terms. He proposed that helpers, including counselors, have unique perceptual sets about themselves and the people they counsel. Specifically, they see themselves as identified with people, trustworthy, liked, accepted, accepting, nonauthoritarian, and valuing open communication. Combs also hypothesized that effective helpers would see others as capable, trustworthy, helpful, nonthreatening, respectable, and worthy.

Research has supported Combs' hypotheses (Carkhuff, 1969b; Ivey, 1983). Kanfer (1980) and Parloff, Waskow, and Wolfe (1978) regret that research has not been successful in identifying additional factors that would enable even more effective matches between specific counselors and clients. However, when one reviews the research literature on effective counselors, one is struck with the consensus that effective helpers have a definite set of traits. Brammer (1985) broke these down into eight categories: (1) self-awareness, (2) sensitivity to cultural differences, (3) ability to analyze one's own feelings, (4) ability to serve as a model, (5) altruism, (6) strong sense of ethics, (7) ability to assume responsibility for self and the person being helped, and (8) ability to assume the role of facilitator of personal growth.

It is obvious, when examining Brammer's list or the one posed earlier by Combs, that two sets of attitudes stand out: one set is related to self and the other is related to how the self treats another person, particularly one that is to be helped. Carkhuff and Berenson (1977) suggest that the latter grow out of the former. To combine much of the thinking on effective counselor characteristics, we will discuss seven traits that seem to portray the effective counselor.

Personal Congruence

Hutchins and Cole (1986) depict the congruent individual by using three rings to represent thoughts, feelings, and actions. In their pictorial representation, these rings have considerable overlap. Historically, personal congruence among emotions, cognitions, and behaviors has been equated with good mental health as well.

Congruent individuals are self-aware, that is, they understand their own values and motivations. They do not meet their own needs at the expense of others. They are open to feedback and act nondefensively and appropriately whenever they receive valid messages. Finally, congruent helpers are self-assured, not in the sense of being a "know-it-all," but they have confidence in their ability to be effective in human relationships.

Empathy/Understanding

In 1951 Carl Rogers wrote:

> *It is the counselor's function to assume, insofar as he is able, the internal frame of reference of the client, to perceive the client himself as he is seen by himself, to lay aside all perceptions from the external frame of reference while doing so, and to communicate something of this empathic understanding to the client (p. 29).*

This definition of empathy has gone virtually unchanged (Carkhuff, 1983).

Brammer and Shostrom (1982) point out that empathy can be equated with understanding. They divide understanding further into two categories: (1) therapeutic understanding, which is similar to Rogers' empathy, and (2) diagnostic understanding. The latter enables the counselor to describe the client in ways helpful to others, to plan meaningful interventions, and to predict client behavior under both current and future conditions. Brammer and Shostrom contend that both therapeutic and diagnostic understanding are important dimensions of effective counselors.

Cultural Sensitivity

In a very real sense, empathy is a core ingredient in cultural sensitivity. But as Brammer (1985) points out, cultural awareness has a knowledge and experience base. Research has shown that cross-cultural counseling, conducted by culturally insensitive counselors, is likely to result in either premature termination by the client or unsatisfactory outcomes (Sue, 1981). Therefore, as Brammer suggests, counselors who expect to be effective with clients from different cultural backgrounds prize diversity and express an interest and commitment to learning about people with diverse traditions.

Genuineness

Truax and Carkhuff (1967) pointed out that genuineness characterizes effective helping relationships. It is the capacity of all persons involved to emerge as real or authentic persons. Carkhuff and Berenson (1977) denote the absence of genuineness as not being fully aware of the here-and-now experience, hiding behind a role as a counselor, doing what one is "supposed" to do as though one were pro-gramed. Obviously, genuineness is correlated closely with congruence and empa-thy. Without the former, it would be difficult to supply the sensitivity necessary for congruence and empathy.

Respect/Positive Regard

Respect refers to the valuing of others, holding them in positive regard because they are human beings. Egan (1975) provides a more operational definition of re-spect. He indicates that being respectful involves being nonjudgmental, being "for" the individual, showing appreciation for the individual, and providing ap-preciative feedback for the efforts of the client. In its most basic sense, respect is communicating to one's clients that they are worthwhile, regardless of back-ground, behaviors, or attitudes.

As Carkhuff and Berenson (1977) note, respect or holding the other person in positive regard has its basis in one's own self-respect. They also point out that there is evidence to suggest that respect is communicated through the warmth the indi-vidual conveys to the client. Spontaneity, commitment, and effort expended seem to be the basis for communicating warmth. Thus, while respect stems from our own feelings of self-worth, directing it outwardly to others requires energy, en-thusiasm, and dedication.

Communication

Effective helpers must be effective communicators. In relating to others they make their intentions clear and concrete. They are able to communicate, both verbally and nonverbally, their empathy, genuineness, respect, and cultural sensitivity.

Communication is a skill that can be taught efficiently through carefully de-signed learning activities (Carkhuff, 1983; Egan, 1975; Hutchins & Cole, 1986). However, communication skills are not executed in a counselor's work without a commitment to helping, an attitude of caring, an optimism about the human con-dition, and a willingness to risk sharing one's self with another person.

Cormier and Cormier (1991) identify three potential problem areas, related to unresolved feelings and needs, that might inhibit this. First, issues related to per-ceived competence might result in "pollyanna" (overly positive) or overly self-crit-ical interpersonal style. Unresolved are issues of incompetence and the fear of failure or success. The second potential problem area relates to the use of power to compensate for feelings of impotence, passivity, and dependence. Relationships may become difficult because the person acts too omnipotent (fearful of losing con-trol) or too weak and unresourceful (fearful of assuming control). The third prob-lem area has to do with being able to deal with intimacy and through it one's vulnerability for rejection.

STUDENT LEARNING EXERCISE
Rate yourself as a helper by responding as honestly as possible to the following items.

	Little	Some	A Lot
1. I understand my values and motives.	1	2	3
2. I understand other people.	1	2	3
3. I can take another person's point of view.	1	2	3
4. I appreciate views that are different from mine.	1	2	3
5. I am aware of my prejudices and how they influence my interpersonal relationships.	1	2	3
6. Lifestyles other than my own are acceptable to me.	1	2	3
7. I try to understand the points of view of people from different racial and ethnic backgrounds.	1	2	3
8. I can be myself with people.	1	2	3
9. When put on a spot, I can respond nondefensively.	1	2	3
10. I work toward equal rights and responsibilities for men and women.	1	2	3
11. I believe that most human beings can solve their own problems if given the opportunity.	1	2	3
12. I can communicate my thoughts and feelings clearly.	1	2	3
13. People have told me that I am a warm person.	1	2	3
14. I am aware of my faults.	1	2	3
15. I am sought out by others as a helper.	1	2	3

Social-Influence

From social psychology we understand the counseling process as one involving social influence. The counselor can be a catalyst in helping the client to make difficult changes by demonstrating expertness (credibility), attractiveness, and trustworthiness (Sommers-Flanagan & Sommers-Flanagan, 1993). From a behavioral counseling perspective these factors in combination greatly increase the reward value of any counselor response. Even brief interest or attention from the counselor can be reinforcing. As a result that client is more likely to remain in counseling, even if some of the issues to be treated are difficult and painful (Mennicke, Lent, & Burgoyne, 1988).

Different theoretical orientations emphasize different counselor characteristics. For example, the degree of emotional closeness between counselor and client varies across different orientations. While a person-centered counselor highly values the expression of warmth and caring, the RET counselor finds it sufficient to assure the client of support, but not to let it get in the way of disputing irrational thinking. Table 4.1 compares the relative value of counselor characteristics discussed in this section across different counseling orientations, expressed by the categories used in Chapter 3 (see Table 3.1). Transference and countertransference, listed in Table 4.1, are discussed later in the chapter.

The Counseling Relationship

The counselor behaviors described assist in building a unique relationship between counselor and client. Most interpersonal relationships have either formal or informal roles prescribed for the participants. For example, when one works for

TABLE 4.1   Counselor Characteristics Across Different Counseling Orientations

Counselor Characteristic	Behavioral	Cognitive	Humanistic	Analytic
Personal Congruence	Not emphasized	Not emphasized	Very important	Very important
Empathy	Valuable early to increase reward value of counselor	Affective domain not strongly emphasized	The single most important factor in counseling	Empathy important, but concealed early to promote transference
Cultural Sensitivity	Important for understanding reinforcement contingencies	Very important	Empathy transcends culture	Not given much attention
Positive Regard	Somewhat important to generate positive expectancies for outcome	Not emphasized	Prizing the client extremely important	Showing neutrality important; need to resolve negative countertransference
Genuineness	Described as interpersonal attractiveness	More important to model rational thinking	Extremely important	More important early to be an ambiguous figure
Communication	Extremely important to be clear and concrete	Very important to look closely at meanings of words	Strong emphasis on nonverbal communication	Verbal interpretations seen as powerful tools
Social Influence	Expertness, attractiveness, and trustworthiness extremely important	Extremely important	Emphasize client freedom of choice	Very important

the Department of State, huge books on protocol govern relationships with members of the international community. In counseling there is a paradox; a role exists for counselors, but if they "play" that role, it is unlikely they will form a therapeutic relationship with clients. Naturalness and authenticity on the part of the counselor govern the favorable formation of a counseling relationship. To practice doing this, one practices approaching people as oneself.

Practically speaking, the counselor does not attempt to consciously rehearse how he or she is "supposed" to be. The counselor acts professionally, but does not put on a professional front, playacting some imaginary expert counselor. As one becomes trained as a counselor, one learns many skills, quite a few of which are taught specifically in the context of structured practice situations. But in the end counselors-in-training must take that repertoire of skills and personalize it, integrating it into the rest of their personality (Evans, Hearn, Uhlemann, & Ivey, 1989).

As this integration becomes increasingly more successful, counselors meet the clients' expectation of assistance from a professionally trained person, but soon learn from experiencing the humanness of the counselor that clients too can be free to be themselves, to be human, to reveal parts of themselves often hidden in other relationships. The natural, nonjudgmental style of the counselor makes it easier for clients to share parts of themselves. As the client becomes able to self-disclose, the relationship deepens (Jourard, 1964).

With these standards modeled by the counselor, both participants can begin to work together in a reciprocal manner, using the reactions to one another as important information. Effective counselors recognize that their greatest resource is the client.

Though such an open relationship exists, it is not without limits. Counseling is still a business relationship occurring in most instances on an "outpatient" basis. The relationship becomes structured within the context of a formal interview, usually lasting forty-five to fifty minutes and scheduled weekly on the hour. For clients to be able to utilize such an arrangement, they must be able to function without professional assistance between interviews. If a client cannot do this, but must frequently telephone the counselor at home, demand frequent emergency sessions, and so forth, that client may need a more protective treatment (e.g., a residential placement).

Such limits demonstrate differences that exist in counseling versus close friendships or families. The American Psychological Association Ethical Standards warn psychologists of the hazards of dual relationships, when one serves a client in two different capacities (e.g., a therapist and a relative). Counselors too are wise to recognize how one relationship can contaminate the other. This is particularly important in counseling because of confidentiality. However, it is important to recognize that counselors also have a right to privacy as do clients. Often beginning counselors have difficulty limiting their availability to clients during nonwork hours. Poor boundary management between private and professional lives is linked to eventual burnout for counselors (Watkins, 1983).

Stages in the Counseling Process

Before we describe a common sequence of events in counseling, it is important to note that many clients, for one reason or another, will not complete all the stages of counseling. The process will be abandoned prematurely, not because something went wrong, but because of factors external to the counselor-client relationship. For example, the school year may end for a student client, or a client or counselor may move away to accept a new job. When counseling is in process and must abruptly end, the participants will feel the incompleteness and loss. For this reason counselors are encouraged to fit all the stages to be described into the time available, no matter how brief it may be. In accordance with this, accurately estimating the probable number of interviews available for working with a client becomes an important skill, especially for practitioners who will do a lot of time-limited counseling (e.g., school counselors).

The Beginning Phase

During the very early interviews the immediate goals become twofold: (1) to begin forming a good working relationship and (2) to explore the reasons the client sought counseling. In the latter, problems and concerns will be uncovered, along with how they affect the client.

To achieve both immediate goals the counselor provides fundamental conditions that create an interpersonal atmosphere characterized by empathy, respect, and genuineness (Rogers, 1951; Carkhuff, 1969a; Carkhuff, 1969b). Central to providing the entire atmosphere is empathy. Briefly, empathy is the ability to understand the subjective experience of the client—to perceive the world as the client does while retaining one's own identity.

Empathy is important because the nature of a client's perceived world dictates how the client will behave. To understand the whys of a client's behavior requires empathetic understanding. In addition, the empathetic counselor becomes a more potent reinforcing agent—something that will become important throughout the rest of the process, but especially as the client acts on the understanding gained in counseling (Corrigan, Dell, Lewis, & Schmidt, 1980).

To be able to empathize the counselor must be able to overcome self-consciousness and devote complete attention to what the client is trying to share. Often beginning counselors do not empathize well because they are trying to think of what they will say to the client, rather than listening to what the client is saying. Listening is the basis for being able to empathize.

In the early phase counselors do a lot of listening. If things go well, clients will realize that counselors appreciate and encourage their participation. It will become clear that there is a dual responsibility for progress in the relationship. The talk ratio early in counseling will be close to 50:50. In addition to listening, counselors will communicate their understanding through reflective statements ("You seem to be feeling . . ."), summaries ("Up to this point we have been talking about . . ."), and clarifications ("Am I hearing you correctly, you seem . . ."). This willingness on the part of the counselor to hear the client's story, rather than being too passive, seems to increase the attractiveness of the counselor, and may increase the counselor's ability to influence client change efforts later in the process (Heppner & Heesacker, 1982).

Counselors will also need to ask questions both to seek clarification and elaboration and to guide exploration into additional areas. However, the beginning phase of counseling is not an interrogation, and it should not seem so as a result of the counselor's asking too many questions. Repeated questions, especially closed-ended ones (questions that can be answered by a simple "yes" or "no"), tilt the responsibility too much toward the counselor. Before long the client will develop an increasingly passive stance in the interview, with the counselor increasingly feeling more pressure to make something happen.

When counselors-in-training attempt their first practice interviews, they often ask too many questions. They do this because they already know how to question, but must learn the skill of active listening in which they paraphrase client statements, reflect feelings, and summarize. A common exercise in counselor training is to prohibit the use of questions in a practice session in order to increase the use of other types of responses. It is like tying one's dominant arm behind the back in order to increase the facility of using the other arm. Later trainees are allowed to use questions after they are confident of their ability to use other responses. This results in counselors becoming versatile interviewers, utilizing a variety of different verbal responses. Their early sessions have a conversational, rather than an interrogative, quality to them. Experienced interviewers may appear informal and relaxed, yet they are able to explore an extensive amount of material in a single interview.

Success in early interviews is judged by the degree to which the client self-discloses. Chit-chat becomes almost nonexistent as the client risks revealing information that could be embarrassing, socially disapproved, or even potentially damaging. Such disclosures will occur only if the counselor proves to be trustworthy.

Beginning counselors, however, should not expect the early phase to be all positive; clients will at times test and challenge, purposely deceive, and resist exploration into sensitive areas. Such negative behaviors may be connected with the very problems the client has come to solve. Thus, learning to relate better becomes a counseling goal for such clients, not a reason to reject or abandon them. That is why counselors are trained to deal with people others would find too troublesome.

With difficult and troublesome clients the counselor's patience may be tested. At times the counselor will feel abused and mistreated. Being able to handle such feelings without punishing the client is important. Because counselors have a genuine liking for people and can see beyond the immediate situation, they are able to respond therapeutically to these difficult situations.

At times a counselor may actually deserve a negative response from the client; often a counselor is mistreated not because of what she or he does, but because the client has projected onto the counselor traits associated with others in the client's life. This is called *transference*. If the client perceives the counselor as an authority figure, the counselor may be treated just as the client has treated other such figures. If the counselor is viewed as a nurturing person, he or she may be treated as the client treats other nurturing persons. On the same note, the counselor may respond emotionally to the client in some overly intense or otherwise unexplainable way, at least by virtue of what has transpired between the two of them. Here the counselor may have projected onto the client undeserved qualities. This is called *countertransference*. In both cases something unresolved from the past may have erupted. In the former, the client needs to work through transferences in counseling; in the latter the counselor needs to work through countertransferences with a supervisor.

Instead of such reactions, hopefully the counselor is able to display genuine caring for the client, even if times occur when scattered negative feelings must be restrained and evaluated. Understanding of clients is served by having counselors evaluate their reactions to them. Overall, the counselor strives in both verbal and nonverbal behavior to show spontaneity, congruence, and good humor. If this occurs with a reasonable degree of regularity during the beginning of helping, increasingly problems are identified and clarified along with unused opportunities to solve them (Egan, 1994). The client makes progress telling his or her story. Complex problems are reorganized into elements that allow one simpler solution to pave the way for other solutions (Egan, 1994). Blind spots inhibiting earlier problem solving are uncovered along with new images and ideas that promote healing.

The Middle Phase

Problem exploration and relationship building, while characteristic of the early phase of counseling, reemerge in later stages as well. But once early exploration has resulted in the uncovering of a quantity of information useful in understanding and treating those problems, the tone of the interviews begins to change. Counselors become more active. They have intently listened to what the client has said, while they have also begun to assess the client's personality or repertoire of adaptive and not-so-adaptive attitudes and behaviors. The client's style of problem solving, mistakes in logic, and faulty habits become more clear. In addition, environmental stressors, bad luck, and other external factors become more fully understood. The counselor must do something with this understanding.

Sharing this understanding may be a simple matter with a client who arrives at the same conclusions as the counselor at roughly the same time. In such situations the counselor could ask the client to draw an obvious conclusion (e.g., "What do you make out of what we have been talking about?"). A client with few blind spots and few rigid defenses can draw a conclusion with which the counselor can agree. Both can then explore what can be done with this new understanding.

Frequently the counselor sees something emerging out of early exploration that the client does not. Often this is connected to how the client contributes to the problems being explored. The counselor in this middle phase of helping must "personalize" the problem for the client (Carkhuff & Anthony, 1979).

Being given such information is often not very pleasant for the client. In fact at a subliminal level clients might be aware that there is something about them that is contributing to their difficulties, but are afraid to face it. It is like realizing over the winter that your clothes are fitting tighter; you know you have gained weight, but avoid stepping on a scale or looking at yourself naked in front of a mirror. The final confrontation of the reality is fearsome.

Part of the reason such confrontations with reality are so fearsome may lie in the fact that individuals in such situations already have lost so much self-esteem; to risk losing more might put them dangerously close to an amount of loss ultimately intolerable. When counselors confront clients with such information they expose clients to pain—pain often understood as necessary for a favorable, final outcome. Yet we know people avoid pain; people avoid going to the dentist, realizing they have decaying teeth, but unable to voluntarily submit themselves to pain. How pain is administered in a voluntary relationship, such as counseling, is crucial in the development of technical competence.

Well-trained counselors are careful and tactful in helping clients to personalize their problems in terms of how they contribute to what is bothering them. This tact pays special attention to timing things said to the client that will be difficult for the client to accept. This means that one waits for an appropriate time to deal with difficult confrontations, a time when the client is more ready to deal with them or when sufficient time exists for the matter to be fully treated. This can be achieved if input from the counselor about client problems points to solutions as well.

Egan (1994) describes the middle phase of helping as eventually constructing a new scenario—how things could be different and better. This can begin by understanding self-defeating behavior in a new, different light. The counselor is able to do this most often through the use of interpretations. Cormier and Cormier (1991) define an interpretation as "a counselor statement that makes an association or a causal connection among various client behaviors, events, or ideas or presents a possible explanation of a client's behavior (including the client's feelings, thoughts, and observable actions)." One language system replaces another. One set of ideas replaces another to explain the client's behavior and situation. The ideas come from the theories counselors study and use to organize their efforts. All counselors interpret; the interpretations change according to the theoretical orientation of the counselor.

With the new understanding gained from confronting and interpreting important client characteristics, the new scenario of how things could be better—how the client could change for the better—emerges. Early in counseling goals were discussed generally in terms of the elimination of various problems and symptoms. In this phase of counseling those goals are revised in terms of more clear, specific statements of how the client's attitudes and behaviors might change to achieve problem resolution.

At this point counselor and client must agree on these revised goals. If the way they were initially cast is not acceptable, they need to be revised until they are. Following this it is important that the client commit to those goals and to the actions required to attain them. Since much of what clients must commit to deals with their willingness to self-manage strategies requiring considerable effort and practice, commitment is especially crucial (Kanfer, 1980).

Achieving a commitment to work at changes based on a new understanding would not be possible were it not for the subtle achievements gained by the client in contact with the counselor. Cavanagh (1982) describes counseling as a new type of learning experience for most people. It is an intense curriculum in oneself. Emerging out of it is more than the recognition of internal conflicts, psychological imperatives ("musts" and "oughts" that govern life), and new insights into self. Clients, according to Cavanagh, experience something in the counseling relationship that offers them a chance for new psychological freedom. Because of this, they can begin to imagine themselves as different, and possibly for the first time in their lives, actually believe that they *can* be different. This is the launching pad for going out and trying to be what one imagines.

In preparing the client for the real-life attempts at change, the counselor has to work hard. In the middle phase the wisdom and experiences of the counselor pay off. More than likely the counselor in the middle phase, compared to the early phase, has initiated more and applied his or her own perspective to that of the client. In a sense the major contributions have been made; it is now up to the client to complete the process by working on permanent personal change that provides solutions to immediate problems and generalizes to other problems in the future.

The Late Phase

According to theoretical orientation, the later counseling sessions vary in content. Some counselors continue themes already developed; they continue to work on the new, emerging self-image of the client with the belief that the cognitive structure representing the self is the key to effective action-taking. Other counselors believe in more structured strategies aimed at action-taking. They emphasize the practice of concrete behaviors directly related to expressed problems and desired goals. Regardless of orientation, what has been talked about in the abstract can be solidified in real client change. Already, to get this far, the client feels better and has more self-confidence and optimism about the future; the client is energized and ready to try things that may have been too demanding prior to counseling.

The client has more endurance and greater tolerance of frustration. If this were not true, neither structured, action-oriented approaches nor less structured, personal encounter approaches would work.

For some counselors a variety of techniques find their way into different sessions. Some of these are role playing, relaxation training, and exercises built around props or materials. Other sessions may be structured around review of diaries or logs the client was requested to keep. In still others readings assigned between sessions might be discussed (Hutchins & Cole, 1986).

All such adjuncts to simple counselor-client interactions are connected to the principal action point in the counseling process: the real, ongoing experience of the client as lived between counseling sessions. At times the counselor may desire to assume some control over this experience by assigning in consultation with the client "homework" to be completed between sessions. A sequential plan for such homework may develop to systematically approach the rehearsal of desired behaviors and roles.

In many instances later counseling sessions consist for the most part of the client reporting to the counselor what transpired over the past week, how difficult situations were managed, how successes could be explained. The counselor in such a situation is expected simply to comment on such experiences in light of what has occurred during counseling and as now a trusted, supportive consultant. Confusing or surprising events are mutually explored and analyzed for the purpose of fine-tuning the new, more effective stance the client has toward life experience.

In other instances there may be a need for the partners to cycle back to exploring or reunderstanding a particular problem, resulting in a need for the counselor to reinterpret a behavior or event. Eventually the client must encounter life on his or her own; that is a goal. As a parent learns to let go of a daughter or son, the counselor must let go of the client. As mentioned earlier, if the counselor has competence, power, or intimacy problems, this letting go will be difficult.

Toward the end of counseling, there is a tendency on the part of clients to forget what it was like prior to treatment. Review of problems and changes made remind clients of what they have achieved and serves as a precaution against their slipping back to less adaptive ways.

Eventually the counselor and client must confront the issue of termination. Ending an especially meaningful, ongoing relationship can be difficult; both members can experience considerable loss. Nevertheless, timing termination so it is neither too soon nor too late hopefully will occur. Ward (1984) lists the following as themes associated with termination: ending, growing up, autonomy, individuation, reviewing, summarizing, consolidating, and saying good-bye. If the client is ready to end, Ward notes that it will not be because of a complete cure; that rarely happens. However, presenting problems will be reduced; the client will feel better; there will be an increase in coping ability, marked also by greater playfulness and improved relationships with others.

STUDENT LEARNING EXERCISE

Read the following statements and indicate whether they suggest appropriate counselor behavior. Circle Y for yes or N for no.

1. A client appears very anxious during the first interview; the counselor interprets this as resistance.   Y   N

2. During one of the final sessions the client asks the counselor if her concerns were typical of someone her age. The counselor answers the question.   Y   N

3. A counselor has interpreted a client's behavior as a consequence of being sheltered as a child, not having the opportunity to learn needed social behaviors. The counselor uses the same interpretation in several later interviews for the same and other behaviors.   Y   N

4. A counselor, fearful of a client's becoming too uncomfortable during an interview, rarely confronts self-defeating actions and beliefs.   Y   N

5. A counselor spends considerable time with a client reviewing real-life experiences since the last interview.   Y   N

Summary

In this chapter a general overview of the counseling process was provided. Emphasis was on the behavior of the counselor as it influences the client immediately and also as it prepares the way for later change efforts. Note was taken on special issues arising during different phases of the process.

Review Questions

1. Construct two lists of client characteristics—one that appears essential for favorable counseling outcome and another that simplifies the counseling process.

2. Write a profile of the effective counselor.

3. Describe characteristics of the counseling relationship that differentiate it from a friendship.

4. Describe early, middle, and late phases of counseling.

References

Brammer, L. (1985). *The helping relationship.* Englewood Cliffs, NJ: Prentice-Hall.

Brammer, L. M., & Shostrom, E. L. (1982). *Therapeutic psychology: Fundamentals of counseling and psychotherapy* (4th ed.). Englewood Cliffs, NJ: Prentice-Hall.

Carkhuff, R. R. (1969). *Helping and human relations, Vol. II: Practice and research.* New York: Holt, Rinehart and Winston.

Carkhuff, R. R. (1983). *The art of helping* (5th ed.). Amherst, MA: Human Resources Development Press.

Carkhuff, R. R., & Anthony, W. A. (1979). *The skills of helping.* Amherst, MA: Human Resource Development Press.

Carkhuff, R. R., & Berenson, B. G. (1977). *Beyond counseling and therapy.* New York: Holt, Rinehart and Winston.

Combs, A. W. (1969). *Florida studies in the helping professions.* Gainesville, FL: University of Florida Press.

Cormier, L. S., & Hackney, H. (1993). *The professional counselor: A process guide to helping* (2nd ed.). Boston: Allyn and Bacon.

Cormier, W. H., & Cormier, L. S. (1991). *Interviewing strategies for helpers: Fundamental skills and cognitive behavioral interventions* (3rd ed.). Pacific Grove, CA: Brooks/Cole Publishing Company.

Corrigan, J. S., Dell, D. M., Lewis, K. N., & Schmidt, L. D. (1980). Counseling as a social influence process: A review. *Journal of Counseling Psychology, 27*(4), 395–441.

Egan, G. (1975). *Exercises in helping skills.* Monterey, CA: Brooks/Cole.

Egan, G. (1994). The skilled helper: A problem-management approach to helping (5th ed.). Pacific Grove, CA: Brooks/Cole Publishing Company.

Evans, D. R., Hearn, M. T., Uhlemann, M. R., & Ivey, A. E. (1989). *Essential interviewing: A programmed approach to effective communication* (3rd ed.). Pacific Grove, CA: Brooks/Cole Publishing Company.

Goldstein, A. P. (1971). Psychotherapeutic attraction. New York: Pergamon Press.

Heilbrun, A. B., Jr. (1982). Cognitive factors in early counseling termination: Social insight and level of defensiveness. *Journal of Counseling Psychology, 29*(1), 29–38.

Heppner, P. P., & Heesacker, M. (1982). Interpersonal influence process in real-life counseling: Investigating client perceptions, counselor experience level, and counselor power over time. *Journal of Counseling Psychology, 29*(3), 215–223.

Hutchins, D. E., & Cole, C. G. (1986). *Helping relationships and strategies.* Monterey, CA: Brooks/Cole.

Jourard, S. M. (1964). *The transparent self.* Princeton: D. Van Nostrand.

Kanfer, F. H. (1980). Self-management methods. In F. H. Kanfer & A. P. Goldstein (eds.), *Helping people change* (pp. 334–389). New York: Pergamon Press.

Kurpius, D. J. (1986). The helping relationship. In M. D. Lewis, R. L. Hayes, & J. A. Lewis (eds.), *An introduction to the counseling profession* (pp. 96–130). Itasca, IL: F. E. Peacock Publishers.

Mennicke, S. A., Lent, R. W., & Burgoyne, K. L. (1988). Premature termination from university counseling centers: A review. *Journal of Counseling and Development, 66*(10), 458–465.

Parloff, M. B., Waskow, I. E., & Wolfe, B. E. (1978). Research on therapist variables in relationship to process and outcome. In S. L. Garfield and A. E. Bergin (eds.), *Handbook of psychotherapy and behavior change: An empirical analysis.* (pp. 233–282). New York: John Wiley and Sons.

Sommers-Flanagan, J., & Sommers-Flanagan, R. (1993). *Foundations of therapeutic interviewing.* Boston: Allyn and Bacon.

Sue, D. W. (1981). *Counseling the culturally different: Theory and practice.* New York: John Wiley and Sons.

Truax, C. B., & Carkhuff, R. R. (1967). *Toward effective counseling and psychotherapy.* Chicago: Aldine.

Watkins, C. E. (1983). Burnout in counseling practice: Some potential professional and personal hazards of becoming a counselor. *Personnel and Guidance Journal, 61*(5), 304–308.

Chapter 5

Group Counseling and Other Group Interventions

Goal of the Chapter

The goal of this chapter is to introduce the various types of groups used by counselors in their efforts to deal with the problems encountered by their clients.

Chapter Preview

- A brief history of the group movement will be provided.
- Several types of groups will be defined and classified.
- The unique skills of the group leader will be presented.
- The process of group counseling will be outlined.
- A brief description of several groups will be presented.

Introduction

The first therapeutically oriented group was provided to tuberculosis patients by Joseph Hersey Pratt in 1905 (Gladding, 1991). Pratt's groups were the forerunners of today's support groups in that they were primarily oriented to offering support and encouragement. Current day extensions of this idea range from support groups for children who are experiencing the break up of their families to groups that offer support to women who have been raped. At approximately the same time (1907), Jessie Davis was preempting English classes at Grand Rapids High School in Michigan to offer students vocational and moral guidance classes (Gladding, 1995), a tradition that is still in place in thousands of U.S. schools.

Alfred Adler may well have been the first mental health professional to employ a group therapy approach, starting as early as 1922. His work with families and other groups was contrary to the individually oriented work of Sigmund Freud that dominated therapeutic thinking in the early part of the twentieth century (Gladding, 1995). However, it was J. L. Moreno who introduced the terms group therapy and group psychotherapy into our vocabularies. He also developed an influential approach to group work known as psychodrama where group members act out their concerns in a group setting and the therapist functions as the director of the "play." The term group counseling was coined in 1931 by R. D. Allen, and Alcoholics Anonymous (AA), which was the first group effort to use peer leaders, was started in 1934 (Gladding, 1991). Overeaters Anonymous and Weight Watchers are groups modeled after the approach pioneered by AA, as are some of the current groups designed to help the adult children of alcoholics.

From the early thirties, group work has grown rapidly. In the sixties, encounter groups became popular as means of promoting personal growth in normal people. These groups were characterized by interpersonal interactions and feedback about the nature of these interactions. In some instances these groups lasted for extended periods of time (e.g., twenty-four hours) and were understandably called marathon groups. However, research regarding these groups was for the most part not supportive, and they have been replaced by groups that are more task oriented such as assertion training groups for adults, friendship groups for children, and groups that deal with phobias and other problems.

The Association of Specialists in Group Work (ASGW), founded in 1973, has provided and continues to provide significant leadership in promoting group work by promulgating training standards for group leaders, and by establishing ethical principles for the leadership of groups. Because of the work of the pioneers mentioned, organizations such as ASGW, and research that is quite supportive of the efficacy of group work, most mental health professionals have received training in this area.

Counseling Theory and Group Counseling

In Chapter 3 the major theories of counseling were outlined and will not be repeated here. Perhaps it will suffice to say that group counselors rely on the same theoretical underpinnings as do individual counselors. However, group counselors must take into consideration another set of theoretical assumptions; those that grow out of group dynamics.

A group is a collection of individuals who interact with each other on a regular basis, are interdependent in some way, share a common set of standards or norms that regulate their interaction, have common goals, and influence each other (Johnson & Johnson, 1991). Group dynamics are the forces that operate on group members as they interact with other group members. Effective groups maintain good working relationships among the members, have clearly defined goals, and move toward the accomplishment of those goals (Johnson & Johnson, 1991). Groups may include or exclude some members. They may become cohesive—that is develop a sense of unity where the members identify with the group—or they may remain a loose collection of individuals. Group members may or may not be committed to the group; they may develop a high level of trust in the leader and other members or they may be distrustful. Group members may grow to like and support each other or they may learn to dislike and be hostile toward each other. The leader may skillfully facilitate the group or fail to recognize the complexities of the group and miss opportunities to be helpful. Inclusion, cohesiveness, commitment, trust, attraction to the leader and the group, and skillful leadership are all positive group dynamics. The leader may have a thorough understanding of Adlerian, behavioral, rational emotive, or some other theory, but unless he or she is able to manage the dynamics of the group, he or she is likely to be unsuccessful.

Classifying and Defining Groups

Classification

As is obvious in the historical overview provided above, there are many types of groups: therapy, counseling, support groups led by peers, self-help, task, etc. These groups can be categorized in many ways. For example, there are groups aimed at primary prevention, that is, oriented to keeping mental health problems from arising. There are secondary prevention groups that are aimed at ameliorating mental health problems that have arisen, but have not advanced to the life threatening stage. Tertiary prevention groups are groups that deal with serious mental health problems that are life threatening. In Table 5.1 various types of groups are classified using this taxonomy.

TABLE 5.1   Groups Classified According as Primary, Secondary, or Tertiary Prevention Groups

Primary	Secondary	Tertiary
1. Classroom guidance in schools	1. Overeaters Anonymous	1. Eating disorders (e.g., bulimia)
2. Assertion training	2. Phobia intervention groups	2. Alcoholics Anonymous
3. Social skills	3. Marriage and family groups	3. Suicide groups with chronic depressives
4. Support groups		
5. Weight Watchers		

Some attempts have been made to classify groups in terms of whether they are counseling or therapy groups. For example, Brammer, Shostrom, and Abrego (1989) contend that counseling groups deal primarily with problems of normal people who require educational interventions (e.g., the dispensation of information), support (encouragement provided, but no intervention), and problem-solving interventions such as choosing a career or a college major. They also suggest that the focus of counseling groups is the present (as opposed to the past) and deals with psychological material that is in the conscious awareness. Psychotherapy, on the other hand, deals more with material from the past, has more of a reconstructive emphasis, is more analytic, and deals primarily with nonnormals, that is people who are dysfunctional in some way and have severe emotional problems. These authors also note that since there is a great deal of overlap between counseling and psychotherapy, the distinction between the two may be hard to make in many instances.

Differentiation among Groups

The seven types of groups that counselors lead (Jacobs, Harvill, & Masson, 1988), some of which have been listed already, are as follows:

- Mutual sharing or support groups—the purpose of these groups is sharing of experiences and the provision of encouragement and support. Stress management groups, groups for children, death and dying groups, victims of personal and natural disasters such as assault or tornados, Viet Nam veterans, and many others join these groups. In some instances these groups may be self-help groups which are led by group members, but typically they are led by counselors and other mental health professionals. Recently, it has been recognized that these groups may be useful in the prevention of post-traumatic stress syndrome (PTSS).
- Educational groups—these groups are formed as an efficient means of delivering various types of information to children and adults, and for the purpose of developing certain skills. Career exploration, the development of employability skills such as interviewing, AIDS and problem pregnancy prevention, study skills, and parenting skills, may be covered in these groups. They are typically led by a professional, but may be led by peer leaders or paraprofessionals.
- Discussion groups—these groups are formed so that people can air their opinions on a host of problems and concerns. They are not oriented toward problem solving and are often led by nonprofessionals. High school groups aimed at improving multicultural relations, college groups focused on rape prevention, and adult groups focusing on neighborhood issues are examples of these groups.
- Task groups—short-term groups that are assembled to solve problems and may or may not be led by a professional. Once the task of improving institu-

tional rules, organizing the career fair, or developing a disciplinary policy is complete, the group disbands.

- Growth groups—these groups are established for people who wish to improve their interpersonal functioning and who are not presently experiencing a psychological problem or major life problem such as a loss. They are led by professionals, and usually last a finite period of time; the length of the meeting may vary from one and one-half hours to several hours. A variation of these groups may involve couples who, while they are not experiencing marital problems, wish to improve the quality of their marriages. These groups are also used to help intact teams such as management teams improve their functioning.

- Counseling/therapy groups—these groups meet primarily for the purpose of helping group members deal with educational or mental health problems. They are led by professionals and may meet for relatively short periods of time, or for years depending on the problems being dealt with and the orientation of the leader. These groups vary on many dimensions including amount of structure, homogeneity of problems experienced by the members, and leader style. Career concerns, depression, interpersonal problems, test anxiety, and eating disorders are but a few of the problems handled in these groups.

- Family/couples counseling groups—these groups are formed because problems have arisen in families that need the attention of a mental health professional. In family counseling the counselor may see individuals as well as the entire family. Couples group counseling involves several couples who are having marital problems.

- Self-help groups—these groups are formed and led by peer leaders, sometimes with the assistance of mental health professionals. Alcoholics Anonymous, Overeaters Anonymous, Weight Watchers, Adult Children of Alcoholics, and Emotions Anonymous are examples of self help groups.

STUDENT LEARNING EXERCISE

Match the purposes of the group listed in the left-hand column to the type of group listed in the right-hand column. Some groups may have more than one purpose.

1. Therapy group	a. Prevent mental health problems
2. Growth group	b. Solve problems
3. Support group	c. Restructure personality
4. Task group	d. Provide emotional support
5. Self-help group	e. Help people without problems function more effectively

What Makes Groups Effective?

Therapeutic Forces

It is likely that if you ask a hundred group leaders why groups are effective, you would get a hundred different answers; especially since there are so many types of groups. However, if you talked to each of them long enough, you would begin to get some consensus on what has been termed the therapeutic or curative factors present in groups. While the titles and the number of these factors vary, eleven curative factors are a representative list. Yalom (1985) believes that some or all of these factors must be present if groups are to be effective.

Factor	*Why Important*
1. Instillation of hope	Members believe they will benefit from the group experience
2. Universality	Individual realizes they are not only one with the problem
3. Information	Members learn about their problems and how to deal with them
4. Altruism	Members learn they have value by helping others
5. Recreation of primary family	Members recreate family problems and resolve conflicts in group
6. Social learning	Members learn social skills
7. Imitative behavior	Members learn from each other
8. Interpersonal learning	Because the group is a social microcosm, members correct faulty interpersonal learnings
9. Cohesiveness	Group members develop sense of belonging and safety that allows them to grow
10. Catharsis	Members are free to share ideas that have been held inside
11. Existential	Accept that life may be unfair but they must face life no matter what pain is involved

The Leader

If we accept Yalom's idea that certain forces must be at work if groups are to be effective, then it becomes the responsibility of the leader to ascertain that the conditions are present in the group that will give rise to these forces. The counselor's characteristics, the leadership strategies employed by the counselor, and the members of the group are the ingredients that give rise to these therapeutic forces. The characteristics of the effective group counselor are no different than those of the effective individual counselor (Corey, Corey, Callahan, & Russell, 1992) discussed earlier in this book. However, group counselors must have the skill to select group members that will work effectively together, and must have a unique set of leadership skills in addition to those employed in individual counseling that will be discussed at this point.

Forming the Group

Some groups fail simply because the members of the group are not carefully selected. Often, unsuspecting school counseling trainees find themselves in the position of leading groups of acting-out aggressive children or adolescents with predictable results. These students are impulsive and have little regard for authority. In the group they often reinforce each other's behavior and generally retard progress. These counselors soon learn that the composition of the group is essential to success.

The criteria to be used in forming groups varies with the type of group being formed, although the principle for composing most groups is homogeneity of problem type and heterogeneity of personality type or behavioral styles. This means that for most groups the people placed in the group should have the same presenting problems (e.g., aggression, depression, anxiety disorder, substance abuse, career selection problems, etc.), but the people with these problems should have different coping styles. Moreover, they should have the social skills needed to function in a group setting. Very aggressive and painfully shy people may need to participate in individual counseling prior to entering a group. Group counselors must be skilled in selecting members that can work together successfully, a task that is typically completed in a pregroup interview. In some instances the initial group is also a screening group in that the leader observes the group and then makes final decisions regarding who will be included in the group.

Determining the Size of the Group

Group leaders must consider several factors such as the age of the clients, the amount of time available for group sessions, and the presenting problem in determining the size of the counseling group. The guiding principle is the amount of air time available for group members. Children with short attention spans must be involved regularly in the group or they lose interest. Children's groups also typically meet for shorter periods of time than adult groups, partially due to the attention span issue. The result is that children's groups are typically no larger than six to eight in size. Counseling groups for adults may be as large as twelve, although ten is the typical recommendation for group size.

Allaying Anxiety

Although a pregroup meeting has been held with each group member, it is likely that the initial group meeting will be characterized by fairly high levels of anxiety.

It is the group leader's responsibility to allay this anxiety by (1) explaining the purpose of the group, (2) establishing expectations for member behavior such as attendance, punctuality, and functioning in the group, and (3) establishing that, at least so far as the leader is concerned, information divulged will be held in confidence. It is also useful to have group members discuss their expectations of the group (Corey & Corey, 1992).

Structuring the Group

Structure in a group setting is the degree to which the leader specifies an agenda for the group. In the sixties and seventies it was not uncommon for leaders of growth groups to enter the group and sit until the group developed its own approach to promoting growth. The opposite of this would be an assertion training group where the leader establishes an agenda for each group meeting and designs assessment and intervention strategies that fill the time. We now know that to totally ignore structure is counterproductive and that structure can allay anxiety, promote self disclosure and cohesion, and contribute to positive outcomes if it is used properly (Bednar & Kaul, 1985). It is the leader's task to establish an agenda for the group and determine the degree of structure that will be needed to ensure that the group functions well and that the members achieve their objectives.

Theoretical orientation plays an important role in the type and degree of structure that is provided. Behavioral counselors provide a great deal of structure, almost to the point to establishing a "teaching" atmosphere. Rational emotive counselors immediately set out to teach the premises of their counseling approach so that members of the group can not only begin to understand their own irrational thinking, but that of others in the group as well. Person centered and psychodynamic counselors provide far less structure.

Establishing Cohesion

Individual counselors must establish a relationship with one client. Group counselors must also establish a relationship with group members. Additionally, the group counselor must be able to establish a feeling of "we-ness" or to put it differently, a sense of relationship among the group members. This process begins by selecting group members who will be attracted to each other based on perceptions of communalities. However, beginning with the first group, the counselor must also facilitate this process by "linking" members together by pointing out the similarities that exist among them. This cannot occur unless members self-disclose information about themselves and their problems. This self-disclosure also allows members to recognize that they are not alone; Yalom's therapeutic force of universality.

Protecting the Welfare of the Individual

Groups can exert tremendous pressure on individuals. In a classic study, Yalom and Lieberman (1971) reported that some members in growth groups characterized by conflict and negative feedbacks were actually harmed psychologically by their experiences. In *Ethical Guidelines for Group Counselor* (ASGW, 1989, Section 6) group counselors are told, "Group counselors protect member rights against physical threats, intimidation, coercion, and undue peer pressure insofar as it is reasonably possible." In order to do this, the same document (Section 6 (f)) states, "Counselors intervene when a member is verbally abusive or inappropriately confrontive to another member."

Facilitate the Movement of the Group from Stage to Stage

Groups move through certain well-defined stages: (1) the initial or formative stage, (2) the transition stage, (3) the working or problem-solving stage, and (4) the termination stage. Some of the issues surrounding the initial stage have already been identified, including allaying anxiety, pointing out similarities to facilitate the development of cohesion, and structuring the group. In the initial stage it is also important that the group counselor model and reinforce appropriate group behavior, including listening, accepting differences, and sharing information. Most importantly, the group leader must maintain what is termed a group focus. This is done by making sure that all members have an opportunity to participate and focus on topics that are of general concern. Inclusion of all members in the dynamics of the group is of major concern in this stage as is ensuring commitment to the group.

The transition stage of groups is the point at which group members decide individually and collectively if they are going to commit to working on the problems they brought to the group. This may be a tumultuous time in some groups, with group leaders being confronted and members openly expressing their ambivalence about the utility of the group. In other groups the members may simply keep their concerns to themselves and verbal participation may decline. Trust is a primary issue and leaders must be able to reassure people that, not only can they be trusted, but others in the group are trustworthy as well.

In the working stage of counseling groups, the focus of the group switches from group concerns to the individual problems of the members. The counselor at this point uses some of the same interventions employed in individual counseling, but has the rich resources of the group membership to draw on to make them more effective. For example, counselors employ role playing on a regular basis as a strategy for helping members deal with interpersonal problems such as spousal concerns. In a group setting many different people might role play with the spouse giving the client different perspectives. Other group members may also be used to model means for dealing with the spouse.

In addition to helping group members solve problems during the working stage of the group, the leader must employ strategies that maintain the group. Some group members may inadvertently sabotage the growth of another member because of issues they brought to the group. This may cause anger and hostility, not only from the member who is trying to make changes and has been sabotaged, but from other group members as well. While these types of situations provide rich learning experiences they must be resolved in a manner that will allow all parties involved to work together therapeutically.

In a very real sense, termination is a stage that is being prepared for at the pre-group meeting with a member. The major task of the group leader is to help members consolidate what they have learned and use it as a foundation for continued growth after the group. They must also help them deal with the anxiety that is sometimes associated with group termination and deal with unfinished group business such as unresolved interpersonal conflicts (Corey & Corey, 1992). To a certain extent, what the leader does is reassure members that they can function well independently. Perhaps more importantly, the group leader needs to help members recognize their strengths and to realize that they can cope.

STUDENT LEARNING EXERCISE
Match the techniques in the right-hand column with the leader's objective in the left-hand column.

1. Ensure cohesiveness	a. Tell own experiences
2. Protect individuals in groups	b. Choose members who are alike in many ways
3. Promote self-disclosure	c. Schedule group for twelve meetings
4. Promote trust in the group	d. Discuss confidentiality
5. Prepare the group for termination	e. Have group discuss importance of accepting others

---

Some Typical Groups

Substance Abuse Groups: Alcoholics Anonymous (AA)

AA is a self-help group and is one of the most successful approaches to treating alcoholics. It has been widely imitated in the treatment for other substance abusers as well as other addictions (e.g., Overeaters Anonymous). AA is frequently referred to as the twelve-step program because it is based on the following steps. Members are asked to:

1. Admit that they are powerless over their addiction to alcohol.
2. Accept the idea that there is a greater power, a power that can help them regain control.
3. Decide to turn their lives over to this higher power as they understand it. (Note: this higher power does not have to be God as He is understood in the Judeo-Christian tradition.)
4. Search their own morality. Be brutally honest in this search.
5. Admit to their higher power and to others their moral flaws.

6. Become ready to have morality corrected by their higher power.
7. With humility ask to be cleansed of moral imperfections.
8. Make a list of those that they have harmed because of their moral flaws and become ready to make restitution.
9. Make amends to people that they have harmed as a result of their moral flaws.
10. Stay fully aware of their morality and admit wrongs whenever they occur.
11. Seek fuller understanding of the will of their higher power through prayer and meditation.
12. Awaken spiritually and take the message to others while practicing moral principles in their day-to-day living.

In AA group meetings members affirm that they are alcoholics and report the length of their sobriety. They also receive support and encouragement from fellow alcoholics and are encouraged to follow the twelve steps to sustained sobriety.

Substance Abuse Groups: Addictions Counseling

Ideally these groups, which are led by professional counselors, are made up of people with substance abuse problems who are at approximately the same level of chemical dependence, have high levels of motivation, and have similar records with the criminal justice system (Clark, Blanchard, & Hawes, 1992). The aim of these groups, like that of AA, is to promote abstinence from substance abuse. One rule that is typically proposed by the counselor and usually adopted by the group, is that members will not come to the group under the influence of drugs or alcohol. Since it is unlikely that all members will conscientiously follow this rule, leaders of the group must be prepared, with the involvement of the group members, to determine what the consequences are for breaking the rule. If group members do have abstinence as their goal, the member who comes to the group under the influence may be asked to begin participation in Alcoholics Anonymous or a similar group, or be dismissed from the group. The latter tactic would be taken only as a last resort.

Support Groups: Children's Divorce Support Groups

Elementary school counselors regularly organize and lead support groups for children who have either experienced or are experiencing a divorce. The objectives of these groups are to provide emotional support, to help children develop coping strategies to deal with the pain inflicted by the divorce, and to help children understand that, as the victims of divorce, they are still worthwhile regardless of what happens. The groups are comprised of six to eight children of approximately the same age and whose families are at the same stage in the divorce process. They meet for approximately eight weeks, typically from thirty to forty-five minutes. Children are encouraged to share their feelings about the divorce and their parents. They are also asked to discuss how the divorce is influencing the way they see themselves and they receive reassurance that they are not responsible for the divorce. Depending on the age of the children, counselors may read stories or show filmstrips to evoke self-disclosure.

Groups for Victims of Abuse

These groups may deal with physical, sexual, or emotional abuse that took place when the member was a child or an adult. Not unexpectedly, members come to the group with a wide variety of negative feelings including guilt, anger, and depression. Their symptoms include low self-esteem, drug and alcohol abuse, sexual dysfunction or extreme sexual promiscuity, and somatic complaints such as headaches and lower back pain (Vinson, 1992).

The goals of groups for people have been abused are threefold: develop an awareness of the impact of their abuse on their current functioning, divest themselves of the thoughts and feelings about themselves that haven arisen because of the abuse, and recover themselves by learning to deal authentically with the present. People who are in crises or are chemically dependent should not be accepted to these groups because they may be unreliable members (Corey & Corey, 1992). It is essential that the group leader develop an atmosphere of trust to ensure the attendance and reliability of group members.

Groups for victims of abuse may last for a year or more, although some short-term group experiences may be helpful (Vinson, 1992). Since much of the material to be dealt with by the members may be painful, leaders must be sensitive to the feelings of those who are participating and must be prepared either to mobilize the members to provide support or to provide it themselves.

Assertion Training for Adolescents

Assertion training groups for adolescents may deal with specific concerns such as refusing offers and pressure to use drugs and alcohol or sexual advances. They may also deal with more general assertion issues. In these groups which are didactic in nature, adolescents are taught to differentiate between aggressive, assertive, and nonassertive behavior. Once they can make these distinctions, the members are encouraged to assess their own assertiveness in several situations and taught assertive ways of responding. The "instruction" is done through readings, modeling by the counselor and other group members, and behavioral rehearsal with feedback about performance. These groups are time limited and rarely take more than eight one-hour sessions that are typically spaced one week apart.

Large Group Counseling for Anxiety Disorders

Anxiety constitutes one of the largest mental health problems and includes simple phobias, agoraphobia with panic attacks, depression, and related problems. Several extremely successful large-group strategies have been developed for people with these problems. For example, both American Airlines and USAir offer seminars for people who are afraid to fly. People who enroll in these seminars are claustrophobic (afraid of closed spaces), acrophobic (afraid of heights), agoraphobic (afraid to leave their safe places), and aviophobics (afraid of airplanes). The length of the seminars varies, but they consist of an educational and a coping skills component plus exposure to flying. The educational component is handled by an American Airlines pilot and consists of information about pilot selection and training, aerodynamics, weather planning and avoidance, turbulence, and maintenance. In the coping skills portion of the seminar, counselors teach people how phobias develop. They learn about their physiological response to fear, how to measure their fear, and how to control their response to fear by the use of thought stopping and controlling their breathing, heart rate, and muscle tension. The culmination of the seminar is a graduation flight. These types of programs have very high success rates.

Individual vs. Group Counseling

Although counseling groups have been used since the turn of the century, counselors and others have generally assumed that individual counseling was superior to group counseling. Various reviews of the literature tell us quite convincingly that this is not true (Capuzzi & Gross, 1992; Gladding, 1995). It is also the case that many of the brief counseling and therapy interventions that Steenbarger (1992) identified as having empirical support, were group interventions. Moreover, many of the individual interventions listed by Steenbarger could have been offered in a group situation. Group counseling is as effective as individual counseling for almost every concern and is probably more effective as a means of treating substance abusers (Vinson, 1992). Perhaps more important in an age of limited resources and growing numbers of mental health problems, is the fact that group counseling is more efficient than individual counseling as a treatment strategy. A counselor may spend one hour with one person or one hour with eight to ten people.

Summary

Group counseling is an extremely useful tool and has been applied with many different types of clients. It is as successful, and in some instances more successful, as individual counseling. However, many types of groups, although not all, require a wider variety of skills than individual counseling. In addition to the skills typically employed in individual counseling, the group counselor must acquire a set of skills that will allow him or her to manage the dynamics of the group.

Review Questions

1. In the early part of the chapter the therapeutic forces that are needed to make groups effective were listed. Subsequently the tasks that the leader must perform to be effec-

tive were listed. Try to determine which tasks might lead to the development of each of these forces.

2. Identify several factors that might increase or decrease group cohesion.

3. How should the leader prepare the group for termination? When should this begin?

4. Negative affect in groups has been associated with harmful effects on group members. If you were the leader what would you do to ensure that this type of atmosphere did not develop in your group?

5. Which types of groups can be led by lay people or peer leaders? Which ones require professional counselors?

References

Bednar, R. L., & Kaul, T. J. (1985). Experimental group research: Results, questions, and suggestions. In S. L. Garfield & A. Bergin (eds.), *Handbook of Psychotherapy and Behavior Change*, (pp. 812–838), New York: Wiley.

Brammer, L. M., Shostrom, E. L., & Abrego, P. J. (1989). *Therapeutic Psychology*, (5th ed.). Englewood Cliffs, NJ: Prentice Hall.

Capuzzi, D., & Gross, D. R. (eds.). (1992). *Introduction to Group Counseling*. Denver, CO: Love.

Clark, J., Blanchard, M., & Hawes, C. W. (1992). Group counseling for people with addictions. In D. Capuzzi & D. R. Gross (eds.), *Introduction to Group Counseling*, (pp. 103–120), Denver, CO: Love.

Corey, M. S. & Corey, G. (1992). *Group Process and Practice*, (4th ed.). Pacific Grove, CA: Brooks/Cole.

Corey, G., Corey, M. S., Callahan, P., & Russell, J. M. (1992). *Group Techniques*, (2nd ed.). Pacific Grove, CA: Brooks/Cole.

Gladding, S. T. (1995). *Group Work: A Counseling Specialty*, (2nd ed.). New York: Merrill.

Jacobs, E. E., Harvill, R. L., & Masson, R. L. (1988). *Group Counseling Strategies and Skills*. Pacific Grove, CA: Brooks/Cole.

Johnson, D. W., & Johnson, F. P. (1991). *Joining Together Group Theory and Group Skills*, (4th ed.). Boston: Allyn & Bacon.

Steenbarger, B. N. (1992). Toward science-practice integration in brief counseling and therapy. *The Counseling Psychologist, 20*, 403–450.

Vinson, A. (1992). Group counseling with victims of abuse/incest. In D. Capuzzi & D. R. Gross (eds.), *Introduction to Group Counseling*, (pp. 165–182). Denver, CO: Love.

Yalom, I. D. (1985). *The Theory and Practice of Group Psychotherapy*, (2nd ed.). New York: Basic Books.

Yalom, I. D., & Lieberman, M. (1971). A study of encounter group casualties. *Archives of General Psychology, 25*, 16–30.

C h a p t e r **6**

Assessing Client Problems

Goal of the Chapter

The purpose of this chapter is to provide an overview of the use of testing and interview assessment by counselors.

Chapter Preview

- The purpose of assessment will be explored.
- The characteristics of standardized tests, their selection, and their use in counseling will be examined.
- The use of computer technology in assessment will be described.
- Nonstandardized or interview assessment will be discussed and exemplified.

Introduction

This chapter will survey the purpose of assessment—its use and value in the counseling profession. Types of assessment procedures will be differentiated. Standardized tests and inventories commonly used by counselors will be discussed. At the end of the chapter the diagnostic interview as a means of assessing clients will be highlighted.

The Purpose of Assessment

Assessment is used to diagnose client problems, to make predictions about clients, and to develop client self-awareness. It is a process not restricted to the client-counselor relationship; organizations such as schools and corporations can follow some of the same assessment practices.

Counselors are constantly processing information related to the welfare of clients. This information is linked to decisions that clients must make, that organizations dealing with clients (e.g., schools and employers) must make, and that counselors must make when treating their clients. Important questions emerge related to such decisions:

- *From clients.* What are the chances that I can be successful in a particular training program? What occupations fit with my talents and interests? Why am I so discouraged about life and my future? What can I do to feel better?
- *From family members.* Is it a good idea to transfer our child to a private boarding school with very high academic standards? Is my spouse just as dissatisfied with our marriage as I am?
- *From schools.* What students should be placed in special classes? Which applicants can succeed in a highly competitive academic program?
- *From employers.* Will your client's past difficulties prevent him or her from fitting into our organization? Which employees have the most advancement potential—the greatest potential to handle top-level positions?
- *From counselors.* Is this client potentially dangerous to himself or to others? Might he kill himself or harm others within the next few days? Why is it that this seemingly bright student is having difficulty in certain of her classes? What goals should I discuss with this client for our counseling relationship?

The parameters of these various questions differ. Some of them demand quick decisions; others can be entertained over time. Some can be made by the counselor alone; others are best handled in consultation with others, including the client. Some allow considerable room for error; others must be made carefully or the client might be put in danger.

The questions posed above are difficult ones to answer. They demonstrate how counselors work with clients and organizations to deal with important issues. In helping to answer such questions, counselors have earned the respect of both their clients and other helping professionals.

Assessment Defined

Assessment is the process by which counselors systematically collect data about clients that can be used to make vital decisions. Assessment can be formal, where carefully developed tests and inventories are administered under carefully controlled conditions. It can also be informal, where the counselor draws conclusions from observing clients both during and outside of interviews.

In counselor-related activities assessment is aimed first at description, then at prediction of client behavior. For example, a high school student might want to learn how her mathematical reasoning compares to other students (description). Based on this information, she may solicit an estimate concerning her chances for admission into a college of engineering (prediction).

In using assessment to help clients make decisions, counselors strive for precision. They want to gather accurate information to predict the future. Prediction of the future is always less than perfect. This is especially true with an individual. For example, when using SAT scores to predict grade point average in college, we can be more accurate for a group of students than for an individual.

Types of Assessment

Standardized Tests

Standardized testing is perhaps the most important approach to assessment used by counselors. Standardized tests provide a sample of behavior, drawn by an examiner in a fixed way, so that results collected at different times and places will be fully comparable (Cronbach, 1984). Hopefully, a standardized test also will be objective in that every observer of the test-taker's performance would report the very same results. In addition, the test will be reliable and valid; that is, it will consistently measure what it is supposed to measure and will truly measure what it says it measures, not something else. If an instrument says it measures trustworthiness, but respondents answer questions primarily to meet socially approved standards, the instrument is not very valid, because it does not measure what it says it measures. If an intelligence test is administered three times at monthly intervals, and it generates discrepant scores, it is not very reliable.

For decades psychologists have been developing standardized tests to sample many different human traits and behaviors. These tests are particularly useful in comparing individuals to larger groups because results are normed. That is, outcomes from using those instruments with different groups of people are described in mathematical terms (statistics), so a counselor can help a client size up her or his performance compared to those norms. This brief review of important assessment concepts demonstrates the existence of a special vocabulary. Table 6.1 provides a glossary of some frequently used assessment terms.

Statistics and Standardized Assessment

Statistics are wonderful tools for accurately describing things. For example, a person could say, "I had a wonderful day," and we would know very little about that day, especially compared to other days. However, if the person says, "On a scale from one to ten, it was a ten day," we would have a more precise representation of her experiences for that day. Statistics do this for us in even more graphic ways; they help achieve greater clarity in description and prediction. It is often unfortunate that many counselors-in-training are afraid of mathematics and subsequently fail to use numbers to full advantage as a way to effectively communicate.

In general, tests are a way of communicating information about both how well a person can do something and what that person thinks or believes, depending on the type of test. Counselors use both tests and inventories. Items on tests usually have right and wrong answers and attempt to measure maximum performance.

TABLE 6.1 Glossary of Selected Assessment Terms

Academic aptitude: A combination of inherited and learned abilities necessary for school work.

Aptitude: A combination of inherited and learned abilities that are known to be predictive of success in a given area of performance (e.g., music).

Battery: A group of several tests usually administered at one time.

Diagnostic test: A test used to locate the particular nature of a strength or weakness—for example, to assess reading or mathematics difficulties.

Norms: Statistics (mean, standard deviations, etc.) used to describe the performance of various groups on a test (e.g., grade, gender, age norms).

Objective test: A test for which the outcome will be exactly the same no matter who scores the test.

Performance test: A test requiring manual responses, such as the manipulation of equipment.

Profile: The results of a series of tests or subtests within a test presented in graphic form.

Reliability: The stability of a test to consistently measure what it is supposed to measure. The freedom of a test from error.

Standardized test: The use of systematic procedures or rules to ensure that the test will be administered in the same way regardless of who is administering the test.

Validity: The extent to which a test truly measures what it is supposed to measure. Valid tests measuring the same trait will achieve the same result.

Items on inventories usually do not have right or wrong answers; they are opinions or judgments, and they sample typical performance.

In most cases standardized tests and inventories are developed to measure lasting characteristics, that is, characteristics that influence long-term adjustment. Clients come to counselors to make long-term plans. Helping clients assess stable characteristics provides information about the personal assets that will be invested in those plans.

Nonstandardized Assessment

Not all important decisions counselors make are related to long-term conditions. For example, when a student comes to a counselor complaining about the erratic behavior of her mother and the potential threat of injury to the student or her siblings, the mother often cannot be assessed through the administration of standardized instruments. There is neither time nor opportunity to do so. Whether a person is actually going to commit homicide has never been effectively measured by an inventory.

Nonstandardized assessment, or what has been called clinical assessment, continually filters through much of what counselors do. Often this assessment is immediate. It is data gathering face-to-face with people. Norms are irrelevant or do not exist for the behavior in question. A computer will not help in making the decision on what to do. However, by training and experience, counselors are able to assess the nature of the situation and decide what to do. The ability to deal with emergencies or one-of-a-kind situations comes from sharpening one's skills in nonstandardized assessment. Both standardized and nonstandardized assessment skills enable counselors to do their job.

Types of Standardized Tests and Inventories

The types of instruments frequently used by counselors include tests of intelligence, aptitude, and achievement. Inventories measuring personality factors, career interests, and attitudes are also common to the assessment repertoire of the counselor.

Intelligence Tests

Anastasi (1992) notes that intelligence tests are most often validated against measures of academic achievement and thus often are designed as tests of scholastic aptitude. Some prefer to call intelligence tests measures of cognitive development. Most intelligence tests emphasize a single numeric score (e.g., IQ) as the outcome. Intelligence tests do not measure the size of one's intellectual capacity. They measure one's potential to do well in life situations valued by our dominant culture, requiring in the majority of cases verbal and mathematical skills. Such skills are developed through opportunity. This is why people continue to argue about whether intelligence tests are measures of aptitude or achievement.

The standards for the measurement of intelligence are found in the individually administered tests of intelligence, such as the Stanford-Binet and the scales developed by David Wechsler (Anastasi, 1988). School and clinical psychologists spend more time administering and interpreting individually administered tests of intelligence than do counselors.

Counselors more often use group-administered tests of intelligence. The Otis-Lennon School Ability Test is an example of such an instrument. Tests developed to screen college students are considered measures of intelligence (Anastasi, 1988). A good example is the Scholastic Aptitude Test (SAT) of the College Entrance Examination Board. It is one of the most researched, technically perfect assessment tools (Anastasi, 1988). Because of the link between intelligence testing and academic achievement, such instruments are most often used to make educational decisions for school-age individuals. Examples of uses include placement into special education, honors programs, and other curricular offerings.

Aptitude Tests

Aptitude tests also are measures of special abilities. They focus on some future behavior that a person is capable of learning with appropriate training (Aiken, 1985). The most frequently used aptitude tests measure multiple factors; that is, they include numerous subtests that assess specialized aptitudes. Results of all subtests form a profile of the multiple factors that can be graphically represented and associated with such important issues as occupational success. An example of a measure of multiple aptitudes is the Generalized Aptitude Test Battery (GATB) developed by the U.S. Employment Service. The GATB measures the following:

1. Intelligence (General learning ability)
2. Verbal aptitude
3. Numerical aptitude
4. Spatial aptitude
5. Perception of geometric forms (form perception)
6. Clerical perception
7. Motor coordination
8. Finger dexterity
9. Manual dexterity

Extensive work has been done associating GATB profiles with success in various occupations. Thus they are useful in making career decisions both in school and work settings.

Industry and vocational rehabilitation often use more specialized instruments to help in job placement. There are many different measures of manual dexterity, eye/hand coordination, clerical ability, and so forth. Some of these tests are paper-and-pencil tests, especially those that measure verbal aptitudes. Others rely on a piece of apparatus to measure motor skills. The device may be as simple as a metal box with holes of different sizes in which the test-taker inserts and tightens nuts and bolts. These tasks are timed and the results compared with norms for employees in various occupations.

Work samples can be used to assess managerial ability. Corporate decision making has been simulated via what is called an "in-basket" technique in which problem situations are presented as if they have just arisen in a worklike situation.

Achievement Tests

Tests of achievement for the most part are intended to be used in education to assess the outcome of various learning activities. Entire school districts in cooperation with state departments of education assess general academic achievement at regular intervals. School counselors usually are involved in this process.

Standardized achievement testing is a big business, with large corporations marketing dozens of achievement test batteries and hundreds of different subject matter tests. Achievement test batteries are supposed to measure what is called general educational development, what we consider to be the basic skills in reading, language usage, mathematics, and general knowledge in science and social studies. The results are used for curriculum evaluation and identification of students for remediation and advanced placement. The Stanford Achievement Tests and the Iowa Tests of Basic Skills are examples of these instruments. The American College Testing Program (ACT) examines college applicants on English usage, mathematics, social studies reading, and natural sciences reading.

Achievement test results can play a role in academic advising, but are of limited use in personal counseling. Some exceptions may be with students who have discrepancies between the grades they receive and the scores they achieve on standardized tests. Sending home a student's test results informs parents of a student's standing but can intensify conflicts between parent and child on school and future planning issues. Often parents take an interest in the test results and change their attitudes toward counseling.

Career-Related Inventories

The administration and interpretation of occupational interest inventories is a key factor in career planning. Through their usage counselors help clients to crystallize their interests, which then become the guide used to explore relevant opportunities in the immense world of work. If one recognizes that *The Dictionary of Occupational Titles* lists more than 24,000 different occupational titles, one begins to visualize the impossibility of exploring all conceivable opportunities for employment. More realistic is the tactic of narrowing down occupations for consideration according to a client's interests.

Popular interest inventories include the Strong Interest Inventory, The Self-Directed Search, The Harrington/O'Shea System for Career Decision-Making, and the Ohio Vocational Interest Survey (OVIS). These inventories generally list household and work tasks, hobbies, school subjects, and various occupations. The person taking the inventory then indicates whether he or she likes, dislikes, or is neutral to the activity. Responses are then normed to various groups. For example, the Strong compares the responses of the person completing the inventory to 211 Occupational Samples (OSs) representing 109 different occupations. In addition, client responses are further compared to General Reference Samples (GRSs) of 9,484 males and 9,467 females (Harmon et al., 1994). These and other results are profiled for use in career decision making. Figure 6.1 shows two pages of the Interpretive Report prepared from computer scoring and analysis for a sample Strong Interest Inventory Profile. Page 3 of this sample profile can be better understood after reading the brief description of John Holland's Career Theory in Chapter 7, pages 125–126. Page 10 of the sample profile describes the occupational

Your General Occupational Theme Highlights

The table below describes the General Occupational Themes in which you showed the most interest. Because these Themes describe broad interests, portions of the descriptions may not fit you exactly. As you read about your Themes, consider whether you would describe yourself with the words in the "Descriptors" column. Do other people see you this way? Have you already considered or actually tried some of the occupational and leisure interests listed here?

Theme	Your Results	Common Occupational Interests	Common Leisure Interests	Descriptors
Artistic	High Interest	Writing Entertainment Commercial or fine arts Music	Attending plays or concerts, visiting museums, painting, playing music	Expressive Unstructured Independent
Social	High Interest	Teaching Health care Counseling Religious vocations	Entertaining Volunteer work Family gatherings	Outgoing Concerned for others Humanistic Verbal Generous
Investigative	High Interest	Research Mathematics Physical, natural, or medical science	Computers Sailing Math games Astronomy	Analytical Achievement- oriented Independent

FIGURE 6.1   Your General Occupational Theme Highlights

scales for which the sample client has the most similar interests to women working in those occupations. The sample client is also a female.

The interest profile serves many purposes. One is to guide career exploration; another is to diagnose the client's readiness to make a career choice. A "flat" or undifferentiated (no low or high interest areas) profile represents people who as yet do not know what they like or dislike. With more life experience they may clarify their preferences. In a sense they need to grow a little more before they are ready to make an important career choice.

Many other factors are related to a person's readiness to make career decisions. To assess many of these, measures of career maturity or career development have been developed. One such instrument is the Career Maturity Inventory (CMI), developed by John Crites (1976) to measure attitudes and competencies

Your Occupational Scales Information Table

Theme Code Occupational Scale DOT Code(s)	Description	Related Occupations
AES Corporate Trainer 166	Develop & conduct training programs for employees Formulate teaching outline & instruction methods Test trainees to measure progress & evaluate effectiveness of training	Career development director Human resources director Technical training coordinator Training instructor Training specialist
ASE English Teacher 091	Teach courses in composition, literature, grammar, poetry, creative writing, & speech Prepare course objectives & course outlines Participate in faculty & professional meetings Advise students	Literature teacher Publications advisor Speech teacher Writing teacher
A Librarian 100	Maintain collection of books, films, periodicals, & recordings Locate & explain references Acquire & prepare materials for use Work with books or computers	Acquisitions librarian Bibliographer Children's librarian Medical librarian Reference librarian
EAS Human Resources Director 166	Organize recruitment, selection, & training of employees Establish employee benefits plans May act as liaison between management & labor	Benefits manager Career development director Compensation manager Job analyst Personnel director
AIR Technical Writer 131	Develop, write, & edit material for technical & administrative publications Observe production & experiments to become familiar with product technologies Interview production & engineering personnel	Computer publications editor On-line documentation writer Scientific copy editor Scientific indexer Software editor
SEA School Administrator 099	Administer school system or primary or secondary school Direct budget, interpret programs & policies of school system Confer with teachers, students, & parents Interview, hire, & evaluate teachers	County school administrator Curriculum director Principal School district administrator Superintendent Vocational education administrator
A Lawyer 110	Represent clients in court Draw up legal documents May act as trustee, guardian, or executor May teach college courses in law	Criminal lawyer Patent lawyer Probate lawyer Real estate lawyer Tax attorney
SEA Social Science Teacher 091	Teach courses such as American studies, economics, geography, civics, history, & political science Participate in faculty & professional meetings Advise students	Career development teacher Criminology teacher Government/civics teacher Psychology teacher Sociology teacher
SE High School Counselor 045	Provide educational & vocational guidance Collect & organizes information for vocational & educational planning Aid counselees in making & carrying out objectives	Dean of guidance Education coordinator Psychologist School psychologist Vocational counselor
A Translator 137	Translate written material from one language to another following established rules in semantics & syntax May specialize in particular type of material, such as news or scientific reports	Editor Foreign language teacher Interpreter Linguist Translation director

FIGURE 6.1 *Continued*

needed to make effective career decisions. The CMI can measure both attitudes and self-reported competencies. Career development competencies assessed include: Self-Appraisal, Occupational Information, Goal Selection, Planning, and Problem-solving. In addition to use in individual and group counseling, measures of career development are useful in assessing needs of client populations as well as outcomes of career guidance programs.

Personality Inventories

Because their reliability and validity tends to be lower than other types of standardized instruments, personality inventories have been a little more suspect than other standardized instruments. Nevertheless, every year dozens of new measures of personality appear. However, most of these are intended for use in research in which they will be administered to groups of subjects for the purpose of norming human factors, and for drawing general conclusions about populations of people. When a counselor uses such instruments to draw conclusions about an individual client, the inventory results should conform closely to other information about the client. As part of an overall evaluation, personality inventories have their place. They can stimulate useful inquiry into dimensions of the client that might otherwise have been avoided.

Some of the most frequently used personality inventories are those that assess psychopathology. The Minnesota Multiphasic Personality Inventory (MMPI) and the more recent MMPI-2 are used for this purpose; extensive, specialized training is required for their use, and considerable experience is needed for its their interpretation.

Traditionally, counselors have served normal populations facing regular developmental challenges. Thus, instruments intended for these populations have been of greater interest for counselors. For example, the California Psychological Inventory (CPI) uses some items from the MMPI, but assesses personality dimensions of interest in everyday interpersonal relationships and work/school situations.

The counseling profession has been able to overcome many concerns about the reliability and validity of personality inventories by the way it uses them as part of an ongoing, interactive relationship with a client. The most common abuse of most tests and inventories results when counselors make judgments about clients in isolation from other information. A counselor who often uses a personality inventory as a point of departure for discussion of issues with the client, probably will avoid these mistakes. The inventory leads to additional subjective data from the client. Together counselor and client find their efforts enriched by the way the inventory may have stimulated additional questions and answers.

An example of this would be the use of the Myers-Briggs Type Indicator in counseling. Based on Jungian Personality Theory, this inventory helps clients arrive at hypotheses about their personality, the kind of cognitive style they might have, and the types of people they might enjoy and complement. At the same time clients learn to appreciate diverse characteristics among people, coming to see the complementarity of these traits, how they enrich social interactions. They learn about themselves through the personality inventory, but also learn a lesson in tolerance of individual differences. The latter may be integral to the overall objective of the counseling relationship, especially if intolerance of others is at the heart of the client's difficulties. A form for reporting the Myers-Briggs Type Indicator is presented in Figure 6.2.

Report Form for the Myers-Briggs Type Indicator®

Name: _____

Sex: ☐ Male ☐ Female   Date: _____

The MBTI® reports your preferences on four scales. There are two opposite preferences on each scale. The four scales deal with where you like to focus your attention (E or I), the way you like to look at things (S or N), the way you like to go about deciding things (T or F), and how you deal with the outer world (J or P). Short descriptions of each scale are shown below.

E — You prefer to focus on the outer world of people and things — or — **I** — You prefer to focus on the inner world of ideas and impressions

S — You tend to focus on the present and on concrete information gained from your senses — or — **N** — You tend to focus on the future, with a view toward patterns and possibilities

T — You tend to base your decisions on logic and on objective analysis of cause and effect — or — **F** — You tend to base your decisions primarily on values and on subjective evaluation of person-centered concerns

J — You like a planned and organized approach to life and prefer to have things settled — or — **P** — You like a flexible and spontaneous approach to life and prefer to keep your options open

The four letters show your Reported Type, which is the combination of the four preferences you chose. There are sixteen possible types.

REPORTED TYPE: ☐☐☐☐

PREFERENCE SCORES: ☐☐

Preference scores show how consistently you chose one preference over the other; high scores usually mean a clear preference. Preference scores do *not* measure abilities or development.

EXTRAVERSION **E**   **I** INTROVERSION

SENSING **S**   **N** INTUITION

THINKING **T**   **F** FEELING

JUDGING **J**   **P** PERCEIVING

60 50 40 30 20 10 0 10 20 30 40 50 60

Each type tends to have different interests and different values. On the back of this page are very brief descriptions of each of the sixteen types. Find the one that matches the four letters of your Reported Type and see whether it fits you. If it doesn't, try to find one that does. For a more complete description of the types and the implications for career choice, relationships, and work behavior, see *Introduction to Type* by Isabel Briggs Myers. Remember that everyone uses each of the preferences at different times; your Reported Type shows which you are likely to prefer the most and probably use most often.

FIGURE 6.2   Reports Form for the Myers-Briggs Type Indicator®

Characteristics frequently associated with each type

Sensing Types

Intuitive Types

ISTJ
Serious, quiet, earn success by concentration and thoroughness. Practical, orderly, matter-of-fact, logical, realistic, and dependable. See to it that everything is well organized. Take responsibility. Make up their own minds as to what should be accomplished and work toward it steadily, regardless of protests or distractions.

ISFJ
Quiet, friendly, responsible, and conscientious. Work devotedly to meet their obligations. Lend stability to any project or group. Thorough, painstaking, accurate. Their interests are usually not technical. Can be patient with necessary details. Loyal, considerate, perceptive, concerned with how other people feel.

INFJ
Succeed by perseverance, originality, and desire to do whatever is needed or wanted. Put their best efforts into their work. Quietly forceful, conscientious, concerned for others. Respected for their firm principles. Likely to be honored and followed for their clear convictions as to how best to serve the common good.

INTJ
Usually have original minds and great drive for their own ideas and purposes. In fields that appeal to them, they have a fine power to organize a job and carry it through with or without help. Skeptical, critical, independent, determined, sometimes stubborn. Must learn to yield less important points in order to win the most important.

ISTP
Cool onlookers—quiet, reserved, observing and analyzing life with detached curiosity and unexpected flashes of original humor. Usually interested in cause and effect, how and why mechanical things work, and in organizing facts using logical principles.

ISFP
Retiring, quietly friendly, sensitive, kind, modest about their abilities. Shun disagreements, do not force their opinions or values on others. Usually do not care to lead but are often loyal followers. Often relaxed about getting things done, because they enjoy the present moment and do not want to spoil it by undue haste or exertion.

INFP
Full of enthusiasms and loyalties, but seldom talk of these until they know you well. Care about learning, ideas, language, and independent projects of their own. Tend to undertake too much, then somehow get it done. Friendly, but often too absorbed in what they are doing to be sociable. Little concerned with possessions or physical surroundings.

INTP
Quiet and reserved. Especially enjoy theoretical or scientific pursuits. Like solving problems with logic and analysis. Usually interested mainly in ideas, with little liking for parties or small talk. Tend to have sharply defined interests. Need careers where some strong interest can be used and useful.

ESTP
Good at on-the-spot problem solving. Do not worry, enjoy whatever comes along. Tend to like mechanical things and sports, with friends on the side. Adaptable, tolerant, generally conservative in values. Dislike long explanations. Are best with real things that can be worked, handled, taken apart, or put together.

ESFP
Outgoing, easygoing, accepting, friendly, enjoy everything and make things more fun for others by their enjoyment. Like sports and making things happen. Know what's going on and join in eagerly. Find remembering facts easier than mastering theories. Are best in situations that need sound common sense and practical ability with people as well as with things.

ENFP
Warmly enthusiastic, high-spirited, ingenious, imaginative. Able to do almost anything that interests them. Quick with a solution for any difficulty and ready to help anyone with a problem. Often rely on their ability to improvise instead of preparing in advance. Can usually find compelling reasons for whatever they want.

ENTP
Quick, ingenious, good at many things. Stimulating company, alert and outspoken. May argue for fun on either side of a question. Resourceful in solving new and challenging problems, but may neglect routine assignments. Apt to turn to one new interest after another. Skillful in finding logical reasons for what they want.

ESTJ
Practical, realistic, matter-of-fact, with a natural head for business or mechanics. Not interested in subjects they see no use for, but can apply themselves when necessary. Like to organize and run activities. May make good administrators, especially if they remember to consider others' feelings and points of view.

ESFJ
Warm-hearted, talkative, popular, conscientious, born cooperators, active committee members. Need harmony and may be good at creating it. Always doing something nice for someone. Work best with encouragement and praise. Main interest is in things that directly and visibly affect people's lives.

ENFJ
Responsive and responsible. Generally feel real concern for what others think or want, and try to handle things with due regard for the other person's feelings. Can present a proposal or lead a group discussion with ease and tact. Sociable, popular, sympathetic. Responsive to praise and criticism.

ENTJ
Hearty, frank, decisive, leaders in activities. Usually good in anything that requires reasoning and intelligent talk, such as public speaking. Are usually well informed and enjoy adding to their fund of knowledge. May sometimes appear more positive and confident than their experience in an area warrants.

Introverts

Extraverts

FIGURE 6.2 *Continued*

Selecting and Interpreting Tests and Inventories

With all the possibilities available, the selection of standardized tests and inventories becomes quite a challenge. Standardized assessment requires in-depth, comprehensive knowledge if its use is to help clients. Continual study is necessary. Counselors using tests are wise to receive current catalogues from the test publishers, tour test-related exhibits at conferences, regularly review tests by reading the *Mental Measurements Yearbook* (Buros, 1978; Conoley & Kramer, 1989), and reviews in professional journals such as *Measurement and Evaluation in Counseling and Development*.

Controversies frequently occur around the use of tests. Thus, counselors at times are faced with angry parents, employees, and students who wish to contest decisions that were based on test data. Anxieties over ensuring confidentiality of results is common. Test results are invalid when instruments have not been administered under conditions specified by the publisher; thus counselors must worry about the administration process.

Tyler (1984) notes a common myth that assumes that test performance results from innate ability when in fact it results more from background and experience. Minorities at times have been deprived of this background and experience. Their families often do not have the economic means needed to supplement classroom learning with learning that occurs during a vacation, summer camp, a house full of stimulating toys and games, and so forth. Such lack of opportunity among racial and ethnic minorities may influence results from standardized assessment (Gregory & Lee, 1986).

In spite of the precautions that must be taken when standardized tests are used, millions of individuals, especially students, are given such tests every year. In a national survey of educational testing (Engen, Lamb, & Prediger, 1982, p. 289), data indicated "that nine out of ten schools provide career guidance tests, three out of four administer achievement tests, and two out of three use aptitude tests." The wide use of standardized testing is in part a reaction to the capricious practices used before its arrival. Standardized assessment techniques, while imperfect, represent an effort to supply objective data for use in equitable decision making.

Because of some of the historic abuse of test results, many counselors and educators have proposed that limitations be placed on the use of tests (Engen, Lamb, & Prediger, 1982). Tinsley and Bradley (1986) argue that some of the pessimism about the use of tests, especially among counselors, results from the underemphasis on test interpretation in counselor education and an over-emphasis on the technical aspects of testing (e.g., reliability and validity). Test results are not damaging, but how those results are communicated and understood determines their value. Greater integration of test results into the counseling process is possible.

One major problem in using information from tests is the tendency of counselors to process it in isolation from other information. Often counselors seem to interrupt what they are doing with clients to interpret tests, rather than integrating them with other aspects of their work with clients. Counselors also forget to use some of their interview skills (e.g., reflective listening) during interpretations. Rawlins, Eberly, and Rawlins (1991) describe in detail a set of procedures counselor educators can use to upgrade the test interpretation skills of counselors-in-training.

Goodyear's (1990) review of the research on test interpretation concludes that it generally has a positive effect on clients. There is little evidence to support one approach to test interpretation as superior to another in terms of client retention of information and achievement of counseling goals. However, evidence suggests that clients prefer individual over group and computer interpretations.

In summary, the effective interpretation of test results is the only way to take advantage of the information offered by these instruments. The following are some suggestions for the interpretation of tests.

1. Always prepare in advance for a test interpretation session by reviewing results for the purpose of arriving at a synthesis of their meaning. Integrate this synthesis with other information (Tinsley & Bradley, 1986).
2. Prepare materials or teaching aides (e.g., miniposters), such as those used by door-to-door salespersons, to assist you in explaining material you will repeatedly need to review (Srebalus, Marinelli, & Messing, 1982). Visual as well as verbal explanations increase the likelihood of the client's remembering the information.
3. Help the client remember the instruments being discussed by showing copies of the test booklets along with sample items.
4. Solicit client recollections of the testing situation to determine whether conditions might have existed that would invalidate the results.
5. Invite client self-estimates of performance on different instruments and subtests. Be alert to discrepancies between self-estimates and actual results. Process them in detail.
6. If time runs short, schedule another interpretive session instead of rushing through the remainder of the results.
7. Before ending, ask the client to summarize the information discussed. This is an important check on the client's comprehension of the material. Ask questions regarding what was useful information and how it will help (Rawlins, et al., 1991).
8. Plan to follow up the session in the future to check on the client's retention of the material.

Using tests in counseling has been viewed historically (Goldman, 1972) as a "marriage that failed." However, with greater attention to the integration of test information, clients can benefit from testing by virtue of its ability to supply data useful in the making of important personal decisions.

STUDENT LEARNING EXERCISE

Read the following statements and indicate whether they reflect an appropriate use of assessment. Circle Y for yes or N for no.

1. A counselor who is uncertain how to handle a client having marital problems administers a marital adjustment inventory.   Y   N

2. A counselor meets with the school's curriculum committee to review the results of achievement tests administered to the sixth grade.   Y   N

3. A counselor working with a group of nondating college males administers a social skills inventory with the plan to interpret the results during the next group meeting.   Y   N

4. A counselor disregards the results of a client's aptitude test results when it is learned that the test administrator was not certified to give the test.   Y   N

Assessment Referrals

There are situations in which the type of assessment needed for a client is not within the job description or the expertise of a counselor, and referral for testing may be made to a school or clinical psychologist. For example, in many states the identification of a student for placement in a special education class must be based on testing conducted by a school or licensed psychologist.

Neuropsychological assessment is another reason for referral. This activity evaluates general changes as well as specific intellectual and emotional functioning of patients suffering from traumatic brain injury, disease, epilepsy, or drug reactions. Tests often used for neuropsychological assessment include the Wechsler scales, portions of the Reitan-Halstead battery, the Wide Range Achievement Test, the Bender-Gestalt, and the Luria-Nebraska Test (Korchin & Schuldberg, 1981). Reitan (1975) presents a clear description of neuropsychological assessment with examples from many of these instruments.

Testing and Computer Technology

Since the 1950s business computers have been used to assist in the scoring of tests and in the compilation and profiling of their results. Testing corporations, such as the Educational Testing Service and Houghton Mifflin, have needed large mainframe computers in order to score and profile instruments from school districts and national testing programs. With the introduction of microcomputers in the 1970s, computer technology has offered yet another dimension in test utilization.

The Effects of Computers on Testing

In general, experts are very optimistic about the potential benefits of computer technology for standardized assessment (Sampson & Loesch, 1985; Matarazzo,

1986; Skinner & Pakula, 1986). The introduction of microcomputers, however, has raised some serious questions in reference to new uses of computers in testing. Micros are used both to administer and to interpret tests in addition to scoring and profiling their results. More and more programs are being marketed by firms other than the established, reputable test publishers. In a sense there is now a "cottage industry" producing software that interprets the significance of test scores. In most cases counselors and psychologists cannot inspect the programs to determine the validity of the judgments made by the programs. It is precisely because computers are now being used to make clinical judgments that concern about them exists (Skinner & Pakula, 1986). Also, there is fear that unqualified practitioners will purchase or illegally copy test interpretation programs and present themselves as competent to use various instruments without real expertise.

The use of test interpretation programs can have some benefits. First, such programs can reduce the cost of test utilization through reduction in professional time needed to interpret, profile, and write test reports. Korchin and Schuldberg (1981) have noted that the cost of thorough assessment has become difficult to justify in relation to the increasing use of briefer therapies. Thus extensive clinical assessment has been on the decline. In national surveys clinical psychologists reported in 1959 that 44 percent of their time was spent in testing, but by 1969 that portion of time was reduced to 28 percent (Korchin & Schuldberg, 1981). This trend has probably continued to the present.

Second, many test interpretation programs supply graphics as part of the package, and this can increase the effectiveness of feedback to the client by creating a visual dimension. Third, administration of an instrument through the console of a microcomputer (keyboard and monitor) has much greater potential than paper-and-pencil to present more varied stimuli. For example, perception and artistic aptitude can be assessed through the presentation of computer-driven images (high resolution graphics) that would be impossible with paper-and-pencil. Where microcomputer and paper-and-pencil versions of instruments exist (e.g., the Ohio Vocational Interest Inventory), the microcomputer version compares favorably to the other versions (Hoyt, 1986). While greater supervision of the use of software may be needed, no one questions the use of computer hardware by the helping professions. Both the use of software and hardware in interpretation of such popular instruments as the MMPI show general customer satisfaction (Green, 1982). Computer technology in testing is here to stay.

Assessing Clients Through Interviews

Earlier in this chapter it was noted that questions regarding clients often dictate informal assessment through an interview. Interactions with clients provide a rich source of relevant data that, if utilized properly, can allow the counselor to draw meaningful conclusions about both immediate crisis situations and the long-term well-being of clients.

Before entering a discussion of informal assessment certain cautions should be noted. First, a counselor's judgment is no better than his or her training and experience. Thus, without a background in mental health problems, it is inappropriate for a counselor to draw conclusions about them. Second, in crisis situations sensitivity to all relevant factors is ensured through consultation with others, if time permits. Third, guidelines offered to assist in making judgments in crisis situations are only guidelines, not recipes that can be followed blindly.

The Intake Interview

Assessment through face-to-face interviewing can occur as part of ongoing treatment or as a function of an interview formally structured for assessment purposes. The most common example of the latter is the "intake" interview. Intakes are used in many treatment settings to assess both client problems and resources in preparation for treatment or referral. Traditionally the intake interview has attempted to generate a comprehensive picture of clients, their current functioning and situation, and a history of their development and adjustment. For this reason the intake is also called the "history-taking interview." Outlines for the intake interview appear in dozens of psychiatric and counseling texts. The most common elements listed for the intake are:

1. The client's presenting problem (complaint)
2. The history of the presenting problem, including efforts to treat or manage the problem
3. Other complaints and problems and previous treatment of those problems
4. Educational, social, and occupational history
5. Family and marital background
6. Medical history
7. The current ability and resources to manage the problems presented

The use of intake interviewing in community mental health is described in Chapter 15.

Historically, the outcome of the intake interview was a diagnosis. The diagnosis was supposed to point the way to treatment. Diagnosis is usually based on some kind of classification system. The most popular system used worldwide in psychiatry, psychology, and mental health counseling is the one presented in the fourth edition of the Diagnostic and Statistical Manual of the American Psychiatric Association (1994). The *DSM-IV* attempts a comprehensive diagnosis by using a multiaxial system to identify presenting problem (Axis I), long-term personality orientation (Axis II), physical/medical condition (Axis III), psychosocial stressors

(Axis IV), and level of adaptive functioning (Axis V). The principal diagnosis (Axis I) identifies a condition from a list of disorders that have been divided into sixteen broad categories. Examples are substance related disorders, schizophrenic and other psychotic disorders, anxiety disorders, sexual and gender identity disorders, adjustment disorders, and so forth.

Making a Diagnosis

The most common situation in which a counselor must make a formal diagnosis occurs in mental health agencies where a DSM-IV diagnosis must be made. Inexperienced counselors often misdiagnose because they do not systematically approach interview assessment. The following is an example of how they might seek to establish a diagnosis:

1. They conduct an initial or intake interview with a client, attempting to explore problems without reference to any interview guide or outline.
2. They rarely take notes of what is discussed in the interview, leaving to their memory the recall of important information.
3. When they have completed the interview, they thumb through the DSM-IV, looking for a disorder that approximates the complaints heard. There is seldom an effort to make a differential diagnosis, that is to include a list of all the possible disorders that might be suggested by the presenting symptoms.

This approach to diagnosis can be improved by following the recommendations of Othmer and Othmer (1989). The authors argue that the interviewer can learn how to be more precise in exploring problems by essentially formulating three lists of problems or disorders as the assessment interview procedes. The lists include: all possible disorders (List #1), disorders eliminated from further consideration (List #2), and disorders yet to be explored (List #3). In beginning the process the interviewer first seeks to make List #1 as long as possible. While this is being done, the interviewer works on defining the content of List #3. As the intake continues, Lists #1 and #3 will get shorter, while List #2 gets longer. Hopefully List #1 gets small enough to make the diagnosis.

When working on the diagnosis, the interviewer should remember that it reflects the client's current problems. Thus, exploration of symptoms and difficulties should be current issues; the assessment should stay in the present.

When the client's current functioning is understood, past history can be explored to complete the picture. Past history confirms a current diagnosis or eliminates a disorder from the differential diagnosis. In taking past history special attention is paid to events and factors that suggest the seriousness of the problem. Intensity and frequency of a problem are important to the determination of seriousness, whether it is part of an acute situation or a chronic condition. Deterioration should also be noted, if it is apparent.

Assessing Emergency Conditions[1]

Regardless of where counselors work, chances are high that they will encounter people in crisis. In times of crisis individuals find that their normal means for dealing with situations do not work. They cannot cope, and some will turn to counselors for help. Two such situations that challenge the ability of the counselor to assess a crisis situation are dangerousness and suicide. Signs of active crisis are listed in Table 6.2.

The Assessment of Dangerousness

People run the risk of being endangered through the prospect of encountering someone who may inflict bodily injury or death. Certain individuals have a history of acting out aggression. According to Gutheil and Applebaum (1982), potentially dangerous persons themselves show a history of being victimized both as a child and as an adult. Poor impulse control is compounded through the use of alcohol and drugs. Dangerous persons tend to harbor persecutory thoughts, lasting grudges, and images of revenge or retribution. Often they have made written or mental lists of people who have harmed them, people they would like to see dead. Investigation often will show a criminal record documenting charges of assault and battery, drunk driving, and property damage. Such people are likely to own weapons, including a degree in the martial arts. Table 6.3 identifies factors to observe in an assessment interview. Chapter 15 describes some issues in the management of potentially dangerous individuals.

The Assessment of Suicide

The incidence of suicide is discussed in Chapter 15. Inspection of that chapter shows that suicide and attempted suicide are serious risks to most client populations, in particular to adolescents, young adults, and the elderly.

TABLE 6.2   Signs of People in Active Crisis

Disorganized thinking
Impulsivity
Hostility and emotional distance
Acute anxiety
Immobilization
Feelings of helplessness
Loss of behavior control
Panic
Conflict and indecision
Escape through substance abuse

[1]The authors are grateful to Dr. Rosemary Srebalus for her assistance with this section.

TABLE 6.3   Assessment of Dangerousness

Appearance: Psychical tension (grimacing, clenching of fists, tightening of jaw, etc.), preoccupation, pacing, presence of real or potential weapons (knife, length of pipe, etc.).

Mood and speech: Angry, threatening, glaring or hostile looks, words, or threats. Answers positively to the question, "Have you ever for any reason, accidentally or otherwise, caused the death of or severe injury to another human being?"

Thought content: Persecutory delusions, command hallucinations directing violent acts, obsessive thoughts, fantasies, and ruminations of assault, loss of control, revenge motives.

Circumstances: Brought to interview in handcuffs, shackles, or by law enforcement officials, or seen raving in restraints.

Note: Adapted from *Clinical Handbook of Psychiatry and the Law* by T. G. Gutheil and P. S. Applebaum, 1982, New York: McGraw-Hill. Reprinted by permission.

According to Gutheil and Applebaum (1982), factors to consider in the assessment of suicide, besides those in Table 6.4 are the following:

1. The presence of severe depression or the lifting of such a depression, making available the energy needed to take one's life. Adding risk are other disphoric feeling states such as rage or panic.
2. The presence of a psychosis, especially with command hallucinations to commit suicide.
3. A history of substance abuse, which increases a history of poor impulse control, especially toward violence.
4. The loss of a loved person, job, residence, academic or social standing.
5. A history of marginal adaptation with few accomplishments.
6. Lacking support and living in a hostile environment (e.g., a teenager who is shy or withdrawn and subject to harassment from neighborhood gangs).
7. Thoughts and fantasies with destructive content, including revenge and "resting in peace."

Assessing a Client's Coping Abilities

Face-to-face interviewing not only can be potent in identifying problems but can also assess client personal and environmental resources. Problem-solving style comes across during an interview. Can the client be decisive? Will he or she re-

TABLE 6.4   Assessment of Suicide Potential

Suicidal intent (decision to die) with decreased tension
Presence of a specific plan
Availability of means to kill oneself
Previous attempts to commit suicide

spond impulsively to pressure? How will the client enlist help from others? Will he or she be able to sustain involvement in executing a long-term solution?

In addition to helping the counselor learn what the client might do, data processed during an interview might hint at the response others might make toward the client's attempt to change. For example, will an adolescent's attempt to lose weight be supported by her family? Will a distressed worker who wants to change occupations get support from his or her spouse?

Few standardized instruments measure such situations. During an interview client and counselor can become very concrete, naming people, places, and events related to counseling objectives. Alternative solutions already attempted or considered can be explored on the spot. Concrete evidence about previous successes and failures can be provided.

Assessment and treatment both rest on the degree to which a counselor has become skilled in interviewing, in dealing face-to-face with people. When those skills are combined with testing and new forms of assessment emerging from computer technology, the counseling profession can increase its responsiveness to human concerns.

Summary

This chapter explored the nature and purpose of assessment, with emphasis on the use of standardized tests and inventories. Nonstandardized assessment through the intake interview was also discussed. Suggestions were made regarding counselor selection, use, and interpretation of tests. Computer applications in assessment were also surveyed.

Review Questions

1. Describe the characteristics of a well-developed test.

2. List the types of standardized tests and inventories commonly used by counselors.

3. What are the advantages and disadvantages of using informal or interview assessment?

4. What issues should be considered in the selection, administration, and interpretation of standardized tests?

5. Give two examples of circumstances in which a counselor might refer a client for testing by a school or clinical psychologist.

6. What are some of the issues in the use of microcomputers for test administration, scoring, and interpretation?

7. List criteria for the assessment of people in active crisis.

8. List criteria for the assessment of dangerousness and suicide.

References

Aiken, L. R. (1985). *Psychological testing and assessment,* (5th ed.). Boston: Allyn & Bacon.

Anastasi, A. (1988). *Psychological testing,* (6th ed.). New York: Macmillan.

Anastasi, A. (1992). What counselors should know about the use and interpretation of psychological tests. *Journal of Counseling and Development, 70*(5), 610–615.

American Psychiatric Association. (1994). *Diagnostic and statistical manual of mental disorders,* (4th ed.). Washington, D.C.: American Psychiatric Association Press.

Buros, O. K. (1978). *The mental measurements yearbook.* Highland Park, NJ: Gryphon Press.

Conoley, J. C., & Kramer, J. J. (1989). *The tenth mental measurements yearbook.* Lincoln, NE: Buros Institute of Mental Measurements.

Crites, J. O. (1976). Career counseling: A comprehensive approach. *The Counseling Psychologist, 6,* 2–11.

Cronbach, L. J. (1984). *Essentials of psychological testing.* New York: Harper & Row.

Engen, H. B., Lamb, R. R., & Prediger, D. J. (1982). Are secondary schools still using standardized tests? *The Personnel and Guidance Journal, 60*(5), 287–293.

Goldman, L. (1972). Tests and counseling: The marriage that failed. *Measurement and Evaluation in Guidance, 4*(2), 213–220.

Goodyear, R. K. (1990). Research on the effects of test interpretation: A review. *The Counseling Psychologist, 18*(2), 240–257.

Green, C. J. (1982). The diagnostic accuracy and utility of MMPI and MCMI computer-interpretive reports. *Journal of Personality Assessment, 46*(3), 359–365.

Gregory, S., & Lee, S. (1986). Psychoeducational assessment of racial and ethnic minority groups: Professional implications. *Journal of Counseling and Development, 64*(10), 635–637.

Gutheil, T. G., & Applebaum, P. S. (1982). *Clinical handbook of psychiatry and the law.* New York: McGraw-Hill.

Harmon, L. W., Hansen, J. C., Borger, F. H., & Hammer, A. L. (1994). *Strong interest inventory applications and technical guide.* Stanford, CA: Stanford University Press (distributed by Consulting Psychologists Press, Inc.).

Korchin, S. J., & Schuldberg, D. (1981). The future of clinical assessment. *American Psychologist, 36*(10), 1147–1158.

Matarazzo, J. D. (1986). Computerized clinical psychological test interpretations: Unvalidated plus all mean and no sigma. *American Psychologist, 41*(1), 14–24.

Othmer, E., & Othmer, S. C. (1989). *The clinical interview using DSM-III-R.* Washington, D.C.: American Psychiatric Association Press.

Rawlins, M. E., Eberly, C. G., & Rawlins, L. D. (1991). Infusing counseling skills in test interpretation. *Counselor Education and Supervision, 31*(2), 109–120.

Reitan, R. M. (1975). Assessment of brain-behavior relationships. In P. McReynolds (Eds.), *Advances in psychological assessment.* San Francisco: Jossey-Bass.

Sampson, J. P., Jr., & Loesch, L. C. (1985). Computer preparation standards for counselors and human development specialists. *Journal of Counseling and Development, 64*(1), 31–33.

Skinner, H. A., & Pakula, A. (1986). Challenge of computers in psychological assessment. *Professional Psychology: Research and Practice, 17*(1), 44–50.

Srebalus, D., Marinelli, R., & Messing, J. (1982). *Career development: Concepts and procedures.* Monterey, CA: Brooks/Cole.

Tinsley, H., & Bradley, R. W. (1986). Test interpretation. *Journal of Counseling and Development, 64*(7), 462–466.

Tyler, L. E. (1984). What tests don't measure. *Journal of Counseling and Development, 63*(1), 48–50.

Chapter 7

Life Career Development and Counseling

Goals of the Chapter

The goals of the chapter are threefold; first, to provide an overview of career and life development; second, to familiarize the reader with work in the United States; and third, to acquaint the reader with some of the approaches that can be used to facilitate career choice and adjustment.

Chapter Preview

- Definitions of the terms associated with life career development will be provided.
- A brief view of the current status of work in the United States will be provided.
- Career information and assistance programs for various age groups will be illustrated along with a discussion of the career development problems of groups such as women and minorities.
- The processes of life career and career counseling will be surveyed.
- A brief summary of computerized information and career assistance programs will be provided.

Introduction

In the past, the counseling profession has only tacitly recognized the interrelationships of various life roles. Within the past ten to fifteen years, this has begun to change, partly because of new theories, and partly because research on areas such as job stress and family relationships has clearly pointed to interrelationships among life roles and their influences on the functioning of individuals.

A number of terms have been presented that were aimed at illustrating the dynamic relationship among life roles. Herr (1986a) and McDaniels (1989) have argued that the term "career" actually has a broader connotation than just the jobs that one holds; it can be used to depict the interrelationship of life roles. Zunker (1986) notes that lifestyle is also a concept that denotes the individual's overall orientation to life roles. However, the term *life career* was chosen here to depict the interrelationship between career and other life roles because it more clearly denotes that career cannot be considered separately from the rest of one's existence (McDaniels, 1989; Okun, 1984).

While many individuals have discussed not only the concept of life career development but also how it can be facilitated, Okun (1984) has provided a visual illustration of this relationship. Her model is shown in Figure 7.1. As can be seen, the individual, his or her career, and the family are part of a broader life system, and they are influenced by the social, cultural, political, and economic aspects of that system. It is important to note that the individual, career, and family subsystems are portrayed in dynamic interaction with each other.

Super (1990) has also provided us with a visual image of the interaction of various life roles in his Life-Career Rainbow (Figure 7.2). He suggests that at various

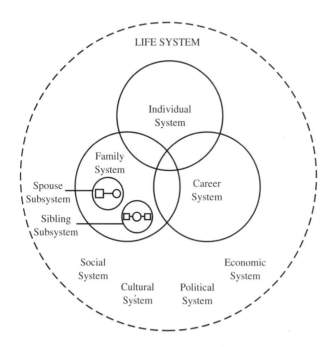

FIGURE 7.1   Life System and Subsystems

Source: Working with Adults: Individual, Family, and Career Development by B. F. Okun. Coypright © 1984 by Brooks/Cole Publishing Company, a division of International Thomson Publishing Inc., Pacific Grove, CA 93950. Reprinted by permission.

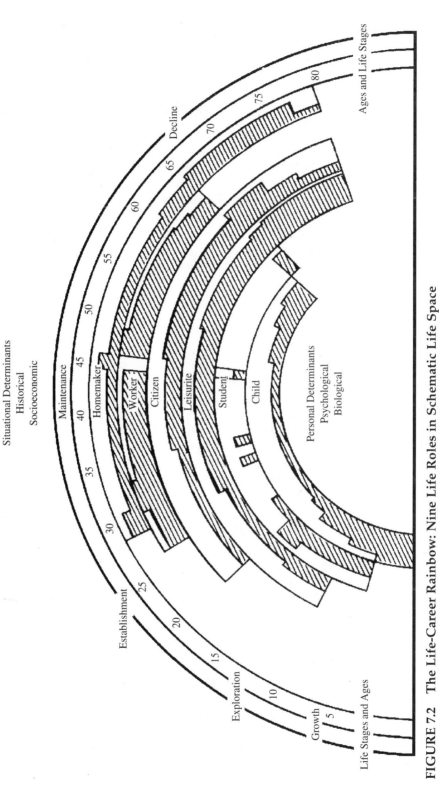

FIGURE 7.2 The Life-Career Rainbow: Nine Life Roles in Schematic Life Space

Source: "A life-span, life space approach to career development," by D. E. Super, (1980), *Journal of Vocational Behavior, 16*, 282–298. Reprinted by permission.

stages of our lives, we fill all the following roles: child, student, leisurite, citizen, worker, spouse, homemaker, parent, and pensioner. He also suggests that at any of the various stages of development, each of us fills a number of these roles. For example, during our middle years, it is likely that a parent, spouse, worker, and citizen are the dominant roles in our lives, but this does not suggest that we are not involved in the roles of child, student, and leisurite. Factors such as age, gender, race, personal characteristics, and economic conditions will influence the extent to which we fill various roles at any given time.

The recognition that life roles are interconnected has slowly begun to change the nature of career and life planning. However, for many individuals, work is still the dominant life role, and some counselors, particularly those working in employment agencies, focus almost exclusively on this role. It would, therefore, be an oversight not to highlight the importance of work and the problems involved in career choice and work adjustment.

Some Definitions

A number of terms and concepts have already been introduced. Before proceeding, it seems prudent to define both the terms that have been introduced to this point and those that will be used later.

- *Work:* A paid or unpaid systematic activity aimed at producing something of value for one's self, others, or a combination thereof.
- *Occupation:* A formally classified work activity that involves a group of people working in different situations. School counseling and social work are occupations.
- *Job:* A specific occupation held by an individual at any given time. Usually used synonymously with occupation.
- *Career:* The totality of work and related experiences held by an individual over her or his life span.
- *Career development:* The sum total of changes that occur in the individual as a result of physiological, psychological, sociological, and economic forces that influence entry into and progression in those occupations that make up the career over the life span.
- *Life-career development:* The totality of the changes that occur as a result of physiological, psychological, sociological, and economic forces that influence individual, family, career, and other life role development and the interaction of these subsystems over the life span.
- *Leisure:* Planned or spontaneous events, usually relatively short-term in nature, aimed at enlightening, entertaining, relaxing, or stimulating the individual.
- *Occupational information:* Materials ranging from single printed pages and extensive directories to computer programs designed to impart data about spe-

cific occupations, including descriptions of the work done, rewards, training requirements, and employment trends.

Work in the United States

No one seems to doubt that the work we perform in our jobs influences our economic, psychological, and sociological functioning. Herr (1986b) suggests that the nature of our occupation is a primary determiner of our lifestyle. Whether or not "work responds to something profound and basic in human nature" (Report of Special Task Force, 1973, p. 1), as was suggested over two decades ago, is open to question. What is not open to question is that most Americans will spend a large part of their waking adult hours involved in some form of paid or unpaid work. Because of this, work will remain a topic of considerable study and concern for psychologists, counselors, and others. Of particular concern to career counselors and others is the nature of the workplace in the future and the impact it will have on the worker.

McDaniels (1989) examined the literature regarding the future of work in U.S. society and has painted three scenarios: green, yellow, and red. In the green scenario, robots and computers will assume many of the roles now filled by people, new careers will replace old ones, entrepreneurial enterprises will flourish, and the Informal Age will replace the Industrial Age. The green scenario is essentially a positive view of the world of work, although only those individuals who are properly prepared will be successful in this dynamic situation.

The yellow scenario can be characterized as a steady-state view. Change is expected, but it will be orderly, and the future will look very much like the present. In this future, not only will occupations appear much as they do today, but they will continue to be open to people of all backgrounds, not just to highly trained individuals. The only negative aspect of this scenario is that new jobs will not be created, and thus opportunity will stem from the replacement of current jobs.

The red scenario projects a bleak future for the world of work. This scenario draws on the spiraling unemployment in this country, the cheap cost of foreign labor, and the negative balance of payments, among other things, to forecast the belief that ten to twenty million members of our future workforce will be chronically underemployed or unemployed, creating an underclass in our society. It is impossible to tell which of McDaniel's scenarios will be realized.

Career Development

Theorists such as Roe and Lunneborg (1990), Super (1990), Bordin (1990) and others trace occupational choice and ultimately career development back to the earliest developmental stages of the individual. Donald Super has been particularly influential as an advocate of career development as a life-long process. He believes that from birth to adolescence, children develop many of the attitudes and values that lead to occupational choice. During childhood, fantasies about the world of work and unbridled interests serve as the bases for thinking about careers.

During adolescence, interests and fantasies are still important, but capacities or abilities also begin to play a major role in the thinking of the adolescent as he or she moves through a succession of reality-testing experiences. The result of this reality testing is a series of tentative choices that lead in turn to a number of trial jobs.

As the young adult gains more experience in the world of work, establishment in a relatively stable work pattern occurs. Establishment is followed by stabilization in the occupation and then advancement.

The middle and later years of life, according to Super (1990), are followed typically by maintenance of one's occupational position. Ultimately, aging produces a period marked by declining interest and involvement in work in most people. These stages are depicted in Figure 7.3.

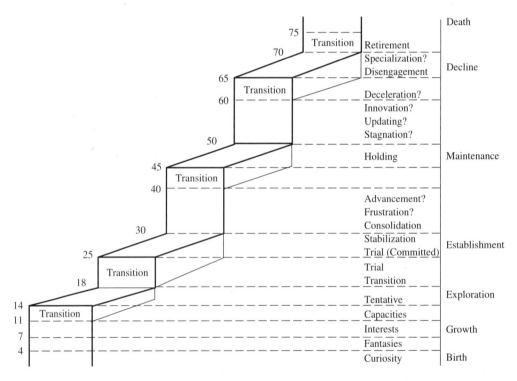

FIGURE 7.3   Life stages and substages based on the typical developmental tasks with a focus on the maxicycle

Source: "Career and Life Development, (p. 201) by D. E. Super. In Career Choice and Development by D. Brown and L. Brooks, eds., 1984, San Francisco: Jossey-Bass. Reprinted by permission.

Super (1990), along with Levinson (1978), Neugarten (1976), Gould (1978), as well as others, realize that many, and perhaps most people do not enter a single career and move through it in linear fashion. As can be seen in Figure 7.3, Super (1990) postulates that transition points in the development of the individual, such as moving from tentative choices to tryouts (trial occupations) are characterized by a minicycle involving some or all of the developmental stages. For example, an adolescent preparing to assume a trial occupation probably passes through the growth stage in which he or she fantasizes about occupations, searches his or her interests, examines his or her capacities, and selects from the options available. Similarly, adults dissatisfied with their jobs may very well recycle through the growth, exploration, establishment, and maintenance stages again. They have already experienced decline and withdrawal from their previous occupation. As can be seen, career development is a process that occurs throughout life. Counselors working with all age groups and populations ultimately become involved with the process.

Career Development at Different Developmental Stages

During the 1970s career development programs flourished in U.S. schools, but as is characteristic of education, these programs were largely swept away by the back-to-basics movement. Currently, thanks in large part to the National Occupational Information Committee (NOIC), career development programming in public schools and elsewhere is on the increase. NOIC has implemented what has been termed the National Career Development Guidelines Project and has pilot programs in elementary, secondary, and post-secondary schools as well as in the community. The emphasis in the elementary school phase is to focus on building self-esteem and to begin to explore the relationship between work and education.

Elementary school counselors are, of course, dealing with children in Super's (1990) growth stage. In some school districts, extensive career education programs have been implemented in which children are systematically exposed to various facets of the world of work in the form of self-awareness activities designed to clarify interests and values. Awareness activities are also aimed at clarifying a vocational self-concept (Super, 1990), that is, having the child project himself or herself into a variety of work roles. The following are illustrations of some of these ideas.

- Children in one school were exposed to increasing numbers of careers in relationship to their social studies curriculum. First graders explored their parents' careers and those of people in their neighborhoods. Second graders studied occupations in their county, while third graders studied careers in their state. Fourth, fifth, and sixth graders studied careers in their geographic region, the nation, and the world, respectively.

- Tools were brought into one classroom, and students took turns using hammers, saws, chisels, and other hand tools to build various projects. Follow-up activities involved discussing types of workers that used the various tools and how the children felt about performing the tasks.
- Counselors in one district conducted extensive field trips designed to show children occupations that were related to each of their subject matter areas.

Junior high school and high school counselors deal with students in Super's (1990) exploration phase, where capacities become more important. As a result, many career development programs at these levels include the administration of tests that provide feedback on interests, aptitudes, and experiences that will enable students to assess how their aptitudes, interests, and values can be realistically utilized in the world of work. In a few schools, students are exposed to simulated work environments. Most approaches involve discussion with workers, job shadowing experiences, where students literally follow workers around, and internship programs, where students can get "hands on" experiences. Computerized systems and other informational approaches can also assist students in assessing their characteristics relative to various occupations.

Counselors working with young adults in college and vocational technical schools often offer programs quite similar in nature to those described for counselors working with adolescents. Counselors working with adults in continuing education centers, employee assistance programs, business and industry, and other settings may also provide career exploration and personal development programs aimed at helping individuals make career choices. They may also be involved in assisting workers cope with job stress and in outplacement counseling. Outplacement counseling, a relatively new activity, is the assistance provided by some employers when an employee is terminated; it helps the employee in the transition from the job he's leaving to another one.

Services to adults involve career exploration and choice making, as well as adjustment to the current work setting (Brooks & Brown, 1986; Brown & Brooks, 1985). When helping adults adjust to a work setting, life planning comes strongly to the fore, since work and other life roles (parent and worker) may be interacting to negatively influence work adjustment. For those stuck in an unrewarding occupation, review of more personally satisfying alternatives may be emphasized.

Occupational Choice Making

Career development is a dynamic, life-long process involving a series of occupational choices. Just as there are theories of career development, so too there are theories of occupational choice making. One of the earliest of these was presented by Parsons (1909). His conceptualization of career choice involved three steps: (1) self-analysis, (2) analysis of the world of work, and (3) matching of one's personal characteristics to those required by occupations through "true reasoning." Parson's tripartite model became the foundation for the trait-and-factor model of occupational choice. E. G. Williamson (1939, 1965) became the best known of the early advocates of this model. He and others who came after Parsons followed the three-step model but had the advantage of aptitude and ability tests, interest and personality inventories to measure traits, and sophisticated occupational information based on a systematic analysis of the skills and personal qualities demanded in a particular occupation.

More recently, John Holland (1985) has presented an elaborate trait-and-factor model of occupational choice. Holland believes that the essence of occupational choice is matching one's personality to a congruent occupational environment. He believes that personalities are comprised of six different types: Realistic, Investigative, Artistic, Social, Enterprising, and Conventional. But an individual is rarely a pure type, and thus the personality is made up of different components of the six types.

Realistic types prefer orderly activities, often involving tools and machines, and have aversions to educational and therapeutic activities. Investigative types also prefer systematic activities, but differ from realistic types in that their preferences are for symbolic activities that lead to the investigation of various social and scientific phenomena. Investigative types have aversions to persuasive, social, and repetitive activities. Artistic types diverge substantially from realistic and investigative types in that they have aversions to systematic and ordered activities. They have preferences for free-flowing, ambiguous activities that involve various art forms.

Social types have deficits in the manual arts and prefer interactions with people aimed at leading, informing, or curing them. They also have aversions to systemic, ordered activities. Preferences for leadership and the development of interpersonal and persuasive skills characterize enterprising types. Conventional types, like realistic and investigative types, prefer activities that involve order and system, particularly those that involve maintaining, reordering, or filing data or materials. Conventional types have aversions to the ambiguous and unsystematic.

Holland (1985) also believes that there are six work environments that correspond to the six personality types, that is, realistic, investigative, artistic, social, enterprising, and conventional. These environments can be so characterized because they are made up of workers with similar personality types. Realistic work environments would be made up of people with realistic personalities, a social environment of people with social personalities, and so forth.

Job satisfaction, career stability, achievement, and reduction of job stress are likely to be enhanced if the individual matches his or her personality to a similar work environment (Holland, 1985).

There are, of course, other ideas about career decision making, most of which use some form of the scientific method as their basis. They hold that good decision making involves a process of (1) identifying the problem, (2) generating alternative solutions, (3) systematically collecting data about the alternatives generated, (4) selecting from among the alternatives, (5) implementing the solution, (6) evaluating the solution, and (7) recycling as necessary. These decision-making models point to the process that one might follow, but do not suggest what factors should be employed in reaching the decision.

Problems in Decision Making

Values can be defined as cognitive structures that influence the way we feel and act and are viewed by many as the key factors in the decision-making process (Rokeach, 1973; Brown, 1986). If our choices do not result in our values being reinforced we will be unhappy with our decisions. For example, many counselors have altruism—concern for the well-being of others—as one of their values. If they find themselves in situations where they are unable to contribute to the well-being of others, they are likely to be at best discontented and at worst very unhappy. Interests are preferences for activities and also influence the decision-making process, as do personality variables such as introversion and extroversion. Accordingly, if people are to make sound decisions they must understand their personal traits and how they relate to careers and other life roles.

Even though counselors have a better understanding of the career decision-making process than ever before, there are many people who still make poor decisions. Why? A survey of adults in the United States found that almost sixty percent of the respondents did not actively engage in a career planning process (NCDA, 1994). Some of these people did not plan because they were not properly apprised of the need to do so. If these people had been aware of the need to plan and had valid information, they could have made good career decisions. However, some people do not engage in career planning because it raises a high level of anxiety (Brown & Kaplan, 1986; Goodstein, 1972); therefore, they may avoid the process altogether. These people are classified as indecisive because, even if they are aware of the need to plan and have the information, they are unable to engage in the process in a thoughtful manner. When forced to make a career decision they may do so impulsively or may rely on others to make the decisions for them. Before this group can make good career decisions the anxiety must be eliminated.

Other Factors in Occupational Choice

Personality, values, and other psychological aspects of the individual play an important role in the choice of occupation. The process followed can also be a major determinant of the outcome. But psychological characteristics and the decision-making process are not the only concern of the career counselor.

Occupational Outlook

The U.S. Department of Labor's Bureau of Labor Statistics (BLS) publishes a wide range of materials that attempt to forecast the future of various occupations. Perhaps the best known of these is the *Occupational Outlook Handbook* (OOH) which contains not only forecasts about job growth and decline, but information about salary, training requirements, working conditions, and other information as well. The BLS also produces information such as that shown in Tables 7.1 and 7.2. These tables contain information about occupations that will have the largest increase in real numbers (7.1) and the occupations that will show the greatest percentage increase (7.2). Both of these tables provide information that is useful to decision makers, but they would also need to know the *supply* of workers available if they are to make decisions about the availability of jobs. The *Occupational Projections and Training Data* publication, along with the OOH, provide data on this issue.

The latest issue of the OOH provides the following information about counselors:

- *Nature of work:* Counselors assist people with personal, family, social, educational, and career decisions, problems, and concerns.
- *Employment:* Counselors held about 144,000 jobs in 1990. School counseling was the largest specialty.
- *Job outlook:* Overall employment of counselors is expected to grow faster than the average for all occupations through the year 2005. In addition, replacement needs should increase significantly by the end of the decade as a large number of counselors now in their forties and fifties reach retirement age.
- *Earnings:* The median salary for full-time educational and vocational counselors in 1990 was about $31,000.

  Other information about training requirements, specialities within the counseling profession, and related occupations is presented in the OOH. Other sources of information are also listed.
- *Gender:* Gender influences occupational choice and must therefore be considered as a special factor in the decision-making process. Brooks (1986) indicates that women often engage in career planning simultaneously and thus may limit themselves unwittingly. The result is that women traditionally choose lower-paying clerical and service jobs while ignoring the sciences and many of the professions, and earn only about two-thirds as much as men earn. While there is evidence that women are increasingly entering occupations that once were almost exclusively the domain of men, such as accounting, veterinary medicine, dentistry, medicine, and law, women are still grossly under-represented in engineering, the sciences, and the skilled trades.

Minority Status

Some research (Brown, Fulkerson, Vedder, & Ware, 1983; Lawrence & Brown, 1976; McNair & Brown, 1983) has shown that African American minorities have deficits with regard to estimating abilities and interests, but generally the differences between blacks and their white counterparts have not been startling. However, as Dil-

TABLE 7.1 Occupations with Largest Increase in Numbers 1990–2005

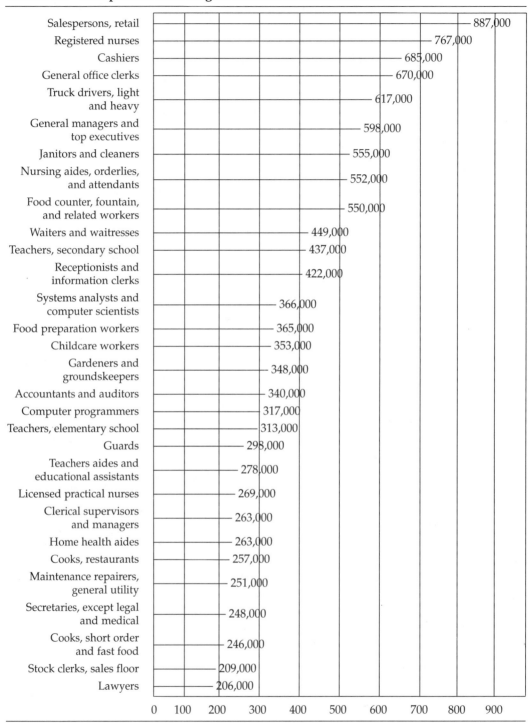

Salespersons, retail	887,000
Registered nurses	767,000
Cashiers	685,000
General office clerks	670,000
Truck drivers, light and heavy	617,000
General managers and top executives	598,000
Janitors and cleaners	555,000
Nursing aides, orderlies, and attendants	552,000
Food counter, fountain, and related workers	550,000
Waiters and waitresses	449,000
Teachers, secondary school	437,000
Receptionists and information clerks	422,000
Systems analysts and computer scientists	366,000
Food preparation workers	365,000
Childcare workers	353,000
Gardeners and groundskeepers	348,000
Accountants and auditors	340,000
Computer programmers	317,000
Teachers, elementary school	313,000
Guards	298,000
Teachers aides and educational assistants	278,000
Licensed practical nurses	269,000
Clerical supervisors and managers	263,000
Home health aides	263,000
Cooks, restaurants	257,000
Maintenance repairers, general utility	251,000
Secretaries, except legal and medical	248,000
Cooks, short order and fast food	246,000
Stock clerks, sales floor	209,000
Lawyers	206,000

0 100 200 300 400 500 600 700 800 900

Source: Occupational Outlook Quarterly/Fall 1991, page 30.

TABLE 7.2   Occupations with Greatest Percentage Increase 1990–2005

Source: Occupational Outlook Quarterly/Fall 1991, page 31.

lard (1980) notes, there are a number of barriers to the career development of African Americans. These include poverty, quality of educational opportunities, and family conditions. Whether other minorities are faced with these same barriers is not clear, but the dropout rate for Hispanic students seems to exceed that of their white counterparts (Bureau of the Census, 1990). Unemployment figures also support the idea that Hispanic and black minorities, in particular, are less able than whites to negotiate the occupational structure of this country (Bureau of the Census, 1990).

Because of the barriers of poverty, lack of family support, decreased educational opportunity and continued discrimination in the work force, some minorities may be apathetic. They may avoid the occupational decision-making process or, at least, not give the process the attention it deserves. They may select occupations stereotypically and may not consider the numerous conditions that influence their lives as workers.

STUDENT LEARNING EXERCISE
True or False

1. The personality types realistic, artistic, investigative, social, and enterprising are a part of Holland's theory of occupational choice.   T   F

2. One major difference between career developmental and occupational choice is the time frame in which they occur.   T   F

3. There is a resurgence of interest in career education in this country.   T   F

4. Work and occupation are interchangeable terms.   T   F

5. Job stress can cause physiological as well as psychological problems.   T   F

6. Technology appears to be the long-term solution for the problems experienced by people in the work environment.   T   F

7. For Super, the vocational concept is the key variable in career decision making.   T   F

8. Realistic types have aversions to education.   T   F

9. Career indecisiveness is caused by lack of information.   T   F

Life Career Counseling

It was suggested at the beginning of this chapter that life career development is a phrase meant to denote the interrelationship of various life roles. Gysbers and Moore (1986) have taken this one step further. More recently they state, "life career development is advocated as an organizing and integrating concept for understanding and facilitating human growth and development" (Gysbers and Moore, 1986, p. 4). Thus far, the emphasis of this chapter has been on the use of the concept as an organizing and integrating concept. This section will focus on life career counseling as a means for facilitating human growth and development.

Recently a number of articles and books have appeared that focus on various aspects of life career counseling. For example, Brown (1985) argued that many problems may appear to be psychological in nature but in fact are work related. He noted that job stress can cause depression, headaches, lower back pain, loss of motivation, and a variety of other problems. Thus career counseling may be a viable form of therapy for many distressed clients. Brown and Brooks (1990) provided a schema for assessing the primary locus of a problem, along with suggesting some interventions for dealing with psychological, career, and interrelated problems. Finally, Brooks and Brown (1986), writing about the career counseling of adults, posed the following definition of career counseling that reflects a life career development perspective.

> *Career counseling is an interpersonal process designed to assist individuals with career development problems. Career development is that process of choosing, enjoying, adjusting to, and advancing in an occupation or occupations. It is a lifelong psychological process that interacts dynamically with other life roles. Career development problems include, but are not limited to, career indecision and undecidedness, work performance, stress and adjustment, incongruence of the person and the work environment, inadequate or unsatisfactory integration of life roles with other life roles (e.g., parent, friend, citizen) (p. 98).*

In the above definition, the focus of counseling is on careers, whether it be choosing a first or a new career, or adjusting to one already chosen. Other life roles become important only when they impinge on the individual's work role which, it should be added, they invariably do. However, life career counseling has a somewhat different emphasis. It has as its primary focus the most salient and troublesome life role while focusing on the interaction of other life roles with the problematic one. The assumptions of life career counseling are as follows:

1. All life roles are interconnected.
2. Individuals strive to attain homeostatis among their life roles.
3. Difficulty in one life role (e.g., career) will have a negative impact on other life roles.
4. Harmony and congruence in one life role will positively affect other life roles.
5. Positive functioning in one life role can attenuate stress brought about by negative aspects of another life role.
6. All life roles offer the possibility of satisfaction and dissatisfaction, although they do not hold the same potential at any given time.
7. Personal perceptions of the importance of a particular life role will be directly related to its potential for satisfaction or dissatisfaction.
8. Intervention in one life role may be made directly in that life role, or indirectly in other life roles. Thus, all problems have multiple solutions.
9. Interventions that bring positive changes in one life role may break the dynamic homeostasis that has developed among various life roles and thus have a negative impact on another.

The Process of Life Career Counseling

As has been noted by a number of authors (e.g., Brooks & Brown, 1986; Brown & Brooks, 1990; Herr & Cramer, 1992), and as will be pointed out directly later in this book, all counseling—career, life career, or personal—begins with establishment of a therapeutic relationship. This relationship will be discussed in Chapter 9.

Assessment or diagnosis of the client's problems begins simultaneously with relationship development and follows after the relationship has been built. Assessment involves identifying the nature of the problem and those causal factors that are contributing to it. Gysbers and Moore (1986), while writing about career counseling, have presented an approach to assessment in life career counseling. They call the approach Life Career Assessment (LCA), and describe it as follows: "The LCA is designed to cover your client's level of functioning in various life roles including the worker, learner, and personal roles as well as yielding information on how they negotiate with their environment" (p. 89). An outline of Gysbers and Moore's LCA can be seen in Table 7.3.

As the table shows, life career assessment begins with an assessment of the personal characteristics of the individual. Any of the major theories described later in this book can be used as the basis for the personal analysis phase of life career counseling. However, as Brown and Brooks (1985) have suggested, one of the basic thrusts in this assessment is to determine the perceptual clarity of the individual.

TABLE 7.3   Life Career Assessment Interview(s)

1. Personal assessment
     Inter- and intrapersonal functioning examined

2. Career assessment (life role = work)
     Totality of work experience examined including likes, dislikes, etc.

3. Education (life role = student)
     Educational and training experiences examined as they relate to work and other life roles

4. Recreation (life role = leisurite)
     Leisure activities including time spent in recreational and social activities

5. Significant others (life roles = child, parent, spouse, friend)
     Spouse and/or significant others examined

6. Community involvement (life role = citizen)
     Examination of citizenship roles pursued

7. Interaction
     The interaction of all life roles examined for positive and negative aspects

Note: Adapted from *Career Counseling: Skills and Techniques for Practitioners* by N. C. Gysbers & E. J. Moore, 1986, Englewood Cliffs, NJ: Prentice-Hall.

Does the person possess the ability to objectively assess his own characteristics (self-awareness), the various aspects of his life (environmental awareness), and how they "fit" into those situations (interactional awareness)?

Once perceptual clarity is ascertained, the counselor must decide whether to proceed to life career planning and adjustment or to deal with the perceptual problems that have been discovered. Mild perceptual problems, such as stereotypical thinking, can probably be dealt with routinely in the role assessment and planning process. Severe problems will need to become the major agenda item in the counseling process and should supercede life career role planning and adjustment work.

The outcomes of life career counseling will quite obviously depend on a variety of factors. An adolescent may simply want to make some tentative plans about various aspects of his or her life, usually beginning with education and work roles, but ultimately including roles involving leisure and significant others. Young adults may be interested in developing some balance among their life roles (adjustment) after being preoccupied with education and work. Older adults may be interested in making a change in a single life role (e.g., leisurite or worker), changing the emphasis among the life roles, or planning to totally deemphasize a life role such as work. Retirees, faced with the loss of the role of worker, may be seeking ways to derive meaning and satisfaction from other life roles, and the aged, faced with the loss of the role of spouse, may have similar concerns.

Life Career Planning Workshops

Zunker (1986) suggests that workshops designed to help adults have been around since the mid-1960s, and that life career planning on some college campuses began soon after. Zunker indicates that some of these workshops are as brief as a single day and involve participants in developing a future orientation, examining life roles in detail, establishing some new life career goals, and developing strategies for pursuing those goals.

Life role planning workshops have been developed for all ages. For college students they focus on integrating career choice with other life roles. Topics might include:

1. Setting life goals
2. Examining values, interests, and aptitudes
3. Exploring occupations and their relationship to education
4. Occupational choice to lifestyle considerations and other life roles such as family and leisure
5. Taking action—goal achievement strategies

A life roles planning workshop was developed for adolescents that included the following (Brown, 1980):

1. Why people behave as they do (understanding motivation)
2. Winners and losers (positive thinking and planning emphasized)
3. Your fantasy life (imagery is the first step in planning)
4. Your real life (how fantasy and reality may vary)
5. Setting life goals
6. Short term planning—high school graduation
7. Long term planning for education, career, family, and leisure

Life roles workshops for retirees have also been developed. These emphasize the pitfalls that can occur when people move from work to leisure, money management, health issues, and other concerns such as relocation, volunteering as a substitute for paid work, and finding a retirement career.

Career Counseling

The discussion to this point has focused on a counseling process that considers and deals with multiple life roles. Career counseling was defined as a process of choosing or adjusting to an occupation with consideration given to other life roles in the process (Isaacson & Brown, 1993). Career counseling varies from life career counseling in that in the former the client's role of worker receives the primary emphasis, and in crisis situations such as those that occur when a client loses his source of livelihood, regaining the work role may be the only emphasis.

STUDENT LEARNING EXERCISE

List five potential explanations for the following presenting problems and think of some possible solutions.

Carlos is a 35-year-old Hispanic laborer who was recently granted citizenship. His wife works as a waitress. They have three children. Lately, Carlos has had difficulty getting himself motivated to go to work. As a result, he has been late on numerous occasions, and has missed five days of work. His supervisor told him three days ago that unless he "shapes up," he is going to be fired.

1.

2.

3.

4.

5.

Computers in Career Counseling

The process of career counseling varies little from that already described for life career counseling except for its narrower focus. However, a number of adjuncts, that include the use of aptitude tests, interest and personality inventories, as well as occupational information and computerized assistance systems have been developed. Tests and inventories will be discussed later but computerized adjuncts to career counseling will be discussed here briefly.

One of the first computerized systems was developed under the direction of David Tiedeman and Robert O'Hara (1963). This system, *Information System for Vocational Decisions (ISVD),* was interactive in nature and assisted students to relate information about themselves to various types of educational career data including those in the military. Students who used *ISVD* were presented interactive scripts in which they were asked to relate data about themselves to educational, career, and military information, with the expected result being that they would develop personalized decisions.

A more current computerized system is the *System of Interactive Guidance (SIGI),* plus *The Next Generation on Computerized Guidance,* which was developed under the leadership of Martin Katz at the Educational Testing Service. *SIGI* was developed for use by college students and includes the following nine sections:

- *Introduction* gives an overview and helps a user decide how best to use the eight remaining sections.
- *Self-assessment* has a user rate of fifteen work-related values, including such specific job-related values as "Staying Put," "Easy Commute," and "Challenge." Interests are examined on two dimensions—fields of knowledge and types of activities. Thus a user can combine an interest in remaining in a particular field with an interest in engaging in different kinds of activities (for example, combining engineering and sales); users can look at classified lists of activities and decide which ones they are good at.
- *Search* allows a user to retrieve occupations from a database of about 230 on the basis of values, interests, skills, and educational requirements. An additional search is available to avoid certain attributes of activities (e.g., doing math, poor outlook).
- *Information* allows a user to ask up to twenty-seven questions about occupations and, in response, to receive national information. If the system has been tailored, local information is also given (e.g., salary figures for jobs within a company might be given along with national estimates for the occupation as a whole).
- *Skills* provides information about the skills required to perform important work tasks and has users assess themselves on these skills. Managerial skills are also described and assessed.

- *Preparing* offers a detailed look at preparation for entry into an occupation. It shows educational and training requirements, plus work tasks that must be mastered. Users then evaluate their readiness to enter.
- *Coping* examines a number of practical considerations (e.g., money, child care, college credit for life experiences) related to career change.
- *Deciding* helps users reach decisions by evaluating and combining (a) the desirability of each occupation they are considering (including their present job) and (b) their chances of success in entering it.
- *Next steps* helps users plan a course of action to meet their objectives.

SIGI's subsystems illustrate the two uses to which computers can be put in the career planning process. The planning subsystem simply presents and sorts information on demand. The strategy subsystem interacts with the user to assist in the choice-making process. One criticism of the strategy subsystems, and others like it, is that the computer has only so many alternatives available and thus acts as a limiting force in the choice-making process.

Discover was developed by the American College Testing Program under the leadership of JoAnn Harris-Bowlsby, and like *SIGI* and *ISVD*, is an interactive program. In the first part of the program users can complete interest and values inventories, and these in turn can be used to generate a list of related occupations. However, it is not necessary to take these inventories if the results of a number of popular interests inventories and aptitude batteries are available, because the results of these can be entered and lists of occupations can be generated with these results. The user has the option of taking the tests and inventories included in *Discover* and entering the results of others.

Once occupational interests are listed, the user of *Discover* may consult the occupational information file and ask up to fourteen questions about each occupation. This exercise can be followed by using a file that contains information on more than 3,000 two- and four-year institutions that may offer courses or programs of study related to occupations users have identified. These files contain data regarding cost, size, admissions policies, minority representation, male-to-female ratios, and so forth.

The *Discover* program for adults varies from the one for young adults in that it contains a section on weathering life transitions. It also allows the adult learner to engage in self-analysis by taking interest inventories, rating his or her skills and experiences, and surveying his or her values. Once this is completed, the adult can obtain a list of occupations related to his or her self-analysis, along with suggestions regarding the training needed. The user can also get detailed descriptions of occupations of interest, training in occupational decision making, assistance with educational planning, and such job-seeking strategies as preparing resumes and job interviews. A retirement planning version is also available.

Choices was developed by the Employment and Immigration Commission in Canada. The user begins by interacting with the system to determine whether or not he or she can benefit from the system. If the user determines that he or she can benefit, self-assessment is pursued. This involves either making self-estimates of various traits or actually taking tests. The user is also asked to complete a "data sheet" that includes information about education and preferences regarding the world of work, such as expected salary, training requirements, and working conditions.

Once all information about the user is placed into the program, the user elects one of four "routes" to complete the career exploration process. The Specific Route simply provides brief informational descriptions of various occupations. The Compare Route allows the user to actually compare various aspects of various occupations, such as training requirements. The Related Route provides a listing of occupations that are similar in nature to those previously explained in the Specific and Compare Routes. The Explore Route is used by the relatively naive user who needs rather extensive career exploration experience.

The foregoing list of computerized systems is not meant to be exhaustive, only illustrative. Other, more sophisticated, computerized systems of career exploration that will soon replace these systems with faster, more creative programs are now being developed. When the *ISVD* was developed, a large mainframe computer was required to handle the system. Current computerized systems are available on microcomputers. The result is lower costs and it is expected that costs will continue to come down.

Computers and Counselors

Will computers replace counselors in the career counseling process? In some instances with some clients, probably yes. Undecided clients who simply need information can certainly benefit from direct interaction with computers. Indecisive clients who have personal deficits are unlikely to benefit to the same degree or, in some instances, not at all. Computers must, therefore, be viewed as one means of expanding counseling services, not as a threat.

Selecting a Computerized System

Maze (1984) suggests seven steps that should be followed in selecting a computerized system. To a certain extent, the following list is based on his recommendations along with the recommendations of Zunker (1986) and Harris-Bowlsby (1984).

First, determine the characteristics of the users. Some systems are geared toward adults, others toward adolescents. Some systems require that each user complete the entire program, while others allow users to access only those aspects of the program that user deems appropriate. In the latter case, time may be saved, but thoroughness may be sacrificed.

Second, determine what the counseling staff wants to accomplish. Should the program be primarily informationally oriented, or is it important to produce high levels of personal self-awareness?

Third, what is the cost? Terminals, microcomputers, programs, computer paper, telephone time if the computer is on-line, costs of updating the program, etc., are all important considerations. Those considering these programs should get a "bottom line figure" before proceeding.

Fourth, how fast is the program? Some computerized systems, particularly those on microcomputers, may operate somewhat slowly, and thus user motivation may wane. Also, and importantly, more systems may be required if the time on machine per user is too long.

Fifth—a consideration related to the fourth point—will the program maintain user motivation? Not all the computerized systems available have the same ability to involve the user. Only "hands-on" experience by users can provide this type of information.

Sixth, does the theoretical rationale of the program correspond to that of the staff? It may come as a surprise to some that theory would enter into computer programs, but in fact most career exploration programs have well-defined theoretical rationales. For example, *SIGI* is predicated on the idea that values are the most salient variable in career decision making. Each counselor and counseling staff need to examine their own beliefs about this process before proceeding to purchase a system.

Seventh, and finally, is there a good technical support system for the program? All computer programs have "glitches" and "bugs." Unless adequate technical support is available, these problems that plague most systems may result in total failure.

Summary

The increasing recognition that work and other life roles are interrelated has been emphasized in this chapter. Various approaches to life career planning and adjustment have been presented, along with some information about career planning.

The fact that work is still the most important life role has been recognized, the importance of job satisfaction has been emphasized, and the processes involved in career development and occupational choices discussed. The importance of occupational information was also touched on.

In the final section of the chapter, a number of computerized and occupational information and career planning systems were outlined, and the relationship of counselors and computers discussed.

Review Questions

1. Discuss the pros and cons of life career versus career planning.

2. How do career and life career counseling differ from personal counseling? Which takes precedence?

3. Discuss the possible advantages and disadvantages of using computers in the career planning process.

4. What are the factors related to job satisfaction? What individual characteristics might influence job satisfaction?

5. On the basis of the information that you learned about trends in the world of work, what personal ideas that you held had to be changed?

6. Will women and minorities need any unusual or different assistance in career planning? If so, specify these differences.

7. Distinguish between Super's minicycle and maxicycle.

References

Bordin, E. J. (1990). Psychodynamic model of career choice and satisfaction. In D. Brown & L. Brooks (eds.). *Career Choice and Development*, (pp. 102–144). San Francisco: Jossey-Bass.

Brooks, L. (1986). Counseling women. Presentation at the University of North Carolina, Chapel Hill.

Brooks, L., & Brown, D. (1986). Career counseling for adults: Implications for mental health counselors. In A. J. Palmo & W. J. Weikel (eds.), *Foundations of mental health counseling*, (pp. 95–114). Springfield, IL: Charles C. Thomas.

Brown, D. (1980). A life-planning workshop for high school students. *Vocational Guidance Quarterly, 29*, 77–83.

Brown, D. (1985). Career counseling: Before, after, or instead of personal counseling? *Vocational Guidance Quarterly, 33*, 197–201.

Brown, D. (1986). Brown's values-based model of career and life role choice and satisfaction. In D. Brown & L. Brooks, *Career Choice and Development* (3rd ed.) San Francisco: Jossey-Bass.

Brown, D., & Brooks, L. (1985). Career counseling as a mental health intervention. *Professional Psychology: Research and Practice, 16*, 860–867.

Brown, D., & Brooks, L. (1990). *Career counseling techniques*. Boston: Allyn & Bacon.

Brown, D., Fulkerson, K. F., Vedder, M., & Ware, W. B. (1983). Self-estimate ability in black and white 8th-, 10th-, and 12th-grade males and females. *Vocational Guidance Quarterly, 32*, 21–28.

Bureau of the Census. (1990). *Statistical abstracts of the United States*, 1990. Washington, DC: Bureau of the Census.

Dillard, J. M. (1980). Some unique career behavior characteristics of blacks. Career theories, counseling practice, and research. *Journal of Employment Counseling, 17*, 288–298.

Goodstein, L. D. (1972). Behavioral views of counseling. In B. Stefflre and W. H. Grant (eds.). *Theories of Counseling* (pp. 243–286). New York: McGraw-Hill.

Gysbers, N. C., & Moore, E. J. (1986). *Career counseling: Skills and techniques for practitioners*. Englewood Cliffs, NJ: Prentice Hall.

Herr, E. L. (1986a). Career development theory: An overview. In R. L. Frank (ed.), *Proceedings of statewide conference on career guidance theory*. Cedar Falls, IA: University of Northern Iowa.

Herr, E. L., & Cramer, S. H. (1992). *Career guidance and counseling through the life span*. (4th ed.). New York: Harper Collins.

Holland, J. L. (1985). *Making vocational choices: A theory of vocational personalities and work environments*, (2nd ed.). Englewood Cliffs, NJ: Prentice-Hall.

Isaacson, L. E., & Brown, D. (1993). *Career information, career counseling, and career development*, (5th ed.). Boston: Allyn & Bacon.

Lawrence, W., & Brown, D. (1976). An investigation of intelligence, self-concept, socioeconomic status, race, and sex as predictors of career maturity. *Journal of Vocational Behavior, 9*, 43–52.

Levinson, D. (1978). *The seasons of a man's life*. New York: Knopf.

Lowenthal, M., & Weiss, L. (1976). Intimacy and crises in adulthood. *The Counseling Psychologist, 6*, 10–16.

McDaniels, C. (1989). *The changing workplace*. San Francisco: Jossey-Bass.

McNair, D., & Brown, D. (1983). Predicting the occupational aspirations, occupational expectations and career maturity of black and white male and female 10th graders. *Vocational Guidance Quarterly, 32*, 29–36.

Maze, M. (1984). How to select a computerized guidance system. *Journal of Counseling and Development, 63*, 158–162.

Naisbitt, J. (1984). *Megatrends: Ten new directions transforming our lives*. New York: Warner Books.

National Alliance of Business. (1986). *Employment policies: Looking to the year 2000*. Washington, DC: National Alliance of Business.

NCDA (1994) Report of the Gallup survey of working adults. Albuquerque, NM: Annual Convention of the National Career Development Association.

Neff, W. S. (1985). *Work and human behavior*. New York: Aldine.

Neugarten, B. (1976). Adaptation and the life cycle. *The Counseling Psychologist, 6*, 16–21.

Okun, B. F. (1984). *Working with adults: Individual, family, & career development*. Monterey, CA: Brooks/Cole.

Parsons, F. (1909). *Choosing a vocation*. Boston: Houghton Mifflin.

Report of a Special Task Force to the Secretary of Health, Education and Welfare. (1973). *Work in America*. Cambridge, MA; MIT Press.

Roe, A., & Lunneborg, P. W. (1990). Personality development and career choice. In D. Brown & L. Brooks (eds.). *Career Choice and Development*, (pp. 68–101). San Francisco: Jossey-Bass.

Rokeach, M. (1973). *The nature of human values*. New York: Free Press.

Super, D. E. (1990). A life-span approach to career development. In D. Brown & L. Brooks (eds.). *Career Choice and Development*, (pp. 197–261). San Francisco: Jossey-Bass.

Tiedeman, D. V., & O'Hara, R. P. (1963). *Career development: Choice and adjustment*. New York: College Examination Board.

Williamson, E. G. (1939). *How to counsel students*. New York: McGraw-Hill.

Williamson, E. G. (1965). *Vocational counseling*. New York: McGraw-Hill.

Zunker, V. G. (1986). *Career counseling. Applied concepts of life planning*, (2nd ed.). Monterey, CA: Brooks/Cole.

Three Counseling Specialties: Couples and Family, Gerontology, and Substance Abuse

Goal of the Chapter

The purpose of this chapter is to introduce three distinct counseling specialties.

Chapter Overview

- The concept of counseling specialties will be discussed briefly.
- An overview of couples and family counseling, gerontological counseling, and substance abuse counseling will be presented.

Introduction

Counselors, like members of other occupational groups in our society, are increasingly specialized. Currently, the National Board for Certified Counselors offers specialty certification in career counseling, mental health counseling, school counseling, gerontological counseling, and substance abuse counseling. The International Association of Marriage and Family Counselors and Therapists (IAMFC/T) is also exploring the possibility of establishing a certification program for marriage and family counselors. However, many states have already established legal guidelines for the certification or licensing of marriage and family specialists. Much of the work on these laws came about as a result of the efforts of the members of the American Association of Marriage and Family Therapists (AAMFT), a group that is not associated with the American Counseling Association. AAMFT has, until recently, provided much of the leadership in promoting the professionalization of marriage and family counselors and therapists. It can be expected that IAMFC/T will share this role in the future. It remains to be seen if regulation of gerontological counseling at the state level in the form of licensure laws will occur. The effort by NBCC, which is purely voluntary, may lead to this type of development.

Why so much specialization? Simply because the body of knowledge and skills required to provide services to clients with diverse problems precludes counselors from being competent to provide all types of counseling services. As will be highlighted later, competency is one of the cornerstones of ethical practice. Moreover, regulatory statutes require specialized course work and supervised practice in order to be approved to provide services in many instances. Students considering becoming professional counselors need to carefully consider the three specialties presented in the sections to follow along with other specialties discussed throughout this book.

Couples and Family Therapy

Overview

Marriage or couples' therapy has almost as long a history as individual counseling and psychotherapy. Since the 1920s ministers, social workers, and marriage counselors have been working with couples. Much of this was outside the established professions of psychiatry and clinical psychology with little recognition being given to it during its early history. Also, these early efforts were not based on any extensive theory, and were without evidence of their effectiveness. Gradually centers and institutes for marriage counseling were established that help professionalize couples' work. In 1942 the American Association of Marriage Counseling was established as part of this trend. In the decades that followed, treating couples as a unit became a well-established part of the counseling profession. Family therapy is somewhat more recent. Nichols and Everett (1986) note that family work, especially in psychiatry, was not welcomed at first. Emphasis among psychiatrists was on psychoanalytic technique and reconstructive work with individuals. Up through the early and middle 1950s researchers and practitioners of family therapy were largely underground. The emergence of family therapy in that decade was stimulated by an increasing concern for marital relationships, child behavior problems, and the origins and treatment of schizophrenia (Broderick & Schrader, 1981). In addition, the helping professions of social work and counseling were beginning to make their presence known. They would put more emphasis on helping with problems of everyday living.

So why would counselors, more than likely first trained in individual work, decide it was important to consider treating couples and families as a unit? Some of the following examples suggest the problems clients bring with them to counseling as having their roots in family interactions.

Imagine working with a motivated adolescent client. Over the first few weeks of treatment the teenager is feeling better, while changing some problem behaviors. You are delighted at this progress. However, you are surprised when you receive a call from the client's affluent parents, who express concern about the cost of treatment and impatience at its progress. In the two sessions that follow the call, you notice your client becoming more demoralized. Some old problems begin returning. After the client fails to return, you wonder what went wrong.

A second situation involves two counselor friends who work at the same clinic. They discover that each is seeing spouses in the same marriage. Neither is getting anywhere in individual counseling, as both struggle to move their clients beyond simply blaming their spouse for the problems in the marriage. In sessions each client is very convincing in his or her stories. Following permission to consult with the other spouse's counselor, the therapists conclude that they don't know who to believe about what is going on in the marriage.

Finally, in our last example you might be working with a client in a long-term, committed relationship. Most of your sessions concentrate on early childhood disappointments and current efforts toward greater self-acceptance. Only occasionally does the client discuss problems in her primary relationship. As your client continues to get better, you learn that her partner is having more emotional difficulties. In a panic the partner calls you to get a referral for her own counseling. In making the referral you want to understand what might have precipitated the crisis. You wonder if the changes your client has made in some way affected the emotional life of her partner.

These examples suggest something more than the simple idea that spouses impact the happiness of their mate, and that the mental health of children is affected by their parents. They point to a far stronger context, one in which individuals construct a social environment with numerous unwritten rules and relational devices. These devices control the way partners and families behave as individuals and as social units. To work only with individual members deprives the counselor access to powerful social forces.

The Family as a System

While most major approaches to counseling and psychotherapy have been adapted to couples and family problems, new approaches were developed that view the family as a system. Systems are units in themselves that are composed of elements that stand in some regular relationship with one another. Systems are organized by this consistent set of interactions among its parts. Thus, a system's operation is predictable via the means by which it is regulated. For example, when we set the thermostat in our house, it regulates the flow of heat from the furnace in order to maintain the set temperature. Family systems set unpublished rules governing the expression of feelings. In the family system only so much anger may be tolerated.

These systems include within themselves subsystems. Thus, a family may be organized by a set of roles each member is supposed to play. In turn new sets of roles are carried out separately among the children and separately among the spouses, demonstrating subsystems within the family.

Consistent with the general idea of a system, families differ by how open or closed their system is. An open family system has boundaries that let in information and feedback. There is regular interaction with the outside. A balance is achieved between protecting the integrity of the system, while embracing new input. Other families are closed, allowing little influence from the environment. While the system is protected, becoming too closed results in less growth and vitality. This may prevent change needed to cope with environmental demands. In turn this destabilizes the system, upsetting the equilibrium within the system (Nichols & Everett, 1986). Troubled families often are closed systems. Besides there being difficulty in getting information from outside, communication inside the family system may be impaired.

By contrast troubled families can be too open. For example a single mother can change live-in boyfriends several times. Each of these males may attempt to establish a father role in different ways. The mother's children may not know which set of rules is in effect, overloading their capacity to anticipate rewards and punishments from the current boyfriend.

The Development of Family Systems Theory

While many individuals have contributed to family therapy practice, Ackerman (1954, 1958) and Satir (1964) were among the first theorists to interview couples and family members together. This form of treatment became referred to as *conjoint* therapy as compared to *concurrent* therapy in which partners were treated simultaneously but separately. It was probably first referred to under that label by Don Jackson in 1959.

Ackerman was a child psychiatrist, who like Salvador Minuchin, emerged from the early child guidance movement to become a family therapist. Virginia Satir would team up with Jackson and Jay Haley. Together they formed a circle of people from many different disciplines. Their group began understanding families as a social system that affects the behavior of individual members in deceptive ways. At times families use covert tactics to manipulate each other. They develop hidden agendas that require subtle maneuvering. This group of family practitioners, originally from Palo Alto, California, became known as the "communications" school because of their emphasis on treating troubled families through improving the way members communicate.

Satir and Haley took different directions after those early years. Communication continued to be the central theme in Satir's view. She also maintained emphasis on self-esteem, another of her own early interests. For Satir, families have difficulty solving their problems when they set up communication rules that obstruct and distort what they want to say. Her therapy looked closely at the process of communication. The therapist observes the family interacting, helping members to understand the feelings behind the messages they and others send (Satir, 1972). The following modes of communication at points of stress were described by Satir (Satir, Stachowlak, & Taschman, 1983): placating, blaming, being super-reasonable, irrelevant, and congruent. She worked with families to help them communicate more congruently. Her writings contain many suggested exercises and role plays to help families become more aware of how they deal with each other.

Jay Haley (1963, 1973, 1976) developed many different strategies to cope with the troublesome maneuvers of family members. Part of this resulted as a consequence of his affiliation with Milton Erikson, an imaginative psychiatrist who also strongly influenced hypnotherapy. Haley's spouse, Cloé Madanes (1981), along with Haley, understood certain aspects of family interaction as maneuvers to usurp and retain power. Their approach has become known as Strategic Family Therapy.

Haley was especially sensitive to the often brief nature of family therapy and the lack of success achieved with conventional interpretative strategies. His approach includes many directive techniques by the therapist. Power and control are key factors in understanding how families function, and Haley worked at means of redistributing power among members. Haley managed resistance to change through a form of reverse psychology he called paradoxical directives. Often he would order someone to do the opposite of what he really wanted to happen. In response to the directive, the family member would resist therapist control by in turn doing the opposite of the directive, ending up doing what Haley wanted all along.

Best known of his techniques, borrowed from Milton Erikson, is prescribing a troublesome symptom. The symptom maintained the balance in the system in a hidden way. When the symptom was prescribed, its role in the system became more apparent. The symptom lost its covert influence, opening the door for change in the family system.

Haley also worked at the Philadelphia Child Guidance Clinic with Minuchin (1974). Salvadore Minuchin developed a theory to understand the various alliances that develop among family members. This includes different coalitions that attempt to isolate other family members. This has led to the notion of structural family therapy that plans its maneuvers based on how the family is socially organized. This organization may be very rigid, producing distance and lack of engagement among family members. In other instances family members may be enmeshed, i.e., their personal identities are blurred together. From Minuchin has come very specific responses for the therapist in given situations. He too emphasizes the importance of communication. If the feedback between members can change, so can the family and its ability to support positive changes in members.

An overview of family systems therapy would not be complete without mention of both Carl Whitaker and Murray Bowen. Both were pioneers of family therapy. Both helped practitioners make the bridge between individual and family therapy. They often worked on family problems by focusing on the treatment of individuals or the marriage unit, and not always on the entire family. Thus, they were not exclusively conjoint in their therapy.

The Family Crucible (Napier & Whitaker, 1980) is one of the best known and most widely read accounts of family therapy. In it a psychology intern and his mentor give us a view of treatment with seriously disturbed families. We see the impact stress has on those families, how it polarizes members on issues, in turn escalating the conflict. The authors treat such important issues as scapegoating, blaming, and the diffusion of individual identities.

Bowen (1978) stands out through his insight into the influence of the extended family. A troubled or ineffectual parent often had the seeds sown for their difficulties in their original family. Thus, family therapy may need to include transgenerational work in which relationships among grandparents and parents are improved. This helps the latter to be more effective with the grandchildren. They are better able to differentiate themselves as individuals, hopefully breaking the generational cycle of corrupted family relationships. To differentiate in this context means to be less emotionally entangled with other family members, better able to attach to new people in stable relationships.

Sketching the Family Therapy Process

In this section we will attempt to illustrate some of the ideas presented earlier through an overview of the conjoint family therapy process. Often family practitioners have been trained in a number of family systems approaches along with family applications of the traditional therapies mentioned in Chapter Three. In their practice, counselors often find it necessary to combine some of the ideas they acquired from different sources.

Assessment

Getting a family together for counseling has more logistic problems than seeing individuals. Because of the stress within the family unit, it is more likely that treatment will end quickly if some assistance does not come soon. For this reason lengthy assessment in advance of actual counseling seldom takes place. Rather, assessment is intertwined with treatment.

Often family therapy begins with a referral of an individual member. Called the "identified patient," this person's problems may provide a window to how the family functions; how it deals with stress; communicates within; solves problems; and interacts with the outside world. Family background related to the identified client very quickly provides an estimate of the degree to which the family may be dysfunctional.

Family functioning runs along a continuum from severely dysfunctional to optimal (Beavers & Voeller, 1983). Parents of severely dysfunctional families often have numerous problems ranging from work history and criminal record to severe mental illness. Moderately dysfunctional families may appear healthy to outsiders, but often have problems in establishing rules or boundaries. Minimally dysfunctional families may also have problems with rules and boundaries, but they are open systems, and thus open to information and skills development. Often parent education is sufficient for these families.

Assessment in family work looks beyond individuals to the way relationships are structured among members. Who is allied with whom? What factions are in conflict? Do these coalitions require the family therapist to give special support to a member whom others are colluding against? What important issues does the family avoid discussing? Are there secrets they all cooperate in keeping?

When individual family members are assessed during sessions, unique roles and uncharacteristic behaviors are noted. For example, a child in the family may have been "parentified" very early. This youngster assumes responsibilities ordinarily a parent would assume. The child in a sense seems too grown up, the parent may be too immature.

Bowen (1978) discusses the importance of triangular relationships. When two persons get into difficulty they often pull in a third person to refocus the attention away from them. A husband may align himself with his mother against his spouse. A mother may use a child against her husband. These triangles form the building blocks for interactions in the system. Identifying them is an important part of assessment with couples and families.

At times a therapist may use role playing as a diagnostic device. One of Kohlberg's moral dilemmas could be given to the family as a whole to solve (Hauser, Powers, & Noam, 1991). In these contrived situations the therapist can focus the family on issues that are slow to emerge on their own. See Figure 8.1 for a summary list of questions for assessing family dysfunction.

Goal Setting

Most couples and family approaches in the beginning have an assumed objective of preserving the unit. Sometimes problems are such that the welfare of members may not make this possible. If so, reducing the damage to the members, and transitioning to new systems become objectives.

In family systems theory the social unit tries to maintain a state of equilibrium. When a crisis or problem develops that upsets the balance, the system attempts to make corrections to reestablish equilibrium. Sometimes initial problems threatening the balance are replaced with other problems. For example, marital discord among the parents may threaten to break up the family. To neutralize it, one of the children might develop a problem (e.g., school phobia). The parents decrease their

1. Does the family have trouble establishing rules and boundaries? Are the boundaries so well developed that information and influence from the outside are not permitted to intrude?

2. What is the nature of the family alliances? Where are the triangles that involve two people allied against one?

3. Are family relationships enmeshed or too distant? Are children encouraged to establish their own identities? Is one person living his or her life vicariously through the life of another?

4. Are subsystems (e.g., parents and children) well established or has one of the children become parentified?

5. Is there a scapegoat for the family problems?

6. Are there "secrets" that the family conspires to keep from the outside world?

7. What are the rules that govern communication? Is there a channel through which all communication must flow (e.g., a parent)? Is communication open and direct and generally supportive or more covert and negative?

8. Are there double binds, such as a child told one thing and reinforced for another?

9. Do relationships with grandparents intrude into the primary family and disrupt the family's functioning?

FIGURE 8.1   Questions that Assess Family Dysfunction

arguing as they combine efforts to take care of the child's problems. The parents originally come to the counselor to get help for their child. The goal of counseling is to get to problems that are behind the original presenting problems. Getting all members to agree on solving the hidden problems is very important in goal setting.

A common goal among many of the family systems approaches is the re-structuring of the rules that govern communication. Rules shed light on boundaries, whether they are too rigid or too diffuse. Boundaries affect the development of each member's identity and autonomy. Families that communicate effectively find it easier to be supportive of one another, and to celebrate everyone's unique-ness. This helps to overcome problems of detachment and enmeshment. Given support and encouragement to be an individual, members are more free to interact with the larger world; form relationships outside the family without threatening relationships within it. In arriving at this, members learn how to negotiate, compromise, share power, and live with differences.

Goal setting with couples and families can be burdened by the tendency of members to project blame or responsibility for the problem, e.g., "If the kids weren't always arguing, I wouldn't stay away so much," "All I want is to get my parents off my back." It is important to get all identified clients to contribute to the desired change (Cormier & Cormier, 1991) and to take responsibility for what they can control. The counselor cannot just say, "what changes do you need to make?" Because of the interrelations of behavior in the family the message becomes, "In order for them to make those changes, what do you need to do as well?"

Plan Implementation

Couples and family counselors help their clients attain the important goal of improved communication by modeling effective communication themselves. The counselor strives to be supportive of everyone in the session, paying particular attention to individuals on the spot, in need of extra support. The counselor may even select where to sit in the room as a way of equalizing differences in power. They may sit close to the family member most under attack as a subtle sign of support. They are good listeners and clarifiers, and they help others put into words what they find difficult to convey. Through the counselor's help with communication, couples and families can begin dealing with issues that were too painful or raised too much anger.

Counselors often begin to help their clients change faulty interactional patterns by relabeling or reframing the situation. Instead of an adolescent client being "stubborn," the counselor helps the parents to see it as becoming more independent (Watzlawick, Weakland, & Fisch, 1974). Reframing accomplishes the same as an interpretation, it helps change the way information is encoded or perceived. A problem often is redefined in a less threatening manner, making family members less defensive, more open to trying different solutions.

Gatekeeping is an important function for the counselor. With several different clients in the same session, family work is group work; hesitant clients are invited to contribute. Those that contribute may alert the counselor to important issues. At first the counselor may observe typical interactions, alert to the risk of getting caught in the same pattern. For example, if one child is being scapegoated, the initial impulse may be to side with the parents or to protect the child. What should be done? The counselor may decide to support the parents, with the hope of opening the door later to marital problems. Typical marital problems center around communication, sexuality, in-laws, and financial matters (Nichols & Everett, 1986). These affect the overall atmosphere in the family.

At times the counselor may have to actively intervene to curtail destructive behaviors. This quickly restructures interactions and the relief it provides may cement the family's engagement in the counseling process. Based on direct experiences with members the counselor may make recommendations regarding the order in which problems are addressed. Counselors can generate optimism in the face of serious conflict by being active and engaging. Clients may need a referee, an ally, or a protector, and the counselor at different times can serve in those roles.

In the middle phase of counseling, after dealing with some conflicts, compromising, and accommodating, families and couples often learn to accept differences. Ironically, while this is happening clients also better recognize the common ground in their relationships. At this point clients are faced with the choice of deepening the relationship by attending to intimacy problems that underly specific points of conflict. This is particularly true of couples work. In a family situation, as the overall system begins to function better, subsystems (e.g., sibling relationships or the marital dyad) can get specific attention.

Termination

Couples and family therapy begins to draw to a close when goals are met. However, families are commonly understood from a developmental perspective. They have a life cycle of their own that involves numerous transitions (Carter & Mc-Goldrick, 1980). Families take on a different character and different problems as they move from a new couple, to one with young children, to raising adolescents, to the empty nest, and so on. For this reason termination becomes more open-ended in anticipation of new developments at different times in the family life cycle.

Termination in family work, especially if the experienced therapist uses para-doxical techniques, may be successful but not satisfying. The directive from the therapist may have been instrumental in a positive outcome, but the family is not grateful. Part of the change was to spite the counselor. This requires counselors to have intimacy needs fulfilled. Without this they may be limited by a need for warmth and acceptance.

Evaluating Couples and Family Therapy

Todd and Bohart (1994) reviewed the research on numerous approaches to couples and family therapy. They conclude that the evidence is positive for marital, family, and strategic approaches, even though much of the data are not scientifically rigorous. Research on these approaches is still in an early stage, so it is premature to dismiss any approach.

Some disadvantages do exist in conjoint couples and family therapy. Counselors need special training to do conjoint work, adding to the cost of their professional development. Second, families often resist treatment, preferring to see problems as only those of the identified patient. Third, adequate attention to personal growth and developmental issues may not be possible. With the whole family present, adequate privacy may not be possible so certain problems are never divulged. Finally, the logistics of getting families together at the same time and place are difficult.

Couples and family therapy have several advantages over individual work. First, they may help us gain a more accurate view of problems, especially among family members. Second, these approaches may help all members assume responsibility for problems and solutions. These treatment strategies also provide a more direct route to relational problems. Transference issues with the therapist are diminished so family members can go straight to their interpersonal conflicts. Finally, these approaches can be cost effective in several ways. Not only do they treat several clients at one time, they also can include healthy members in the process, a real asset for the treatment.

STUDENT LEARNING EXERCISE

Respond to the following statements by indicating whether they are true or false.

1. Conjoint and concurrent therapy are essentially the same.   T   F
2. When a troubled family member begins to feel better, this improvement may lead to problems in other family members.   T   F
3. Improving communication is one of the main goals of couples and family therapy.   T   F
4. Counselors play many different roles when working with couples and families. T   F
5. Family counselors are often trained in many different theoretical approaches, and often blend elements of several approaches in their work.   T   F

Counseling Substance and Alcohol Abusers

Overview

Alcoholism has been studied extensively and to a large extent the findings from that research are generalizable to drug addiction (Muisener, 1994). It seems quite likely that people are predisposed to develop these problems by heredity. Modeling by parents also seems to play a major role in the development of addictions. These two bits of information go a long way toward explaining why abuse problems run in families. However, if the home environment is unstable, the risk of developing some type of addiction is enhanced.

The extent of the problems associated with alcohol and drug abuse is staggering and it is unlikely that anyone in our society is totally unaware of the problem. It has been estimated that 100,000 people die because of alcohol consumption, mostly because of automobile accidents and fires. Perhaps more importantly, as many as ten million people may suffer from what the World Health Organization has termed the alcohol dependence syndrome (ADS) (Velleman, 1992). This concept is quite different than the one of an alcoholic which conjures numerous stereotypes, most of which are inaccurate (Rollinick & MacEwan, 1991). Alcoholics may have physical dependence but no psychological dependence. Some have both psychological as well as physical dependence and lose control whenever they drink. They may drink to the point of physical impairment but suffer no dependency at all. They may be able to abstain for long periods of time and then binge, or they may not be able to abstain for even short periods of time (Velleman, 1992). However, persons with ADS abuse alcohol in some fashion that causes problems in their lives, yet they may not be alcoholics in the traditional sense of the term.

People with alcohol-related problems come to counselors on their own, via referrals from friends, relatives, and employers, and as a result of court ordered treatment. Drunk drivers, spouse and child abusers, and others are often directed by courts to seek some type of treatment.

The figures for substance abusers are just as staggering. While alcohol is the most popular drug in our society, millions of Americans have problems with drugs ranging from crack cocaine to marijuana. This group has an additional problem—breaking the law—and risk arrest for possession of an illegal substance. Not surprisingly, many substance abusers are directed to counselors by the courts. However, like those who have problems with alcohol, self referral and referrals by concerned family members and others, may also bring the substance abuser to the counselor.

There are two types of treatments for people with alcohol and drug-related problems: counseling and programs such as Alcoholics Anonymous or Narcotics Anonymous. Often both approaches are employed, however, only the counseling approach will be discussed at length with only a brief overview of Alcoholics Anonymous.

Counselors who work with substance and alcohol abusers may work in several settings including employee assistance programs in business and industry, mental health centers, private practice settings and hospitals, and similar settings that have treatment programs for abusers. Traditionally people who have health insurance or the money to pay for treatment have enrolled in private programs while others have enrolled in publicly supported programs. Because these programs are expensive, the result has often been that poorer people in our society have not received the quality of treatment needed to overcome this serious problem.

Issues

Alcoholics Anonymous was started in 1935, in Ohio. Narcotics Anonymous was started some 18 years later in 1953. Both programs follow the so-called 12-step program and have been instrumental in helping millions of people deal with their abuse problems. These programs rely on lay leaders exclusively. Perhaps because of the success of these programs, many of the rehabilitation hospitals in this country hire nonprofessional counselors or, perhaps more appropriately technicians, to provide counseling to abusers. Often these leaders have no formal education and are ex-addicts or ex-alcoholics. Defenders of this practice claim that professionals are condescending, lack understanding of the experience of the abuser, and attempt to look for underlying medical or psychological problems, when in fact the problem is the substance that is being abused. Professionals often charge nonprofessional counselors with applying simplistic solutions to complex problems and express concern about matters such as the ethics of the nonprofessionals. It is unclear how this issue will be resolved although licensing laws are forcing some treatment centers to abandon the use of nonprofessionals.

The Counseling Process

The steps in the counseling process for clients with alcohol- and drug-related problems are (1) develop trust, (2) assess problem, (3) establish goals, (4) implement plan, (5) relapse training, and (6) termination. Developing trust requires essentially the same skills as those described in Chapter Four and will not be repeated here. However, counselors need to be aware that clients may come to them at various stages, including a dawning awareness that they have a problem and a high degree of awareness that their abuse problem is linked to other problems. However, they may not be ready to move into the stage of doing something about the problem because of their dependence on alcohol or drugs.

Structuring the Sessions

Most counselors who deal with substance abusers try to establish certain guidelines at the outset. One of these is come to counseling sober or "straight." The smell of alcohol or marijuana, the slurring of speech, constricted (opiates) or dilated pupils (cocaine, stimulants, or marijuana), runny nose or eyes, and slowed physical reactions are signs that the client has not lived up to this stipulation. These counselors also make it clear that clients are to follow through on homework assignments such as attending AA or NA, or developing exercise regimens if counseling is to be successful. Depending on the approach used and the setting, counselors may not agree to continue counseling past the first session if the client cannot agree to these requests.

Assessment

The assessment process is quite specific and several questions must be answered during the assessment process, not the least of which is, to what degree has the problem developed. Initially, abusers learn that these substances cause mood changes. As the problem advances they begin to seek these changes, become preoccupied with them, and use alcohol and drugs to make themselves feel normal (Muisener, 1994). Ultimately, psychological and physical dependence are the result of the abuse syndrome.

To a certain extent, the question about stage of development can be answered by determining how long the client has been a user, how often drugs or alcohol are used, what amounts are consumed, and determining if there have been unsuccessful attempts to stop (Muisener, 1994; Velleman, 1992). It is also important to determine the impact of the use on physical and psychological health, behavioral function (e.g., job performance), and social and interpersonal functioning (relationships with significant others).

One of the confounding problems when trying to assess abusers is the possibility of the coexistence of a mental health problem such as depression or personality disorder. Gone (1994) emphasizes that the assessment of these problems cannot be done reliably until the abuse problem is stabilized.

Goal Setting
Goal setting is to some extent related to the stage to which the problem has developed. Typically, the goal for drug abusers is complete abstinence. However, for people with alcohol-related problems the goal may be controlled drinking as opposed to total abstinence. Goals may also include intrapersonal change to deal with feelings of helplessness, behavioral changes such as assertiveness, or lifestyle changes that involve avoiding people or places where the possibility of relapse is heightened. Gone (1994) suggests that one of the problems that occurs at this time is a well-refined defense mechanism that has been developed to justify the continuation of drinking or substance abuse. Even though the counselor may be able to easily identify the rationalization that is advanced, Gone warns against premature confrontation of the abuser because of the increased risk of relapse.

Plan Implementation
Prior to plan implementation, clients who are physically and psychologically dependent on drugs or alcohol may need to enroll in a detoxification program for thirty to ninety days so that they will have the support they need to deal with the severe trauma that can result from withdrawal. If this is not required, plan implementation can start immediately after goals have been established and client can begin attending Alcoholics or Narcotics Anonymous, participating in support groups, and/or taking Antibuse. Antibuse, which makes the client violently ill if alcohol is consumed, is indicated if client feels that he or she cannot control the impulses to drink. Once all the pieces of the plan are in place the client enters a long maintenance period until changes that are made are solidified. During this time, relapse prevention training may begin.

Relapse Prevention
Relapses are most likely to occur during the first six months of treatment, but can occur at any time. The counselor's task is to help the client anticipate those situations and circumstances that might lead to a relapse. For example, times of high stress often lead to relapse. Clients need to be aware when these times might occur (e.g., break-up of a relationship) and be prepared to deal with them. Clients also need to be able to cope with pressures from peers and families to resume the abuse, and be aware when they are making a high-risk decision such as visiting a bar or a friend who regularly uses drugs. Perhaps most importantly, counselors need to help clients break the expectation that drugs and alcohol will solve their problems (Velleman, 1992).

Termination

At the point of termination both the counselors and the clients feel that clients are ready to cope with the stresses of their lives without the aid of alcohol. If a client is in a 12-step program such as AA, then this part of the treatment continues, perhaps with the client attending fewer meetings. Antibuse may also be continued in some instances, and in this event continued observation by a physician is required.

STUDENT LEARNING EXERCISE

Respond to the following statements by indicating whether they are true or false.

1. The main concern of counselors who deal with alcohol abuse is physical addiction.   T   F

2. Alcoholics fit a narrow stereotype, that is they have similar psychological characteristics.   T   F

3. Drugs have replaced alcohol as the leading addiction problem in the U.S.   T   F

4. Confronting the substance user early and often is sound treatment strategy.   T   F

5. Alcohol abusers have been studied extensively and much of what has been learned can be applied to drug abusers.   T   F

Gerontological Counseling

Overview

The aging of the U.S. population has received increasing attention because of the strains that it places and will continue to place on the social security and medicare programs. One startling statistic, according to the most recent report from the U.S. Census Bureau, is that the fastest growing segment of our population is the over eighty group. In spite of this interest, it is the case that the elderly receive less attention in research, in writing, and in training than other groups. This may be because many stereotype old age as a time of decline, and thus do not see the optimistic approach that counselors bring to most client groups as useful for the elderly. Nothing could be further from the facts. While there is an inevitable decline in functioning and ultimately activity, many people view the later years of their lives as wonderful opportunities to develop new careers, pursue long neglected leisure activities, or to improve family relationships and seek help with these concerns (Riker & Myers, 1990; Wolinsky, 1990). Stereotypes of "old people" will not be very helpful for would-be gerontological counselors simply because most are faulty. In fact Salamon (1986) reports that older adults report fewer worries and have higher self-esteem than their younger counterparts, while noting that loss of physical functioning constitutes a real problem for the older group.

Counselors, like other mental health professionals, have been increasingly aware of the aging of the U.S., and a few counselor education programs offer specialties in this area. In the future, graduates of these programs may find themselves working in mental health agencies, hospices, hospitals, and retirement communities. In many instances they will find themselves working both with the aging person and that person's family because, for many older persons in the last stages of their lives, they reverse roles with their children and they assume a parenting role.

Kirchofer and Plumb (1989) suggest that it is useful to think about older Americans as young-old—those in their sixties and early seventies, old-old—those in their late seventies and early eighties, and very old—those in their late eighties and beyond. Gerontological counselors are generally more concerned with those groups that Kirchofer and Plumb classify as old-old and very old. However, since aging, like other aspects of development, may be more of a developmental than a chronological issue, gerontological counselors concern themselves with people, either who have concerns about growing older, or for whom the toll of the aging process has become a barrier to functioning. In performing in this role, gerontological counselors will need to fill the following roles (Riker & Myers, 1990):

1. Individual counselor
2. Bereavement counselor
3. Leisure counselor
4. Services coordinator
5. Counselor of dying
6. Client advocate
7. Nursing home consultant
8. Psychological educator
9. Financial counselor
10. Preretirement counselor
11. Marital and sex counselor
12. Family counselor
13. Educational counselor

The Counseling Process

Like other forms of counseling, gerontological counseling goes through certain stages, namely (1) relationship development, (2) assessment, (3) goal setting, (4) plan implementation, and (5) termination. Perhaps the only unique aspect of the relationship stage is that, depending on the physical and psychological functioning of the client, a relationship with the family members supporting the client may also have to be developed. This process is not unlike the one outlined in the first section of this chapter. Waters and Goodman (1990) also suggest that counselors need to be careful that the older client does not become overly dependent. In particular, emotional dependence can develop if the counselor becomes a major part of the client's support network.

Assessment
Smyer (1984) notes that numerous concerns must be considered when assessing the older person's problem, but that counselors should not lose sight of the fact

that people function holistically. Waters and Goodman (1990) seem to follow this guideline when they suggest that in the assessment process, the variables of general health, ability to care for self, emotional stability, cognitive ability (e.g., memory), and extent of social support be considered. Kirchofer and Plumb (1989) take a decidedly different tack. They stress the importance of determining the coping mechanisms, or lack thereof, that have been developed by the older adult to deal with the presenting problem. Tiggs (1989) also takes a more circumscribed approach to assessment and stresses the importance of focusing on self-esteem during the assessment process. He suggests that the aging process may compromise self-esteem with varying results including feelings of helplessness, hopelessness, and uselessness.

According to Tiggs (1989) helplessness manifests itself in increasing demands, diminished ability to control emotions, and perhaps withdrawal from social interaction. Helplessness may stem from the loss of independence, loss of physical ability, and dependence on medication. Hopeless people have no goals, may be angry and resentful, have increased psychosomatic problems, and be increasingly anxious. Feelings of hopelessness, according to Tiggs, stem from loss of primary life roles such as being a spouse, physical problems, and recognition of impending death. Feelings of uselessness may be manifested in depression, lack of eye contact, lowered communication, and general unresponsiveness. This is likely to occur because the person feels he or she is a burden to their family, a loss of personal security, and the general feeling that the person has lost control of the direction of his or her life.

Ebersole and Hess (1990) also focused to some degree on the importance of self-esteem in the functioning of the elderly. They suggest that symptoms such as apathy, rigidity, boredom, paranoia, indecisiveness, anger, and delusions may be linked to loss of self-esteem.

When considering the assessment process it is also important to note that depression is the leading psychological problem of older adults. The assessment of this problem is complicated by the need to differentiate it from dementia which has organic roots (Kirchofer & Plumb, 1989; Salamon, 1986). The most common cause of dementia is probably Alzheimer's disease which afflicts four to six percent of persons over age sixty-five. This disease, which ultimately results in death for most victims, is characterized by confusion, forgetfulness, and anxiety at the outset, moodiness and clear signs of forgetfulness as it develops, and memory loss and other problems that lead to institutionalization as it completes the earliest phases of development. During the middle stages of development of Alzheimer's disease, which may last from five to ten years, the older person begins to lose awareness of his or her surroundings. In the last stage of the disease, the victim may lose his or her ability to walk, may become incontinent, and lose interest in food.

Alzheimer's disease is not the only cause of dementia. Major strokes or a series of mini-strokes occurring over time can lead to lack of blood to the brain, and can in turn impair brain functioning and lead to some of the Alzheimer's type symptoms, some of which appear to be depression.

Clinical depression can be brought on by the adult's reaction to loss of physical functioning such as a hearing loss or incontinence, loss of a spouse or friends, the onset of diseases such as arthritis or various types of heart diseases, and the loss of independence (Ebersole & Hess, 1990; Tiggs, 1989). This and other psychological problems can be treated using standard psychological and psychopharmacological approaches. However, depression can also be brought on by the presence of subclinical diseases, too much or too little of certain medications, and poor nutrition (Ebersole & Hess, 1990). These issues should be ruled out prior to embarking on other approaches to treatment.

Goal Setting

Sherman (1981) along with Waters and Goodman (1990) and others, have set forth numerous goals that may be established by older clients. Many times, older adults will want to reduce the stress associated with certain life events such as the death of a friend or a heart attack. Others may wish to reduce their dependency on emergency support systems. Increasing self-esteem and enhancing social skills as a means of extending or enhancing the social support network may be another goal that develops in counseling. Communication with family members and resolving family conflicts may also be concerns. Counselors may also find themselves working with the elderly to improve their memory, a task that can be attained as long as the basis for the problem is not organic. Identifying leisure pursuits, finding part-time jobs, and locating volunteer opportunities may also become goals for older clients. Finally, older clients may need help adjusting to physical and sexual decline, accepting loss of independence, and dealing with the inevitability of death.

Plan Implementation

Waters and Goodman (1990) suggest that the plan to remedy the problems that older adults experience should be linked to the degree to which they are impaired. Self-esteem may be restored by strategies such as helping clients identify creative pursuits, learning new skills, learning to deal with anxiety through relaxation, helping others through volunteer work, and regaining control of money (Ebersole & Hess, 1990). Feelings of depression may be reduced by involvement in support groups, encouraging increased family support, and engaging in activities such as caring for a plant or pet.

When counseling strategies are required they can be based on any of the theoretical positions presented in Chapter Three. For example, Sherman (1981) built an entire approach to counseling older persons on the work of Beck (1976), perhaps because of the prevalence of depression among this group and the efficacy of this approach in treating this problem. However, given the prevalence of family-related problems and the need to make interventions at a more systemic level, it seems likely that the gerontological counselors need to include some of the strategies described earlier in this chapter as well. Bereavement counseling will also be needed at times, thus helping the older adult move through the stages of grief and on to reorganizing their lives by expanding their social networks and letting go of their grief will be important strategies (Waters & Goodman, 1990).

In situations where the older adult is seriously impaired by medical problems such as Alzheimer's, interventions may include day care programs, support groups for the family, arranging for home health care, placement in a mental hospital, hospice care, and other similar approaches.

Termination

While gerontological counselors will, at termination, experience many of the same feelings of satisfaction that other counselors enjoy because of their ability to help their clients open new doors, resolve personal conflicts, and enhance their quality of life, some terminations will occur because of the death or impairment of clients. If the family of the older person is the client, then death or severe impairment may lead to further work to help resolve the conflicts that arise because of these events.

STUDENT LEARNING EXERCISE
Respond to the following statements by indicating whether they are true or false.

1. Many of the stereotypes of older adults have a strong basis in reality.   T   F
2. One problem for the gerontological counselor is who should be the "client."   T   F
3. Gerontological counselors have much more restricted roles than other counselors.   T   F
4. In many ways counseling older adults is simpler because of the restricted set of interventions available to the counselor.   T   F
5. Dementia is the leading cause of psychological problems in adults.   T   F

Summary

Three counseling specialties have been discussed in this chapter. Of these, family counseling is probably the most divergent from other approaches to counseling because it is based on systems theory as opposed to theories of individual functioning. The three specialties have been discussed separately although there is some overlap among them. For example, gerontological counselors also need some family counseling skills because of the likelihood that the older adult's family will often need to be involved at some point in the counseling process. It is also the case that substance abuse counselors need to understand family dynamics and be able to work with families because of the relationship between family dynamics and substance abuse. Substance abuse problems may also play a major role in family problems and the difficulties of the elderly. While it is unlikely that one counselor will be dealing with family problems, the problems of the elderly, and be actively involved in the treatment of substance abusers, the counselor must be familiar enough with each field so problems can be detected and appropriate referrals made.

Review Questions

1. Describe what is meant by a family system, and how it influences the counseling process.

2. Describe three techniques used by family therapists.

3. What are some advantages and disadvantages of couples and family therapy?

4. What are the symptoms that may be displayed by an alcoholic? Someone with Alcohol Dependence Syndrome?

5. What are the stages in counseling the substance abuser, and how do they differ if at all from other approaches to counseling?

6. Identify the major reasons abusers return to alcohol and drug use.

7. How would you go about assessing a substance abuser's problem? What interventions would you suggest for each type of problem?

8. Is the concept of classifying older adults as young-old, old-old, and very old useful to gerontological counselors? Can you think of a more useful way to classify the elderly?

9. Identify the roles that gerontological counselors may fill.

10. Describe the assessment process for the older adult.

11. Why do gerontological counselors need family counseling skills?

12. Gerontological counselors have been called resource linkers. Why do you think they were labeled as such?

References

Ackerman, N. W. (1954). The diagnosis of neurotic marital interaction. *Social Casework, 35,* 139–149.

Ackerman, N. W. (1958). *The psychodynamics of family life.* New York: Basic Books.

Beavers, W. R., & Voeller, M. N. (1983). Family models: Comparing and contrasting the Olson circumplex model with the Beavers systems model. *Family Process, 22*(1), 85–97.

Beck, A. (1976). *Cognitive therapy and emotional disorders.* New York: International Universities Press.

Bowen, M. (1978). *Family therapy in clinical practice.* New York: Jason Aronson.

Broderick, C. B., & Schrader, S. S. (1981). The history of marriage and family therapy. In A. S. Gurman & D. P. Kniskern, (eds.), *Handbook of family therapy* (pp. 5–35). New York: Brunner/Mazel.

Carter, E. A., & McGoldrick, M. (eds.). (1980). *The family life cycle: A framework for family therapy.* New York: Gardner Press, Inc.

Cormier, W. H., & Cormier, L. S. (1991). *Interviewing strategies for helpers: Fundamental skills and cognitive behavioral interventions,* (3rd ed.). Pacific Grove, CA: Brooks/Cole Publishing Company.

Ebersole, P. & Hess, P. (1990). *Toward healthy aging,* (3rd ed.). St. Louis, MO: C. V. Mosby.

Gonet, M. M. (1994). *Counseling the adolescent substance abuser.* Thousand Oaks, CA: Sage.

Haley, J. (1963). *Strategies for psychotherapy.* New York: Grune & Stratton.

Haley, J. (1973). *Uncommon therapy.* New York: W. W. Norton.

Haley, J. (1976). *Problem solving therapy.* San Francisco: Jossey-Bass.

Hauser, S. T., Powers, S. I., & Noam, G. G. (1991). *Adolescents and their families: Paths of ego development.* New York: The Free Press.

Jackson, D. D. (1959). Family interaction, family homeostasis, and some implications for conjoint family psychotherapy. In Masserman (ed.), *Individual and family dynamics.* New York: Grune & Stratton.

J. H. Kirchofer, M. & Plumb, M. (1989). Psychological aspects of aging. In Diechman, E. S. & Kociecki, R. (eds.), *Working with the elderly,* (pp. 43–66). Buffalo, NY: Prometheus Books.

Madanes, C. (1981). *Strategic family therapy.* San Francisco: Jossey-Bass.

Minuchin, S. (1974). *Families and family therapy.* Cambridge, MA: Harvard University Press.

Muisener, P. P. (1994). *Understanding and treating the adolescent substance abuser.* Thousand Oaks, CA: Sage.

Napier, A. Y., & Whitaker, C. A. (1980). *The family crucible.* New York: Bantam Books.

Nichols, W. C., & Everett, C. A. (1986). *Systemic family therapy: An integrative approach.* New York: The Guilford Press.

Riker, H. C. & Meyers, J. E. (1990). *Retirement counseling: A practical guide for action.* New York: Hemisphere.

Rollinick, S. & MacEwan, I. (1989). Alcohol counseling in context. In Davidson, R., Rollinick, S., & MacEwan, I. (eds.), *Counseling problem drinkers,* (pp. 97–114). New York: Tavistock/Rutledge.

Salamon, M. J. (1986). *A basic guide to working with the elderly.* New York: Springer.

Satir, V. (1964). *Conjoint family therapy.* Palo Alto, CA: Science & Behavior Books.

Satir, V. (1972). *People making.* Palo Alto, CA: Science and Behavior Books.

Satir, V., Stachowlak, J., & Taschman, H. A. (1983). *Helping families to change.* Northvale, NJ: Jason Aronson Inc.

Sherman, E. (1981). *Counseling the aging.* New York: Free Press.

Smyer, M. A. (1984). Life transition and aging: Implications for counseling older adults. *The Counseling Psychologist, 12,* 17–28.

Tiggs, K. N. (1989). Therapy and the health care practitioner. In Diechman, E. S. & Kociecki, R. (eds.), *Working with the elderly,* (pp. 171–193). Buffalo, NY: Prometheus Books.

Todd, J., & Bohart, A. C. (1994). *Foundations of clinical and counseling psychology,* (2nd ed.). New York: Harper Collins College Publishers.

Velleman, R. (1990). *Counseling for alcohol problems.* Thousand Oaks, CA: Sage.

Waters, E. & Goodman, J. (1990). *Empowering older adults.* San Francisco: Jossey-Bass.

Watzlawick, P., Weakland, J., & Fisch, R. (1974). *Change: Principles of problem formation and problem resolution.* New York: Norton.

Wolinsky, M. A. (1990). *A heart of wisdom: Marital counseling with older adults.* New York: Bruner/Mazel.

Chapter *9*

Counseling in a Multicultural Society

Goal of the Chapter

The aim of this chapter is to survey cultural issues and their impact on the practice of counseling.

Chapter Preview

- The concept of culture will be defined.
- Multicultural counseling will be described.
- Barriers to multicultural counseling will be examined.
- Counseling of populations with special issues will be examined.
- Particular attention will be given to the counseling of women.

Introduction

Much of the counseling literature focuses on the YAVIS client, that is, the young, attractive, verbal, intelligent, and successful individual. Most counselors freely admit that some of their most difficult clients are those that fall outside this group, including the physically and mentally handicapped, clients mired in poverty, and individuals who are part of minorities not fully supported by our society.

It is also true that historically much of the counseling literature has focused on white males to the detriment of the counseling of women and ethnic and racial minorities. Research and practitioners' observations have shown that theories and practices developed for white males and YAVIS clients do not necessarily generalize to the many client groups that exist in our culture. As immigration to this country continues, especially from the Far East, and as birthrates of other racial and ethnic groups exceed that of the white population, counselors will have to serve these individuals differently than their traditional clients. It is the purpose of this chapter to discuss some of the counseling issues that must be addressed if one is to provide effective services to clients who belong to ethnic and racial minorities, or who are women, gay or lesbian, aged, or disabled.

Cultural Differences and Counseling

The Concept of Culture

Defining culture is no easy task, as Copeland (1983) notes. As early as 1952, Kroeber and Kluckhohn identified more that 150 different definitions of culture. However, as Copeland (1983) did, so did Herskovits (1955) define culture as the human made part of the environment. Cultures form when people share common experiences, history, language, and geographic location, although national boundaries often contain more than one culture. Common experiences and social tools such as language used to describe experience affect the perceptions of the people in a culture, and thus culture contains many subjective elements.

Ibrahim (1985) describes culture-building as a process in which a group of people form a world view, a philosophy of life. Important elements in this philosophy are (1) a characterization of human nature, (2) a definition of the goals of human relationships, (3) the relationship of people to nature, (4) the relationship of people to time, and (5) the goals and implications of human action.

Table 9.1 lists the differences that exist among various cultural groups in this country. One can see from the table that cultural influences on an individual affect basic values and beliefs. When individuals from different cultures attempt to relate to one another, they may begin with very different perceptions about the nature of people, what people need, how people succeed, and the relationship of people to nature.

Multicultural Counseling

Multicultural or cross-cultural counseling are labels for the same process. Its history and development parallels the political and social movements of the last three decades, sensitizing counselors to the cultural differences clients bring to treatment (Fukuyama, 1990). Many definitions exist for multicultural counseling; they all deal with cultural differences between counselor and client; they differ according to how inclusive or exclusive the definition is.

Ridley, Mendoza, and Kanitz (1994a) note that inclusive definitions offer a view in which many different cultural characteristics affect the counselor-client dyad. These include racial/ethnic identity, religious affiliation, gender and gender

TABLE 9.1   Individuals Affected by Cultural Barriers in Counseling

Barrier	Most Affected	Least Affected
Language	Not English-speaking English second language	English predominant language
Values	Other-directed Noncompetitive Time unimportant Have strong traditions	Self-oriented Competitive Time conscious Self-disclosing
Stereotypes	All affected	
Race	African American Asian American Latino American Native American	White American
Social Class	Inner-city poor Rural poor	Middle-class Suburban
Gender	Females	Males
Sexual orientation	Gay, lesbian, bisexual, transgender	Heterosexual
Age	Elderly	Young adults
Handicapping conditions	Deforming conditions	With "normal" appearance

identity, physical ability, socioeconomic status, geographical location, national identity, and so on. Pedersen (1988), Vontress (1988), and Fukuyama (1990) represent this position.

Exclusive definitions of multicultural counseling restrict its scope to racial and ethnic factors as they impact the counselor-client relationship. The latter argue that too broad a definition will blur the focus on important racial/ethnic concerns, particularly of the four visible minority groups in America—African, Asian, Latin, and Native Americans (Ridley, et al., 1994a). Locke (1990) and Lee (1991) represent this position.

To have a multicultural sensitivity as a counselor begins with a recognition of the cultural bias in counseling as it emerged in the U.S. and Europe. Sue (1981) argued that underlying the practice of counseling were such cultural-bound values as individualism, rationalism, and self-determination, frequently assumed to be correct and preferred.

Locke (1986) suggests that there is a multicultural counseling awareness continuum (Figure 9.1) through which a counselor should pass before engaging in cross-cultural counseling. This development begins with self-awareness, including, one presumes, an awareness of prejudices that one holds. Self-awareness should be followed by the development of an awareness of one's own culture; increased sensitivity to the presence of racism, sexism, and poverty in our society;

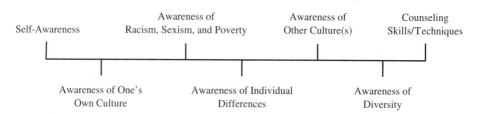

FIGURE 9.1   Cross-Cultural Awareness Continuum

Source: "Cross-cultural Counseling Issues" (p. 122) by D. C. Locke. In *Foundations of Mental Health Counseling* (pp. 119–137) by A. J. Palmo and W. J. Weikel, (eds.), 1986, Springfield, Illinois.

awareness of individual differences; awareness of other cultural groups and the diversity within those cultures; and, finally, the development of counseling techniques that will enable the counselor to bridge the gaps that exist between self and culturally different clients.

Sue (1981) has elaborated extensively on the counseling skills that are needed in multicultural counseling. He stresses that the culturally skilled counselor must have a basic understanding of counseling techniques and must be culturally sensitive enough to apply those techniques appropriately. For example, most counseling techniques are oriented toward inducing increasing self-disclosure on the part of the client. But according to Sue (1981), "Self-disclosure may be incompatible with the cultural values of Asian Americans, Chicanos, and Native Americans" (p. 107).

It is also worth noting that traditional insight-oriented therapy, such as that emphasized in the traditional therapies, may be inappropriate for certain cultural groups since economically and educationally disadvantaged clients may be uncomfortable in a role that requires extensive verbalization. Also, many minority clients prefer the more action-oriented approaches characterized by the behavior and cognitive therapies, as opposed to the longer, more deliberate approaches (Sue, 1981).

Sue and Sue (1990) suggest that there are four scenarios that may evolve from cross-cultural counseling, only one of which is positive. In that positive scenario, the process engaged in by the counselor is appropriate with regard to the cultural background of the client, and the goals pursued are also in keeping with the cultural situation and sociopolitical realities of the client's existence. The other outcomes of cross-cultural counseling described by Sue are (1) appropriate process, inappropriate goals, (2) inappropriate process, appropriate goals, and (3) inappropriate process, inappropriate goals.

In the first of these negative situations, a cross-cultural counselor might engage in a more active process with a Native American client and help him or her pursue counseling goals that are compatible with his or her view of the relationship of humans to nature and time. One community college counselor reported trying to help Native Americans reconcile a desire to achieve in academic arenas that required punctuality and attendance with beliefs that the annual salmon runs also demanded their attention and, of course, absence from the academic setting.

An appropriate process coupled with an inappropriate goal is illustrated by an active counseling process engaged in by a middle-class white counselor with a poor white fourth-grade boy in which she attempts to teach him to stop fighting. In this situation, fighting skills are necessary if the child is to get to school with his lunch. An appropriate goal for the counselor would be for her to help the child discriminate between appropriate and inappropriate fighting. However, the middle-class white counselor may still use an inappropriate process by attempting to justify not fighting as a civilized means for solving problems.

Sue and Sue (1990) believe that premature termination of counseling is likely to occur when the process is inappropriate, even though the goals of the counseling situation are appropriate. A nondirective counselor working with clients who are black and poor, regardless of the goal being pursued, is likely to be ineffective, as is the counselor who chooses the wrong counseling process as well as an inappropriate goal.

Yau, Sue, and Hayden (1992) cite numerous references that recommend directive/structured forms of counseling for the four visible minority populations in this country. However, their own research shows no overall preference for counseling style. Their international student clients changed their rating of different counseling styles from session to session. Different styles were seen as complimentary rather than as antagonistic. Again, it is difficult to make universal statements about diverse client groups.

Developing Cultural Sensitivity

One of the principal goals of multicultural training for counselors is the development of cultural sensitivity (Ridley, Mendoza, Kanitz, Angermeier, & Zenk, 1994b). This is based on the assumption that better outcomes can be achieved with diverse client populations if cultural insensitivity is reduced. Defining cultural sensitivity has not been easy; it seems that many terms implying cultural sensitivity have been used interchangeably; they include: cross-cultural competence, cross-cultural expertise, cultural responsiveness, cultural awareness, and being culturally skilled (Ridley, et al., 1994b). Being culturally sensitive is part of the way one cognitively processes information. To be sensitive means that counselors first of all are alert to cultural stimuli and aware of their own values, beliefs, and expectations; secondly, they are fluid or flexible in being able to structure and restructure information as the counseling process continues. Finally, culturally sensitive counselors are motivated to expend effort in formulating these changes in their understanding, based on knowledge of a client's unique cultural background.

Barriers to Multicultural Counseling

Language

Conversation is the most fundamental tool utilized by counselors. In multicultural counseling, a major obstacle to be overcome is often a language difference. Even though this country is understood to be an English-speaking nation, millions of its citizens regularly use other languages. In fact, many individuals are far more fluent in a language other than English and are therefore handicapped in their ability to take advantage of opportunities available to those who are fluent in English. Among those who do speak English, many use a nonstandard form with word connotations and slang phrases that are quite different from those in standard English. Language barriers must be overcome if counseling is to be successful.

Minorities have been underrepresented in the counseling profession. At present only a few counseling practitioners are bilingual, even though we are becoming a bilingual nation (Arrendondo-Dowd & Gonsalves, 1980). Legislation has recognized this situation, including a need to provide counseling services to non-English-speaking clients. The amended Bilingual Education Act of 1978 specifically named counselors as recipients of federal funds to develop better bilingual programs, including programs to train bilingual counselors. However, providing bilingual counseling will not solve the problem that exists between a counselor who speaks standard English and a client who speaks a nonstandard form. Only cultural sensitivity and hard work can bridge this gap.

Related to language use are differences in general communication style. Sue (1990) lists proxemics (the use of physical distance), kinesics (body movements), and paralanguage (verbal cues other than words) as important nonverbal forms of communication that take on cultural significance and can disturb client-counselor communication. He cites research that suggests women and minorities as better readers of nonverbal cues than white males.

Values

As has already been noted, culture-bound values are an important impediment to cross-cultural counseling. As was also noted, one of the most valued behaviors related to the counseling process is self-disclosure. Therapists believe clients benefit more from counseling if they are willing to share hidden thoughts and feelings, but clients may not share this value.

Sue (1977) notes how threatening the expectation of self-disclosure is to Chinese American clients who have been raised to minimize the expression of feelings. More recently, Sue and Sue (1990) compared the typical American therapist with the typical Chinese American. The former often prizes being open, competitive, verbally direct, and independent minded; the latter learns through cultural conditioning to revere solidarity, adherence to roles, conformity, and continuity within a kinship system. As an example, Sue presented the conflict of diverse values at a conference in which professional papers are read. Typically, the work of even a revered scholar will receive direct, open criticism by a reactor. This is completely contrary to Asian tradition.

Even the most conscientious counselors from the dominant culture may unknowingly alienate a minority client. They fail to see that what they take for granted as the clearly superior standard is nothing more than one of many options. For example, the counselor may value competition in the classroom, while his Native American client values cooperation and thus sees direct competition as inappropriate. Unless the counselor perceives the client's point of view, the result of counseling is likely to be less than satisfactory.

Stereotypes

Much has been written about the potential dangers of stereotypes. Usually defined as generalizations one group of people make about another group, stereotypes at first do not seem so negative. However, stereotypes are usually oversimplified opinions that do not receive critical examination. Thus, stereotypes misrepresent individuals from the group being typed.

When counselors use stereotypes, they lose flexibility in responding to the needs of their clients. Noted throughout this text are the efforts of the American Counseling Association (ACA) and the American Psychological Association (APA) to establish commissions and task forces to minimize the damage of cultural stereotypes. While this effort has been successful to some degree, it also seems likely that counselors now more effectively conceal their stereotypes. Paradis (1981) documents the reluctance of counselor/therapists to admit to stereotypes. In his study many reflect repressed hostility toward other cultural groups. However, problematic overgeneralization in the profession is probably a two-way street. White middle-class counselors should be aware that their clients hold stereotypes of them, and counselors must be prepared to deal with these views.

STUDENT LEARNING EXERCISE

Read the following descriptions and indicate whether you think the counseling profession has been successful in dealing with the issue identified. Circle Y for yes or N for no.

1. There is an emerging definition of what constitutes effective cross-cultural counseling. Y N
2. Self-disclosure is not a problem in cross-cultural counseling. Y N
3. There are adequate numbers of bilingual counselors today. Y N
4. Counselors are rarely affected by cultural stereotypes. Y N
5. Differences in cultural background between counselor and client often lead to premature termination of counseling. Y N

Social Class

Low social class or poverty appears to affect both the rate of diagnosed mental health problems and access to treatment. Studies tend to show an inverse relationship between social class and such disorders as schizophrenia, alcoholism, drug abuse, and antisocial behavior (Dohrenwend & Dohrenwend, 1974). In part, this has been explained as a function of the stressors related to poverty.

In the counseling process, the different experience levels of the client and counselor, and thus their perceptions or world views, may pose the greatest barriers. The middle-class counselor may not have learned that deciding to delay gratification is of doubtful value to the poor because experience has taught them that promises of future rewards never materialize. These differences, when encountered, must be processed.

Race and Ethnicity

Much attention has been given to the cultural differences of racial minorities and the effect of these differences on counseling-related issues (Atkinson, Morten, & Sue, 1979; Marsella & Pedersen, 1981). Evidence does show that minority clients are more likely to drop out of therapy early, miss scheduled appointments, and verbalize greater dissatisfaction with the treatment process (Raynes & Warren, 1969; Sue, 1977; Acosta, 1980). In addition, they are likely to be assigned lower level staff as therapists and are more often assigned inpatient treatment. This suggests that in the past minorities have felt undervalued and mistreated when seeking mental health services (Korchin, 1980).

The process of counseling itself may be problematic to minority clients. Most therapy systems emphasize introspection, assuming responsibility for life's consequences, and the necessity for arriving at personal decisions and solutions. Minority clients, on the other hand, recognize well their identity as an oppressed people. They can point to a social environment outside themselves as the source for much of their hardship. Thus much of the theory underlying client involvement in therapy is at odds with core elements of minority group identity.

Minority individuals often want more from their therapists than is given. In part this includes more direct intervention—more explicit advice, financial counseling, and vocational help (Korchin, 1980). Most counselors, since they do not really understand the stressors affecting minority clients, find it difficult to provide such direct assistance.

Such issues point out again the need for cross-cultural counselors. As Locke (1986) noted, fundamental to cross-cultural involvement is the recognition of group identity as well as individual differences. Tolerance of both represents an ethical necessity for counselors (Pedersen & Marsella, 1982).

Important in understanding clients from different racial backgrounds is the development of one's own racial identity, something not fully mature in many white counselors (Ponterotto, 1988). Research has shown that racial identity attitudes, that is the acceptance, consciousness of, and celebration of one's own racial heritage, may better predict multicultural effectiveness than amount of multicultural education and length of experience as a practitioner (Ottavi, Pope-Davis, & Dings, 1994). This suggests that being "color blind" actually mitigates against one's cultural skillfulness.

Gender

One of the most powerful influences on our culture and our profession in the last two decades has been the women's movement. Feminist counselors and psychologists have been extremely important in mobilizing the helping professions to respond to sexist practices.

In 1970 therapists were shocked into the reality of sexist attitudes in the helping professions by the historic study by Broverman and coworkers (Broverman, Broverman, Clarkson, Rosenkrantz, & Vogel, 1970). This investigation documented not only the presence of gender stereotypes among therapists, but also the devalued nature of the female stereotypes. In this study counselors viewed healthy adults as different from healthy females but not from healthy males; by implication counselors viewed women as less psychologically healthy than men. Women, in the minds of therapists at that time, were less independent and adventurous than men; they were seen as easily influenced and overly emotional. Additional studies in the mid-1970s supported the continuation of these gender-related stereotypes among counselors (Moore & Strickler, 1980).

While the presence of such stereotypes became a source of concern in itself, the helping professions were faced with the question of whether or not their presence led to negative outcomes for women who had undergone counseling or psychotherapy. Over the past decade and a half this issue has been hotly contested and examined. It seems that a review of the evidence (Whitley, 1979; Smith, 1980) does not support the view that therapy is unhealthy for women. On the other hand, many issues remain regarding the ability of the therapy professions to respond to the unique needs and aspirations of female clients.

The alarm set off regarding sexist practices in the helping professions has been responded to vigorously by our professional associations and the federal government. The Education Amendments Act of 1972 opened many new opportunities for women. Early in the sexism debate the American Counseling Association (then the American Personnel and Guidance Association) published the following strong position papers on sex-fair counseling practices: "Standards for the Preparation of Counselors and Other Personnel Services Specialists" (ACES, 1973); "Career Guidance: Role and Function of Counseling and Guidance Personnel Practitioners in Career Education" (APGA, 1974); and "Position Paper on Counselor Preparation for Career Development/Career Education" (ACES, 1978).

The American Psychological Association in turn has addressed sexism with the following: the report from the National Conference on Levels and Patterns of Professional Training in Psychology (APA, 1973); the report of the Task Force on Issues of Sex Bias in Graduate Education (APA, 1975a); the report of the Task Force on Sex Bias and Sex Role Stereotyping in Psychotherapeutic Practice (APA, 1975b); and APA Division 17's "Principles Concerning the Counseling and Therapy of Women" (see Table 9.2).

In addition, these professional associations attempted to promote sex-fair practices through the use of nonsexist language in their publications and in efforts to revise ethical standards in accord with nonsexist principles. Moore and Strickler (1980) document numerous other professional efforts to eliminate sex bias from the helping professions.

In 1980 Worell reviewed more than 500 articles dealing with ideologies, goals, needs, rationales, strategies, and research findings related to counseling women. Johnson (1979) notes this explosion of literature as a true beginning of a feminine psychology and outlines the topics such a psychology can explore with direct attention to treatment. Dupuy, Ritchie and Cook (1994) surveyed counselor education programs regarding women's and gender issues. They found the most frequently required texts for counselors-in-training on gender issues to be *In a Different Voice* (Gilligan, 1982), *Women's Ways of Knowing: The Development of Self, Voice, and Mind* (Belenky, Clinchy, Goldberger, & Tarule, 1986), and *Handbook of Feminist Therapy* (Rosewater & Walker, 1985).

Much of this effort appears necessary in the helping professions in light of the fact that historically most therapy approaches emerge out of the study of males (Hare-Mustin, 1983), leaving many feminine lifestyle issues still undertreated. This applies especially to career development and counseling, where sex-bias may have had its most significant impact (Fitzgerald & Crites, 1980). Female theories of career development have begun to emerge (e.g., Astin, 1984; Poole, Langan-Fox, Ciavarella & Omodei, 1991), and gender-fair interpretations are more a part of standardized career assessment (Gilbert, 1991).

Areas of high relevance to women include marital and family relations, reproductive problems, physical and sexual abuse, depression, diagnosis based on sexist tenets, and problems associated with eating (Hare-Mustin, 1983). Fitzgerald and Crites (1980) note that women may follow a wider variety of lifestyle patterns, making adaptation more of a challenge. A key issue for women is the merging of career and family. Gray's (1980) review of the literature shows that working women still shoulder most of the burden of managing a household. Women are often put in a position of multiple-role involvements, with high expectations from themselves and others for each separate role. Helping women, then, often involves working not only with the women themselves but also with their families, friends, or associates.

Much has been accomplished in the almost two decades since the study by Broverman and coworkers. Through the efforts of mostly women, there has been

TABLE 9.2 Principles Concerning the Counseling and Therapy of Women

Preamble

Although competent counseling/therapy processes are essentially the same for all counselor/therapist interactions, special subgroups require specialized skills, attitudes, and knowledge. Women constitute a special subgroup.

Competent counseling-therapy requires recognition and appreciation that contemporary society is not sex fair. Many institutions, test standards, and attitudes of mental health professionals limit the options of female clients. Counselors/therapists should sensitize female clients to these real-world limitations, confront them with both the external and their own internalized limitations, and explore with them their reactions to these constraints.

The principles presented here are considered essential for the competent counseling/therapy of women.

1. Counselors/therapists are knowledgeable about women, particularly with regard to biological, psychological, and social issues that have an impact on women in general or on particular groups of women in our society.
2. Counselors/therapists are aware that the assumptions and precepts of theories relevant to their practice may apply differently to men and women. Counselors/therapists are aware of those theories and models that proscribe or limit the potential of female clients, as well as those that may have particular usefulness for female clients.
3. After formal training, counselors/therapists continue to explore and learn of issues related to women, including the special problems of female subgroups, throughout their professional careers.
4. Counselors/therapists recognize and are aware of all forms of oppression and how these interact with sexism.
5. Counselors/therapists are knowledgeable and aware of verbal and nonverbal process variables (particularly with regard to power in the relationship) as these affect women in counseling/therapy so that the counselor/therapist-client interactions are not adversely affected. The need for shared responsibility between clients and counselors/therapists is acknowledged and implemented.
6. Counselors/therapists have the capability of utilizing skills that are particularly facilitative to women in general and to particular subgroups of women.
7. Counselors/therapists ascribe no preconceived limitations on the direction or nature of potential changes or goals in counseling/therapy for women.
8. Counselors/therapists are sensitive to circumstances where it is more desirable for a female client to be seen by a female or male counselor/therapist.
9. Counselors/therapists use nonsexist language in counseling/therapy, supervision, teaching, and journal publications.
10. Counselors/therapists do not engage in sexual activity with their female clients under any circumstances.
11. Counselors/therapists are aware of and continually review their own values and biases and the effects of these on their female clients. Counselors/therapists understand the effects of sex-role socialization on their own development and functioning and the consequent values and attitudes they hold for themselves and others. They recognize that behaviors and roles need not be sex based.
12. Counselors/therapists are aware of how their personal functioning may influence their effectiveness in counseling/therapy with female clients. They monitor their functioning through consultation, supervision, or therapy so that it does not adversely affect their work with female clients.
13. Counselors/therapists support the elimination of sex bias with institutions and individuals.

These principles were endorsed unanimously by the Division 17 Ad Hoc Committee on Women, the Executive Committee of Division 17, and the entire membership of Division 17 during the August 1978 meeting of APA in Toronto as necessary for responsible professional practice in the counseling and therapy of women. Reprinted with permission of the American Psychological Association.

a moderating of gender stereotypes in the helping professions (Brodsky & Hare-Mustin, 1980). O'Malley and Richardson (1985), in a replication of the Broverman study, found that many therapists still hold gender stereotypes, as they did in 1970. However, such stereotypes no longer cast women as less psychologically healthy. The achievements noted raise hope for other special groups in their contact with help-givers.

Feminist and Nonsexist Therapy

While one might have expected feminist therapies to be efforts by counselors to correct some of the weaknesses noted earlier in providing treatment for women, they in fact evolved out of the wide range of political, sociological, and philosophical perspectives within the feminist movement (Brown, 1990). Like feminist philosophy, feminist therapy is diverse and multifaceted.

Enns (1992) summarizes a number of varied feminist philosophies, two of which we will discuss briefly. Liberal or "mainstream" feminism emphasizes inequalities in educational opportunities and civil rights, working toward legal and educational reform to achieve a sex-fair society, much in accord with the liberal philosophies of the eighteenth and nineteenth centuries. In the second philosophy, radical feminism, the guiding assumption is that the earliest and most pervasive form of oppression has been of women. Since it is the most widespread, it is the hardest to eradicate; it is rooted in patriarchy—marked by male dominance, competition, and heterosexism. The term radical in this form of feminism does not mean "extreme" as much as it captures the sense of "getting to the root causes of gender inequality" (Enns, 1992). This view calls for radical cultural changes, since such institutions as family and church are so permeated by patriarchal thinking that they need to be augmented with new structures (Donovan, 1992).

When these ideas are applied to counseling, to some degree all feminist therapists would focus on a client's gender role socialization and the barriers the client experiences in achieving personal goals. Because liberal feminism is closely linked to a humanistic model of personhood, its related therapy often is much like other humanistic therapies, emphasizing personal growth and wholeness, nurtured through an accepting, empathic therapeutic relationship. Also, since it recognizes that thinking and behavior patterns learned through gender socialization produce cognitive injunctions limiting growth, cognitive-behavioral techniques also might be viewed as useful (Enns, 1992). Counseling that follows the direction of liberal feminism is often called "non-sexist therapy," while psychotherapy following the tenets of radical feminism is frequently called "feminist therapy" (Enns & Hackett, 1990). The latter is better understood by first reviewing its historic development.

The precursors to feminist therapy were consciousness-raising groups (Enns, 1993). In the feminist movement support, equality, and sharing stood as the antidote to the power-oriented, male-dominated, hierarchical system that it was determined to change. Groups symbolized this different order. While consciousness-raising groups were not considered to be therapy, many members reported important personal changes as a result of their participation. When feminist therapies began to emerge in the 1970's, and individual therapy joined group work, there remained an emphasis on therapy as democratic, as an interactive process among equals (Enns, 1993). By the close of the first decade of feminist therapy there was an effort to integrate it with existing forms of counseling and psychotherapy.

In the 1980's, as the ratification of the Equal Rights Amendment failed, and rightist accusations mounted regarding feminism as a threat to family-oriented values, women became painfully aware of power politics and realized that neutral forms of therapy that supported the concept of androgyny (balancing masculine and feminine characteristics) really could not overcome the sexism inherent in society. Neither could educational programs, assertiveness training, or other conventional procedures create satisfactory solutions to the abusive position women experienced in the overall mental health system. Diagnostic systems needed to be overhauled, and new theories of feminine personality development needed to be written, so therapists would not merely influence women to adopt male-style lives. Thus, some practitioners of nonsexist counseling searched for different strategies to help clients.

As these theoretical foundations came into place, feminist therapy became more active. Radical feminist therapists were more likely to point out social barriers and encourage clients to alter both their behavior and environments, at times emphasizing political activity (Enns & Hackett, 1990). For more detailed reading of nonsexist and feminist therapy protocols, Enns recommends Marecek and Kravetz (1977) and Rawlings and Carter (1977).

When one considers the assumptions on which feminist therapy is based, the preference for female therapists as role models for female clients is clear. However, it may be possible for males to offer a form of profeminist therapy (DeVoe, 1990). The research evaluating the many forms of feminist and nonsexist therapy is showing the favorable outcomes regarding the credibility of feminist and profeminist therapists (Enns & Hackett, 1990). To date, much of this research tests analogues (e.g., videotapes of counselorlike behavior) to real therapy. However, future research activity should be vigorous, utilizing both traditional quantitative methods along with qualitative methods preferred by many researchers in women's psychology.

Sexual Orientation

Coming to grips with one's sexuality is an issue commonly explored in counseling. It concerns recognizing sexual feelings, assimilating them into one's self-image, and making decisions on how to act on one's feelings and identity. This process is difficult enough when one receives considerable support from others; it can be overwhelming when the direction taken runs counter to carefully guarded norms.

Developing a lesbian or gay identity runs counter to current societal norms. The individual grappling with such an identity often finds little support. The penalties for this sexual orientation have been severe. Evolving out of this has been what Weinberg (1973) coined as *homophobia:* a strong, irrational fear of homosexuality and homosexuals. Advanced by the dominant culture, it is an attempt to establish control over the incidence of a gay or lesbian sexual orientation. Beane (1981) describes how both clients and counselors can bring a homophobic presence into the counseling process. Counselors often do not understand that cultural conditioning also has created an internalized form of homophobia in a gay, lesbian, or bisexual client.

While the evidence shows that many well-adjusted gays follow diverse lifestyles consistent with their varied personalities (Bell & Weinberg, 1978), accepting and maintaining a gay identity and lifestyle are particularly troublesome because of the negative pressures already cited. It has been the experience of gay men and women (Groves & Ventura, 1983) that little help will result from counseling with someone other than a gay therapist; this is because of the homophobic issue. This challenges nongay counselors to evaluate themselves regarding this factor, and determine if they can be gay affirmative in their practice. It also demonstrates the expanse of multicultural counseling; cultural differences between counselor and client may result from sexual orientation as well as from racial or ethnic background.

Helping with the Coming Out Process

The process of gay self-identification (coming out), compared to other gay issues, has received the most attention in the counseling literature (Beane, 1982; Sophie, 1982; Groves & Ventura, 1983). Coming out often begins with anxiety and self-rebuke as attraction toward friends of the same sex can no longer be denied. With the pressure to conceal such feelings, adolescents especially remain isolated and lack the opportunity to discover the varied nature of the gay community. Often they retain the negative stereotypes they learned earlier about that community.

When a person who is coming out turns to a counselor for help, several precautions must be mentioned. Like other important parts of one's identity, sexual orientation deserves extended deliberation. Young people often have so little experience in sexual matters that they cannot establish a position on the matter. Thus, the counselor, especially the nongay counselor, needs to be gentle, accepting, nonhomophobic, and *informed.* Clients can directly benefit from some straightforward information; in some instances information regarding how to contact the gay community to learn more about it is sufficient.

A gentle, caring counselor, dealing with the issue of coming out, shows the same sensitivity as in other situations. This includes avoidance of vocabulary likely to raise anxiety, avoidance of premature labeling, recognition of the oppression of gay men and women, and the realization that the establishment of a sexual orientation is just one small part of each person's existence. For the nongay therapist, helping with the coming out process requires much self-reflection and reading and some contact with the gay community.

Understanding the Nature of Sexual Identity

Reiter (1989) describes the coming out process as one that begins with a diffuse sense of difference that is without a label. Ultimately, it will get a label followed by the individual self-labeling. When that occurs the person begins to develop a sexual identity as a lesbian, gay male, or bisexual. Research suggests that this identity will not become positive and self-affirming until years later, due to the socially mandated and enforced heterosexuality (McDonald, 1982; Riddle & Morin, 1977).

A gay or lesbian identity involves much more than erotic tendencies, interests, and attachments; it is only the heterosexual community that often sees it so restrictively (Elliott, 1985). In addition, it would be an error to think that a gay or lesbian identity develops only in later adulthood, and is not an issue with adolescent clients (Coleman & Remafedi, 1989). For that matter, one of the common biases of therapists is a lack of understanding regarding identity development and the importance of a positive one for overall psychological adjustment (Garnets, Hancock, Cochran, Goodchilds, & Peplau, 1991; Miranda & Storms, 1989). The development of a positive identity most often is achieved through contact with the gay/lesbian community where sexual orientation becomes normalized, and role models can help provide answers to a broad range of life issues (Cass, 1979).

Helping Gay Couples

Winkelpleck and Westfeld's (1982) review of the literature indicates that the majority of gay people eventually enter into a relationship with the thought of making it work and last. Yet many factors mitigate against that outcome. Besides dealing with prevailing prejudice in society, gay couples often find that they lack role models from whom to learn relationship coping skills. Gay people have no terminology (e.g., "engaged," "premarital," "marriage") to express the nature of their relationships.

The patterns of forming relationships vary. Groves and Ventura (1983) cite literature that shows that gay men enter committed relationships after establishing a gay identity; women, on the other hand, often enter into a committed relationship with another woman before accepting themselves as lesbians. While heterosexual partners have available many sources of assistance with such problems as sexual dysfunction, gay couples do not. Gerontological counseling for gay couples is another area not being addressed (Winkelpleck & Westfeld, 1982).

Alternate Lifestyles

It seems that the counseling profession has taken the position that the overall interests of individuals and society are served more effectively in a pluralistic culture that recognizes the validity of multiple lifestyles than in a culture that has a narrow view of acceptable lifestyles. Patterns of living or lifestyles can be divided into traditional ones, supported openly by the majority, and alternative ones, occurring less often and usually not endorsed by society at large. If marriage and children represent the core of a traditional lifestyle, some alternatives include communal living, single living, and child-free marriages. To any of these can be added such conditions as celibacy, living together without formal marriage, or simple nonmaterialistic living—lifestyles that have been difficult to understand and accept not only by society in general, but by some counselors as well.

It is important to recognize that many social institutions support and actively assist persons leading traditional lives, but few do the same for those adopting alternative patterns. It makes sense to see that counselors are needed to fill the gap.

To meet this need, counselors must accept any lifestyle in itself that is not better or worse than any other, except for those that violate the rights of others (e.g., survivalists). Yet a particular lifestyle, including a traditional one, can be better or worse for a given individual than another lifestyle. A person's potential may be advanced by access to an alternative lifestyle that provides personal meaning and fulfills social needs.

The Single, Never-Married Lifestyle

This lifestyle is an example of an alternative lifestyle that is often misunderstood in the helping professions. It is commonly held that married persons are better adjusted, happier, and more well-rounded. Single, never-married individuals are supposed to be lonely, conflicted, narcissistic, and possibly schizoid. In reality, single people are a diverse group, coming from a variety of backgrounds, and manifesting heterogeneous demographic characteristics (Stein, 1978). Johnston and Eklund (1984), in their careful review of the literature on the life-adjustment of never-marrieds and marrieds, show no clear support for the above stereotypes. While the research tends to support single males as less well-adjusted than married males, nonmarried females seem to be better adjusted than married females.

Counseling single individuals should have the same goal as all counseling; helping the client more fully develop within the context of a valid chosen lifestyle. Assumptions about the lifestyle by the counselors need to be examined carefully. Like all lifestyles, being single has its advantages and disadvantages (Edwards & Hoover, 1974).

Johnston and Eklund (1984) note that social support and satisfaction of intimacy needs are key issues in working with singles. In an adult society dominated by couples and extended family contacts, singles often need creative methods for ensuring contact with others. Such contacts need to be planned and regularly scheduled, especially if one is out of school or away from settings in which many other singles are present. Diversified friendship networks that allow for intimate sharing might even be something counselors actively promote as part of their service to singles.

Using single persons as an example of an alternate lifestyle makes the point that social roles are often a veneer under which lie universal strivings for meaning. Cross-cultural counselors are good at seeing those strivings.

STUDENT LEARNING EXERCISE

Read the following descriptions of situations and indicate whether you think the counselor responded effectively. Circle Y for yes or N for no.

1. The counselor working in a women's center specializes in such issues as marital/family relations, eating disorders, sexual abuse, and depression.   Y   N

2. A counselor generalizes characteristics of relationships of gay men to gay women.   Y   N

3. A counselor interprets a celibate lifestyle as indicative of sexual problems.   Y   N

4. A group of college counselors hold a discussion group with minority students to broaden the counselors' understanding of cross-cultural issues in hopes of being more help to the students.   Y   N

Old Age

The historic roots of counseling lie in the service of adolescents and young adults making key decisions about their lives. As the profession has grown, new populations have been added so that now clients of all ages are served. In the future, aged clients will likely make up a large part of a counselor's caseload. This will be true especially because of the increasing lifespan of people as a result of medical breakthroughs in the treatment of cancer and heart disease.

Counselor stereotypes of the aged are likely to be the most challenged stereotypes in the future. The Social Security Administration (Irelan, Motley, Schwab, Sherman, & Murray, 1976) found that major differences occurred every six years among groups of retirees seeking benefits. This evidence may well challenge the validity of most theories on old age. At a minimum, what we have considered the problems of the aged will likely apply to increasingly older individuals.

Glass and Grant (1983) attend specifically to some of the issues affecting persons beyond seventy-five years of age. While chronological age is often not a reliable index of the issues associated with the last stage of human development, the likelihood for such clients experiencing significant physical and social loss are greater than for younger clients. Institutionalization of this age group is often done inappropriately, without consideration of less restrictive but effective service (Subcommittee on Human Services of the Select Committee on Aging, 1980). Counselors can ally themselves with other professionals to increase their knowledge of gerontology (i.e., the study of the aging process) to further ensure the meaningfulness of this life stage. In part this may mean the support of the continued independence of clients in advanced age. This support can be operationalized in terms of adequate income, quality health care, social involvement, a variety of housing arrangements, and reinforcement of coping skills associated with younger groups.

Handicapping Conditions

With the implementation of the Rehabilitation Act of 1973 (P.L. 93–112) and the Education for All Handicapped Children Act of 1975 (P.L. 94–142), the legal mechanisms to more fully integrate disabled adults and children have been established. The counseling profession needs to continue its efforts to maximize the intents of these laws.

Nathanson (1979) reviews some of the literature on the attitudes of professionals who deal with individuals with disabilities or handicaps. Not immune to bias, counselors often unconsciously reveal their problems with such conditions. Nathanson identifies the following as common counselor violations of the integrity of disabled persons:

1. To perceive one handicapping condition as spreading to other aspects of the person so that the whole individual is evaluated by a single physical characteristic.
2. To falsely pity the individual by seeing him or her as fragile, hopeless, suffering, frustrated, and rejected.
3. To damage the individual's opportunity for accountability and self-reliance by too readily encouraging others to give the disabled person "a break."
4. To dampen the enthusiasm and optimism of the client by too quickly setting limits on action in hopes of avoiding failure.
5. To reject the client by being unable to cope with a client's physical deformity without displaying revulsion and disgust.
6. To overvalue the achievements of a client as "amazing" or "outstanding" with the implication that most disabled persons are inferior.

To effectively deal with disabled populations, counselors need considerable background knowledge and a variety of skills, in addition to an examination of their own attitudes. With an emphasis on the younger client, Hosie (1979) lists the following areas of emphasis in pre- and in-service training:

1. Federal and state legislation, guidelines, and local policies relating to programs and services for the handicapped.
2. Rights of handicapped children and their parents, and the skills necessary to advise parents and enable them to exercise their rights.
3. State guidelines for classification, diagnostic tools and their limitations, and the skills necessary to relate these to learning characteristics and the common elements of correction.

4. Informal assessment procedures and the skills necessary to relate these to the special learning strategies of the handicapped.
5. Growth and development process, characteristics, and the impediments of the handicapped, and the skills necessary to relate this knowledge to developmental learning tasks and strategies.
6. Characteristics and development of the learning disabled and the skills necessary to diagnose why the individual is failing tasks and to change methods and objectives when necessary.
7. Sensory impairments, speech disorders, and communication deficits, their effect on diagnosis and remediation, and the skills necessary to overcome or lessen their effect in learning and counseling settings.
8. Input, structure, and potential outcomes of the Individual Educational Program (IEP), and the skills necessary to consult and assist in the construction of such a program for the mainstreamed student.
9. Ability, learning rates, and modes of learning of the handicapped, and the skills necessary to utilize these factors in recommending educational placements and environments.
10. Attitudinal biases of teachers and others and the skills necessary to teach and consult with regular and special educators to produce a facilitative learning environment.
11. Learning disorders, the social and emotional behavior problems of handicapped students, and the skills necessary to instruct and consult with teachers, using behavior modification and management principles to enhance academic learning and social behavior.
12. Potential growth and development of the handicapped child; fears, concerns, and needs of the parents; and the skills necessary to consult, counsel, and teach parents regarding methods to facilitate their child's academic and social development.
13. Characteristics of the handicapped related to employment skills, training programs, and potential occupational and educational opportunities, and the skills necessary to assist the individual in career decision making and development.
14. Roles and skills of other personnel within and outside the institution and the skills necessary to refer them or work with them to enhance the learning and development of the handicapped individual.

Preparing Counselors to Work with Special Populations

Whether one is preparing to enter the counseling profession or is a veteran striving to develop further as a cross-cultural counselor, there are a number of general strategies that augment practice with diverse client populations. First and foremost is a journey inward for the examination of hidden prejudices and misconceptions. There exists a wealth of literature to bombard those beliefs.

Second, contact with members of minority groups and the development of close friendships can provide personal "interpreters" for various subcultural issues. Preparation programs can assist by working actively to recruit minority candidates. Friends can warmly challenge one another and provide access to broadly based experiences with numerous subcultures. This can help members of these interactions to further develop their own racial and ethnic identities, that research suggests helps one be more culturally sensitive.

Third, with greater experience as a transcultural person, comes the need to analyze and synthesize those adventures. Important questions need to be answered: How far do cultural differences go in actual work with clients? What about common human traits that transcend culture? Where are we in history regarding the rapprochement of cultures? In the future, how much further will we advance toward such things as androgeny, transnationalism, or are these goals inappropriate or unattainable? What is the formula for maintaining unique background and heritage and universal humanness in one's identity?

The ending has not been written for the counseling profession in its effort to serve special populations. However, the beginning, the ideal, and the direction are clear. Counselors as human beings *are* striving to achieve more fully what has begun.

Summary

This chapter explored the evolution of the counseling profession in its attempts to meet the needs of special client populations. Cross-cultural counseling was described. Barriers that can affect clients and counselors from different cultural backgrounds were examined.

Review Questions

1. Define cross-cultural counseling and contrast it to counseling lacking sensitivity to cultural issues.

2. List and briefly describe barriers to cross-cultural counseling.

3. Describe some of the issues related to gender that have influenced the counseling profession and other helping professions.

4. How does sexual orientation of the client influence the delivery of counseling profession?

5. What special sensitivities are important for counselors working with physically disabled clients?

6. How might a counselor-in-training prepare to meet cross-cultural issues?

References

Acosta, G. (1980). Self-described reasons for premature termination of psychotherapy by Mexican-American, Black American, and Anglo-American patients. *Psychological Reports, 47*(3), 435–443.

American Personnel and Guidance Association. (1974). Career guidance: Role and function of counseling and guidance personnel practitioners in career education. Washington, D.C.: American Personnel and Guidance Association.

American Psychological Association. (1975). Report of the task force on sex bias and sexrole stereotyping in psychotherapeutic practice. *American Psychologist, 30*(12), 1169–1175.

Arrendondo-Dowd, P. M., & Gonsalves, J. (1980). Preparing culturally effective counselors. *Personnel and Guidance Journal, 58*(10), 657–661.

Association for Counselor Education and Supervision. (1973). Standards for the preparation of counselors and other personnel services specialists. Washington, D.C.: Association for Counselor Education and Supervision.

Association for Counselor Education and Supervision. (1978). Position paper on counselor preparation for career development/career education. *Counselor Education and Supervision, 17*(3), 178–179.

Astin, H. S. (1984). The meaning of work in women's lives. *The Counseling Psychologist, 12*(4), 117–126.

Atkinson, D. R., Morten, G., & Sue, D. W. (1979). *Counseling American minorities: A cultural perspective.* Dubuque, IA: Wm. C. Brown.

Beane, J. (1981). "I'd rather be dead than gay": Counseling gay men who are coming out. *Personnel and Guidance Journal, 60*(4), 222–226.

Belenky, M., Clinchy, B., Goldberger, N., & Tarule, J. (1986). *Women's ways of knowing: The development of self, voice, and mind.* New York: Basic Books.

Belkin, G. S. (1984). *Introduction to counseling.* Dubuque, IA: Wm. C. Brown.

Bell, A. P., & Weinberg, M. S. (1978). *Homosexualities.* New York: Simon and Schuster.

Brodsky, A. M., & Hare-Mustin, R. T. (1980). *Women and psychotherapy: An assessment of research and practice.* New York: Guilford.

Broverman, D. M., Broverman, I., Clarkson, F. E., Rosenkrantz, P. S., & Vogel, S. (1970). Sex-role stereotypes and clinical judgments of mental health. *Journal of Clinical and Consulting Psychology, 34*(1), 1–7.

Brown, L. S. (1990). The meaning of a multicultural perspective for theory-building in feminist therapy. *Women and Therapy, 9*(1), 1–22.

Cass, V. C. (1979). Homosexual identity formation: A theoretical model. *Journal of Homosexuality, 4*(2), 219–235.

Coleman, I., & Remafedi, G. (1989). Gay, lesbian, and bisexual adolescents: A critical challenge to counselors. *Journal of Counseling and Development, 68*(1), 36–40.

Copeland, E. J. (1983). Cross-cultural counseling and psychotherapy: A historical perspective. *Personnel and Guidance Journal, 62*(1), 10–15.

DeVoe, D. (1990). Feminist and nonsexist counseling: Implications for the male counselor. *Journal of Counseling and Development, 69*(1), 33–36.

Dohrenwend, B. P., & Dohrenwend, B. S. (1974). Social and cultural influences on psychopathology. *Annual Review of Psychology, 25*, 417–452.

Donovan, J. (1992). *Feminist theory: The intellectual traditions of American feminism.* New York: Continuum Publishers.

Dupuy, P. J., Ritchie, M. H., & Cook, E. P. (1994). The inclusion of women's and gender issues in counselor education: A survey. *Counselor Education and Supervision, 33*(4), 238–248.

Edwards, M., & Hoover, E. (1974). *The challenge of being single.* Los Angeles: J. P. Tarcher.

Elliott, P. E. (1985). Theory and research on lesbian identity formation. *International Journal of Women's Studies, 8*(1), 64–71.

Enns, C. Z. (1992). Toward integrating feminist psychotherapy and feminist philosophy. *Professional Psychology: Research and Practice, 23*(6), 453–466.

Enns, C. Z. (1993). Feminist counseling and therapy. *The Counseling Psychologist, 21*(1), 3–87.

Enns, C. Z., & Hackett, G. (1990). Comparison of feminist and nonfeminist women's reactions to variants of nonsexist and feminist counseling. *Journal of Counseling Psychology, 37*(1), 33–40.

Fitzgerald, L. F., & Betz, N. E. (1984). Astin's model in theory and practice: A technical and philosophical critique. *The Counseling Psychologist, 12*(4), 135–138.

Fitzgerald, L. F., & Crites, J. O. (1980). Toward a career psychology of women: What do we know? What do we need to know? *Journal of Counseling Psychology, 27*(1), 44–62.

Fukuyama, M. A. (1990). Taking a universal approach to multicultural counseling. *Counselor Education and Supervision, 30*(1), 6–17.

Garnets, L., Hancock, K. A., Cochran, S. D., Goodchilds, J., & Peplau, L. A. (1991). Issues in psychotherapy with lesbians and gay men. *American Psychologist, 46*(9), 964–972.

Gilbert, L. A. O., Osipow, S. H. (1991). Feminist contributions to counseling psychology. *Psychology of Women Quarterly, 15*(4), 537–547.

Gilligan, C. (1982). *In a different voice.* Cambridge, MA: Harvard University Press.

Glass, J. C., & Grant, K. A. (1983). Counseling in the later years: A growing need. *Personnel and Guidance Journal, 62*(4), 210–213.

Gray, J. D. (1980). Counseling women who want both a profession and a family. *Personnel and Guidance Journal, 59*(1), 43–45.

Groves, P. A., & Ventura, L. A. (1983). The lesbian coming out process: Therapeutic considerations. *Personnel and Guidance Journal, 62*(3), 146–149.

Hare-Mustin, R. T. (1983). An appraisal of the relationship between women and psychotherapy: 80 years after the case of Dora. *American Psychologist, 38*(5), 593–601.

Herskovits, M. (1955). *Cultural anthropology.* New York: A. A. Knopf.

Hosie, T. W. (1979). Preparing counselors to meet the needs of the handicapped. *Personnel and Guidance Journal, 58*(4), 271–275.

Ibrahim, F. A. (1985). Effective cross-cultural counseling and psychotherapy: A framework. *The Counseling Psychologist, 13*(4), 625–638.

Irelan, L. M., Motley, D. K., Schwab, K., Sherman, S. R., & Murray, J. (1976). *Almost 65: Baseline data from the retirement history study.* Report no. 49/HEW, Publication No. (USA) 76-11806. U.S. Department of Health, Education and Welfare.

Johnston, M. V., & Eklund, S. J. (1984). Life-adjustment of the never-married: A review with implications for counseling. *Journal of Counseling and Development, 63*(4), 230–236.

Korchin, S. J. (1980). Clinical psychology and minority concerns. *American Psychologist, 35*(3), 262–269.

Lee, C. C. (1991). Cultural dynamics: Their importance in multicultural counseling. In C. C. Lee & B. L. Richardson, (eds.), *Multicultural issues in counseling: New approaches to diversity,* (pp. 11–17). Alexandria, VA: American Association for Counseling and Development.

Locke, D. C. (1986). Cross-cultural counseling issues. In A. J. Palmo & W. J. Weikel, (eds.), *Foundations of mental health counseling,* (pp. 119–137). Springfield, IL: Charles C. Thomas Publisher.

Locke, D. C. (1990). A not so provincial view of multicultural counseling. *Counselor Education and Supervision, 30*(1), 18–25.

Marecek, J., & Kravetz, D. (1977). Women and mental health: A review of feminist change efforts. *Psychiatry, 40,* 323–329.

Marsella, A. J., & Pedersen, P. B. (1981). *Cross-cultural counseling and psychotherapy.* New York: Pergamon Press.

McDonald, G. J. (1982). Individual differences in the coming out process for gay men: Implications for theoretical models. *Journal of Homosexuality, 8,* 221–227.

Miranda, J., & Storms, M. (1989). Psychological adjustment of lesbians and gay men. *Journal of Counseling and Development, 68*(1), 41–45.

Moore, H., & Strickler, C. (1980). The counseling profession's response to sex-biased counseling: An update. *Personnel and Guidance Journal, 59*(1), 84–87.

Nathanson, R. (1979). Counseling persons with disabilities: Are the feelings, thoughts, and behaviors of helping professionals helpful? *Personnel and Guidance Journal, 58*(4), 233–237.

O'Malley, K. M., & Richardson, S. (1985). Sex bias in counseling: Have things changed? *Journal of Counseling and Development, 63*(5), 294–299.

Ottavi, T. M., Pope-Davis, D. B., & Dings, J. G. (1994). Relationship between white racial identity attitudes and self-reported multicultural counseling competencies. *Journal of Counseling Psychology, 41*(2), 149–154.

Paradis, F. E. (1981). Themes in the training of culturally effective psychotherapists. *Counselor Education and Supervision, 21*(2), 136–151.

Pedersen, P. (1988). *Handbook for developing multicultural awareness.* Alexandria, VA: American Association for Counseling and Development.

Ponterotto, J. G. (1988). Racial consciousness development among white counselor trainees: A stage model. *Journal of Multicultural Counseling and Development, 12*(2), 146–156.

Poole, M. E., Langan-Fox, J., Ciavarella, M., & Omodei, M. (1991). A contextualist model of professional attainment: Results of a longitudinal study of career paths of men and women. *The Counseling Psychologist, 19*(4), 603–624.

Rawlings, E. I., & Carter, D. K. (1977). Feminist and nonsexist psychotherapy. In E. I. Rawlings & D. K. Carter, (eds.), *Psychotherapy for women,* (pp. 49–76). Springfield, IL: Charles C. Thomas.

Raynes, A., & Warren, G. (1969). Some distinguishing features of patients failing to attend a psychiatric clinic after referred. *American Journal of Orthopsychiatry, 41*(4), 581–588.

Reiter, L. (1989). Sexual orientation, sexual identity, and the question of choice. *Clinical Social Work Journal, 17*(2), 138–150.

Riddle, D. I., & Morin, S. Removing the stigma: Data from individuals. *APA Monitor,* (November, 1977), p. 16, 28.

Ridley, C., Mendoza, D. W., & Kanitz, B. E. (1994a). Multicultural training: Reexamination, operationalization, and integration. *The Counseling Psychologist, 22*(2), 227–289.

Ridley, C. R., Mendoza, D. W., Kanitz, B. E., Angermeier, L., & Zenk, R. (1994b). Cultural sensitivity in multicultural counseling: A perceptual schema model. *Journal of Counseling Psychology, 41*(2), 125–136.

Rosewater, L. B., & Walker, L. E. (1985). *Handbook of feminist therapy: Women's issues in psychotherapy.* New York: Springer.

Smith, M. L. (1980). Sex bias in counseling and psychotherapy. *Psychological Bulletin, 87*(3), 492–507.

Sophie, J. (1982). Counseling lesbians. *Personnel and Guidance Journal, 60*(6), 341–345.

Stein, P. J. (1978). The life-styles and life choices of the never-married. *Marriage and Family Review, 1*(1), 1–11.

Subcommittee on Human Services of the Select Committee on Aging, U.S. House of Representatives, 96th Congress, (1980). *Future directions for aging policy: A human services model.* Washington, D.C.: U.S. Government Printing Office.

Sue, D. W. (1981). *Counseling the culturally different: Theory and practice.* New York: John Wiley and Sons.

Sue, D. W. (1990). Culture-specific strategies in counseling: A conceptual framework. *Professional psychology: Research and practice, 21*(6), 424–433.

Sue, D. W., & Sue, D. (1990). *Counseling the culturally different,* (2nd ed.). New York: John Wiley and Sons.

Sue, S. (1977). Community mental health services to minority groups. *American Psychologist, 32,* 583–592.

Vontress, C. E. (1988). An existential approach to cross-cultural counseling. *Journal of Multicultural Counseling and Development, 16*(1), 73–83.

Weinberg, G. (1973). *Society and the healthy homosexual.* Garden City, NY: Doubleday/Anchor.

Whitley, B. E. (1979). Sex roles and psychotherapy: A current appraisal. *Psychological Bulletin, 86*(4), 1309–1321.

Winkelpleck, J. M., & Westfeld, J. S. (1982). Counseling considerations with gay couples. *Personnel and Guidance Journal, 60*(7), 294–296.

Worell, J. (1980). New directions in counseling women. *Personnel and Guidance Journal, 58*(7), 477–484.

Yau, T. Y., Sue, D., & Hayden, D. (1992). Counseling style preference of international students. *Journal of Counseling Psychology, 39*(1), 100–104.

10

Consultation

Goals of the Chapter

The primary aims of this chapter are to introduce the major models of consultation and to illustrate how these might be employed.

Chapter Preview

- Three major models of consultation will be presented: mental health, behavioral, and organizational.
- The stages of consultation will be reviewed along with salient research findings.
- Consultation will be contrasted with other interventions employed by counselors in terms of its efficiency, effectiveness, and acceptability.

Introduction

When used colloquially, "consultation" is often seen as synonymous with "advice giving." People regularly consult with their banker, stock broker, physician, and so forth. The type of process envisioned in these consultations, which involves relying on an expert, is an accepted model of consultation among human services workers. However, consultation has taken on a much broader meaning for most. Perhaps the best way to proceed with defining consultation is not to describe what it is, but rather to tell what it is not.

First, consultation and supervision are not the same (Brown, Pryzwansky, & Schulte, 1995; Caplan, 1970). Supervision is a process that involves a superordinate-subordinate relationship in which one party, the supervisor, has an evaluative role. Consultants, however, usually attempt to develop collegial relationships and have no evaluative role (Brown et al., 1995; Caplan, 1970). Consultation and supervision do generally converge on one point: the recipients of the processes, the consultee and the supervisee, are expected to gain knowledge and skills as a result of their interaction with the consultant and supervisor, respectively.

One process that is often confused with consulting is training. It is not uncommon to hear counselors indicate that they have entered into a consulting relationship when in fact the service they are going to deliver involves a seminar or workshop. Training is a direct service and "is a process of imparting, in a planned, systematic way, a specified body of information" (Conoley & Conoley, 1992, p. 4). Consultation diverges from training in that it is an indirect service since the focus of the consultation (the client) is not present when the consultant and consultee meet. In addition, trainers often rely on one-way communication, are generally in positions of authority, and have set agendas. None of these conditions apply to consultation. It should be noted that while consultation and training are not analogous, it is not uncommon for consultants to employ training as an adjunct to consultation (Brown et al., 1995).

Consultation and organizational development (OD) are also frequently confused. "Organizational development" is a term used to depict a variety of services aimed at improving the functioning of organizations, including training (teaching), applied research and evaluation, and consultation (Lippitt & Lippitt, 1986). Organizational development is an umbrella under which a variety of developmental processes may be placed and in which counselors will be involved.

Perhaps the helping process that diverges most sharply from consultation is counseling. Consultation is an indirect service in that its aim is to help the consultee develop the skills needed to assist a client. Counseling is a direct service to clients. The aim of counseling is to assist clients with psychological difficulties that have already manifested themselves to some degree. Consultants refrain from dealing with the psychological difficulties of consultees, although they may have as one of their objectives helping consultees develop strategies to assist clients with psychological problems. When counseling and consultation are aimed at ameliorating an existing psychological difficulty, they are secondary or tertiary mental health prevention approaches. Secondary prevention efforts are aimed at eliminating problems before they have serious consequences, and tertiary prevention efforts have as their objectives the reduction of debilitating psychological problems, such as alcoholism, to reduce their overall impact. While consultation can be used as a secondary or tertiary mental health intervention, it can also be used as a primary prevention strategy, that is, one aimed at preventing the onset of mental health problems (Brown et al., 1995).

Consultation Defined

What then is consultation? It is first and foremost a problem-solving process with a twofold aim: (1) to help consultees acquire the knowledge and skills needed to solve a problem of concern to them, and (2) to help consultees implement what they have learned to assist a third party, the client. The client may be an individual (a child), a group, a family, an organization, a business, or an entire community (Lippitt & Lippitt, 1986).

The consulting relationship, which is often referred to as "triadic" because of the focus of the consultant and consultee on the client, is an egalitarian one, and as a result, consultation must be viewed as a totally voluntary process (Gallessich, 1982; Reynolds, Gutkin, Elliot, & Witt, 1984). In addition, effective consulting relationships are characterized by a collaborative spirit in which the consultant and consultee often share the responsibility for identifying the problem at hand, generating solutions to the problem, and implementing those solutions (Brown et al., 1995; Randolph, 1985). It should be pointed out that some consultants, most notably Caplan (1970), disagree with the idea that the consultant should be involved in implementing the intervention strategy. However, the rationale for this position is that the limited empirical data available on this issue suggest that consultees prefer this approach (Babcock & Pryzwansky, 1983).

Caplan's (1970) definition of consultation indicates that it occurs between two professionals (e.g., a counselor and a social worker), as opposed to between a professional and a layperson (e.g., a counselor and a parent). A number of authorities (Lippitt & Lippitt, 1986; Randolph, 1985) have taken issue with this assertion and have posited that consultation can occur between a consultant and either a professional or a layperson. Whether consultation occurs between a professional or a layperson, its purpose is to solve a "work problem" being experienced by the consultee. A teacher might be concerned about a misbehaving child, or a plant manager might focus on the productivity of his or her operation. Parents might seek consultation regarding an adolescent who is a drug abuser, and the head of a neighborhood action group might ask a consultant to assist the group to become more influential in the city's problem-solving strategies (Heller, 1985; Snapp & Davidson, 1982).

Consultants can operate effectively from either outside (external) or inside (internal) the agency or organization employing the consultee (Lippitt & Lippitt, 1986). Tradition has held that effective consultants can only operate from an external frame of reference (Caplan, 1970; Gallessich, 1982). However, during the past ten years this position has given way to one that recognizes that the locus of the consultant, while influencing such factors as consultant status, knowledge of the consulting setting, ability to relate to individuals in authority positions, and a number of others, may not be the major factor in consultants' ability to function (Brown et al., 1995).

Finally, consultation moves through a number of rather well-defined stages, although not necessarily in lockstep order. These stages are relationship, problem identification, goal setting, strategy development and implementation, and evaluation.

STUDENT LEARNING EXERCISE

Read the following descriptions of incidences and indicate whether what the counselor is doing is actually consultation or not. Circle Y for yes or N for no.

1. A mental health counselor is asked by a halfway house for alcoholics to assist in its staff development program by providing assertation training for all house parents.   Y   N

2. A school counselor helps a teacher develop an achievement motivation program for underachieving mathematics students.   Y   N

3. A college counselor works with a group of residence assistants to help them develop a study skills program for the students in their respective residences.   Y   N

4. A mental health counselor routinely assists the mental health workers in his agency to assess the severity of eating disorders and to design appropriate treatment or referral programs.   Y   N

The Consulting Process—General Considerations

In the preceding section, an overview of consultation was presented along with a discussion of three major models of consultation. In the models sections, some insight was provided regarding the consulting process that was defined at the outset as being roughly analogous to problem solving. In this section, more attention will be accorded the process. The intent here is to provide a generic overview of the steps in consultation and some of the significant empirical findings regarding them.

The Consulting Relationship

The nature and quality of the consultation relationship are as important in consultation as they are in counseling and, not surprisingly, the development of this relationship requires many of the same types of skills needed in other helping relationships such as empathy and warmth.

Similarly, structuring the consulting relationship is viewed as essential to effective consultation (Brown et al., 1995). This involves establishing role relationships, agreeing that problem solving is important, making a commitment to spend the time needed to pursue problem resolution, and planning for termination. Of these aspects of structuring, two probably require further elaboration: role relationships and planning for termination.

In the definition set forth in the early stages of this chapter, the consulting relationship was characterized as collaborative, which in this context is translated literally as assuming a joint responsibility for each phase of the consultation. Research has supported this idea (Babcock & Pryzwansky, 1983). One barrier to this is that consultees often ascribe expertise to the consultant, thus tilting the power relationship to the consultant. If this happens the consultee may be reluctant to take an active part because he or she is intimidated by the consultant's knowledge or may feel coerced into accepting the consultant's suggestions because of the so-called expertise of the consultant. This can lead to lack of participation on the part of the consultee, and thus lack of ownership of the process by the consultee. Not only must consultants "structure in" egalitarianism, they must practice it as the relationship evolves (Brown et al., 1995).

It is also important that, at the outset, the consultant and consultee plan for termination. The goal of consultation is to produce a consultee who can function independently of the consultant. Establishing the expectation that termination will occur at the point the presenting problem has been resolved can assist in the attainment of this goal.

Problem Identification

Problem identification depends on the ability of the consultant and consultee to generate sufficient information about the client, the consultee's interaction with the client, and the consultee to provide an adequate database for assessment. A facilitative relationship will enhance this process. So will the ability of the consultant to introduce consulting leads that will elicit the needed information. Bergan and Kratochwill (1990) suggest that these leads or elicitors, as they term them, must be focused on seven categories. These are defined as follows:

1. *Background-environment:* historical variables that might influence the current situation.
2. *Behavior-setting:* the immediate environment in which the problematic behavior occurs.
3. *Behavior:* precise description of the client's problematic behavior.
4. *Observational data:* reports of systematic observation of the client.
5. *Client characteristics:* personality variables, intelligence, physical impairments, and so on.
6. *Plans:* reports of what the consultee has tried.
7. *Other:* material not falling into the foregoing categories.

Early research by Bergan and Tombari (1976) found that consultants who were either inefficient or ineffective in identifying the client's problem were unable to make much progress in consultation. Erchul & Chewning (1990) also found that the consultant's verbalizations can influence the manner in which consultees conceptualize problems and whether they expect to solve them. It appears that Bergan's beliefs about the importance of eliciting information from the consultee have some validity.

Goal Setting

Once the problem has been defined, the goals of consultation must be established. Unlike the counseling process, where the only concern is the client's objectives, in consultation, goals need to be established for both the consultee and the client. Client goals are similar to those established for counseling clients; that is, they involve facilitating the development of coping cognitions and behaviors that will reduce stress and enhance overall adjustment. Consultee goals are analogous in many ways to those established by teachers since they involve the acquisition of skills and attitudes that will enable the consultee to deal with similar problems without the consultant in the future.

The precision of the goals of consultation is to a large extent dependent on the consultant and consultee. However, most consultants opt for specific objectives since this eases the evaluation process.

Strategy Selection/Implementation

Once goals are established, the consultant and consultee must select a strategy to achieve these goals. Strategies used depend on a number of factors, including the biases of the consultant and consultee, the setting in which the consultation is occurring, and the wishes of the client (Bergan & Kratochwill, 1990; Brown et al., 1995). This last variable in strategy selection, the wishes of the client, may come as a bit of a surprise since consultation has been characterized as an indirect process. It should be noted, however, that it is indirect only insofar as the consultant is concerned. Consultees, whether they be parents, teachers, psychologists, or managers, must ultimately become directly involved with the client or client groups. Therefore, since good "therapeutic" practice requires involving clients in designing their own treatment, this rule applies in consultation as well.

As was shown earlier, Caplan (1970) recommended that consultants not become involved in the implementation process. Certainly there are times when, even in a collaborative approach, involvement in strategy implementation will not be necessary. However, the educational goals, that is, the goals for the consultee, can probably be better attained through collaborative efforts, although there is limited empirical support for this.

The techniques utilized to attain consultee goals are fairly standard, regardless of the approach to consultation utilized. Modeling, role playing, bibliotherapy, and feedback seem to be effective. Techniques to be avoided as much as possible are those that will foster a dependency relationship, such as too much advice giving or assuming the consultee's responsibility for action when she is prepared to take action herself.

Evaluation

The consultant is a counselor/scientist at work. Specific problems are identified and solutions are advanced. Good science requires that the outcomes be systematically evaluated. Brown and coworkers (1987) suggest that a number of evaluation designs can be employed in the evaluation of consultation. Some of these will be discussed later in this book.

Termination

Termination occurs under a variety of circumstances, the most obvious of which is when goals have been attained. However, termination may also occur when it is obvious that the consultee does not have the necessary commitment, when the consultant or consultee cannot agree on goals for the client, and when the consultee wants assistance with an unethical/illegal act (e.g., establishing personnel procedures that will discriminate against a particular group).

The consulting process can be laid out in a series of neat steps, but in reality it rarely follows them precisely. It is certainly possible that a consultant and consultee could be assessing one problem while intervening on another. It is also likely that, once having moved into assessment, goal setting, or strategy implementation, factors such as resistance or interpersonal conflict may crystallize a need to return to relationship building.

Models of Consultation

Earlier in this book an overview of a number of major counseling theories was presented. This section is analogous to that presentation. Because the theoretical formulations regarding consultation are in a relatively early stage, the term "model" has been selected to describe the formulations that guide consultants rather than the term "theory" because of the connotations of the terms. One author, Gallessich (1985), has decried the current state of theory building in consultation and asserted that the lack of adequate models may lead to poor consultation practice. Admittedly, Gallessich's point about consultation models has some validity, particularly as it relates to the availability of a single model that can be generalized to all situations and to the clarity of the formulations. However, existing models, if used judiciously, can provide adequate guidelines for practice.

Overviews of the three major models of consultation—mental health, behavioral, and organizational development consultation—will be presented in this section. Of these, mental health consultation (Caplan, 1970) has probably had the greatest impact on the consultation of human services professionals.

Mental Health Consultation

Following World War II, Gerald Caplan worked in a child guidance center that had responsibility for providing mental health services to 16,000 children that had fled to Israel in the aftermath of the Holocaust. To complicate matters, the children were housed in a number of facilities covering a wide geographic area. Once a referral was made, members of the team of psychiatrists, social workers, and psychologists would travel to one of these cities to deliver the service. It soon became obvious that traditional diagnostic and therapeutic services were impossible, and thus the mental health workers began to "counsel" the professionals such as social workers about ways to manage the referrals rather than provide direct services themselves. Mental health consultation was born (Caplan, 1970; Caplan & Caplan, 1993).

As indicated earlier in this chapter, Caplan (1970) defines consultation as an interaction between two professionals for the purpose of solving a work problem being encountered by the consultee. Caplan maintained that the relationship between the consultee and consultant must be coordinate (egalitarian) in nature, but structured so that the consultant would not get involved in implementing the solution to the problem derived in consultation. Finally, Caplan asserted that, in order to be effective, consultants should come from outside the employing agency of the consultee.

Caplan's (1970) general model actually includes four types of consultation. The type selected depends on whether consultees have concern with a particular problem, are experiencing administrative difficulty, need information in their area of specialization, or need to improve their problem-solving skills. These four approaches are discussed further below.

Client-Centered Case Consultation

The primary objective of this form of consultation is to develop a plan to deal with a particular client or group of clients. In this mode, the consultants are very much in the expert role. They diagnose the nature of the client's problem and prescribe a treatment. In some instances, the treatment is to be carried out by the consultee, in others a referral will be made for the treatment. While Caplan generally views consultee skill development as an important aspect of consultation, consultee skill development is of secondary nature in client-centered case consultation. A part of the consultation process will necessarily focus on the skills of the consultee, since consultants must devise a treatment plan, and it is likely that the consultee will carry out the plan. But since much of the consultant's time is spent with the client performing diagnostic duties, consultees may benefit little from the process.

The typical tools used in the assessment of the client's problems are clinical interviews with the client, psychological and educational tests, and verbal reports from the consultee. The consultant also seeks to understand the work setting of the consultee in order to discern whether it is supportive of the work that needs to be conducted on the client. Once the diagnosis is completed and recommendations arrived at, this information is provided to the consultee, often in written form. Consultants may conduct information-giving sessions with consultees to make certain that they completely understand the recommendations that have been made (Caplan, 1970; Caplan & Caplan, 1993).

Consultee-Centered Case Consultation

Unlike client-centered case consultation, the primary goal of this form of consultation is the amelioration of the weaknesses of the consultees that contribute to their inability to deal with particular cases (Caplan, 1970). Caplan provides four diagnostic categories:

1. Lack of knowledge of psychological or social factors that are contributing to the problem or information that might contribute to the resolution of the concern.

2. Lack of skill. In this situation, the consultee seems to understand the psychological or social factors contributing to the problem, but does not possess the skill to implement a solution.
3. Lack of confidence. In this case the consultee does not feel he or she can adequately deal with a problem even though he or she has the knowledge base and skills to do so.
4. Lack of objectivity. Here the consultee's perceptions do not correspond with objective indicators regarding the client's problem.

Assessment in consultee-centered case consultation requires that the consultant ask the consultee to furnish descriptions of the difficulty that he or she is experiencing. When lack of objectivity appears to be the consultee's problem, the consultant may ask for repeated descriptions in order to make sure that the individual does in fact lack objectivity.

Lack of knowledge and skills deficits may be handled rather straightforwardly by supplying the knowledge needed or by developing the skills required to deal with the client. However, Caplan (1970) believes that when a number of knowledge and/or skills deficits are encountered within an organization, a better approach to dealing with them is program-centered consultation. A school counselor who encounters a number of teachers with classroom management deficits might want to become involved in program-centered consultation with the school's principal in order to begin an in-service offering that would resolve the difficulties rather than deal with each teacher individually.

Caplan (1970) does not believe that consultants should become overly involved in providing support to the consultee who lacks self-confidence. Rather he suggests that the consultant attempt to identify sources of support within the organization and link the consultee to them. For example, a mental health counselor might be linked to a marriage and family therapist who would assume responsibility for helping the counselor gain confidence in the area of family therapy.

Caplan (1970) believes that there are five underlying causes of lack of objectivity: (1) personal involvement, (2) identification, (3) transference, (4) characterological distortion, and (5) theme interference. A counselor who, out of concern for a child, takes that child into his or her home has become personally involved. Caplan suggests that the consultant's role in dealing with this concern is to encourage the individual who has become personally involved to resume her or his professional role. This can be done by simply reviewing the importance of maintaining one's personal role or by providing a model of how a professional person would react in this situation.

Identification with the client may occur when the consultee has had a similar life experience to that of the client. For example, a manager who is unable to reprimand an alcoholic employee because he himself once had a drinking problem has an identification problem. Caplan (1970) again recommends that the consultant model appropriate objective behavior for the consultee.

Transference results from unresolved personality conflicts and usually is characterized by inaccurate perceptions of the client. A consultee who has an unresolved conflict with her mother may become hostile toward a secretary in her office who is having a similar problem even though that secretary is functioning effectively. Consultants should ask consultees to observe the secretary more closely, perhaps even suggesting that the consultee collect objective data about the secretary's performance. The consultant may also offer objective observations of the secretary's performance.

Characterological disorders are rather severe personality disturbances. While it is outside the consultant's role to deal with the disorder itself, Caplan (1970) believes that consultants can offer assistance by providing a model of objectivity. A mental health counselor, consulting with the supervisor of a group care home for emotionally disturbed adolescents, might discover that the consultee lacks the ability to establish meaningful relationships. The consultant in this case might assist the consultee in dealing with his or her anxiety in this area and model an effective means of relating to adolescents.

Theme interference is one of the most frequently occurring contributors to lack of objectivity, and Caplan (1970) believes it is fairly normal. Theme interference, like some of the other concerns mentioned, stems from an unresolved personality conflict and manifests itself in the form of a syllogism characterized by a faulty premise and an illogical conclusion. For example, a teacher might believe that all persons who make low grades will end up as failures in life. Thus, poor grades (A) always lead to failure in life (B). This syllogism is impenetrable by logic since some unresolved conflict provides the "logic" for it. Persons who experience theme interference may try a number of ill-conceived solutions to the problem they perceive and may report these "extensive" efforts to the consultant.

Two solutions to theme interference are possible: unlinking the faulty premise from the conclusion and theme interference reduction. Unlinking occurs when the consultant persuades the client that A and B are not necessarily related in the particular case (i.e., poor grades do not dictate failure in life). Caplan believes that unlinking is a gross error because it leaves the theme intact. He suggests that the consultant reduce the theme as follows.

The first technique for reducing theme interference is to examine case details in detail and consider all the possible outcomes and causes of the problem as presented. Thus, a consultant could help a teacher understand that a variety of correctable factors may be the cause of the problem as well as the possibility that outcomes other than failure are possible. Consultants may also tell parables based on their own experiences that contradict the inevitable outcome seen by the teacher. For example, to reduce theme interference in our hypothetical teacher, the consultant might tell of a situation in which a teacher predicted a gloomy outcome for a poor student in class. Later the student became motivated, did well, and was successful.

The consultant may also communicate to the consultee that his or her expectations regarding the client are unrealistic. Caplan (1970; 1993) cautions that this should not be done in a confrontive manner. Finally, Caplan notes that consultee's themes may manifest themselves in the consulting relationship. A police officer consultee—one who is absolutely certain that all juvenile delinquents will end up as convicted criminals—may have difficulty with authority. (A = People who defy authority by breaking the law; B = criminals incarcerated for their crimes.) The consultee might manifest this theme by taking issue with suggestions made by the consultant. The consultant should not engage in disputes with the consultee, that is, should not disprove the "logic" and utilize the interpersonal relationship as a means of theme reduction.

Program-Centered Administrative Consultation

This form of consultation is most analogous to client-centered case consultation in that the consultant's role is to assess a current situation, diagnose the problem, and make recommendations regarding either the remediation of an existing problem or the initiation of a new one. It is characterized as program-centered administrative consultation because the "client" is a mental health program and the consultee is an administrator of that program.

During the problem assessment phase of program-centered administrative consultation, the consultant must be able to examine the characteristics of an organization (such as the counseling center of a community agency in which the program functions or is to function); make judgments about the human, fiscal, and physical resources available to support the program, and assess the managerial ability of the person or persons responsible for the program under consideration. As Caplan (1970; 1993) notes, this form of consultation requires far more than the usual clinical skills possessed by most mental health professionals. Caplan also notes that a number of specific factors must be examined during the assessment stage. Among these are the history of the organization, its goals, the support of the top administrator for the change being considered, as well as the aforementioned resources and managerial expertise.

Once initial judgments are made, it is recommended that the consultant seek staff input regarding them because successful outcomes are not likely to result unless individuals in the organization have some personal investment in the program. These judgments are then used to modify the tentative plan and a report is filed. As is customary in Caplan's model, the consultant does not participate in the implementation of the program.

Consultee-Centered Administrative Consultation

Like its counterpart, consultee-centered case consultation, the goal of this approach to consultation is to improve the functioning of a member or members of the administrative team. Consultee-centered administrative consultation may develop as a result of other types of consultation. However, as Caplan (1970; 1993) specifies, it differs in many ways from any of the foregoing models.

During the initial or entry phase of consultee-centered administrative consultation, the consultant needs to seek sanctions from the chief administrator and then work to understand the function of the organization and the consultee(s). Ultimately, consultations may occur with one or more members of the administrative team, but it must be made clear that consultation is a voluntary process. Thus, the consultant works to uncover difficulties that are precluding the organization from delivering mental health services, brings these to the attention of the administrators, and hopes that they will volunteer for consultation. This process is necessarily a long-term one.

During the assessment phase, the consultant examines the personalities of the key administrators, the manner in which subgroups within the organization function internally, and how they relate to other groups within the organization. In addition, the consultant looks at vital organizational processes such as communication, leadership, decision making, role assignments, and organizational patterns in order to identify problems in organizational functioning.

In keeping with the overall model of mental health consultation, the consultant intervenes with individuals either to increase their effectiveness or to develop an awareness of organizational difficulties in vital areas of functioning. The consultant does not design organizational interventions and does not participate in the implementation of interventions designed by the consultee.

STUDENT LEARNING EXERCISE

The following is a brief description of a mental health agency that is functioning below its potential. On the basis of the description, decide which of the mental health consultation approaches would be most acceptable to Caplan himself.

1. An external consultant has been called in because case loads are so heavy the staff cannot provide individual therapy. As a result, the waiting list is very long, and many people in the community are questioning the management of the agency. The director has proposed alternative approaches to counseling (e.g., group counseling) a number of times without result. Preliminary interviews with the staff reveal that the director is viewed as a "political hack." Which approach should be used in light of the fact that the director has three years left on his contract?

2. Several counselors have had difficulties with cases involving PCP abuse. They have treated the cases in the same manner as other substance abuse cases, but without result. Which of Caplan's approaches fits the situation best?

3. It is clear that a teacher who is constantly referring poor children to the school counselor for help has a real "hang-up" when it comes to children who are not middle class.

4. A wave of referrals dealing with stepfamilies engulfs a family counseling agency. Results of the contacts meet with mixed results at best.

Behavioral Consultation

Three behaviorally oriented models of consultation have surfaced to date. Bergan (1977) articulated a model that relies primarily on operant learning theory, a model that was extended to some degree by Bergan & Kratochwill (1990). Keller (1981) set forth a behavioral-eclectic model that draws on a number of learning theories for its conceptualization, and Brown and Schulte (1987) formulated a cognitive-behavioral model. While these models differ significantly in a variety of ways, they share the behavioral tradition of emphasis on empirical support for their propositions and allegiance to a strict problem-solving model based on the scientific method.

Background

Behavioral consultation is a relatively new phenomenon that grew out of the behavior modification movement of the 1960s and early 1970s. However, a growing realization that personal variables such as cognitive and environmental factors beyond those related to immediate rewards and punishers caused most behaviorists to rethink their formulations. Bergan (1977) can justifiably be viewed as one of the genuine innovators in this area, in that he focused on the importance of the consultant-consultee relationship as a key variable in the consultation process. His view, which is somewhat controversial (Gallessich, 1982), is that the consultant essentially controls the consulting process through verbal processes such as eliciting key information through careful consulting leads and thoughtful input regarding psychological processes. Bergan does maintain that consultants should apprise the consultee of their intentions and that consultation must be a purely voluntary process.

More recently, Brown and Schulte have set forth a social learning model (SLM) of consultation based on the thinking of Albert Bandura (1977). Bandura's social learning theory emphasizes that the environment, cognitions, and behaviors are all key variables in the functioning of human beings and has increasingly emphasized the importance of self-efficacy, or the confidence that one can perform in a specific situation (e.g., working calculus problems).

Relationship

Brown and Schulte (1987) depart from the behavioral tradition, particularly that of Bergan (1977), in one significant way: the nature of the consulting relationship. They assert that the bases for the consulting relationship are the traditional facilitative conditions of empathy, warmth, and genuineness. Their point of view is simply that the presence of these conditions facilitates the free flow of ideas in consultation in much the same way that they do in counseling or therapy.

Assessment

Assessment is a twofold process in the SLM. One aspect focuses on assessing client variables, including behavioral deficits, cognitions that relate to the problem, and environmental factors that may facilitate or impede the functioning of the client. When consulting with the parents of an alcohol abusing adolescent, the consultant might wish to know the rate, incidence, and circumstances under which alcohol is consumed (when, where, with whom, and how much), the adolescent's thoughts regarding the importance of drinking and confidence that he or she can stop (self-efficacy), and the environmental variables that may contribute to or act to maintain the drinking (e.g., alcoholic intake of parents, peers, etc.). The SLM consultant would also want to examine other personal variables such as health and alcohol dependency.

Similarly, the second aspect of the assessment focuses on the behavior, environmental variables, and cognitions of the consultee. What behaviors are now employed to deal with the problematic adolescent? How confident are the parents that they can cope with the problem? What environmental variables impinge on them that will influence their own functioning? Are there physiological variables (e.g., alcohol dependency) that preclude altering certain home conditions.

Goal Setting

Goal setting may focus on one or more of the variables identified as contributing to the problem. The goal for the client is, of course, to reduce the problematic behavior by intervening in what appears to be the dominant factor in the problem. Similarly, the goal for the consultee is to develop the behavioral and cognitive behaviors needed to cope with the problem being presented by the client.

Strategy Selection and Implementation

In the SLM, the client is constantly apprised of the consultation conversation by the consultee. Thus, when the problem has been identified and strategies for correcting the client's problem are being selected, input is solicited from the client. In the final analysis, the selection and implementation of the intervention is a collaborative effort. However, the SLM consultant insists that the consultee handle as much of the intervention as his or her cognitive and behavioral repertoire permit, since successful performances are the key to building self-efficacy or the confidence that one can function in a specific area (Bandura, 1977).

Generally speaking, interventions are selected from among the following techniques (Brown & Schulte, 1987).

1. Participant modeling—Guided practice includes coaching, rehearsal, and feedback.
2. Symbolic modeling—Desired behavior presented via audiovisual devices or through bibliotherapy.
3. Covert modeling—Involves imagining desired behaviors.
4. Cognitive modeling—Talking through desired cognitions by the consultant.
5. Cognitive restructuring—Involves identifying thought patterns surrounding problematic behaviors, including antecedents, performance related thoughts,

and those that follow problem behavior, and then teaching new thoughts, often using cognitive modeling procedures.

6. Self-monitoring—Having an individual monitor one problematic behavior in order either to identify its dimensions *or* to determine progress toward goals.

7. Desensitization—Involves a family of procedures designed to eliminate phobic behavior, including approaches using imagery and *in vivo* (in the real situation) techniques.

STUDENT LEARNING EXERCISE

Complete the following quiz relating to Bergan's behavioral model and the SLM model outlined above. Circle T for true and F for false.

1. Bergan emphasizes a traditional or egalitarian consulting relationship in his model while the SLM approach does not.   T   F

2. Objective data are important in both behavioral models outlined, but Bergan emphasizes observational data more.   T   F

3. The client is involved in the intervention effort in both models (Bergan and SLM).   T   F

4. Cognition is a more important variable in the SLM model than in Bergan's behavioral model.   T   F

5. Neither approach emphasizes affect in the counseling relationship.   T   F

Organizational Consultation

Organizational consultation models are those most analogous to Caplan's consultee-centered administrative consultation, discussed earlier. However, as we shall see, organizational consultation grew out of a different background and is conceptually different from mental health consultation approaches to organizational change. The organizational development consultation model discussed here is based partly on the work of Huse (1980), Beer (1980), Lippitt & Lippitt (1986), and Morasky (1982).

Background

Organizational development consultation has a number of historical antecedents, including scientific management, the field theory of Kurt Lewin, and the humanism of Carl Rogers (Stryker, 1982). However, there can be little doubt that systems theory is having great impact on current thinking in this area. Systems theory holds that organizations are open systems that receive products from the environment (inputs), transform them as a result of technology and human processes (throughput), and export them back to the environment (output) (Katz & Kahn, 1978). Organizational development consultants hold that the human processes are most vital to the efficiency and effectiveness of the organization.

Certain key principles must be considered when examining organizations (open systems). These include the following:

1. There is a tendency for organizations to differentiate functions, thus creating specialization in roles.
2. All parts of the organization are interdependent. A problem in one part (subsystem) will inevitably be experienced in another. Because of the interdependence of the parts, solutions to problems in one subsystem may cause negative consequences in another. (See Figure 10.1.)
3. There is no single best solution to a problem (the principle of equifinality).
4. Effective organizations are adaptable. Adaptability requires that the organization respond to shifting external and internal conditions and change to meet the resulting demands.
5. Organizations have a tendency toward entropy or loss of energy. Adaptable organizations avoid entropy through change.

An Overview

Organizational development consultants may be employed to function as a part of the sensing mechanisms needed to identify internal and external changes that may negatively influence the welfare of the organization. Often consultants who serve to identify shifts in demands are internal consultants employed by the organization on a full-time basis. In other situations, consultants may be external, in that they are not employed by the organization as regular employees. These consultants may also act in a preventive way (i.e., may be employed to monitor organizational health), but they are more likely to be employed to assist with organizational problems *once they have developed.* There is nothing that precludes internal consultants from dealing with problematic situations, however, and in fact that is often the case. Regardless of the locus of the consultant (internal or external), certain steps must be followed. A description of these follows.

Entry

Entry in the organizational consultation process can be broken down into a number of substages. A consultant, whether internal or external to the organization, may be contacted by an employee, usually a manager, because of a concern, either because a problem has arisen or because the manager wants to prevent difficulties. The manager may have identified a specific problem and may have made his or her own diagnosis of the basis for the problem. Most consultants resist accepting this diagnosis, insisting that they be allowed to work collaboratively with the organization to arrive at a mutual assessment of the concern. Some technical con-

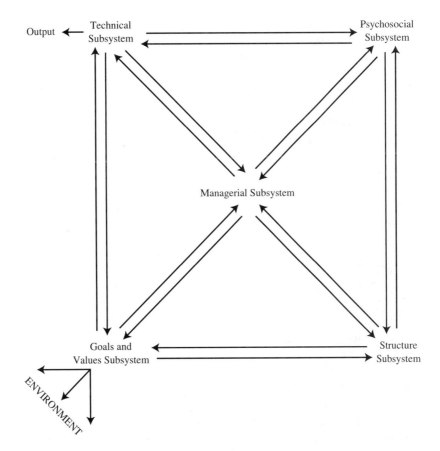

FIGURE 10.1   A Systems View of Organizational Functioning

Source: Psychological Consultation: Introduction to Theory and Practice (p. 101) by D. Brown, W. B. Pryzwansky, and A. C. Schulte (1987). Needham Heights, MA: Allyn & Bacon. Reprinted by permission.

sultants (e.g., systems analysts) may assume full responsibility for this assessment.
However, for the most part, consultants go through a process of reconnoitering
prior to agreeing to becoming involved in a particular process. The objective of this
reconnoitering process is to determine whether or not sufficient commitment and
resources are available to deal with the problem at hand. If, in fact, motivation to
solve the problem exists and human and fiscal resources are available to focus on
the problem, the consultant contracts with the organization to assist with its problems (Beer, 1980; Lippitt & Lippitt, 1986).

Assessment
Morasky (1982) suggests that the beginning point in assessing organizational problems is to identify the goals of the organization in order to determine whether they

are clearly stated and are being followed. In some instances goals have been distorted. In others, they are not clearly stated and thus are misunderstood.

The second step in assessment, according to Morasky, is to examine the input/output boundaries. Inputs come into the organization in the form of (1) technology/information, (2) human resources, and (3) raw materials. If an organization has not kept abreast of the latest technology, cannot attract the needed labor supply, or has either inadequate supplies or inferior raw materials, it is unlikely to function effectively.

The examination of output boundaries is in reality looking at the marketing function. Is the product produced by the organization being "purchased" by the market? This may be easily discerned in the case of profit-making organizations. Nonprofit organizations such as community mental health centers and school counseling programs also have a marketing function (i.e., they need to sell their programs to different audiences). Needless to say, it is more difficult to determine whether the products of these organizations are being accepted in the "marketplace." Consultants may assist organizations to identify groups to which their products are to be marketed and identify marketing devices (Brown et al., 1995).

Third, organizational consultants need to examine the production processes. In community mental health centers, the focus of this investigation would be on the therapy, outreach, and consulting services. In goods-producing organizations, the consultant might look at the technology employed and how this interacts with the human side of the production.

Fourth, the consultant should look at the basic organizational processes (e.g., communications, decision making, incentives system, etc.). Poor vertical communication plagues many bureaucratic organizations. Noninvolvement in the decision-making process can lower morale and generalize to the quality of the product produced. Disparate pay systems can have the same result.

Fifth, and finally, the consultant needs to examine the overall constraints on the system. Geography can serve as a barrier to the recruitment of personnel or to securing raw materials. Public agencies are often underfunded. Air pollution standards can result in the need to modernize. Zoning laws can preclude needed expansion. For example, a counselor who provided organization consultation to a small electric utility in a mideastern state identified the inability to recruit qualified technical staff as a major impediment to the functioning of the organization.

Problem Identification and Goal Setting

Once the foregoing steps have been completed, the consultant and members of the organization must evaluate a mass of data. Lewin's (1951) force field analysis can be used for this purpose (Table 10.1). Driving forces are those identified that exert pressure to solve a problem. Staff morale, low profit, poor corporate image, and so forth are driving forces. Restraining forces are barriers to problem solving such as unavailability of sufficiently trained personnel, outdated equipment, space, and other similar factors. The result of the force-field analysis is to identify specific dri-

TABLE 10.1   Example of Force-Field Analysis Technique

Step 1:   Identify problem and set goals

Current Situation: Low worker morale, resulting in higher turnover and low productivity

Preferred Situation: High worker morale, low turnover, high productivity

Step 2:   List forces that will influence problem resolution

Driving Forces	Restraining Forces
1. Low profit	1. Competition that requires low pay
2. High cost of recruiting and training new workers	2. Outdated company policies regarding work schedule
3. Desire to meet workers' needs, i.e., produce a desirable work environment	3. Available expertise
	4. Current management system

Step 3:   Identify strategies to alter forces

(For example, explain technology that will increase productivity, redo company personnel policies, etc.)

ving forces that can be accelerated and/or restraining forces that need to be reduced that will lead to problem solving. The goals of consultation then become to increase or decrease certain forces that exist within the organization.

Problem Solving

Once driving and restraining forces are identified, specific strategies for dealing with the problem are generated by the consultant and members of the organization. Lippitt & Lippitt (1986) and Kurpius (1985) have classified these interventions according to their focus. Interventions such as skills development or attitudinal change are aimed at individuals who may be impairing the organization's functioning. Group interventions such as team building and collaborative problem solving focus on enhancing the effectiveness of problems with work groups. Mediation and conflict resolution are interventions aimed at improving intergroup relations. Finally, survey information feedback, culture building, and installing new communications systems attempt to positively influence the total organization.

STUDENT LEARNING EXERCISE

Complete the following quiz pertaining to systems theory and organizational consultation. Circle T for true and F for false.

1. The principle of equifinality suggests that the stages through which organizational consultation passes follow a linear model.   T   F

2. Most organizations have a tendency to lose energy. This is referred to as movement toward entropy.   T   F

3. Organizational consultants, after entry has been completed, may begin their work at a variety of places. Morasky suggests that they begin by identifying organizational boundaries.   T   F

4. Throughput and production are analogous terms.   T   F

5. The principles of product marketing are similar for goods and services producing as well as profit and nonprofit organizations.   T   F

6. A positive intervention is one subsystem that may have a negative impact on another.   T   F

The Efficacy of Consultation

Three questions should be asked in the evaluation of any intervention used by counselors. First, is it effective in achieving the changes sought? Second, compared to other approaches, is it more or less efficient? Does it take more or less time, energy, resources, etc.? Third, is it acceptable to the potential client group involved? In other words, will clients or consultees participate? None of these questions can be answered definitively for consultation.

There is a substantial amount of evidence that consultation is an effective means of influencing human behavior (Henning-Stout, 1993). The efficiency of consultation versus other types of interventions has not been addressed as systematically, however. Certainly Caplan's (1970) observations about the increased efficiency that occurred when mental health professionals started functioning as consultants instead of providing therapeutic services supports the idea that consultation is a more efficient use of the professional's time than direct service. However, much research is needed in this area. Finally, little research has been done about the relative acceptance of consultation by caregivers and others, although experience suggests that whenever a potential consultee views consultation as a means of solving a critical problem they are quite open to the process.

Summary

Three approaches to consultation have been discussed in this chapter along with a general discussion of the process of consultation and an examination of its efficacy. What should be obvious is that consultation is a relatively new intervention and, as such, is in a state of flux with regard to both conceptualization and practice. What should be just as clear is that consultation offers the counselor another approach to dealing with complex mental health concerns.

Review Questions

1. Contrast the definition of consultation presented in this chapter with that advanced by Caplan. Speculate on why Caplan has taken the position he holds.

2. Outline the principles of systems theory. Tell how these might be applied to the assessment of an organizational problem.

3. Compare the diagnostic categories set forth by Caplan in his consultee-centered consultation model to the "diagnostic categories" that might be used in the social learning theory of consultation. Which provides the best background for designing an intervention? Why?

4. Caplan recommends that consultee-centered administrative consultation will necessarily be long-term in nature. Speculate on the reasons for this recommendation.

5. Outline the steps in consultation. Identify the prerequisite conditions that must be met at each step before one can move to the next step (except for termination, of course).

6. Caplan identifies five reasons why he believes consultees lack objectivity. Identify these and tell how a mental health consultation would deal with each.

7. Discuss the problem-assessment process in the social learning model of consultation.

8. In organizational consultation, the consultant examines each of the subsystems along with the entire structure of the organization. Why examine the entire system as opposed to concentrating on a single problematic subsystem such as production?

References

Babcock, N., & Pryzwansky, W. B. (1983). Models of consultation: Preference of educational professionals at five stages of service. *Journal of School Psychology, 12,* 359–366.

Bandura, A. (1977). *Social learning theory.* Englewood Cliffs, NJ: Prentice-Hall.

Beer, M. (1980). *Organizational change and development: A systems view.* Santa Monica, CA: Goodyear.

Bergan, J. R. (1977). *Behavioral consultation.* Columbus, OH: Charles E. Merrill.

Bergan, J. R., & Kratochwill, T. R. (1990). *Behavioral consultation and therapy.* New York: Plenum Press.

Bergan, J. R., & Tombari, M. L. (1976). The analysis of verbal interactions occurring during consultation. *Journal of School Psychology, 13,* 209–226.

Brown, D., Pryzwansky, W. B., & Schulte, A. C. (1995). *Psychological consultation: Introduction to theory and practice,* (3rd ed.). Boston, MA: Allyn & Bacon.

Brown, D., & Schulte, A. C. (1987). A social learning model of consultation. *Professional Psychology Research & Practice, 18,* 283–287.

Caplan, G. (1970). *The theory and practice of mental health consultation.* New York: Basic Books.

Caplan, G., & Caplan, R. B. (1993). *Mental health consultation and collaboration.* San Francisco: Jossey-Bass.

Conoley, J. C., & Conoley, C. W. (1992). *School consultation: A guide to practice and training,* (2nd ed.). New York: MacMillan.

Erchul, W. P., & Chewning, T. G. (1990). Behavioral consultation from a request-centered relational communications perspective. *School Psychology Quarterly, 5,* 1–20.

Gallessich, J. (1982). *The profession and practice of consultation: A handbook for consultants, trainers of consultants, and consumers of consultation services.* San Francisco: Jossey-Bass.

Gallessich, J. (1985). Toward a meta-theory of consultation. *The Counseling Psychologist, 13,* 336–354.

Heller, K. (1985). Issues in consultation to community groups: Some use distinctions between social regulations and indigenous citizens groups. *The Counseling Psychologist, 15,* 403–409.

Henning-Stout, M. (1993). Theoretical and empirical basis of consultation. In J. E. Zins, T. R. Kratochwill, & S. N. Elliot, (eds.), *Handbook of Consultation Services for Children*, (pp. 15–45). San Francisco: Jossey-Bass.

Huse, E. F. (1980). *Organizational development and change*, (2nd ed.). St. Paul, MN: West Publishing Company.

Katz, D., & Kahn, R. L. (1978). *The social psychology of organizations*. New York: John Wiley and Sons.

Keller, H. R. (1981). Behavioral consultation. In J. C. Conoley, (ed.), *Consultation in the schools: Theory, research and practice*, (pp. 59–99). New York: Academic Press.

Kurpius, D. J. (1985). Consultation interventions: Successes, failures, and proposals. *The Counseling Psychologist, 13,* 368–384.

Lewin, K. (1951). *Field theory in social sciences*. New York: Harper and Row.

Lippitt, G., & Lippitt, H. R. (1986). *The consulting process in action*, (2nd ed.). San Diego, CA: University Associates.

Morasky, R. L. (1982). *Behavioral systems*. New York: Praeger.

Randolph, D. L. (1985). *Micro-consulting: Basic psychological consultation skills for helping professionals*. Johnson City, TN: Institute of Social Sciences and Arts.

Snapp, M., & Davidson, S. L. (1982). Systems interventions for school psychologists: A case study approach. In C. R. Reynolds & T. B. Gutkin, (eds.), *The handbook of school psychology*, (pp. 858–961). New York: John Wiley and Sons.

Stryker, S. C. (1982). *Principles and practices of professional consulting*. Glenelg, MD: Bermont Books.

Chapter **11**

Ethical Principles of the Counseling Profession

Goal of the Chapter

The purpose of this chapter is to identify the major principles that guide counseling professionals.

Chapter Preview

- The major purposes of codes of ethics will be discussed with an emphasis on the benefit of a code of ethics to a professional and the potential benefits to client groups served by the profession.
- The principles of ethical conduct will be discussed and illustrated.
- Initiating and adjudicating ethical complaints will be discussed.

Introduction

Ethics is the branch of philosophy devoted to the study of moral decision making. Philosophers concerned with ethics dedicate themselves to the understanding of the rise and implementation of moral standards among various societies and subgroups within those societies, including professions. Perhaps it goes without saying that cultures, subcultures, and occupational groups generate different sets of moral imperatives. However, professional groups (e.g., law, medicine, and psychology) within the United States have generated surprisingly similar ethical codes. These codes are the embodiment of the moral standards of these groups. While the general aim of a code is to provide practitioners with a guide to making ethical decisions, a code of ethics serves several other purposes.

Purposes of Ethical Codes

The first purpose of a code of ethics is to provide a basis for regulating the behavior of the members of the professional group. Codes of ethics provide standards of practice regarding activities ranging from fee setting to deciding on which clients to serve. They also provide guidelines for action when certain types of difficult decisions arise (e.g., what to do with a suicidal client). These codes also tend to clarify the responsibilities of professionals to clients, to their employers, to society at large, and to their professional group.

However, as noted earlier, the purposes of codes of ethics are not restricted to providing guidelines for ethical decision making and to regulating the behavior of members of the profession. A code of ethics also protects the profession that promulgates it. All professional groups strive for autonomy from external regulation, particularly regulation by governmental agencies. In order to maintain their independence from regulatory bodies, a professional group must demonstrate not only a willingness to police itself, but also a method for self-regulation. The adoption and enforcement of a code of ethics is a clear signal to the public in general, and governmental regulatory agencies in particular, that this method is in place.

A code of ethics also enhances internal professional harmony because it establishes guidelines for professional practices and regulates intermember interactions such as referral of clients, consultation, and recruiting of new clients. Ethical guidelines for practice also protect the profession by establishing standards of practice that are often used in the adjudication of liability suits. For example, in the case of *Roy v. Hartogs* (1976) the judge ruled in favor of the client because her therapist had violated the professional standards of his field regarding sexual contact with a client. Conversely, counselors, psychologists, and other mental health professionals have routinely been absolved from guilt in liability suits when they have been found to be functioning ethically.

To summarize, a code of ethics is a set of moral guidelines designed to protect the professional, the profession, and the public served by the group. In 1988 the American Counseling Association adopted a revised set of *Ethical Standards* (see Appendix B) that at once reflects the values of the counseling profession and fulfills the functions of a code of ethics. The code is divided into nine sections: (1) preamble, (2) general concerns, (3) counseling relationship, (4) measurement and evaluation, (5) research and publication, (6) consulting, (7) private practice, (8) personnel administration, and (9) preparation standards.

At the time of this writing these standards are once again being revised and while the exact standards that will be adopted are unknown, there are important similarities and some major differences between the Proposed Standards of Practice and Ethical Standards (ACA, 1994) that is presented in Appendix B, and the code of ethics that is currently in effect. The major difference is that ACA is attempting to specify precise behavioral guidelines for counselors to aid them in making decisions. Some of these Standards of Practice will be discussed in this chapter. The major similarity between the proposed code of ethics and the one currently in effect is that principles of ethical behavior still are the framework on which the code is developed.

Principles of Ethical Conduct

Principle One: Responsibility

Professional counselors have various responsibilities, including those to clients, to the public at large, to other counselors, to the institutions that employ them, and to themselves. These responsibilities are enunciated generally in the preamble of the code in the following statement: The American Counseling Association (ACA) "is an educational, scientific, and professional organization whose members are dedicated to the enhancement of the worth, dignity, potential, and uniqueness of each individual and thus to the service of society."

Overall, the ACA statement of *Ethical Standards* emphasizes the responsibility of counselors to their clients. The statement, "The member's *primary* obligation is to respect the integrity and promote the welfare of the client(s). . ." (Section B1) certainly makes this clear. When ethical decisions are to be made by professional counselors, the client's welfare and well-being should take precedence in the decision-making process.

The Proposed Standards of Practice and Ethical Standards identifies the responsibilities of the professional counselor in very clear language in the initial section called Standards of Practice. A standard of practice is an appropriate way of functioning in a specific situation such as supervision or testing. A standard of practice varies from an ethical principle in that it is more specific.

One area of responsibility to individual clients that is particularly highlighted in the current *Ethical Standards* pertains to recognizing individual differences, particularly as they relate to racial and sexual stereotyping. In the introduction to the code the counselor is told that an awareness of the negative impact of stereotyping helps guard "the individual rights and personal dignity of the client" (Section 10). Later, in the section on measurement and evaluation, counselors are warned to use the tests cautiously with minorities or others who are underrepresented in norm groups. These and other statements in the *Ethical Standards* caution counselors against stereotyping individuals while advocating deep respect for the uniqueness of the individual.

Several counselors have asserted that current ethical standards regarding culturally different groups do not go far enough and that changes need to be made to clarify the ethical issues in this area. Cayleff (1986) believes that counselors need an appreciation for the belief systems of culturally different clients and suggests that ethical guidelines should caution against imposing dominant cultural beliefs on culturally different clients. Casas, Ponterotto, and Gutierrez (1986) also believe that a change in the current ACA *Ethical Standards* is necessary. They think that the

Standards need to be more specific with regard to research with culturally different clients and preparation for working with cross-cultural clients, a position echoed by Ibrahim and Arrendo (1986).

One unusual aspect of the current ACA code of ethics has to do with counselors' responsibilities regarding referral should a satisfactory arrangement not be possible because of finances. With regard to the latter, the statement of *Ethical Standards* specifies that, in the event that a fee suitable to the client cannot be established, assistance must be provided in finding comparable services at acceptable costs. This responsibility has been eliminated in the proposed changes (ACA, 1994). However, the proposed changes do not go beyond the current ethical standards in regard to cultural sensitivity.

Counselor's responsibilities to institutions or agencies are also addressed in the *Ethical Standards.* In general, counselors are advised that acceptance of employment is essentially an agreement with the principles and policies of the institution. They are also admonished that if there is a conflict between the institution's practices and those standards established by the code, resignation from employment should be strongly considered.

Professionals who accept administrative jobs are also advised to foster accountability by making the organization's goals and policies explicit. Counselors who function as personnel administrators also have many other responsibilities, including developing an in-service training program for themselves and others, making the goals of their program known to the staff, and designing programs that guarantee the rights of the client group served. These responsibilities would, in all likelihood, be rather easy to meet. However, one ethical guideline that may be problematic for professional counselors can be found in Section G3. It states, "Members *must* alert their employers to conditions that may be potentially disruptive or damaging" (italics added). Would a school counselor inform the administration that a student was going to phone in a bomb threat or pull the fire alarm? Would a counselor working in a prison inform the administration that a sit-down strike was about to occur in protest of the overcrowded conditions? And how are these types of situations balanced against the directive regarding counselors' primary responsibility to clients? These questions cannot be answered without more information. Are people likely to be harmed if a fire alarm is sounded or a sit-down strike begins? With this and other information a plan of action can be developed. In many instances ethical principles provide guidelines for decision making; they do not provide answers.

Counselors also have the responsibility to inform their employers of conditions that may impair their functioning as employees. This guideline is generally interpreted to mean that counselors who develop emotional problems, alcoholism, drug addiction, or related problems should report these difficulties because they may hamper their work. Counselors are naturally reluctant to place this type of information in the hands of employers since it may result in dismissal.

The *Ethical Standards* places a great deal of emphasis on responsibilities to institutions, primarily because many counselors are employed in institutional settings. At the conclusion of the section on the counseling relationship, it is indicated that if the work setting calls for a variation in the guidelines established in the section, consultation with other professionals should be initiated *"whenever possible"* (italics added) to consider justifiable alternatives. This sentence has been dropped in the proposed changes (ACA, 1994).

As would be expected, ACA's *Ethical Standards* deal extensively with counselors' responsibilities to the profession. Two general areas of emphasis are obvious in the current standards and are continued in the proposed revisions. First, counselors are expected to influence the profession by exerting efforts that will improve both professional conduct and practice. As we shall see, practicing ethically and working to ensure that others do as well are two of the efforts expected of professional counselors. These two responsibilities may be the greatest expected of any professional. However, exerting effort to continuously maintain and improve one's competency is also a major responsibility of the professional counselor. This means not only engaging in continued study, but also continuously evaluating the effectiveness of one's own work.

STUDENT LEARNING EXERCISE

Principle One

Indicate whether the following actions are ethical (E) or unethical (U).

1. A counselor fails to regularly upgrade his training.   E   U
2. A counselor utilizes an aptitude test for a multicultural group that has no
    Hispanics in the norm group.   E   U
3. A counselor ignores continued violations of a client's confidences by another
    counselor.   E   U
4. A white counselor, trained in cross-cultural counseling, takes a job in an all-
    black institution.   E   U
5. A student personnel administrator decides that staff in-service is each person's
    responsibility and eliminates staff development from her budget.   E   U
6. A counselor who is an alcoholic continues to work.   E   U

Principle Two: Competence

In the foregoing section it was mentioned that counselors have a responsibility to the profession to develop and maintain their own competencies. A professional group cannot exist if there are substantial concerns in society about the competence of its members. The ACA code, both current and proposed, is very clear on this matter. For example, counselor educators are told that it is important that programs, insofar as possible, be competency based. In this way the profession attempts to ensure that counselors possess the needed competencies when they enter the field. In Section A1 of the code, counselors are advised that professional growth is expected throughout their careers, presumably as a means of maintaining competence. Competence is alluded to again in that same section, but in the context of representing one's own skills accurately. This theme is echoed again in the sections on private practice and personnel administration. The section on measurement and evaluation addresses the area of competence even more directly. It states (in regard to test usage), "Members must recognize the limits of their competence and perform only those functions for which they are prepared" (Section C4).

In sum, the ACA ethical guidelines indicate that ethical behavior requires that competency be developed in the training programs, that counselors have a responsibility to maintain their competency through continuous professional growth, and that their competency level should be represented accurately to clients, employers, and the general public.

STUDENT LEARNING EXERCISE

Principle Two

Indicate whether the following actions are ethical (E) or unethical (U).

1. A counselor gives an individual intelligence test for which she has little preparation.   E   U

2. After attending a workshop on hypnosis, a counselor engages in the activity under the supervision of the workshop leader.   E   U

3. An elementary school counselor attends an hour-and-a-half session on music therapy. She then tries out what she has learned on her students.   E   U

4. A white counselor who has no cross-cultural counseling training is asked to counsel a "difficult" black client. He agrees to do this.   E   U

5. A counselor who has no training in counseling homosexual clients continues to counsel a gay client but consults an expert after every session.   E   U

Principle Three: Confidentiality

A hallmark of a professional group is when clients can discuss personal issues and have those disclosures kept in confidence. It should be noted that while a professional group can assert that it is necessary to safeguard clients by keeping personal disclosures in confidence, only a legislative body can grant the right to make disclosures privileged information. This point will be discussed in detail in the next chapter, but the reader should be aware that unless privileged communication has been granted by legislative decree in a particular jurisdiction (normally a state), counselors may find themselves in conflict with the legal system since the ethical expectation of keeping confidences is not supported legally.

As would be expected, the *Ethical Standards* addresses confidentiality in numerous ways. However, and not unexpectedly, the strongest language is found in the section dealing with the counseling relationship. It indicates that information disclosed by the client must be kept in confidence *unless* "there is clear and imminent danger to the client or others" (Section B4). Counselors are told to take reasonable action whenever danger arises, presumably to prevent clients from harming themselves or others. Counseling records, data collected in the counseling relationship, and specific subject data collected in the course of the research project are also viewed as confidential information and, therefore, should be protected against disclosure.

The section of the code dealing with confidentiality also addresses group counseling. The current guidelines suggest that the group leader should establish a norm of confidentiality in the group. Obviously the developers of the revised code of ethics (ACA, 1994) feel that the statements about confidentiality in groups are not sufficient in the 1988 code because they have added this statement in Section B: "The fact that confidentiality cannot be guaranteed in group counseling must be clearly communicated to group members."

One apparent oversight in the current ethical statement but not the proposed ethical codes is the failure to address confidentiality in the consulting relationship. While it would generally be assumed that information resulting from a consultation relationship with an individual would be accorded the same status as that disclosed during counseling, no guidelines are provided in this area. The proposed code of ethics (ACA, 1994) is a bit better in this regard than the 1988 statement. This statement appears in *Ethical Standards* section B.6.a: "Information obtained in a consulting relationship is discussed for professional purposes only with persons clearly concerned with the case. Written and oral reports present data germane to the purposes of the consultation, and every effort is made to protect client identity and avoid undue invasion of privacy."

Unfortunately this statement is so vague that it would be impossible to develop a set of personal standards based on it. What does, "for professional purposes" mean? Who are "people clearly concerned with the case"? And what is "undue invasion of privacy"?

STUDENT LEARNING EXERCISE
Principle Three

Indicate whether the following actions are ethical (E) or unethical (U).

1. An organizational consultant informs the plant manager that a number of the supervisors believe the manager is incompetent but does not reveal which ones hold that belief.   E   U

2. A school counselor fails to contact authorities after she learns that students intend to construct a barricade made of straw on a nearby interstate highway. E   U

3. A school counselor informs the playground supervisor that John and Jim intend to throw rocks at three of the fourth-grade girls.   E   U

4. A counselor consults with the school social worker regarding one of his clients and gives detailed case information.   E   U

5. A counselor reveals interest test scores of one of his clients to an army recruiter. E   U

Principle Four: Public Statements

Historically, ethical codes have been quite definitive about the types of public statements that could be made. Until recently, physicians, dentists, lawyers, and other professionals were precluded from advertising and were permitted only to make announcements regarding the opening of their practices. However, court cases and governmental rulings have changed this situation. All professional groups are entitled to advertise, and ethical codes have been revised to provide guidelines for these advertisements and other public announcements.

Both the 1988 and the proposed (ACA, 1994) ACA code of ethics emphasizes accuracy as the most important ingredient in advertising and public statements. In part, it states that "the member must advertise the services in such a manner so as to accurately inform the public as to services, expertise, profession, and techniques" (Section F2). Claiming credentials as a mental health counselor when one has been prepared as a school counselor would be unethical, as would offering services for which one has no expertise. More obviously, claiming degrees, preparation in areas outside of counseling (e.g., psychology), or other qualifications that are unearned would be unethical.

Figure 11.1 shows an advertisement used by a counselor in private practice to announce the opening of her practice. This advertisement follows ethical guidelines.

Advertisements are not the only form of public statements made by counselors. School counselors and others often make public statements about test scores and other data regarding the students they serve. In these instances counselors should give complete information and provide data that will allow the public to draw accurate conclusions. The ACA code of ethics makes particular mention of the need to avoid possible misinterpretation of information such as I.Q. test scores. Providing accurate and unbiased data to the general public, regardless of the nature of the information, is also stressed.

An example of an unethical statement by a counselor was published recently in a southern newspaper. The counselor, who works for a private academy, proudly announced that twelve of the school's students had qualified as National Merit Semifinalists on the basis of the Preliminary Scholastic Aptitude Test (PSAT) scores. The counselor went on to suggest that the high proportion of National Merit Semifinalists was the outcome of the academy's superior curriculum and outstanding instruction. Since the academy only accepts very bright students who

Business Card

Certified Clinical Mental Health Counselor
National Certified Career Counselor
SONDRA VAN SANT, M.ED
licensed professional counselor

address   telephone

Announcement

CAREER SUCCESS WORKSHOP
Strategies to:
- identify and market your strengths
- find unadvertised jobs
- improve your resume
- map your career path

conducted by
SONDRA VAN SANT, M.ED
National Certified Career Counselor
6 Thursday Evening Sessions Sept. 29 – Nov. 3
CALL 967-3605

7:30–9:30   Fee $75

For Information and Reservations

Yellow Pages Advertisement

VAN SANT SONDRA S. M.ED
Licensed Professional Counselor
Certifications: Career and Mental Health Counseling
— for —
Career Choice, Changes, and Work-Related Stress

address   telephone

FIGURE 11.1   Ethical Business Card, Workshop, and Yellow Pages Listing

Used by permission.

normally come from middle-class and upper-middle-class homes, there is some likelihood that a number of them would have had outstanding PSAT scores regardless of where they went to school. Thus the conclusion that the scores were the result of the student's experiences at the academy was unsubstantiated and it is unethical to state this publicly.

STUDENT LEARNING EXERCISE

Principle Four

Indicate whether the following actions are ethical (E) or unethical (U).

1. A counselor in private practice indicates that the course he offers will raise college entrance examination scores "significantly" for those who complete it.   E   U

2. A MA-level mental health counselor indicates that his training is equivalent to that of a clinical psychologist.   E   U

3. An AACD member, trained as a school counselor, hangs out a shingle as a career counselor/consultant.   E   U

4. A person who is untrained as a counselor but is a member of ACA uses the following statement when opening a private job placement bureau: "Staffed by a member of the American Association for Counseling and Development. Skilled counseling and placement services offered to the job hunter."   E   U

5. An agency director, advertising drug rehabilitation services staffed by "experienced, qualified counselors," fails to mention that the staff is made up of paraprofessionals who were once themselves substance abusers.   E   U

Principle Five: Relationships to Client Groups

One of the important aspects of the client-counselor relationship, confidentiality, was discussed above. However, other guidelines are provided for dealing with clients. For example, clients are to be advised of the nature of techniques to be used *prior* to initiating the counseling relationship. In addition, a counselor who determines that the counseling relationship cannot be helpful to the client is obligated to terminate the relationship. And in those counseling relationships that involve a fee, counselors are advised that the financial position of the client is to be considered in the fee-setting process. Counselors are also told to avoid relationships in which they might not be totally objective. These would most typically involve what are classified as "dual relationships," which are counseling relationships with friends, relatives, and business associates. Finally, counselors are admonished that sexual intimacies with clients are to be avoided.

Counselors are involved with client groups other than those being seen in counseling relationships. Subjects in research projects must be conscientiously safeguarded so that no possible psychological or physical damage will result from the research procedures. For those counselors consulting with organizations, a clear understanding of "problem definition, change goals, and predicted consequences" (Section E2) must be developed. The ACA (1988, 1994) code of ethics, unlike many other ethical statements, deals with training. It also specifies that in preparation programs, students should receive an integrated academic and supervised practice, exposure to varied theoretical orientations, training in the ethical standards of their profession, and instruction from skilled teachers and practitioners.

Many of these guidelines obviously provide counselors with some difficult decisions to make. For example, when does one know that a particular counseling relationship will fail to be productive? It is not unusual for some psycho-analytically oriented therapists to see their clients several times a week for years. Therefore, the counselor's theoretical orientation comes into play in the decision-making process, along with that person's judgment about expected outcomes.

Protecting the welfare of clients involves taking a number of other steps, including explaining counseling techniques that might prove harmful or embarrassing. In general, the explanation should provide enough information so that the client can make an informed decision. For example, if a client will receive negative feedback in a group counseling environment, this should be explained and illustrated if necessary so the client can anticipate the situation and decide whether he wants to participate. Protecting clients also means not using them to meet one's own needs, such as sexual needs. One research study indicated that nearly 5 percent of the 507 male psychologists responding to a survey regarding sexual intimacies with clients indicated that they had been so involved. A significantly lower percentage (0.08 percent) of the female psychologists indicated that they had been involved sexually with their clients (Bouhoutos, Holyroyd, Lerman, Forer, & Greenberg, 1983). As Coleman and Schaeffer (1986) point out, however, sexual contact is not the only way that clients can be abused by counselors. Hugs, fondling, seductive behavior, and professional voyeurism (unnecessarily exploring intimate areas) may all lead to client confusion and disrupt the therapeutic relationship. As these authors point out, the counselor can avoid overt sexual abuse and psychological harm to clients by establishing clear boundaries between the counseling and the personal relationship. If this cannot be accomplished, the relationship should be terminated.

STUDENT LEARNING EXERCISE
Principle Five

Indicate whether the following actions are ethical (E) or unethical (U).

1. A counselor conducts several sessions with a client and then discovers that she is seeing a psychologist for the same problem. The counselor decides to continue counseling. E U

2. A school counselor accepts as a client the daughter of his best friend even though he has given his friend "advice" about the problem with the daughter for a number of months. E U

3. A school counselor accepts as a client the son of one of his best friends when he learns that the young man has a serious drinking problem that has been undetected by his parents. E U

4. A counselor becomes involved with one of his clients, stroking and embracing her, because he believes this will help her overcome her shyness with other males. E U

5. A counselor who leads growth groups based on encounter procedures does not inform a client that some sessions may involve intense negative feedback. E U

Principle Six: Relationships to Colleagues and Other Professions

The success of a professional group depends to a large degree on the extent to which there is harmony within the profession and with other similar groups. In two obvious attempts to maintain inter- and intraprofessional harmony, the current ACA code of ethics specifies that (1) the member may not knowingly enter into a counseling relationship with a client who is being seen by another professional, and (2) if a counselor discovers that a client is being seen by another professional after the counseling relationship has been initiated, the relationship must be terminated (if permission to continue cannot be gained from the second professional or unless the second relationship is terminated by the client). This has been changed in the proposed code (ACA, 1994, Section C, SP-27) to read, "Professional counselors must inform other mental health professionals that a counseling relationship exists."

The ACA ethical statement also addresses the relationships among professionals in the area of research and publication. Counselors engaged in research have the responsibility to accord appropriate credit for research projects including joint authorship if the results are published (1988, 1994). They must also communicate the full results of research to other counselors, even if that research reflects negatively on particular practices employed, services offered, and on the institutions generally.

When engaging in private practice involving other professionals, counselors must make clear the responsibilities of each, both among themselves and to the clients they serve. In the supervision of others, counselors are advised to "establish interpersonal relations and working agreements with supervisors and subordinates" (Section G2). In this context "supervisors" refers to secondary or field supervisors. These types of relationships are deemed necessary so that ethical behavior can be maintained and so that competencies can be developed. Other intraprofessional relationships are covered by the code, including a section on the relationship between counselor educators and *students*. This section specifies that students should be the recipients of a well-designed and well-taught program. These statements and the ones alluded to earlier in this section should make it apparent that it is the intent of the code to regulate certain aspects of counselors' behavior as they deal with other counselors, counselor trainees, and professionals. Of particular concern is functioning in those areas that might result in ethical breaches or failure to fulfill responsibilities to client groups.

STUDENT LEARNING EXERCISE
Principle Six

Indicate whether the following actions are ethical (E) or unethical (U).

1. A mental health counselor tells a group of people at a cocktail party that social workers are not really prepared to perform psychotherapy.   E   U

2. Even though a student counselor has done a majority of the work on the research, a professor insists that he be senior author on the manuscript that has resulted from their collaboration. The student capitulates. E U

3. A professor in a theory of counseling class proclaims that there is only one theory that has been empirically validated and that is the one the class will study. E U

Principle Seven: Relationships of Ethics and the Law

Most codes of ethics, including the ACA (1988, 1994) code, either tacitly or directly recognize the relationship between the law and the profession. For example, the provision in Section B (Counseling Relationships) indicating that the counselor has a duty to warn others in the case of imminent danger to a client or others comes about as a result of a famous court case *(Tarasoff v. Regents of the University of California)* that will be discussed in detail in Chapter 12. A second provision of *Ethical Standards* deals with "the appropriation, reproduction, or modifications of published tests or parts thereof without acknowledgment and permission from the previous publisher" (Section C15). This is of course a recognition of copyright laws. References are also made to local statutes in the section dealing with private practice. Counselors are urged to be in compliance with local regulations in the establishment of corporations and to adhere to local regulations in the pursuit of their private practice. All of these admonishments came about partially to regulate member behavior, but also as means to make counselors aware of certain legal regulations that, if violated, would endanger the individual and demean the profession.

Future versions of the ACA code of ethics, and other such codes, will undoubtedly be shaped by legislature and governmental regulations just as the current version has been. In this way the profession can demonstrate to regulatory agencies not only an awareness of existing laws and governmental policies but also an intent to enforce them without assistance.

Principle Eight: Research and Publication

Section D of *Ethical Standards* deals with research and publication. In general, this section holds that counselors are to adhere to sound scientific principles when designing and conducting research, are to report their results fully, including results that are contrary to expectation, and are to assist other researchers who want to replicate or extend the research by providing original data and other types of assistance. Researchers are also advised to report results clearly so no misinterpretation is possible.

Another area of concern that is alluded to has to do with subjects in research studies. As was noted in the section on confidentiality, the anonymity of subjects is to be protected in the release or publication of all data. However, the guidelines address a broader set of issues than confidentiality. Researchers are also responsible for protecting the welfare of clients, which means that research subjects are not to be exposed to conditions that would result in psychological or physical harm. One means of assuring that subjects are protected is to fully inform them of the purpose of the research and to gain informed consent to participate. Informed consent is generally interpreted to mean that a prospective subject fully understands the nature and consequences of participation.

There is one equivocation about informed consent, however. The statement found in Section D5 (ACA, 1988) indicates that subjects may be misinformed or not fully informed if such action is necessary to achieve the purposes of the investigation. This statement in no way lessens the investigator's responsibility to protect the welfare of the client. It does allow the continuation of research in which subjects are "blind" to the purposes of the investigation. Subjects in this type of research must be debriefed immediately on completion of the research project. This debriefing process typically involves providing a full explanation of the purposes of the research and offering assistance if any psychological distress has occurred as a result of participation. Guidelines specify that both full explanation and assistance be provided. The proposed ethical standards echo the 1988 guidelines.

STUDENT LEARNING EXERCISE
Principles Seven and Eight

Indicate whether the following actions are ethical (E) or unethical (U).

1. A research team decides not to report the outcomes of two analyses that, while they do not contradict the overall results of the research, do alter the conclusions that can be drawn.   E   U

2. A researcher does not write up a research study in which she obtained no significant results.   E   U

3. Aware that a few high school students have become mildly depressed after a study on the etiology of suicide, as a precaution researchers offer counseling services to students who participated in the study.   E   U

4. A school counselor promises that all information will be held in confidence even though the legislature has not granted privileged communication to school counselors.   E   U

Some Problems with the Code

In the foregoing discussion, several references were made to problems and deficiencies within the ACA (1988) *Ethical Standards*. As Mabe and Rollin (1986) note, not all situations can be covered by an ethical statement, but an attempt will be made to clarify what are viewed as potential areas of difficulty in functioning as an ethical counselor. It is also the position taken here that the current code of ethics, as it now stands, provides some problems for counselors as they present themselves to governmental agencies, health insurance carriers, and others, and as they claim parity with other mental health service providers who have clearer statements of ethical guidelines. Only by clarifying and/or eliminating certain sections can these problems be eliminated.

Conflict Between Client and Institution

Guidelines within the code of ethics indicate that the client is the primary concern of counselors. However, if a counselor is obligated to report a potential disturbance to his employer, there will probably be times when there will be conflicts of interest between the client and the institution. Counselors need to clarify the apparent contradiction that exists in the proposed ACA (1994) code as well. This equivocation may be misinterpreted by the public or by counselors. It also provides problems for counselors who rely on the code as a decision-making tool. It is suggested that counselors make it clear that the client comes first and institutional concerns are secondary. A statement such as the following could be included in the preamble: The essence of the counseling profession lies in assisting the clients that it serves; therefore in all matters the first responsibility of the professional counselor is to the client.

Enforcing the Code of Ethics

The first question to be answered in enforcement is, "Who is covered by the ACA *Ethical Standards?*" The apparent answer is: anyone who calls himself or herself a counselor—but this is incorrect. Persons covered by the *Ethical Standards* include members of the American Counseling Association, its divisions and state branches, counselors who are licensed or certified by state licensing/certification boards that have adopted this code of ethics, and counselors who have been certified by national organizations such as the National Board for Certified Counselors that have adopted the ACA code of ethics.

The first line of enforcement of any code of ethics rests with the moral and ethical values of the individual counselor. As Gallessich (1982) aptly notes, self-discipline is the primary means by which any code of ethics is enforced. It is the basic responsibility of a training program not only to teach the principles of ethical conduct, but also to socialize neophyte counselors in a manner that will result in the internalization of the moral and ethical principles of the code of ethics (Tennyson & Strom, 1986). While there are no clear-cut guidelines for this socialization process, it seems that trainers (1) stimulate ethical sensitivity by emphasizing ethical dilemmas in all classes, (2) involve students in ethical decision-making processes, and (3) develop a tolerance for the ambiguities involved in ethical decision making by modeling these difficulties (Kitchner, 1986).

But what if breaches in ethical standards do occur in practice? Just as counselors' self-discipline and personal ethical standards are the primary basis of ethical functioning, their vigilance against unethical practice among their colleagues is the basic safeguard against widespread unethical practice. Counselors must be alert to and act when unethical practice occurs. Since many ethical errors are simply oversights on the part of counselors, a reminder of the provisions of the code will suffice as an enforcement strategy in many instances. However, in the case of flagrant violations of various aspects of the guidelines, or when unethical behavior continues after it has been brought to the attention of the counselor, stronger steps must be taken to correct the behavior. This means reporting the behavior to the state division of the ACA Ethics Committee or, if the state does not have a committee formed, to the ACA Ethics Committee.

The ACA Ethics Committee has established guidelines for adjudicating complaints regarding ethical misconduct, and these guidelines have been widely adopted by approximately twenty-four states at this writing. It is anticipated that all organizations affiliated with ACA will have ethics committees in place within the near future.

The first step in the adjudication process is the filing of a written statement with the state division ethics committee charging a member with unethical behavior. This complaint may be filed by either an ACA member or a nonmember. At this time there is no statute of limitations on filing these complaints. Therefore, a counselor who acts unethically is at risk for an indefinite period of time. Complaints should provide a detailed description of the unethical behavior and, when possible, indicate the section of *Ethical Standards* that has been violated. One warning is appropriate at this juncture. Counselors should *not* file complaints of ethical misconduct without carefully verifying through first-hand information that a violation of the *Ethical Standards* has occurred. To do otherwise is to run the risk of incurring a defamation suit.

Once the complaint is received, it is the ethics committee's responsibility to contact the accused member, inform him or her of the complaint, and ask him or her for information regarding the allegations. The committee may also collect data from other sources such as clients, other counselors, noncounselors, employers, etc. Once all data are collected, the committee considers the facts and reaches a decision.

If a counselor is found guilty of an ethical breach, a number of consequences may result. The mildest of these is a letter reprimanding the counselor, explaining the code of ethics, and warning the counselor to refrain from unethical conduct in the future. However, the ethics committee may also recommend delicensure or decertification, removal from registries, and suspension or expulsion from ACA. The groups to whom the recommendations are made would then have to take up the matter and render a decision. At this point in time we have insufficient data to indicate what these boards and organizations would do. However, in a sister discipline, psychology, the recommendation of the ethics committee is often followed and appropriate disciplinary action taken.

As was indicated in the foregoing paragraphs, dealing with ethical conduct is a rather new phenomenon for the counseling profession. Indeed, while the first ethics committee was established in 1953 (Allen, 1986), it has only recently become active in the enforcement area. However, the enforcement of the code of ethics is one of the most important activities for counselors since it is one of the factors that can be used to establish the status of counseling as a profession. A record of enforcing the code is also important as counselors seek parity in treatment from insurance companies, legislatures, and other governmental agencies.

Summary

This chapter began with a review of the purposes of ethical codes that were stated generally to be the protection of the public and the profession. This discussion was followed by the presentation of eight general principles of ethical functioning, including professional responsibility, maintaining competence, confidentiality, public statements, relationships to client groups, relationships to colleagues, ethics and the law, and ethical practice in research. The final two sections of the chapter dealt with some problems with the ACA ethical code and the enforcement issues.

Review Questions

1. What are the goals that professional groups have in mind when they adopt a code of ethics? To what degree have these been achieved by the counseling profession?

2. Most professional groups now require continuing education for maintenance of licensure or certification. Which ethical principles can be cited as support for these requirements?

3. Outline the steps in the adjudicating of ethical complaints.

4. Why is the individual practitioner the most important ingredient in maintaining the ethical posture of a group?

5. Discuss the interface between the law and codes of ethics.

6. What are the differences and similarities between the ACA and APA codes of ethics?

References

ACA (1994). Proposed standards of practice and ethical standards. *Guidepost, 45,* 16–22.

Allen, V. C. (1986). A historical perspective of the AACD ethics committee. *Journal of Counseling and Development, 64,* 293.

American Association for Counseling and Development. (1988). *Ethical Standards.* Alexandria, VA: Author.

Bouhoutos, J., Holyroyd, J., Lerman, H., Forer, B. E., & Greenberg, M. (1983). Sexual intimacy between psychotherapist and patient. *Professional Psychology: Research and Practice, 14*(2), 185–196.

Casas, M. J., Ponterotto, J. G., & Gutierrez, J. M. (1986). An ethical indictment of counseling research and training: The cross-cultural perspective. *Journal of Counseling and Development, 64*(5), 347–349.

Cayleff, S. E. (1986). Ethical issues in counseling gender, race, and culturally distinct groups. *Journal of Counseling and Development, 64*(5), 345–347.

Coleman, E., & Schaeffer, S. (1986). Boundaries of sex and intimacy between client and counselor. *Journal of Counseling and Development, 64*(5), 341–344.

Gallessich, J. (1982). *The profession and practice of consultation.* San Francisco: Jossey-Bass.

Gibbs, J. T. (1985). The training and supervision of consultants: Must we continue to be class bound and color blind. *The Counseling Psychologist.*

Ibrahim, F. A., & Arrendo, P. M. (1986). Ethical standards for cross-cultural counseling: Counselor preparation, practice, assessment, and research. *Journal of Counseling and Development, 64*(5), 349–352.

Kitchner, K. S. (1986). Teaching applied ethics in counselor education: An integration of psy-chological processes and philosophical analyses. *Journal of Counseling and Development, 64*(5), 30–310.

Kurpius, D. (1978) Consultation theory and process: An integrated model. *Personnel and Guidance Journal, 56*(6), 335–338.

Mabe, A. R., & Rollin, S. A. (1986). The role of a code of ethical standards in counseling. *Journal of Counseling and Development, 64*(5), 294–297.

Robinson, S., & Gross, D. (1985). Ethics in consultation: The Canterville ghost revisited. *The Counseling Psychologist.*

Roy v. Hartogs, 381 N.Y. S. 2d 590 (1976).

Tarasoff v. Regents of the University of California, S.F. No. 23042, Superior Court No. 405694, 441 P. 2d. 345 (1976).

Tennyson, W. W., & Strom, S. M. (1986). Beyond professional standards: Developing responsibleness. *Journal of Counseling and Development, 64*(5), 298–302.

Chapter **12**

Legal Issues in the Counseling Profession

Goal of the Chapter

The goal of this chapter is to present an overview of the major legal issues confronting professional counselors.

Chapter Preview

- The terms "privileged communication" and "confidentiality" will be discussed and the legal issues surrounding privileged communication presented.
- Malpractice liability will be discussed in terms of the conditions under which it may occur and methods for avoiding legal liability outlined.
- Defamation will be defined as a special case of potential legal liability and circumstances that might lead to slander and libel discussed.
- Legal issues that confront school counselors will be presented, particularly those that may arise as a result of labeling, failure to provide due process, freedom of speech, right to services, records, dress codes, and abortion counseling.
- Issues that should be of concern to private practitioners will be outlined, including honesty in labeling and breach of contract.
- The final section of the chapter will deal with ethics and the law.

Introduction

Twenty-five years ago this chapter would have been unnecessary. Today legal concerns stand as one of the most serious issues confronting counselors. The dramatic rise in the importance attached to legal concerns can be attributed to two factors: the status of the counseling profession and the "legalizing" of American society. Even the most casual observer of current news events is aware that civil liability is of great concern to professionals, corporations, municipalities, and private citizens. This is primarily because juries have awarded increasingly large sums of money to plaintiffs when physicians, psychologists, or others have been found liable for damages in malpractice cases. But liability suits are not the only types of legal problems that make newspaper headlines. An associate superintendent of schools is prosecuted for not reporting a case of child abuse and subsequently is convicted. A state psychological licensing board is sued for defamation of character by a psychologist accused of unethical behavior. Parents file suit against two researchers because they allegedly have invaded the privacy of their child. The list of legal actions taken against all types of professionals is seemingly endless.

The "legalizing" of society is not the only reason that counselors need to be concerned about legal issues, since many legal developments have been quite positive. The last twenty-five years have brought about substantial change to the point that Hopkins and Anderson (1990) observe that the emerging counseling profession of the 1960s and 1970s is the recognized profession of today. Many of the indicators of this recognition are legally based. Licensure laws are one example; privileged communication laws are another. But this recognition has also brought increased expectations with regard to the level of practice since counselors have argued convincingly that high levels of performance are the hallmark of their functioning. When high standards of practice are not adhered to, successful litigation can result.

As a result of increased recognition and increasingly aggressive lawyers, professional counselors need to be aware of laws that pertain to them, sources of civil liability, and the interaction of legal and ethical guidelines. The first section of this chapter will deal with laws that direct and/or restrict counselor practice, primarily in the areas of privileged communication and civil malpractice. The sections that follow will deal with legal issues for two groups of counselors in specialized settings: school counselors and counselors in private practice. Finally, a brief discussion of the interaction of ethics and law will be presented.

Legal Restrictions/Directions

Privileged Communication

As we saw in Chapter 11, confidentiality is an important consideration in the ethical practice of counselors. Counselors are admonished to keep information gained in counseling relationships in confidence. "Confidentiality," then, is an ethical term having its origins in the codes of ethics of professional groups, including physicians, lawyers, counselors, and others. "Privileged communication," on the other hand, is a legal term, and was first granted to lawyers by the New York legislature in 1828 (Hopkins & Anderson, 1990). "Privileged communication" is a narrower term than "confidentiality" and refers to a privilege granted to a client to have information divulged in a professional relationship withheld from the courts. Normally, courts have a right to all evidence related to a particular litigation, and privileged communications statutes run contrary to this tradition (Hopkins & Anderson, 1990; Knapp & VandeCreek, 1983).

The rationale for awarding privileged communication to any group, including counselors, is that the communication must originate with the expectation that it will be kept in confidence, that confidentiality is essential to the maintenance of the relationship in which the communication occurs, that there is a belief in the community (legal jurisdiction) that the client-professional relationship ought to be fostered, and that the injury to the relationship resulting from the disclosure of the information gained would be greater than the benefit that would be derived from the impact of the disclosure on the litigation to which it pertains. Simply, a court or a legislature confronted with granting privileged communication must consider the nature of the relationship, the value placed on it by the community, the positive consequences involved in helping a relationship, and the negative consequences to litigation if privilege is awarded (Hopkins & Anderson, 1990; Knapp & VandeCreek, 1983).

Since 1828 most state jurisdictions have awarded privileged communication to the clients of physicians, lawyers, clergy, and psychologists. Many states have also extended privileged communication to counselors; for example, all licensure and registry laws for counselors contain provisions extending privileged communication to clients of the licensees. However, some states without licensing laws have privileged communication acts.

Privileged communication laws, whether they be freestanding or a part of another law, are of two general types: those granting absolute privilege and those granting some form of partial or limited privilege. Absolute privileged communication is rare, but is most often extended to the lawyer-client relationship or to those individuals who seek help or solace from the clergy. When absolute privileged communication is extended, presiding judges may not compel disclosure of the information, and even statutes such as those that dictate reporting child abuse often do not pertain to relationships so protected.

Most privileged communication statutes pertaining to mental health practitioners, including counselors, can be characterized as limited or qualified in nature. As Knapp and VandeCreek (1983) point out, the limitations applied to privileged communication are so diverse, the only way to ascertain those pertaining to the individual counselor is to consult those statutes that pertain to his or her jurisdiction (state) and situation. However, one of the major legal qualifications imposed on privileged communications where counselors are involved has to do with the right of a presiding judge to order disclosure of information gained in the confidential relationship, either in pretrial investigations or during the trial itself. Disclosure in this case pertains both to the verbal communication (counseling) and to the records kept regarding counseling. In these cases, the judge decides whether disclosure of information in the possession of the counselor is "in the best interest of justice" and makes a ruling regarding disclosure.

In addition to limitations placed directly on the privilege enjoyed by counselors and their clients within the privileged communication legislation itself, other legislation and case law also limit the degree of privilege extended. For example, all 50 states now have child abuse laws that require individuals who work with children (e.g., counselors, teachers, social workers, physicians) to divulge knowledge or suspicion of child abuse. It is also necessary to report criminal activity in some states (Hopkins & Anderson, 1990). These legal mandates override privileged communication statutes for counselors and their clients in many instances.

The Duty to Warn

Case law, in particular *Tarasoff v. Regents of the University of California,* also has influenced the actual practice followed regarding privileged communication. In the Tarasoff case, a mental health worker was seeing a foreign student in an outpatient setting operated by the University of California at Berkeley. The student disclosed that he intended to kill a former girlfriend who, although not identified by name, could easily be identified by the therapist as Ms. Tarasoff. Subsequently, the therapist asked the campus police to detain Mr. Poddar, the client, which they did for a brief period of time. Mr. Poddar was released on order of the head of the psychiatric unit of the facility where he was confined, and he proceeded to kill Ms. Tarasoff. Her parents subsequently filed suit claiming that the therapist had a duty to warn both the parents and the intended victim.

The California Supreme Court upheld the suit, noting that when a special relationship exists between two persons, and the conduct of one of the persons needs to be controlled, a duty to warn is established. The therapeutic relationship was viewed as a special relationship. Mr. Poddar's explicit threats to kill and the identification of a specific, foreseeable victim established a duty to warn in the eyes of the court (Gehring, 1982).

The result of the Tarasoff case has been widely interpreted to imply that mental health workers have the duty to take appropriate steps to warn either the victims of a client or the clients themselves in the case of potential suicides (Denkowski & Denkowski, 1982). Hopkins and Anderson (1990) report that the result of the Tarasoff case has been tempered somewhat by a 1983 Colorado decision (*Brady* v. *Hopper*), which found that liability was dependent on identification of "a specific threat to a specific person" (p. 15).

The counselor's duty to break confidentiality in cases in which clients may commit suicide has been established in a number of court cases. Earlier in a Wisconsin case (*Bogust v. Iverson*, 1960), a counselor was absolved from liability because the court held that he was not a psychiatrist and thus not qualified to make a diagnosis of potential suicide. However, this ruling probably has little relevance today because of the increase of recognition of the counseling profession. Liability can be avoided if the suicide is unforeseeable (e.g., no threats have been made), reasonable professional steps are taken to stop the suicide (e.g., a no-suicide contract is developed), and the counselor uses reasonable judgment in determining that the client can be depended on to follow the contract (Gable, 1983). If a client threatens to commit suicide, and there is likelihood that the threat will be carried out regardless of the steps taken in counseling, the counselor should take appropriate steps to stop the suicide, including informing parents or guardians and/or seeing that the client is detained.

The AIDS epidemic has raised new issues about the need to disclose information or break confidentiality (Hopkins & Anderson, 1990). What should the counselors do if they learn that one of their clients who is infected with the human immunodeficency virus (HIV) is having unprotected sex with one or more partners? Hopkins and Anderson contend that precedents such as *Tarasoff* did not establish the duty to warn in this case. They note that legal dictates vary from those that preclude warning to those that require it. While it is likely that there will be some convergence of legal thinking about this issue in the years ahead, counselors will have to rely on ethical guidelines as the basis for making these decisions until laws are passed that can guide their thinking. After an exhaustive review of the literature, Harding, Gray, and Neal (1993) concluded that in deciding whether to disclose information that a client has HIV, the welfare of the client and those in danger must be weighed and a decision reached. They also suggested that this is one area where the welfare of the individual may eventually become secondary to that of society.

Permission and Privilege

Since privileged communication is granted to the client, not the counselor, a counselor may be freed from that restriction if permission of the client is obtained. Normally, the permission to breach the privilege would be obtained in writing and involves little difficulty if the client is an adult. But a client who has not reached the age of majority (eighteen in most instances) may not be able to provide permission to divulge privileged information. It is probable that only a parent or legal guardian will be able to give this permission.

Finally, counselors who carelessly divulge privileged information are guilty of unethical practice and, in addition to receiving professional sanctions, may find themselves accused of crimes or the subject of civil legal action because of malpractice.

Malpractice Liability

Malpractice liability grows out of four interrelated conditions. These are:

1. A counselor has a duty to a client to offer services that meet a standard of skill or care.
2. There has been a dereliction or breach of the duty.

3. Harm or injury results to the client or a member of society as a result of the breach of duty.
4. A causal link between the injury or harm and the breach of duty can be established. (Gable, 1983, Hopkins & Anderson, 1990).

Although in the Tarasoff case cited in the preceding section, the mental health worker charged with malpractice was a psychologist, this case is illustrative of the relationship of a counselor's duty, a breach of duty, and a causal relationship between the breach and harm. As Gable (1983) notes, malpractice involves negligence, a failure to act according to accepted professional standards. Gable also points out that it is generally expected that professionals will have the skills necessary to provide reasonable care. In the Tarasoff case, possessing the skills to provide reasonable care involved being able to predict homicidal behavior and following acceptable professional standards to prevent the murder. The duty, then, was to diagnose and prevent homicidal behavior. The duty was breached, harm occurred, and a causal link was established between the dereliction of duty and Ms. Tarasoff's murder. As a result the courts ruled in favor of the plaintiffs, Ms. Tarasoff's parents.

Malpractice liability can result from a number of situations, including suicide (Berman & Cohen-Sandler, 1983), sexual intimacy with clients (Bouhoutsos, Holyroyd, Lerman, Forer, & Greenberg, 1983), faulty supervision (Cohen, 1979; Cormier & Bernard, 1982), failure to get informed consent from children in a research project, improper diagnosis or evaluation of physical injury (Gable, 1983), providing abortion and birth control information, defamation, invasion of privacy, or breach of contract (Hopkins & Anderson, 1990; Slimak & Berkowitz, 1983). This list is lengthy, but it is not exhaustive. In the section on some special legal considerations for school counselors, other sources of malpractice liability will be discussed.

Just as certain conditions must be met before malpractice liability can be established, so are there major areas from which malpractice suits against counselors might result: (1) not following standard practice, (2) using procedures or techniques for which one is untrained, (3) failure to select the best procedure, (4) failure to explain the consequences of treatment, (5) defamation, (6) invasion of privacy, and (7) dereliction of duty. An eighth category, breach of contract, will be discussed in a later section.

Following Standard Practice

A standard of practice is a recognized approach to treating a particular concern. As Hopkins and Anderson (1990) note, determining a standard of care in a malpractice suit against a counselor is difficult. Most persons familiar with the counseling profession are aware that there are competing ideas about the most appropriate way to conduct individual and group counseling, consultation, and testing, although the standard practice regarding testing is probably less debatable.

However, while there is no single way to conduct counseling, ethical guidelines establish some standards of care that must be followed. For example, sexual intimacies with the clients are prohibited. As Gable (1983) notes, sexual intimacy with clients, even in the guise of treatment, has consistently resulted in successful liability suits against mental health workers. In addition, in a number of cases in which therapists have engaged in sexual intimacies in the name of treatment, criminal suits have resulted.

Gable (1983) also indicates that innovative therapy involving physical contact with clients can be the basis for malpractice suits, particularly when the contact is extreme (e.g., hitting, choking).

While deviation from standard practice by hitting a client or becoming involved sexually is extreme, it seems likely that such practices occur, based on the data regarding other professions (Bouhoutos et al., 1983; Gable, 1983). However, failure to properly administer and interpret tests and inventories, and failure to warn to take appropriate steps in the face of homicide and suicide threats, appear to be areas in which counselors are more likely to fall short of recognized standards of care.

Training and the Use of Technique

During the past twenty years, a number of new counseling, consultation, and testing techniques have been developed and popularized, including most of the behavioral techniques, many group counseling techniques, some of the currently used interest inventories, and almost all of the computer assisted techniques (e.g., test administration). As a result many counselors either were not exposed fully to some of these techniques during their training or have little preparation in their use. These people are vulnerable to malpractice suits if damage results from the use of the procedures. A historical case in point is the encounter groups of the 1960s and 1970s that were often led by counselors without proper training. A current-day example is the number of counselors using desensitization procedures to deal with phobic clients, again, in some cases, without proper training.

The question is, how does one attain a skill and demonstrate that he or she has applied it in a reasonable fashion? It seems that the courts have varying opinions about this matter, depending on one's profession, one's geographic location, whether one belongs to a professional organization (e.g., Association of Specialists in Group Work), and whether one claims to be a specialist (e.g., career counselor). The ACA (1988) and the proposed changes (ACA, 1994) to the code of ethics specifies that the members shall not claim or imply qualifications that exceed those possessed. The courts would carry this one step further. Counselors shall not engage in practices that require skills beyond those possessed. Those who do, run the risk of professional malpractice if damage results from that practice.

Failure to Select Best Procedure

Counselors are confronted each day with decisions regarding the best approach to use with their clients. Since there is little evidence to support, say, group counseling over individual counseling, or counseling over consultation, there is little likelihood that malpractice suits will result from these types of decisions. However, a report in a major eastern newspaper gives an example of a decision made by a therapist that might lead to a malpractice suit. In this situation, a psychoanalytically oriented psychotherapist used traditional psychoanalytic procedures to treat a middle-aged woman with agoraphobia (fear of open places) for a number of years and at great expense. The woman did not improve and subsequently discontinued her psychotherapy, engaged a behavior therapist, and was cured in eighteen months. The pain and expenses endured by the woman as the result of inappropriate treatment certainly are the basis for a malpractice suit. Counselors who continue to see clients when others might provide better assistance run the risk of malpractice suits, as does the person who selects the least potent treatment approach.

Failure to Explain the Consequences of Treatment

Few of the treatment strategies employed by counselors will cause the dangerous side effects of medical treatments, where this category of malpractice liability is of greatest concern. However, there are documented cases in which counselors have utilized techniques—such as nudity in groups, self-awareness techniques, touch exercises—that have caused psychological distress that might be interpreted by the courts as harm growing out of a breach of duty. Counselors need to recognize that when they are planning counseling activities, clients need to be fully aware of the nature and potential consequences (e.g., personal embarrassment) of the approach.

Defamation

Defamation of character involves slander, defaming someone orally, or libel defamation using the written word (Gable, 1983). Defamation occurs when information provided to a third party exposes the client to hatred, contempt, or pecuniary loss as a result of the communication. The defamed person must be alive and must suffer a loss, although the loss may be real or psychological (e.g., loss of job or reputation). As Hopkins and Anderson (1990) indicate, some states carry the definition of defamation a bit further, in that counselors and others can be found guilty of defamation if they give false information that (1) a client has committed a serious crime, (2) a client has a venereal disease, (3) negatively affects a person's business or profession, or (4) indicates that a female is promiscuous.

Hopkins and Anderson (1990) go on to indicate that there are two areas in which counselors may become involved in defamation: exposure of records and inadvertent disclosure of information received in counseling. To these should be added the area of recommendations, since many counselors are asked to attest to the character, work habits, academic ability, and other factors relating to clients' worth as students or employees.

Undoubtedly, the best defense against defamation is truth. However, the matter of truth and damage can be interpreted by the courts. In addition, the intent of the communication is of major concern in defamation cases. Successful defamation suits usually result from malicious statements, that is, those that are intended to harm one's client. However, false statements, regardless of content, that impugn the reputation of one's clients (particularly those that relate to a woman's reputation or a client's ability to function on the job) may result in successful suits. Truthfulness and honoring the privilege accorded the communications of one's clients are always in order.

Invasion of Privacy

In 1970, the Russell Sage Foundation published a set of guidelines for collecting, filing, and maintaining student data because, as they noted, their current data-collection and record-keeping procedures constituted a serious threat to the privacy of individuals. In 1974 the Protection of the Rights of Privacy of Parents and Students Amendment to Education was passed with the intention of protecting students and parents from invasion of privacy. Invasion of privacy occurs when information about a client is gained without the client's full knowledge and consent or when the client is a minor or is impaired and is unable to give consent and the consent of parents or guardians is not obtained. Invasion of privacy can also occur when derogatory information gained with the consent of the client is knowingly *or* accidentally provided to another person (Hopkins & Anderson, 1990). In such cases, should either psychological or real damage result, the counselor may be held liable, even though the information disclosed is true.

Counselors are routinely involved in situations in which invasion of privacy might occur. The most obvious of these is the counseling situation, particularly if the counselor's duty to maintain confidence is breached.

The obvious defenses against malpractice liability action for invasion of privacy are keeping confidences and making certain that informed consent is received prior to collecting information. Informed consent depends on competency, knowledge, and voluntariness. Competency is affected by two factors—age and ability—with the latter being related to intellect and state of psychological functioning. In general if a student has not reached eighteen years of age, parents or legal guardians must give consent for data collection or transmittal. Intellectual and psychological competence must also be established before informed consent can be established. Intellectual competence relates to individuals' ability to comprehend the purpose and nature of the data to be collected about them and its use. Mental illness may also impair a client's ability to comprehend the nature of a data-collection strategy.

Knowledge is also a prerequisite for informed consent and relates to the nature of the disclosure to a client about a data-collection procedure in a research project. Clients or research subjects must have enough knowledge about what is to be done to understand the personal ramifications of the procedure. For example, inmates in a minimum security prison who are to be given a personality inventory have a right to know the nature of the inventory (types of questions that are to be asked), what is to be done with the data once it is collected, and how the inventory profiles will be stored. In reality, full knowledge is often not provided to students, inmates, or other subjects in research experiments.

Voluntariness is the final condition that must be met in order to ensure informed consent. Voluntariness means that implicit and explicit coercion are not used to force compliance with a data-collection approach or participation in a research experience. It was not uncommon in the 1950s and 1960s for professors of psychology and counselor educators to require students to participate in three or four experiments as part of a course. (This is still a practice in some universities.) It would be hard to claim that consent in these cases meets the criterion of voluntariness, just as it might be difficult to convince a jury that many of our clients and subjects participate totally on a voluntary basis if teachers or guards suggest that involvement is a "good idea."

Failure to Provide Services

An area that has received little attention is the potential liability growing out of failure to provide the necessary services to students, particularly in the presence of state statutes or school board policies that indicate that certain types of counseling services should be made available to students or others. One set of parents brought a suit, which was dropped prior to litigation, against a counselor for not providing "adequate vocational guidance." Some schools are now initiating programs aimed at providing human sexuality and birth control information, suicide prevention programs, and a vast array of other services designed to combat drug and alcohol abuse, dropping out of school, etc. As long as these programs meet reasonable professional standards and are delivered in good faith, it seems doubtful that the circumstances needed for malpractice liability will be met. But, should programs not be properly and judiciously delivered, or not delivered at all in the face of policies to do so, the counselor and others could be found liable.

STUDENT LEARNING EXERCISE

Indicate that a statement is true by circling T or false by circling F.

1. The type of privileged communication afforded clients of most counselors is limited.   T   F

2. When a counselor-client relationship has been accorded limited privilege, the counselor must refuse to testify in a court of law unless a release is secured from the client.   T   F

3. If a counselor fails to provide some form of desensitization for phobic clients, which is documentably the best approach, legal liability may result, even if the client is helped by the alternative treatment.   T   F

4. Defamation may be either written or spoken.   T   F

5. A true report by a counselor indicating that a student has a venereal disease may be the basis for a defamation suit if the report harms the student.   T   F

6. Since counselors have very few standards of care to follow, they are, relatively speaking, free from successful malpractice suits.   T   F

7. A counselor may be found guilty of defamation if he writes a report indicating that a student performed poorly in a certain area when, in fact, he excelled in that area.   T   F

8. Current case law indicates that counselors must only inform the intended victim of a crime if their client is homicidal.   T   F

9. A researcher who works with children need only get permission from school officials to conduct research.   T   F

Legal Issues and School Counselors

In a provocative article, Talbutt (1983) raised a number of special legal issues confronting school counselors, including those relating to search and seizure, labeling students, corporal punishment, dress, rights to due process, and a number of other areas. These will be discussed in this section.

Search and Seizure

As Hopkins and Anderson (1990) note, concerns about search and seizure grow out of the Fourth Amendment to the U.S. Constitution, which prohibits unreasonable search and seizure. As these authors and Talbutt (1983) also point out, the U.S. Supreme Court has consistently held that minors have the same protection growing out of the Fourth Amendment as adults. For example, the Supreme Court has ruled that the use of dogs trained to sniff out various drugs does not constitute a violation of Fourth Amendment rights, but that strip searches of those individuals identified by the dogs in the absence of a prior history of drug abuse, is an infringement of those rights. The key phrase in the foregoing has to do with the history of drug abuse because this relates to probable cause. Probable cause is evidence or likelihood that a crime has been committed and must be established before searches can occur (Kaplin, 1985). Thus random searches of school lockers for contraband such as weapons and drugs would probably constitute illegal search, but spot checking lockers of individuals who have histories of consistent drug abuse would in all likelihood not be illegal (Talbutt, 1983).

Labeling

An often debated issue in public schools today is the labeling of students. Generally the courts have supported the labeling of students for academic purposes (e.g., educably mentally retarded) because some reasonable basis exists for the process. However, the U.S. Supreme Court (*Merrihen v. Cressman*, 1973) has ruled that it is an invasion of privacy to label a student as a *potential* drug user on the basis of a test that has "error" in it because misclassification may result.

Due Process and Punishment

Both the Supreme Court and lower courts have consistently ruled that schools have the right to administer corporal punishment. The courts have also ruled that paddlings may be administered in the absence of due process, that is, without the student's facing his accuser and having the opportunity to rebut the charges brought against him (Talbutt, 1983).

The U.S. Supreme Court has also ruled (*Goss v. Lopez*, 1975) that students who are to be suspended from school have a right to know the charges against them, a chance to answer the charges, including reviewing the evidence against them, and an opportunity to present evidence on their own behalf (Talbutt, 1983). It should also be noted that while courts have consistently upheld the right of students to due process in matters of suspension, they have accepted situations in which students have been given very little notice of the intent to suspend in some cases.

Freedom of Speech

The U.S. Supreme Court has guaranteed students' First Amendment rights to freedom of speech in a number of cases, the most famous of which was *Tinker v. Des Moines Independent Community School District* (1969). In this landmark case the Tinker children wore black arm bands to school to protest the Vietnam War and were subsequently suspended. The U.S. Supreme Court held that the suspension was a violation of their constitutional right to free speech. However, freedom of speech is not a license to disrupt the activities of the school. The courts have consistently held that the school has the right to take appropriate action to maintain order (Kaplin, 1985).

Right to Services

In 1977 P.L. 94-142, Education of the Handicapped, became effective. The thrust of the law is to guarantee that handicapped students receive free and appropriate education. The law also has a built-in assurance that the rights of handicapped students will be protected, because parents are given far-reaching powers to participate in the design of the education of their children. Specifically the law requires that parents be included in the development of an individualized education program (IEP) and the right to appeal to a state agency if they are not satisfied with the quality of the education being provided to their children.

Counselors have become involved with P.L. 94-142 in numerous ways. In some instances counselors are charged with the responsibility of overseeing the development of IEPs and thus must be familiar with the content of the law. IEPs require careful and systematic drafting of an educational plan for the handicapped child, according to Sproles, Panther, and Lanier (1978). These authors go on to indicate that the IEP must contain the following ten components:

1. A statement of the child's current levels of academic performance (including academic achievement, social adaptation, prevocational skills, psychomotor skills, and self-help skills).
2. A statement of annual goals describing year-end educational objectives.
3. Statements of short-term instructional objectives to be met before annual goals.
4. Statements of the specific educational services needed by the child (determined without regard to the availability of those services).
5. Any special instructional media and materials needed.
6. The date and length of time the services will be given.
7. A description of the extent to which the child will participate in regular educational programs.
8. A justification of the record of educational placement the child will have.
9. A list of the individuals who are responsible for the implementation of the IEP.
10. Objective criteria, evaluation procedures, and schedules for determining (on at least an annual basis) whether the short-term instructional objectives are being achieved.

Not only does the IEP have to contain the aforementioned components, it must also be developed in a manner that will guarantee due process of laws to parents and children. Sproles et al. (1978) also identify ten steps that must be followed to ensure that this provision of the law is met. These steps include (1) an annual review of the IEP, (2) scheduling a meeting to initiate the process of developing an IEP within thirty days after identification as a handicapped student, (3) involvement of all relevant individuals, including the parents, in the development of an IEP, and (4) complete disclosure of information to the parents in their native language. Other provisions regarding the IEP meeting itself are (5) gaining informed consent from parents, (6) involving surrogate parents (e.g., foster parents) if the biological parents are unable to act in an advocacy role for the student, and (7) scheduling meetings at places that are reasonably accessible to all parties. Finally, in order to ensure due process parents need to know that (8) they have a right to challenge both the evaluation of their child and the IEP, (9) they may access and review records regarding their children, and (10) all educational procedures initiated on behalf of their children will be fully documented and easily accessible to them.

Records

In 1974, another law with far-reaching implications for counselors, P.L. 93-380, Family Educational Rights and Privacy Act, was passed. This act applies to all public and private institutions that receive federal funds and has become the major legal consideration where student records are concerned (Kaplin, 1985).

The major provisions of P.L. 93-380 are as follows:

1. Parents have the right to access the records of their children until the student reaches the age of majority (eighteen), at which time that right to access passes to the student. This right to access contains five exceptions: personnel and private records of institution employees, some law enforcement records, some student employment records, alumni records, and some records regarding health care (Kaplin, 1985).
2. Parents of students have the right to challenge the content of their children's records.
3. Disclosure of personally identifiable information to persons outside the school is forbidden unless permission is given by the student or, if the student is under eighteen, the parent.
4. School personnel have restricted right of access. Right of access should be determined on a "need to know" basis, that is, those personnel who are directly involved with the student are typically those who need information about the student.
5. Schools have an obligation under the provisions of P.L. 93-380 to make parents and students aware of their rights regarding student records.
6. Students and/or parents have legal recourse if the provisions of the law are violated by filing a complaint to the Department of Education.

Dress Codes

Dress codes have been a part of most school policies for decades. These have included such odd requirements as requiring boys to wear socks and the exclusion of shorts and hats for both boys and girls. As a protest against what appeared to be discriminatory rules forbidding boys to wear shorts to school, a group of young men in Pennsylvania appeared in school in miniskirts, clothing that had been ruled as acceptable for girls. The boys were immediately suspended. Other protests against dress codes have found their way into the courts.

Courts have generally upheld school dress codes that are promulgated to protect the health and safety of the students, such as special clothing in physical education, where strenuous physical activity is required, or in shops and laboratory areas, where danger may be present (Talbutt, 1983). In some cases courts have gone beyond the health and safety guidelines to decide in favor of school rules that relate to maintaining decorum. In the case of *Fowler v. Williamson* (1979) the court held that a student could be barred from graduation for failure to follow dress-code requirements.

Abortion Counseling

Hopkins and Anderson (1990) believe that providing counseling to minors who are interested in having an abortion may have a number of legal implications, primarily because laws and court rulings regarding those laws vary from state to state. One particular concern raised by these authors is that a counselor might negligently interfere with parental rights to advise their children, either by giving inappropriate advice, overly influencing a student in favor of an abortion, or dissuading a student from having an abortion. In these cases the counselor may be held liable in a civil malpractice suit.

In the situation involving inappropriate advice, liability may result if the counselor fails to establish conditions in which the abortion decision could be fully considered. Options in these cases involve abortion, having the child and keeping it, or bearing the child and putting it up for adoption. A counselor who wrongfully uses his or her influence to persuade a client to have an abortion would be guilty of malpractice. Finally, a counselor who dissuades a student from having either the child or an abortion, particularly if the arguments involve any false information, is in legal peril.

Perhaps the best advice that can be offered with regard to dealing with clients who are considering abortions is to be fully familiar with local statutes and court decisions regarding them before proceeding. Also, as is the case in all matters, ethical guidelines should be carefully followed. Finally, personal values and opinions of the counselor should not interfere with professional duty in dealing with clients considering abortion (Hopkins & Anderson, 1990).

STUDENT LEARNING EXERCISE
Indicate that a statement is true by circling T or false by circling F.

1. P.L. 93-380 stipulates that parents have access to their children's records as long as they are in school.   T   F

2. P.L. 93-380 stipulates that all persons working in a school may have access to the records.   T   F

3. If a student in your school has applied for a scholarship from University X, a representative of that school automatically has access to the student's records.   T   F

4. Probable cause relates to the likelihood that a crime has been committed.   T   F

5. Students who are not yet age eighteen have approximately the same constitutional rights as those over age eighteen.   T   F

6. A principal who suspends a student for wearing clothes that distract others is probably on safe legal grounds.   T   F

7. A student who asks to face his or her accuser prior to being suspended probably is on solid legal ground.   T   F

8. Freedom of speech is a right of students, as long as they do not upset other students or the staff.   T   F

9. Generally speaking, the courts have held that spankings are cruel and unusual punishment.   T   F

Private Practice

Increasingly counselors are entering private practice. Two major legal concerns relating to this area of practice will be discussed in this section: honesty in labeling and breach of contract.

Honesty in Labeling

Winborn (1977), Trembly (1977), and Eberlem (1977) were among the first to comment on legal and ethical concerns regarding consumers' rights, although Gill (1982) and others have commented on this issue since. As Winborn states, "Consumers must have accurate information if they are to make informed choices about goods and services" (p. 206). This need extends to counseling and other services provided by counselors. Gill, drawing on the work of Witmer and others, has drafted a suggested list of factors that might be included in a professional disclosure statement. These include (1) a statement of the purpose of counseling, (2) what the expected outcomes of counseling are, (3) the counselor's and the client's responsibilities during counseling, (4) a description of the counselor's methods and techniques, (5) the types of clients with whom the counselor is most effective, (6) when referrals are to be made (e.g., need for medical treatment), and (7) the limits of confidentiality.

To date, no cases in which counselors have been sued for not making the type of disclosure described above have surfaced, although they may have occurred. One way of avoiding the possibility of being sued is for counselors to draft disclosure statements and establish formal contracts with their clients.

Breach of Contract

A breach of contract occurs when either party fails to meet either their implicit or their explicit obligations. For their part counselors are expected to deliver the services contracted for and to do so using reasonable standards of care. To do otherwise is to court breach of contract suits.

Legally speaking, contracts may be of two types, expressed or implied. The result is that a counselor may be sued for breach of contract, even though no formal contract exists. Counselors and other helping professionals enter into implied contracts with their clients regarding the benefits that the client will receive from counseling and in a number of other areas including confidentiality, quality of care to be provided, and techniques to be employed. As can be readily seen, the recommendations made in the preceding section that relate to professional disclosure statements have direct implications for the types of contracts that counselors need to establish with their clients.

Contracts protect clients by delineating the nature of the service to be provided. They also protect the counselor by setting forth length of treatment and terms of payment, although clients' liability with regard to the length of treatment is limited since they terminate treatment at will without incurring liability. However, a contract does legally obligate the client to pay for services received.

Gable (1983) warns against entering into implicit special agreements with clients such as reassurance that the treatment will be effective or that "everything will be fine." The courts have held that these types of reassurances constitute warranties when given by other professionals such as psychiatrists. Thus a counselor who provides reassurances may be in breach of contract should the treatment not be effective. Gable suggests that some assurances can be given to clients that counseling is effective, but that these should not overshadow the fact that counseling can fail. The counselor should also inform the client of the risks involved in the treatment if they exist.

Ethics Versus the Law

Mappes, Robb, and Engels (1985) contend that there are apparently a number of conflicts that exist between the ethical and legal expectations of counselors. In fact, a relationship exists between statutory and case law and ethics, and this is that the former restricts or shapes the latter. Court cases such as *Tarasoff v. Regents of the University of California* have resulted in the reshaping of ethical statements regarding confidentiality to conform to apparent legal expectations. Child abuse reporting laws simply supercede codes of ethics and thus restrict the extent of a client's privilege. Similarly, P.L. 93-380 gives the parents of minor children and adults the right to access their records, which again shapes counselors' ethical behavior with regard to records. Finally, legislative bodies are continuously reviewing the privileged communication laws and reshaping them based on their view of the best interest of justice and clients. For example, the privileged communication law for school counselors in North Carolina was recently amended to make it possible for judges to order disclosure of information in pretrial investigations. Previously, disclosure could only be ordered at the trial stage.

Legal action by the Antitrust Division of the U.S. Department of Justice has also restructured ethical codes and thus ethical behavior in the area of advertising (Mappes et al., 1985). It can be expected that this type of incursion into the ethical conduct of counselor behavior, and those already mentioned, will continue. While some may see these incursions as negative, the result in some cases has been better services, more disclosure of information, and greater protection of the client.

Summary

During the past two decades, juries have awarded huge sums of money to successful plaintiffs in malpractice suits. As a result, mental health practitioners have become increasingly aware of their legal obligations to their clients. Avoiding liability suits involves practicing ethically and following standards of care where they exist. It also involves offering only those services that one is qualified to deliver.

Counselors in schools and in private practice have some particular concerns. School counselors need to be aware of the constitutional and statutory rights of their clients with regard to search and seizure, freedom of speech, protection from invasion of privacy, and rights to services, to name a few of the more important areas. Private practitioners have many of the same legal concerns that other counselors have, but need to be particularly concerned about breach of contract and honesty in advertising.

Finally, the relationship between ethics and law is a dynamic one. Both statutory law and case law will continue to shape the code of ethics and thus the definition of ethical behavior of counselors.

Review Questions

1. Contrast confidentiality and privileged communication.

2. Outline the conditions that must be present before legal liability can be proven and the steps that should be taken to avoid malpractice suits.

3. What are the conditions to the steps outlined in number 2?

4. Distinguish between slander and libel.

5. Define due process and tell the conditions that must be met in a school setting to ensure that students are guaranteed their constitutional rights in this area.

6. Identify the major areas in which statutes and case laws have changed the ways that counselors function.

References

ACA (1994). Proposed standards of practice and ethical principles. *Guidepost, 45,* 16–22.

American Association for Counseling and Development. (1988). *Ethical Standards,* Alexandria, VA: Author.

Berman, A. L., & Cohen-Sandler, R. (1983). Suicide malpractice: Expert testimony and standard of care. *Professional Psychology: Research and Practice, 14,* 6–19.

Bogust v. Iverson, 102 N.W. 2d, 228 (1960).

Bouhoutsos, J., Holyroyd, J., Lerman, H., Forer, B. R., & Greenberg, M. (1983). Sexual intimacy between psychotherapists and patients. *Pro-*

fessional Psychology Research and Practice, 14, 185–196.

Brady v. Hopper, 83-JM 451 (D. Colo) Sept 14, 1983.

Cohen, R. J. (1979). *Malpractice: A guide for mental health professionals.* New York: Free Press.

Cormier, L. S., & Bernard, J. (1982). Ethical and legal responsibilities of clinical supervisors. *Personnel and Guidance Journal, 60,* 486–491.

Denkowski, K. M., & Denkowski, G. C. (1982). Client-counselor confidentiality: An update of rationale, legal status, and implications. *Personnel and Guidance Journal, 60,* 371–375.

Eberlem, L. (1977). Counselors beware! Clients have rights! *Personnel and Guidance Journal, 56*(7), 219, 223.

Fowler v. Williamson, 251 S.E. 2d, 889 (1979).

Gable, R. K. (1983). Malpractice liability of psychologists. In B. D. Sales, (ed.), *The Psychologists' Handbook* (pp. 460–491). New York: Plenum.

Gehring, D. D. (1982). The counselor's "duty to warn." *Journal of Counseling and Development, 61*, 208–212.

Gill, S. J. (1982). Professional disclosure and consumer protection in counseling. *Personnel and Guidance Journal, 60*, 443–446.

Goss v. Lopez, 419 U.S. 565 (1975).

Harding, A. K., Gray, L. A., & Neal, M. (1993). Confidentiality limits with clients who have HIV: A review of ethical guidelines and policies. *Journal of Counseling and Development, 11*, 297–305.

Hopkins, B. H., & Anderson, B. S. (1990). *The counselor and the law.* (3rd ed.). Alexandria, VA: ACA Press.

Kaplin, W. A. (1985). *The law of higher education,* (2nd ed.). San Francisco: Jossey-Bass.

Knapp, S., & VandeCreek, L. (1983). Privileged communications and the counselor. *Personnel and Guidance Journal, 62*, 83–85.

Mappes, D. C., Robb, G. P., & Engels, D. W. (1985). Conflicts between ethics and law in counseling and psychotherapy. *Journal of Counseling and Development, 64*, 246–258.

Merrihen v. Cressman, 364 F. Supp. 913, (E.D. P.A. 1973).

Russell Sage Foundation. (1970). Proposed principles for the management of school records. Excerpt. *Personnel and Guidance Journal, 49*, 21–24.

Slimak, R. E., & Berkowitz, S. R. (1983). The university and college counseling center and malpractice suits. *Personnel and Guidance Journal, 61*, 291–294.

Sproles, H. A., Panther, E. E., & Lanier, J. E. (1978). PL 94-142 and its impact on the counselor's role. *Personnel and Guidance Journal, 57*, 210–213.

Talbutt, L. C. (1983). Recent court decisions: A quiz for APGA members. *Personnel and Guidance Journal, 62*, 355–357.

Tarasoff v. Regents of the University of California, 551, p. 2d 334 (Cal. Sup. Ct., 1976).

Tinker v. Des Moines Independent Community School District, 393 U.S. 503, 506, 89S. Ct. 733, 21 L.Ed.2d 731 1969.

Trembly, E. (1977). Three steps toward consumer advocacy. *Personnel and Guidance Journal, 56*, 214–218.

Winborn, B. B. (1977). Honest labeling and other procedures for the protection of consumers of counseling. *Personnel and Guidance Journal, 56*, 210–213.

Chapter 13

Credentialing Counselors and Program Accreditation

Goals of the Chapter

The purposes of this chapter are to present an overview of individual credentialing and program accreditation in the counseling profession and to discuss the implications of credentialing for the profession.

Chapter Preview

- A brief history of credentialing in the counseling profession will be presented. The intention of this presentation is to illustrate both the recency of the movement and the rapidity with which credentialing is being adopted by the profession.
- The terminology of individual credentialing (e.g., licensure, certification, etc.) will be defined and illustrated.
- Program accreditation will be discussed, including its purpose and the processes involved.
- Implications of credentialing for the counseling profession will be examined.

Introduction

We live in a credential-conscious society. Physicians display their certificates and licenses on office walls. Termite exterminators paint local permit numbers and state certification numbers on their vehicles. Barbers, beauticians, real estate sales people, and nurse practitioners all are credentialed by regulatory bodies in the states in which they practice. The result is that credentials have taken on a variety of meanings. The most important one is that these certificates are now viewed, by both the public and the occupational groups involved, as indicators that those who hold them are legitimate practitioners.

Credentialing began to protect the public at large, and this continues to be its main purpose. Unscrupulous individuals have performed surgery, accepted construction jobs for which they had no expertise, sold worthless property to unsuspecting clients, and practiced psychotherapy. Professional groups and legislators alike view credentialing as a means of identifying those individuals who possess the needed skills and expertise to perform certain services, such as the general practice of medicine.

Credentialing serves other purposes as well. It is a means by which professional groups act to communicate which of its members meet certain specialty standards (e.g., plastic surgery or career counseling). It is also used by professional groups to restrict entry into certain job markets by unqualified individuals. Finally, credentialing provides state legislators with a means by which they can control the entry into, and practice of, various professional groups.

As is perhaps obvious from the foregoing discussion, the impetus for credentialing can come from two sources: professional groups and governmental agencies. Often these two groups work in concert. For example, in one state the attorney general's office received more than 400 complaints within a relatively short period of time regarding the nature of career counseling and placement by private employment agencies. Lawyers in the attorney general's office contacted members of the professional association in the state, and legislation to regulate career counselors via licensing was drafted. However, in another state that was experiencing the same problem, the attorney general's office successfully promulgated legislation that was totally unsatisfactory to professional counselors. As early as 1976, MacKin warned counselors to monitor themselves or run the risk of governmental intervention. Certainly his warning seems appropriate given the turn of events described above.

Credentialing involves more than issuing licenses or certificates to individuals, however. Training programs have also come under scrutiny by professional groups, and the counseling profession is no exception. In addition to the credentialing of individuals, the accreditation of counselor preparation programs will also be discussed in this chapter.

A Brief History of Credentialing: Counselors and Programs

The movement to credentialing in the counseling profession has been dramatic. While some of the background of the credentialing effort was presented in Chapter 1, a brief history of this effect should graphically portray the priority placed on credentialing within the profession. Material in this section was abstracted in part from publications by Warner, Brooks, and Thompson (1980), and McFadden and Brooks (1983).

- 1972—*Welden v. Virginia Board of Psychological Examiners.* John I. Weldon was enjoined from practicing as a counselor by a Virginia court because counseling used the tools of psychology but was unregulated by statute.
- 1973—The Commission on Rehabilitation Counselor Certification met for the first time in Chicago. Four years later credentialing of rehabilitation counselors (Certified Rehabilitation Counselors) began.
- 1973—The Southern Association of Counselor Education and Supervision adopted a position supporting licensure efforts.
- 1974—A special issue of the *Personnel and Guidance Journal*, "Licensure and the Helping Professions," was published under the editorship of Sweeney and Sturdevant.
- 1974—The American Personnel and Guidance Association, APGA (now the American Counseling Association) called for licensure legislation efforts in all fifty states.
- 1975—The APGA (ACA) Senate established a licensure commission with Thomas J. Sweeney of Ohio University as its chair.
- 1975—*State of Ohio v. Culbreth B. Cook.* Mr. Cook was charged with practicing psychology without a license by the Ohio State Board of Psychology, arrested, and tried. Mr. Cook did not represent himself to be a psychologist but was engaged in private practice as a counselor specializing in assessing children in academic difficulty. The court found Mr. Cook not guilty.
- 1976—Virginia passed the first counselor licensure law.
- 1977—Licensure and certification issues were addressed in a special issue of *Personnel and Guidance Journal* edited by Gerald R. Forster.
- 1977—Bruce Shertzer of Purdue University was appointed to head a special committee to study credentialing. Later that year the committee recommended continued efforts in support of licensure, accreditation of counselor education programs, and the development of a national registry for professional counselors.
- 1977—Association for Counselor Education and Supervision (ACES) adopted *Guidelines for Doctoral Preparation in Counselor Education*. These along with the *Standards for the Preparation of Counselors* and *Other Personnel Services Specialists*, adopted in 1973, would underpin program credentialing efforts.
- 1978—*Personnel and Guidance Journal* published a third special issue on licensure and credentialing.
- 1978—Acting on the recommendation made by the committee chaired by Bruce Shertzer, the APGA Board of Directors approved committees for Counselor Preparation and Standards, Licensure, and Registry. ACES was directed to proceed with the accreditation of preparation programs.
- 1979—Idaho State, Ball State, University of Washington, and University of Virginia began the first ACES accredited counselor education programs.

- 1979—The National Academy of Certified Mental Health Counselors administered its first examination.
- 1979—Arkansas passed a second licensure law in March. In July, Alabama became the third state to achieve licensure.
- 1981—Twenty-one states announced their intention to introduce counselor licensure laws at the APGA convention.
- 1981—In June, Texas became the fourth state to pass a licensure bill. In July, Florida became the fifth.
- 1981—CACREP held its first meeting. It became the official accreditation arm of AACD.
- 1981—National Vocational Guidance Association (NVGA) initiated NCCC, the Nationally Certified Career Counselor program.
- 1982—Idaho became the sixth state to pass a licensure law.
- 1982—The National Board of Certified Counselors (NBCC) held its first meeting. More than 3,000 counselors submitted applications for certification that year.
- 1983—North Carolina passed the first counselor registry law.
- 1984–85—Nine additional states pass licensure laws: Ohio, Tennessee, Georgia, Mississippi, Montana, Oklahoma, South Carolina, Missouri, and Oregon.
- 1985—The National Career Counselors certification program merged with the National Board of Certified Counselors. After July 1, eligibility for certification was dependent on prior certification by NBCC.
- 1985—The NBCC newsletter *NBCC News Notes* reported that more than 1,400 counselors had qualified for certification.
- 1986—Nebraska and West Virginia became the seventeenth and eighteenth states to pass counselor licensure or registration laws.
- 1987—Forty-eight counselor education programs had been accredited by CACREP. Washington, Wyoming, Kansas, Delaware, and Rhode Island have passed credentialing laws.
- 1991—Two new specialties are adopted by the National Board for Certified Counselors: Gerontological Counseling and School Counseling.
- 1993—The National Academy of Mental Health Counselors merged with NBCC.
- 1994—One hundred counselor education programs are currently accredited by CACREP; forty-one states and the District of Columbia have passed licensure or registry laws for counselors (Appendix A); approximately 21,000 counselors NCCs—National Certified Counselors.
- 1995—NBCC announced a new specialty certification in addiction counseling.

In approximately thirty years, the counseling profession has advanced from a position of no credentialing of individuals or accreditation of programs to a fully developed program accreditation effort and 80 percent of the states having credentialing laws in place.

State-Level Credentialing for Individuals

The credentialing movement has resulted in a plethora of titles that are at times confusing to both professionals and laypeople alike. In this section the various titles connected with the state-level credentialing of counselors will be identified, defined, and where possible, illustrated. (See Appendix C for listing of credentials for each state.)

Licensure: Title and Title/Practice Laws

A license is a credential authorized by a state legislature that regulates either the title, practice, or both of an occupational group. As a result, there are title acts and title/practice acts. Acts that license counselors, psychologists, social workers, and marriage and family therapists are typically title acts since they usually do not set forth areas of practice, but they do reserve the use of the title to the professional groups. Licensure laws for dentists are title/practice acts since they restrict the use of the title "dentist" to qualified individuals *and* set forth the parameters of dental practice. For example, dentists are entitled to prescribe certain types of medicines, but only those related to their practice. While most states have title restriction acts in place, the movement is to restrict counselors' practices as well. For example, section 4757.01 (A) H.B.205 of the Counselor and Social Work law states,

> *"Practice of professional counseling" means rendering or offering to render to individuals, groups, organizations or the general public a counseling service involving the application of clinical counseling principles to assist individuals in achieving more effective personal, social, educational, or career development and adjustment. "Practice of professional counseling" does not include the diagnosis and treatment of mental and emotional disorders unless a professional counselor has received from the counselor or social worker board created in section 4757.03 of the revised code the endorsement provided for under division B of section 4757.07 of the revised code, or unless a professional counselor is supervised by another professional counselor who has that endorsement, a licensed psychologist, or a psychiatrist.*

Another section of the Ohio statute deals with the title. Section 4757.02 (A) of H.B. 205 states,

> *Except as provided in section 4757.16 of the revised code, no person shall engage in or hold himself out as engaging in the practice of professional counseling under the title of "professional counselor" or "counselor assistant" or any other title or description incorporating the word "counselor" for a fee, salary or other consideration unless he is currently licensed as a professional counselor or registered as a counselor assistant under this chapter and rules adopted under it.*

The above section of the Ohio statute restricts the use of the title to licensed professionals, although a number of exemptions, such as school counselors, are provided for in the act. Section A of the statute also defines counseling practice and provides that only licensed counselors may engage in that practice unless they are exempted by the law. By setting forth these standards the Ohio statute becomes a title/practice licensing act.

A number of states have adopted title restriction licensure laws. Section 490.12 of Florida's bill to license mental health professionals (S.B.82) illustrates the language used in these acts to preclude the use of the title by unlicensed persons. It states,

> No person shall hold himself out by any title or description incorporating the words, or permutations of them, ..."mental counseling," "marriage therapist," "marriage counselor," "marriage consultant," "family therapist," "family counselor," "family consultant," "mental health counselor," "sex therapist," or "sex counselor," unless such a person is licensed under this chapter or is exempt from the provisions of this chapter.

The last sentence in the passage of the Florida mental health licensing law should be noted since it indicates that exemptions from the law are possible. This is a typical statement. To date, counselor licensure laws have been aimed primarily at regulating private practice only; that is, counselors in public agencies do not have to be licensed in most states where licensure laws exist.

Licensing legislation, in addition to restricting the use of title and/or practice, establishes a licensing board that is a quasi-legislative body empowered to establish rules that govern the licensing and delicensing process. This board is typically appointed by the governor of the state, is comprised largely of members of the professional group being regulated by the licensing legislation, and may have a representative of the public at large as a member. Including laypeople on licensing boards is increasingly popular because the basic purpose of licensure boards is to protect the welfare of the public in a particular state, and some legislators feel that licensing boards have become too concerned with the welfare of their own occupational group. The Texas licensure law is illustrative. SB606, Section 4 Nature and Composition of Board states,

> (a) The board is composed of nine members appointed by the governor with the advice and consent of the senate; (b) Not later than the thirtieth day after the effective date of this Act, the executive committee of the Texas Counseling Association shall submit to the governor a list of qualified candidates for the board, including the names of four qualified counselor educators and twelve qualified practicing counselors. Not later than the sixtieth day after the date the list is received, the governor shall select from the list the membership of the board consisting of one counselor educator and four counselors to provide practice. The governor shall appoint four citizens from the general public who have no direct or indirect affiliation with the practice of counseling or delivery of mental health services.

Section 6 of SB606 delineates the responsibilities of the board: These are to (1) hold at least two regular board meetings per year, (2) keep an information file about each complaint filed, (3) "determine the qualifications and fitness for licenses, renewal of licenses, and reciprocal licenses," (4) develop rules that enable the board to carry out the intent of the Act, (5) "examine for, deny, approve, issue, revoke, suspend, and renew licenses," and (6) make consumers of counseling services aware of the purposes of the board and means by which they may register complaints.

Certification: State Level

Of all terms dealing with credentialing, none is more confusing than certification. Because certification has been used historically in connection with the process of becoming qualified to practice in public schools, this is the usual connotation of the term. However, certification laws have been passed that have essentially the same impact as licensure laws. It is therefore necessary to distinguish between these two types of certification.

Certification for Schools

The U.S. Constitution empowers states to regulate education within their jurisdiction. Typically, legislators have delegated this authority to state boards of education who, in turn, establish certification standards for counselors, teachers, administrators, and others. Representatives from state departments of education are then charged with enforcing the rules that have been established by the state board of education. This is accomplished in two ways. The most popular is the approved program approach in which a team from the state department of education peruses the course offerings, field experiences, laboratory facilities and experiences, and other factors related to the quality of preparing educators and approves a certification program in a particular area such as school counseling. A recommendation from that program results in certification.

A second approach is for a Division of Teacher Training and Certification or a similar named office within the state department of education to review credentials of prospective educators and render decisions regarding whether they are qualified to perform in the public schools.

Two things need to be emphasized about the foregoing presentation. First, the constitutional authority of the state and its designee(s) to regulate entry into the public schools is absolute if it chooses to maintain that authority. Licensing laws passed to regulate the use and/or practice of psychology or counseling cannot generally supersede this authority. Therefore, many licensing laws make note of this authority or contain some form of caveat regarding holding the title of counselor or psychologist in the school. Second, state boards of education have little control over private schools, particularly those that are church-related, and thus these schools are usually able to set training standards for their counselors and other personnel independently.

Certification for Title Restrictions

Some occupational groups have petitioned legislatures for permission to designate individuals that have met higher standards. Often these standards are higher than those for other members of that occupational group and involve passing a competency examination, completing a distinct number of years of practice, and holding a graduate degree. Probably the best known occupational group that has pursued this route are the accountants, with only those accountants who have met the higher standards allowed to use the title "certified public accountant." Some states have a similar provision for marriage and family counselors. Any mental health professional may advertise that he or she performs work in those areas, but only those practitioners who have met the standards established by the certification board may advertise themselves as certified marriage and family counselors. In other states, marriage and family counselors are licensed, so the procedure for designating professional groups is not the same from state to state.

Registry for Title Restriction

Another way of allowing an occupational group to designate individuals who have met a set of specified standards is for a state legislature to pass a registry law. A register is a document that lists by name and other pertinent information those individuals who have been certified by a professional certification board (ACA, 1985–86, p. 9). Nursing has traditionally used this means to identify those individuals who meet high standards (registered nurses). At least one state, North Carolina, originally passed a registry law that empowered a registry board to set standards and establish and publish a listing (register) of registered practicing counselors. That law has been converted to a licensing law.

Generally speaking, registry laws are less restrictive than licensing laws. However, wording in the Idaho Licensure Law (HB492) illustrates how title licensure acts and registry acts converge, since the Idaho law is considerably less restrictive in its intent than the Florida law. It states,

> *Chapter 34—section 54-3402*
> *It shall be unlawful for any person to represent himself/herself to be a licensed professional counselor or licensed counselor unless he/she shall first obtain a license pursuant to this chapter. Nothing in this chapter, however, shall be construed to limit or prevent the practice of an individual's profession or to restrict a person from doing counseling provided that the person or individual does not hold himself/herself out to the title or description as being a licensed counselor or a licensed professional counselor.*

Implications: State Level Credentialing

It is obvious that licensure laws that restrict the title, certification, and registry laws perform very much the same function: They identify those professionals who can utilize certain titles (e.g., professional counselors). One important difference among them that has already been noted is that licensure has more status. This is probably because medicine, law, and dentistry have been granted licensure privileges, and licensure laws are typically more preclusive in that they often totally restrict the use of the title "counselor" *or* its derivatives, as is obvious in the Ohio and Florida counselor licensure laws cited earlier. Certification and registry laws only restrict the use of the title certified public accountant or registered practicing counselor, while permitting almost anyone to use the generic occupational title in context (e.g., sales counselor, credit counselor, etc.). Therefore, most occupational groups, and particularly counselors, are striving to secure licensing in all fifty states. Currently, nearly 80 percent of the states have licensing laws in place.

Credentialing for Individuals: National Level

In many ways, state level laws that give counseling groups the right to set standards within that jurisdiction are the most important because of the legal penalties (typically a violation is a misdemeanor) that can be imposed by a licensing, certification, or registry board for individuals who violate the regulations governing the group. However, many occupational groups, including counselors, have initiated additional credentialing efforts at the national level that promote excellence within the group by promoting standards of training, requiring that counselors demonstrate a knowledge base, and asking individuals to maintain their qualifications through in-service training. Within the counseling profession these efforts are in the form of certification boards that offer credentials to qualified individuals.

ACA (1985–86) defines certification as "a process by which the professional certifying board grants formal recognition to an individual who has met certain predetermined professional standards as specified by that group" (p. 9). Currently, there are four boards certifying counselors at the national level: The Commission on Rehabilitation Counselor Certification, the National Academy of Certified Clinical Mental Health Counselors, the National Council for Credentialing Career Counselors, and the National Board for Certified Counselors (NBCC). Because the last of these, NBCC, is generic in nature, it will be discussed first.

NBCC

NBCC was established in 1982. The purposes of the certification, according to NBCC (1994a), are to

- Promote professional accountability and visibility;
- Identify to the public and professional peers those counselors who have met specific professional standards;
- Advance cooperation among groups and agencies actively involved in professional credentialing activities;

- Encourage the continuing professional growth and development of National Certified Counselors;
- Ensure a national standard developed by counselors.

Eligibility

NBCC offers four routes to certification. The first of these is obtaining a graduate degree in a counseling or related field that has been accredited by CACREP. Applicants must submit an official transcript, have supervised counseling experience, document their training, and pass the National Counselor Examination (NCE).

The second certification option is for those people who do not graduate from CACREP accredited programs. These applicants must have earned a graduate degree in counseling or a related professional field, document that coursework has been completed in counseling theory and supervised practice as well as six other areas, complete two years of at least half-time work, and pass the NCE. The third option is available to persons who have passed the NCE and received licensure in states affording that option. These people were exempt from the NBCC exam, but had to meet the coursework requirements listed under option two, and hold licensure as a professional counselor in a state requiring the NCE. The fourth option is for people who have a master's degree in counseling or closely related field and have not yet accrued the required postgraduate experience of two years of at least half-time practice. If these people pass the NCE they are issued a certificate that indicates they have attained NBCC board eligible status and, on completion of the experience requirement, become National Certified Counselors.

Certificate

Counselors meeting eligibility requirements are credentialed as National Certified Counselors (NCC) for a period of five years. Renewal of the certificate requires completion of one hundred clock hours of continuing education or reexamination and continuing ethical practice.

NCCC

In 1981, the National Vocational Guidance Association (now National Career Development Association) established the National Council for Credentialing Career Counselors (NCCC) as a means of improving career development practice. Originally, this council operated independently, but on July 1, 1985, it merged with NBCC. One of the results of this is that NCCC credentialing currently requires NBCC certification as a prerequisite to certification. Other eligibility requirements follow (NBCC, 1994b).

Eligibility

In addition to the NBCC certification requirements already listed, individuals seeking certification as a career counselor must demonstrate that they have compiled coursework in career development, assessment, and fieldwork that includes 25 percent time focused on career counseling or equivalent experience. Additional coursework in career counseling procedures, education and labor market structure and trends, consultation strategies and methods, and career development program management and implementation is also required. Applicants must also pass a National Career Counselor Examination and document that they have at least two years of professional career counseling experience in at least a half-time position.

Certificate
Counselors who meet the requirements are designated as Nationally Certified Career Counselors (NCCC) for a period of five years. In addition to completing one hundred clock hours for NBCC recertification, career counselors must complete an additional twenty-five hours of continuing education. Fifty hours of the total (125) must focus on career development. In addition, NCCC recertification requires continuing ethical practice throughout the certification period.

NACCMHC

The National Academy of Certified Clinical Mental Health Counselor (NACCMHC) published its first registry in 1979. In 1993 the Academy, in cooperation with ACA and the American Mental Health Counselors Association, merged its certification effort with NBCC. The purpose of the certification is to increase the visibility of mental health counselors, enhance public awareness of the specialty and promote professional growth (NBCC, 1994c).

Eligibility
In order to become a Certified Clinical Mental Health Counselor (CCMHC) a counselor must first complete the NCC requirements. Additionally, the eligibility for CCMHC certification specifies that the master's degree must have included at least sixty hours of coursework in counseling or a closely related mental health specialty. Applicants must also demonstrate that they have completed nine to fifteen semester hours of clinical training in fieldwork that is relevant to providing mental health counseling. Finally, applicants must successfully complete the National Clinical Mental Health Counseling Examination.

Certificate
Counselors who meet the requirement for certification as a CCMHC are certified for a period of five years. Renewal of the CCMHC requires that of the one hundred hours of continuing education required for renewal of the NCC, thirty-five hours must be in the clinical mental health counseling area. An additional twenty-five hours of clinical mental health training must also be acquired for recertification.

NCSC

In 1991 NBCC, along with ACA and the American School Counseling Association, established a certification, the National Certified School Counselor, aimed at enhancing the professional identity and identity of school counselors. NBCC also sought to provide an avenue for school counselors who wished to do so to demonstrate that they have met national standards (NBCC, 1994b).

Eligibility
Must meet all the requirements for the NCC and meet the following criteria: (1) two years of full-time school counseling experience, (2) completion of specified course work dealing with school counseling, (3) completion of a self-assessment, and (4) two external assessments, one by a supervisor and one by a counselor who holds the NCSC credential.

Certificate
Successful applicants receive the NCSC for five years. Renewal requires completion of the one hundred hours necessary for the NCC, twenty-five hours of which must be in the area of school counseling.

NCGC

The National Certified Gerontological Counselor (NCGC) was developed by NBCC in cooperation with ACA and the Adult Development and Aging Association for the purpose of promoting the identity of gerontological counselors and enhancing their identity. The NCGC credential was also seen as a means of encouraging professional growth in this group and raising public awareness of this group of counselors (NBCC, 1994b)

Eligibility
In order to become a NCGC counselors are first required to become NCCs. Then they must meet the following requirements: (1) three graduate courses in gerontological studies or 120 hours of continuing education in this area, (2) two years of work in the specialty after completion of coursework, (3) a 600-hour internship under the supervision of a NCGC or similarly credentialed individual. At least 25 percent of the internship must have been in a gerontological setting, (4) a self-assessment, and (5) two professional assessments by a supervisor and a colleague.

Certificate
On completion of the requirements, the NCGC is awarded for five years. To renew the credential the counselor must complete the one hundred hours necessary for renewal of the NCC, at least twenty-five of which must deal with gerontological counseling.

CRCC

The Commission on Rehabilitation Counselor Certification (CRCC) was established in 1974 (CRCC, 1994), and thus is the oldest of the counselor credentialing agencies. The primary purpose of the program "is to provide assurance that professionals engaged in rehabilitation counseling will meet acceptable standards of quality in practice" (CRCC, 1994, p. 1). A second purpose is to provide agencies that employ rehabilitation counselors with a standard against which applicants can be compared.

Eligibility

CRCC delineates six routes to certification and specifies that an applicant must meet *all* requirements listed within one of the categories. All applicants must complete a certification examination. The first of the paths to certification is completion of a master's degree program in a rehabilitation counselor preparation program fully accredited by the National Council on Rehabilitation Education (CORE) and completion of an internship (480-hour quarter system, 600-hour semester system) supervised by a Certified Rehabilitation Counselor (CRC). No employment experience is required under this option. The second option for certification is similar except that provision is made for graduates from programs not accredited by CORE, in which case the applicant must have one year of experience under the supervision of a CRC. Option three, like option one and two, is designed for graduates of rehabilitation counseling programs. However, in the event that the program is not accredited by CORE and the individual has no internship, two years of experience supervised by a CRC are required as a prerequisite to certification.

The fourth option for certification is for students and specifies that students must be enrolled in an accredited rehabilitation counseling program, have completed 75 percent of his or her coursework, have completed the internship under the supervision of a CRC, and provide a letter verifying that he or she is a student in good standing. While this is a special category for students seeking certification, examination results profiles and certificates are not released until students have completed the master's degree. Thus, the effect is to give students a head start on the certification process, not to actually certify them.

The final two categories of certification are for individuals who do not hold U.S. citizenship and for individuals who hold a doctorate in rehabilitation counseling. In both cases, the general requirements set forth for the other categories must be met.

Certificate

Successful applicants are credentialed as Certified Rehabilitation Counselors and the certificate is valid for five years. In order to receive recertification without reexamination, applicants must complete 150 contact hours of approved continuing education credit.

Summary of Individual Credentialing

The numbers and forms of licenses and certification are considerable. What is obvious is that the counseling profession as a whole, and the subgroups within the profession, are enthusiastically pursuing various forms of credentialing. The rationale for this movement was set forth in the introduction: legitimizing the profession and its specialties to the public at large. Other implications of the credentialing movement will be discussed in the final section of this chapter.

STUDENT LEARNING EXERCISE

Match the answers in the right-hand column with the credentials listed in the left-hand column.

___ 1. Title licensure act	a. voluntary rehabilitation counselor certification program
___ 2. Title/practice licensure act	b. aimed at improving vocational counseling
___ 3. Registry/certification laws	c. precludes the use of the term counselor by unqualified individuals
___ 4. Certification for school counseling	d. generic national certificate
___ 5. NCC	e. state level voluntary credentialing effort
___ 6. NCCC	f. preclusive acts that specify areas of practice as well as title usage
___ 7. CCMHC	g. credential sought by counselors who work in community agencies
___ 8. CRC	h. usually given by approved counselor preparation programs
___ 9. NCGC	i. concerned for the elderly
___ 10. NCSC	j. might be interested in children

Training Program Accreditation

The roots of accreditation of counselor education programs can be traced in part to the 1964 adoption of "Standards for Counselor Education in the Preparation of Secondary School Counselors" by the Association of Counselor Education and Supervision (ACES) and the American Personnel and Guidance Association (now ACA) (Stripling, 1978). Today, two accrediting bodies are involved in approving counselor preparation programs. CORE accredits rehabilitation counselor preparation programs and CACREP accredits school, mental health, and related counselor preparation programs. Standards used in the latter process were first adopted in 1973 (ACES, 1977).

The Accreditation Process

Wittmer and Loesch (1986) identify six features of the accreditation process. The first of these is that accreditation is voluntary. In some of the older, more established professions, training programs must be accredited before graduates can practice. However, this is not the case in the counseling profession. The result is that fewer than 25 percent of counselor preparation programs are accredited at this juncture, although this number is expected to rise dramatically in the next decade.

The second and most obvious of the points made by Wittmer and Loesch (1986) is that accreditation is based on standards. These standards address a number of features of the training program, ranging from the care with which program objectives are spelled out to the quality of the faculty. Consideration is also given to the quality of students enrolled in the program, the curriculum offered, the nature of the field experiences, the facilities available to students and faculty, administrative support for the program, and a variety of other factors. To some degree, the standards are aimed at quantitative factors (e.g., number of hours spent in field experience), but for the most part the concern is on qualitative factors (e.g., are students adequately prepared to perform as counselors?).

If a program faculty determines that they wish to become accredited, they conduct an intensive self-study using the aforementioned standards as a guide. This self-study is presented to, and reviewed by, CACREP. CACREP has three courses of action at this point in the process. One of these is to accept the application and send an accreditation team to the university or college housing the applicant program. This team's responsibility is to verify that the information contained in the self-study is accurate. CACREP may also reject the application on the grounds that the program clearly does not meet standards *or* the council may request more information (CACREP, 1994).

If an accreditation team is sent to a program, it interviews faculty, students, administrators, and field supervisors, and conducts a review of appropriate records to determine whether CACREP standards have been met. The team files a report with CACREP that is considered along with the original application. Here again, the council has three options: denial, provisional accreditation, or full accreditation. Full accreditation indicates the program under consideration has fully met accreditation standards. Provisional accreditation is awarded when a training program has met all but a few of the accreditation standards and shows clear promise of remedying its deficiencies within the two-year period for which accreditation is given (CACREP, 1985). Programs that are denied accreditation are provided precise feedback about their deficiencies and encouraged to reapply once problems have been addressed.

The third feature of the accreditation process is that it costs money (Wittmer & Loesch, 1986). One of these costs is the application fee. If the program is approved, a continuing fee must also be paid each year. However, these are not the major costs of accreditation. High-quality counselor education programs cost considerable amounts of money to staff and support because of faculty teaching student loads, the employment of higher-quality faculty, increased expenditures for facilities, and so on. It is the increased cost that precludes some counselor education programs from pursuing the process.

As we have seen, accreditation requires self-study. This is the fourth feature of the process delineated by Wittmer and Loesch (1986). However, the self-study does not end with accreditation. In fact, the self-study at the outset is barely the beginning of this process. Each year, the faculty, field supervisors, and students of a CACREP approved program review the status of each program to make certain that they are still in compliance with the standards.

Wittmer and Loesch (1986) point out a fifth aspect of the accreditation process: It has a geographic limit. However, unlike the Department of Education program approval process described earlier in this chapter, accreditation has a national geographic limit.

Sixth, accreditation is not reciprocal (Wittmer & Loesch, 1986). The American Psychological Association or the American Association of Marriage and Family Therapists will not recognize the accreditation given by CACREP and, of course, CACREP does not recognize APA's or AAMFT's accreditation processes either. Perhaps this can best be understood when one considers that the various accrediting agencies represent different professional groups, and thus reciprocity would, to a very large degree, be inappropriate.

A seventh and final feature of the accreditation process is that it is curriculum specific. Many counselor education programs offer specialties in school counseling, mental health counseling, gerontological counseling, student affairs in higher education, etc. Accreditation is awarded not to an entire department, but to the specialty curriculum (CACREP, 1994). Thus it is entirely possible that one program within a counselor education program unit could be accredited and another not.

There are a number of results of the adoption and implementation of accreditation standards for the preparation of counselors. First, the profession has an adopted set of criteria for judging preparation programs that may be utilized by prospective students, employees, and clients, and by insurance carriers and others to evaluate the quality of preparation of counselors. The criteria also provide a set of standards by which counselors and others may compare their preparation to that of other mental health professionals. Finally, and as already noted, these standards allow credentialing bodies to make judgments about the preparation of persons who apply for certification and licensure. The result is typically preferential treatment for graduates of these programs.

STUDENT LEARNING EXERCISE

Read each statement and place a T in the blank if it is true, and an F if it is false.

___ 1. Program accreditation and individual credentialing are often linked in some manner.

___ 2. Program accreditation is primarily a quantitative effort, that is, aimed at auditing credit hours, examining the credentials of instructors, and examining facilities.

___ 3. Evidence has been advanced that students completing accredited programs are better prepared than those completing nonaccredited programs.

___ 4. AAMFT will accept graduates of CACREP-approved programs for credentialing.

___ 5. At this point, program accreditation by CACREP is a voluntary process.

___ 6. One of the primary reasons for advancing program accreditation is to increase the credibility of counselors.

Implications of Credentialing

Any discussion of the implications of credentialing must be divided into two sections: those for the individual and those for the profession. Students and others often ask, "If I am licensed or certified, what does it mean for me?" In a number of instances, particularly with regard to certification, the answer is that in tangible terms it means nothing. In professional or personal terms, the benefit to the individual may be substantial. Let us look at the tangible rewards for the individual first.

Licensing for counselors in states like Virginia and Florida may mean that the individuals can receive payment for the provision of mental health services specified in the health insurance coverage of a client. Since fees for counseling vary widely, from as little as $15 per hour to as much as $100 per hour, it is difficult to estimate what the actual tangible return might be.

The intangibles of meeting the highest standards of one's professional group are the reward sought by most counselors. Licensure in many states and certification by NBCC or CCRC carry no automatic reward, yet thousands of counselors have pursued these credentials to illustrate their commitment to professionalism.

The implications of credentialing for the counseling profession are profound. One of these that is relatively certain is that both program accreditation standards and certification requirements will continue to escalate. This will place increasing pressure on counselor education programs because higher standards translate also quite directly into increased costs in many instances. Since accreditation, licensure, and certification are linked, preparation programs unable to meet accreditation standards may be less able to compete for prospective students. These are points of conjecture, to be sure, since there is no evidence that program accreditation improves the quality of the graduates.

It is also quite likely that licensure and certification will become hiring requirements for some types of counseling jobs in the future. For example, the American Rehabilitation Counselor's Association has lobbied unsuccessfully to require that all counselors hired under the auspices of the Rehabilitation Act of 1973 be Certified Rehabilitation Counselors (Guidepost, 1986). There are also movements afoot in some states to require that mental health counselors working in state agencies be certified or licensed. These initiatives will continue to intensify and be successful in some instances.

It can also be expected that the counseling profession will gain in stature with the public at large, among mental health professional groups, and among legislators as a result of credentialing. The result will be an extension of professional self-control and rewards such as third-party payments from health insurance carriers. This is not to suggest that these things will occur just because of credentialing. However, credentialing efforts will provide counselors interested in advancing the profession with the rationale and support needed to convince legislators that the profession meets the criteria necessary for further recognition.

Summary

The history of individual and program credentialing in the counseling profession is a brief one when compared to many professional groups. However, given its brief history, credentialing is also a highly successful movement, and one with so much momentum that it is likely to accelerate in the future.

Credentialing varies from state to state, with a large number of states having no licensing or regulatory statutes for counselors in place at this time. However, in almost all states that have no licensing laws in place, movements are underway to correct this situation.

Program accreditation began officially in 1979, although concern about formal training standards in the profession can be traced to the early 1960s. Program accreditation, like licensure and certification processes, is a quality control measure.

Review Questions

1. Compare and contrast title/practice and title licensing laws.

2. How do certification and licensing laws differ? How are they similar?

3. Discuss the pros and cons of credentials such as NCC, given that there are few tangible benefits associated with holding these certificates.

4. What are the advantages that accrue to the accredited counselor education program? What are the disadvantages? What are the advantages and disadvantages to the student, given the fact that there is no assurance that he or she will actually be better prepared to function as counselors?

5. If all states adopted licensure laws such as the one in Ohio that precludes certain counselors from diagnosing mental health problems, what would be the impact on the counseling profession?

6. Given the definitions set forth, is the Idaho law a licensure law or a registry/certification act, even though it is called a licensure law?

References

American Association for Counseling and Development (ACA). (1985–86). *American Association for Counseling and Development, 1985–86.* Alexandria, VA: Author.

Association for Counselor Educational Supervision. (1977). Standards for the preparation of counselors and other personnel services specialists. *Personnel and Guidance Journal, 55*(10), 596–601.

Commission on Rehabilitation Counselor Certification. (1994). *Guide to rehabilitation counselor certification.* Arlington Heights, IL: Author.

Council for Accreditation of Counseling and Related Educational Programs. (1994). *CACREP Accreditation and Procedures Manual.* Alexandria, VA: Author.

Guidepost. (1986). ARCA pursues rehabilitation bill. *Guidepost, 28,* 2.

MacKin, P. K. (1976). Occupational licensing: A warning. *Personnel and Guidance Journal, 54,* 507–511.

McFadden, J., & Brooks, Jr., D. K., (eds.), (1983). *Counselor Action Licensure Packet.* Alexandria, VA: AACD.

NBCC. (1994a). *General Practice Counselor Certification.* Greensboro, NC: Author.

NBCC. (1994b). *Specialty Certification 1994: NCC, NCGC, and NCSC,* Greensboro, NC: Author.

NBCC. (1994c). *Specialty Certification 1994: Clinical Mental Health.* Greensboro, NC: Author.

Stripling, R. O. (1979). Standards and accreditation in counselor education: A proposal. *Personnel and Guidance Journal, 56*(10), 608–611.

Warner, Jr., R. W., Brooks, Jr., D. K., & Thompson, Jean A., (eds.), (1980). *Counselor licensure: Perspectives and issues,* Falls Church, VA: AACD Press.

Wittmer, J. P., & Loesch, L. C. (1986). Professional orientation. In M. D. Lewis, R. L. Hayes, & J. R. Lewis, (eds.). *An Introduction to the Counselors Profession,* (pp. 301–330). Itasca, IL: F. E. Peacock Publishers.

Chapter 14

Counselors in Educational Settings

Goal of the Chapter

The goal of this chapter is to describe the functioning of counselors in various educational settings.

Chapter Preview

- The controversy regarding the roles of counselors in educational settings will be presented.
- Counselor functions in elementary, junior high, high school, and postsecondary educational institutions will be discussed.
- The diverse factors that influence counselor functioning will be discussed.

Introduction

The latest *Occupational Outlook Handbook* reports that of the approximately 150,000 counselors working in the United States, nearly two-thirds were working in educational programs, primarily in elementary and secondary schools, colleges, and universities. This means that the number of counselors working in educational institutions exceeds 100,000 at this point, a number that increases daily. It is a major objective of this chapter to examine the diverse functions these counselors perform and to give the reader a sense of both the commonalities and differences that exist both across and within educational levels. It is not the intention of this presentation to infer that there are prototypical ways of functioning, or that one function (e.g., counseling) is superior to another (e.g., consultation), although there are those within the profession who would do so, and with good reason.

Counselors' Roles and Functions: An Overview

The matter of counselors' roles has not been overlooked by professional organizations, particularly the American School Counselor Association (ASCA), which has continuously provided leadership in the area of clarifying the role of counselors in educational institutions. This association began its discussion of roles with two publications, "The Unique Role of the Elementary School Counselor" (Lamb & Deschenses, 1974) and "The Role and Function of Postsecondary Counseling" (ASCA, 1974). It continued with a revision of the elementary school role statement in 1978 (ASCA, 1978) and publication of "The Role of Secondary School Counselors" (ASCA, 1977). Another document, "The Role of the Middle/Junior High School Counselor," was also developed, but never published, in the 1970s. The 1981 statement, "The Practice of Guidance and Counseling by School Counselors," consolidated all previous role statements into a single document as does the latest statement, "Role Statement: The School Counselor" (ASCA, 1990). Before discussing the specific roles of the elementary school, middle/junior high school, high school, and college counselors, some of the generic aspects of counselor functioning set forth in this latest document will be discussed.

Perhaps the most interesting aspect of ASCA's (1990) latest statement regarding the role of the school counselor is that there is very little differentiation among the roles of counselors functioning at various levels. The statement says that "School counseling is developmental by design, focusing on the needs, interests, and issues related to the various stages of student growth," and school counselors are employed in elementary, middle/junior, senior, and postsecondary schools. Their work is differentiated by attention to age-specific developmental stages of growth and related interests, tasks, and challenges. The statement goes on to identify five basic interventions employed by counselors to deal with students' needs: (1) individual counseling, (2) small group counseling, (3) large group guidance, (4) consultation, and (5) coordination.

While ASCA has decided not to differentiate among the roles of counselors working at various levels, almost every issue of *The School Counselor* contains a new suggestion for counselor functioning. Recent articles have focused on the counselor's role with college-bound students who are learning disabled (Satcher, 1993), counseling the occult-involved student (Carmichael, 1993), and dealing with children who have been sexually abused (Minard, 1993). Over the past fifteen years other authors have recommended that counselors at various levels have a role with families and stepfamilies (Lutz, Jacobs, & Masson, 1981; Wilcoxen, 1986), emotionally disturbed students (Levinson, 1985), special education students generally (Skinner, 1985), potential dropouts (Gadwa & Griggs, 1985), students suffering from eating disorders such as anorexia nervosa (Hendrick, 1984) and bulimia (Hendrick, 1985), and students who are potentially suicidal (Delisle, 1986; Wellman, 1984).

Preoccupation with Role

Counseling is relatively new and, as such, is an evolving profession. Counseling services were first offered extensively on college campuses in the late 1940s, although there were a number of campuses with counseling centers prior to 1945 (Heppner & Neal, 1983). As was pointed out in Chapter 1, counseling in public schools has been available since the turn of the century, but it was not until the late 1950s and early 1960s that counseling services were widely offered in high schools and junior high schools. Although there has been a rapid growth in the number of counselors in elementary schools, many schools are still without the services of counselors. The newness of counseling services in our educational institutions almost mandates that there be an ongoing search for more effective means of delivering services to client groups.

The nature of the clients served has changed over time, and this has also changed perspectives on counselor functioning. Veterans returning to college campuses with their spouses after World War II increased concerns about marriage and family counseling services in institutions of higher education. This concern has been so greatly amplified today that it is not uncommon for job announcements for college counselors to specify that applicants have skills in marriage and family counseling. Similarly, elementary school counselors find that a variety of society trends, including increased divorce rates and both parents working, have increased their need to offer services to parents in the form of parent education, parent consultation, and, in some instances, family counseling. Skyrocketing increases in teenage pregnancy have forced high school counselors to alter their activities to include support groups for pregnant teenagers and to become involved in human sexuality programs. As these changes have occurred and will continue to occur, counselors may have to continue to shift the focus of their activities.

Another factor that contributes to the concern about roles is a sense of vulnerability among counselors in educational institutions. This perception was heightened in the late 1970s and early 1980s when economic recession brought cutbacks in public school and university counseling staffs in states such as Michigan and Pennsylvania, and property tax reduction referendums in California and Massachusetts lowered public school revenue, resulting in a reduction in counselor positions. Gladding and Hageman (1984) characterized the situation as "a professional season of fading. It is a crisis" (p. 166). Crabbs (1984) blamed not only the economic cycle, but increasing social and political conservatism for the current situation, and offered an accountability model for counselors that would enable them to justify their positions and stem the outward tide of reduction in force.

While there is no question that counseling services are to some extent vulnerable since they do not represent instruction—the major function of educational institutions—a countertrend has developed in the nineties, a growing awareness of the need for counseling services. As Herr (1986) observed a decade ago, the doomsayers are not accurate forecasters of the demise of counseling in educational institutions. There are many current indicators that counseling services are valued. Herr cites as one source of support, the prestigious Carnegie Foundation document *High School, A Report on Secondary Education in America* (Boyer, 1983), which recommends that high school counseling loads be reduced to one counselor for each hundred students, a position adopted by ASCA in 1988. Of note also are a modest expansion of college counseling centers in many institutions and the passage of legislation in some states. Virginia, Tennessee, and North and South Carolina recently have required the addition of school counselors to educational staffs.

Another factor that continues to fuel counselors' concerns about their roles is a certain amount of discrepancy between what the public perceives them to do and what professionals themselves believe they are about. Recently, Bishop (1986) found that 85 percent of the faculty on the University of Delaware campus were aware of the services offered by the counseling center. Most (81 percent) also knew that personal counseling was offered to students, and 62 percent knew that educational counseling was offered to the same group. However, only 30 percent recognized that consultation services were available to them, and 17 percent believed that they could receive personal counseling, a service not offered by the center. Bishop concluded that faculty members were not aware of the career development services offered by the counseling center since only 52 percent knew that career counseling for students was available.

Ibrahim, Helms, and Thompson (1983) studied the role perceptions of high school counselors held by students, administrators, members of the business community, and counselors themselves and, like Bishop (1986), found some discrepancies. For example, counselors saw research and consulting with the staff as less important than administrators. It should be pointed out, however, that these two groups agreed on a majority of the functions of the high school counselor.

In the aforementioned study, counselors and administrators had significantly different perceptions from parents or members of the business community with regard to providing help to parents, public relations, educational and occupational planning, and referral of problems to outside agencies. Counselors and administrators attached more importance to public relations and helping parents, and parents and members of the business community placed greater emphasis on career and educational planning and referral (Ibrahim et al., 1983).

A study conducted in Indiana (Schmidt, 1994) found that many parents and students were unhappy with the services that they were receiving from their counselors. For example, only about one-third of the parents in the survey felt they received enough information from counselors to help their students make wise curricular choices. Perhaps more to the point, the study concluded that counselors were often trapped in a no-win situation of trying to be all things to all people with the result being that they were involved in activities for which they were undertrained (dealing with anorexic clients) and overtrained (clerical tasks). Given the lack of clarity about the role counselors should fill, and the wide ranging expectations held by the publics of school counselors, the conclusions in the Indiana study are not surprising.

Partin (1993) studied another problem that plagues school counselors when trying to implement their roles: time robbers. Partin defined a time robber as anything that took time away from professional functioning. He found that 16 percent of the time spent by the counselors he surveyed went into activities that could be classified as time robbers.

What is missing from the literature on counselor role is a set of guiding principles that would help counselors prioritize the functions they perform. In the absence of this statement, counselors often find themselves trying to perform a myriad of functions and performing none of them well. It is also the case that school counselors often serve at the "will and pleasure" of their principals who may have a very different idea about their role than they do and have the power to force unwanted roles on counselors. Because of these and other factors it seems likely that the roles school counselors should fill will be a point of contention, study, and professional deliberation well into the future.

Counselors in Elementary Schools

As was noted in Chapter 1, elementary school counselors are the newest addition to the cadre of counselors working in school settings. As was also noted earlier in this chapter, elementary school counselors represent the fastest growing group of counselors at this juncture, partially because there is increasing recognition of the impact of certain societal problems such as family breakup on children and, to some degree, because there is an expectation that elementary school counselors will prevent serious educational and psychological problems from arising. While there are numerous expectations of how elementary school counselors should function, the fact is that they operate quite differently.

Marsha is the only counselor in an elementary school with an enrollment of 650 pupils. Her district requires that every counselor deliver classroom guidance activities to every classroom each week. The result is that the majority of Marsha's time is spent preparing for or delivering units on topics dealing with friendship, values clarification, understanding and appreciating people who are different (e.g., from different ethnic groups, with handicaps), self-concept development, and an array of others to the thirty classrooms in her building. In her remaining time, she runs small groups dealing with classroom achievement, consults with parents and teachers, serves on the committee to accept and process referrals for students who may need placement in special education classes, and does a limited amount of individual counseling, primarily with students who are having educational adjustment problems. Students with moderate or severe psychological problems are referred to private practitioners or to the local community mental health center.

Sarah's school, like Marsha's, enrolls more than 600 students. However, Sarah has more freedom to design her own program and has elected to work collaboratively with teachers to incorporate units into the regular curricular activities. As a result, all teachers include units on career-related activities such as parent's careers (kindergarten), community helpers (first grade), and workers in our state (fifth grade). Teachers have also incorporated into the curriculum units on study skills and how to take tests. Sarah also coordinates the sex education program for fifth and sixth graders. In all of these activities, Sarah acts as a resource person in that she helps teachers locate appropriate materials and she often acts as an active participant in that she is a copresenter. These coordination/consultant activities take up well over 50 percent of Sarah's time. The remainder is spent in individual and group counseling, conducting parenting skills classes, designing and delivering in-service training for teachers on topics such as creative discipline, conferencing with parents, and developing communications skills.

Tom serves a school of 350 students, and his role is probably more in keeping with the stereotypical role of the elementary school counselor. Classroom guidance takes only about 25 percent of his time, while small groups based on the needs of students occupy another 30 percent. Tom also sees three to four individuals per day for thirty to forty-five minutes, consults with teachers and parents, and serves on the special education screening team.

- *Individual Counseling*—These sessions, lasting from thirty to forty-five minutes, depending on the age of the child, range in focus from support for the child who has experienced a loss such as a death in the family, to skills building for the child who has difficulty making friends. The duration of counseling may be from one to several weeks.
- *Group Counseling*—These sessions typically involve six to eight children and revolve around a central theme such as school achievement, friendship, coping with stepfamilies, etc. Usually, they are scheduled once a week for six to eight weeks, but may last longer.
- *Consultation with Teachers*—These sessions may be initiated by either counselor or teacher and focus on a concern that will assist the teacher to be more effective with students. Counselors act collaboratively, in that they become actively involved in all phases of the process.
- *Consultation with Parents*—This activity may also be initiated by either a counselor or a parent. Consultation is typically short term and focuses on a specific process in the family that is leading to difficulty for the child. An example might be that a child who is undisciplined at home exhibits unruly behavior at school.
- *Classroom Guidance*—These sessions, which typically last from thirty to forty-five minutes, focus on developmental issues confronted by most youngsters such as communication, decision making, getting along with others, etc.
- *Coordination*—This involves the identification and facilitation of activities that will promote the child's development. Elementary school counselors may coordinate the testing program, career development activities, and referral to community agencies.
- *Orientation*—Students new to the school are presented information about their new environment in small groups and by other means. They are also given an

opportunity to explore their feelings about their new experiences. Students leaving the school are familiarized with the middle/junior high school, generally in cooperation with counselors from that level.

- *Educational Activities*—In-service training activities are conducted with teachers in order to increase their skills and enable them to be more effective with students. Similarly, parent education activities are held to develop parenting skills.
- *Other*—Elementary school counselors fill a number of other roles such as serving on committees charged with screening students referred for special services, serving as advisors to student councils, and acting as the school's liaison with community agencies such as the Department of Social Services.

Counselors in Middle/Junior High School

It is true that middle school (typically grades five through eight) and junior high school (seven through nine) counseling have received short shrift in terms of attention and concern. It seems to be the case that most authors believe that material from both senior high school and elementary school will generalize to these grade levels. However, students at this educational level are undergoing some dramatic physical and psychological changes that place unique demands on counseling staffs. The functioning of a middle school counselor and two junior high school counselors is illustrative of the impact of the setting and the students on counselor functioning.

Doug is responsible for 350 students and spends more than 50 percent of his time counseling individual students in the school where he works because "it is virtually impossible to get groups of students together." He does run two support groups per week, one for new students and another for minority students. He is involved in teacher consultation and has been instrumental in getting drug and alcohol abuse units strengthened in health and biology classes. He also has been successful in getting English and social studies teachers to develop units on careers that extend over a nine-week grading period. Doug coordinates the achievement and aptitude testing program, as well as the administration of interest inventories to all first-semester ninth graders. The remainder of his time is spent in scheduling, working with community agencies, "administrivia" (filling out forms), and general school responsibilities.

Julia, formerly an elementary school counselor, now works in a new middle school that enrolls more than 900 students. She has been assigned half of these students. She has found that students have less free time to see the counselors than those in the elementary school where she had worked. She has designed classroom guidance units for students, and each year, each class will receive a nine-week unit based on the developmental needs of the students. Units include human sexuality (conducted with the health educator), school and you, boy-girl relations, getting along with parents, and career exploration. Individual counseling, some group counseling, teacher consultation, parent education, serving on the special education referral committee, scheduling, and referral make up the bulk of the remainder of Julia's schedule.

Sharon works in a rural area where she has responsibility for more than 700 students. She has convinced the administration to make students available for group work and spends more than 35 percent of her time in group counseling. Fifty percent of her time is spent in individual counseling, with the rest spent on parent and teacher consultation, scheduling, and referral of students to community agencies. She spends no time in the classroom, but she believes this is a weakness in her program because she feels she is not reaching all the students.

In summary, the functions that comprise the middle school/junior high school counselor's role are as follows.

- *Individual Counseling*—Sessions are geared to school periods or parts of school periods (thirty to fifty-five minutes) and, for the most part, are spread over a few weeks. Problems discussed typically focus on peers, boy-girl relationships, family concerns, and adjustment in school.
- *Group Counseling*—Group counseling sessions, like individual counseling sessions, have to be tailored to the school day. Problems discussed in groups are similar to those addressed in individual counseling.
- *Teacher Consultation*—Generally, consultation sessions are short term in nature and focus on educational concerns such as discipline, parent relationships, and curricular concerns such as integrating career development concepts into the curriculum, strengthening drug abuse programs, and developing programs such as those involving study skills.
- *Classroom Guidance*—This is not a major role for many junior high school counselors, although many middle school counselors are extensively involved in delivering classroom units. Topics parallel those offered in elementary schools, with more emphasis on career development, life planning, human sexuality, drug abuse prevention, and dealing with parents.
- *Parental Consultation*—Topics involved range from motivating students to do school work to dealing with rebellious adolescents. Generally, consultation is relatively short term, and some of the sessions may be followed up with telephone calls to offer support or assistance.
- *Referral*—A number of serious problems arise among young adolescents, including bulimia, anorexia nervosa, and suicidal ideation. Depending on the severity of the problem, counselors may refer these types of problems to outside agencies because of time constraints.
- *Coordination*—Many counselors working at this level are charged with extensive scheduling responsibilities or, at the very least, coordinating the scheduling process. Counselors also coordinate testing and career development programs in many instances.
- *Orientation*—A part of orientation may come in the form of support groups for new students. However, middle and junior high school counselors, in collab-

oration with elementary and high school counselors, are often involved in the orientation of new students or preparing students for the next level.
- *Research and Evaluation*—These activities are not emphasized in many school districts, but they do occupy a portion of most counselors' time.

High School Counselors

Counseling services have been available in some high schools for approximately a century. Even though these services are the oldest, the roles of counselors working at this level are the most problematic because of the pressures to fill nonprofessional roles and because of the amount of time needed to handle scheduling and related activities (Partin, 1993). What follows are some vignettes that deal with the roles of some "typical" high school counselors.

Sandra is a high school counselor who rotates with her class each year, following sophomores until they are seniors and then picking up another group of sophomores. Because of this rotation, her role varies considerably from year to year. One constant is her involvement in scheduling and general educational planning, which culminates with assisting seniors and those who leave school prior to graduation with selection of postsecondary educational opportunities. Another constant is a steady stream of personal counseling clients who are seen, for the most part, individually. Group counseling focuses on career planning, race relations, and, from time to time, problem pregnancies. Referral of students involved with drugs and alcohol abuse and those who have relatively severe personal problems, such as suicide threats, bulimia, and anorexia nervosa, also occupy a fair amount of each day. Finally, because so many of her students go on to college, writing recommendations, seeing that transcripts are mailed, and helping students with financial aid applications also take much of her time.

Jerry is a vocational counselor in a large high school and works only with vocational students. Although he helps students with personal, educational, and vocational problems, a great deal of his time is spent on career planning, job placement, testing, and the development of employable skills. He also has developed and maintains an extensive career information library. Because Jerry's program is partially supported by federal funds, he spends a small amount of time completing forms such as activity reports.

Marian's principal sees her as an extension of the administration in her school and, as a result, she spends nearly half of her time in scheduling, drop-add, telephoning students who are absent, record keeping, and computing grade point averages. The remainder of her time is spent in individual, educational, and career planning, disseminating postsecondary educational and career information, coordinating the program, serving as a member of the curriculum reform committee, and meeting with parents, usually about students with academic problems or for college planning. She admits to being frustrated by her inability to meet the vast number of personal-social needs among the study body.

The functions filled by secondary school counselors can be summarized as follows.

- *Individual Counseling*—These sessions, usually spanning a few weeks, deal with a wide range of developmental and moderately severe personal problems. Sessions are geared to school schedules and typically last from thirty to fifty-five minutes. Typical problems addressed include making educational choices, career planning, family concerns, drug and alcohol abuse, and peer relationships.
- *Group Counseling*—Like individual counseling, group counseling addresses a wide range of developmental and personal problems. Group counseling typically lasts from eight to ten weeks but may be somewhat shorter or longer depending on the school situation.
- *Teacher Consultation*—Consultation with teachers focuses on such topics as the infusion of activities such as study skills programs into the curriculum and, to a smaller degree, classroom management and the motivation of students.
- *Parent Consultation*—This function typically occupies less of the counselor's time than at other levels. The focus ranges from assisting parents in dealing with alcohol and drug abuse to educational planning.
- *Orientation*—Orientation of new students to the high school is a continuing problem for counselors in this setting because of the frequent arrival of new students. Counselors at this level are also often involved in orienting students to postsecondary educational institutions and the world of work. To cope with the latter, counselors arrange seminars in which graduates of the school discuss work situations with current students; they also plan field trips, internships, career days, and other relevant activities.
- *Educational Planning and Advising*—These activities range from assisting in course selection and registration on a semester-by-semester basis to activities focusing on long-range planning such as planning a high school course of study and selecting a postsecondary educational program. In some instances, this planning is coordinated with career planning, particularly as students near graduation. Some of these activities result in considerable clerical work such as duplicating and mailing transcripts to colleges and universities.
- *Coordination*—Counselors may coordinate such activities as the testing program, career development activities, substance abuse programs, and other similar programs.
- *Job Placement and the Development of Employable Skills*—Some high school counselors are charged with identifying job opportunities in the community, placing students in jobs in the community, and preparing students to secure jobs and be successful in them.
- *Referral*—Students with serious psychological problems such as severe depression, anorexia nervosa, or bulimia are typically referred to outside agencies. Secondary school counselors often are continuously involved with identifying and making referrals to appropriate external agencies and with follow-ups to those referrals.

Counselors in Postsecondary School Settings

Counselors are widely found in vocational-technical schools, community colleges, four-year colleges, and universities. Research regarding counselors in postsecondary institutions has focused for the most part on college counselors. Some of this research has focused not on the role of the college counselor but on certain aspects of the agency itself. For example, Brown and Chambers (1986) found that students indicated that they would be more willing to go to a counseling center called a Personal and Career Counseling Service than they would a service named Psychological and Career Counseling Service; Counseling, Career, and Consultation Service; or Psychological and Career Exploration Service. The authors concluded that their research supported earlier findings that the name of a counseling center influences how it is perceived by students and faculty.

Because some college counseling centers have large staffs, counselors can specialize and thus role definitions may vary widely. More typically, particularly in community colleges and small college counseling centers, counselors perform many duties, some of which may not be related to counseling at all. Some postsecondary counselors find themselves recruiting new students, administering the financial aid offices, and filling any number of other roles.

One of the fairly unsettling trends among college counselors is what can best be described as a growing disinterest in career counseling because of the lack of importance of career counseling among college students. Pinkney and Jacobs (1985) found that new counselors ranked titles that involved career counseling (e.g., job placement) lower than those relating to personal counseling (e.g., psychological counselor). This same group of counselors was also less interested in narrative descriptions of cases involving career-related problems.

The three vignettes that follow illustrate the diversity among the roles filled by college counselors.

Gary is a career counselor in a relatively large counseling center. More than 50 percent of his time is actually spent in career counseling, with the remainder being spent in leading career exploration groups, teaching a career exploration class for undergraduates, and working collaboratively with the Career Planning and Placement Service to develop employable skills such as resume preparation and interviewing behaviors in students.

Lorraine works in the same center and spends three-quarters of her time seeing individual clients with personal adjustment problems. Problems that require long-range treatment (more than twelve weeks) are referred to the local mental health center because of time constraints. Personal development groups, such as those dealing with sex role identity and becoming more assertive, occupy her remaining available hours.

John works in a small community college and wears a "number of hats," including recruiter, job placement officer, and, of course, counselor. Much of his time is spent with orientation and registration activities as well as with those already mentioned. He estimates that he spends less than one-quarter of his time counseling and this is mostly focused on educational and career planning.

The major functions of counselors in postsecondary institutions can be summarized as follows.

- *Individual Counseling*—These activities typically are longer term in nature than individual counseling in other educational institutions and embrace a wider variety of problems. Personal adjustment counseling makes up the bulk of the counseling activity in many agencies, but career counseling is still a very important activity.
- *Group Counseling*—Group counseling may span an entire semester or more. Topics addressed include career exploration, assertiveness, bulimia, anorexia nervosa, developing a sex role identity, and a host of other problems growing out of educational and personal experiences and problems of students.
- *Consultation and Outreach*—Counselors consult with faculty, residence hall personnel, and others involved with students. They also develop educational programs such as those designed to make residence hall advisors better able to identify and refer students who are manifesting psychological problems.
- *Training and Supervision*—Some, but not all, college counselors have adjunct appointments in training programs and are actively involved with teaching courses and the supervision of the field experiences of counselors in training.
- *Research and Evaluation*—A substantial number of college counselors have ongoing research programs and contribute regularly to the professional literature. Some of these and others also are involved in periodic or continuing efforts to evaluate the impact of their agency on the setting where it is located.
- *Testing*—Larger counseling services often employ psychometrists to administer tests. However, in small centers counselors administer tests to their own clients. In community colleges, it is not uncommon for counselors to be charged with the administration of the screening tests used to place students in mathematics and English classes.
- *Referral*—Because of the availability of staff, most counseling centers find it necessary to refer certain types of clients to external agencies. On large college campuses, the counseling center may be one of several agencies delivering services to students, with each agency specializing in a particular function such as career counseling or dealing with pregnant students. In these situations, in-house referral systems are developed and utilized to make appropriate referrals.

Factors that Influence Role and Function

In the preceding sections of this chapter, concerns about the role and function of counselors in educational institutions were discussed first. This was followed by a look at the role and function of counselors at various levels of the educational enterprise. Three different types of information were included in each of the discussions of counselors' roles at the various levels: professional recommendations, roles suggested by research, and brief narrative descriptions of the function of counselors at each of the levels. It is the position here, and one held over a long period of time by the authors (Brown & Srebalus, 1973), that counselors are professionals and thus must be involved in shaping their own role to suit their personal characteristics and those of the institution in which they are employed. This process is ultimately a reciprocal process, with the professional counselor exerting influence based on a variety of factors and the institutions placing demands on the individual that must be met. It should also be noted that the reciprocal process is a dynamic one and thus the role of a counselor is likely to shift over time as the individual and the institution change. At this point, some of the factors that influence this dynamic process will be examined.

The needs of the client groups to be served are among the most influential of the factors shaping the counselor's role in a given institution. On an informal basis, needs may be perceived quite differently by counselors, administrators, parents, and the community. Increasingly, counselors are involved in needs assessment programs that involve approaches such as surveying students, parents, teachers and administrators to ascertain perceptions of student, parent, and teacher needs, examining school records to identify needs (e.g., look at the dropout rate), and perusing test information to identify academic deficiencies. Once needs are developed, mutually agreed on strategies can be developed to meet the needs.

While it would seem logical that the needs of the clients to be served would dictate counselor functioning, this may not be the case. Often preferences for various functions are based on the skills of the counselor, and probably on the personality of the counselor as well.

Not only do the preferences of counselors influence their roles, but so do the expectations of administrators and other role senders. It may be recalled that Marian, a high school counselor, found herself extensively involved in administrative duties because her principal viewed her as an extension of his office. Other counselors have found themselves in similar circumstances.

Tradition is also a powerful force in determining how the counselor will actually function. All too often, counselors hear, "We've always done it this way." Assertive professionals are able to break with tradition and function in different ways over time if they can convince the persons around them that a new method is more effective.

The resources of the institution also are tremendously important determiners of the counselor's roles. Underfunded community colleges press counselors into roles in financial aid, recruitment, registration, etc. Elementary school counselors find themselves checking on truants and giving psychological tests because of the unavailability of attendance officers and school psychologists. High school counselors confronted with massive numbers and no secretarial help may be reduced to functioning as registrars and college placement officers because of the demands placed on them.

Professional organizations such as the American School Counselor Association influence roles by the development of role statements. These statements provide baselines by which professional counselors may judge their own functioning against that established by their peers.

Finally, training programs exert considerable influence on the function of counselors by the selection of areas to be emphasized in the training programs. School counselors have been critical of training programs for being too theoretical and not providing enough techniques that have practical application. However, it is probably not accidental that in the surveys cited earlier in this chapter individual counseling was viewed as the most important activity in which counselors engage and emphasis is placed on this activity in training programs.

Summary

School counselors represent a significant portion of the counseling profession. Because they are employed largely in public institutions, their functioning is influenced by the same societal forces that have an impact on schools. Cutbacks in funding for schools have resulted in reduction in force among counselors in some places, but in many states the number of school counselors is advancing steadily.

The functioning of counselors in educational settings varies tremendously, depending on such factors as student needs, administration expectations, counselor preferences, and the availability of other resources. It seems likely that a number of current issues such as the "back to basics" movement will continue to influence how counselors in educational settings function.

STUDENT LEARNING EXERCISE

After you have read this chapter, the following activities may help you understand more completely the functioning of counselors in educational settings.

1. Interview practicing counselors from various levels that interest you. Ask them the following questions:
   a. How much time do you spend on various counseling related activities? Non-counseling related activities?
   b. Which of your activities is the most rewarding?
   c. If you could change your role, what would you do?
   d. What impact does your supervisor have on your role? Your setting? The age of the client group?
   e. What changes have you seen in your role since you became a counselor?

2. Interview a school psychologist or a mental health counselor and contrast their roles to those of school counselors.

Review Questions

1. Identify the major roles of counselors in educational institutions. Then discuss how each role might be used to meet student needs. Finally, rank those roles you personally would like to offer to students and tell why.

2. Discuss counseling and consultation as possible intervention strategies. Tell how the educational level would have an impact on your use of these two interventions.

3. Outline the pros and cons of school counselors' providing therapeutic services to bulimics, potential suicides, and others who would require large amounts of the counselors' time.

4. Which counselors working in educational settings are in the best position to have an impact on the mental health of their clients? Why?

5. Some have argued that counselors working in K–12 settings do not need to be as rigorously trained as counselors working in mental health settings. Do you agree? Why or why not?

6. Counselors working in some educational settings are saddled with many noncounseling duties. How would you avoid having that happen to you?

References

American School Counselor Association. (1974). The role and function of postsecondary counseling. *The School Counselor, 21,* 330–334.

American School Counselor Association. (1977). Role statement: The role of the secondary school counselor. *The School Counselor, 24,* 228–233.

American School Counselor Association. (1978). The role of the elementary school counselor. *Elementary School Guidance and Counseling, 13,* 91–96.

American School Counselor Association. (1981). Role statement: The practice of guidance and counseling by school counselors. *The School Counselor, 29,* 7–12.

ASCA. (1988). The school counselor and counselor/pupil ratio. In *Position Statements of American School Counselor Association,* Alexandria, VA: Author.

ASCA. (1990). Role statement: The school counselor. In *Guide to Membership Resources,* Alexandria, VA: Author.

Bishop, J. B. (1986). A faculty review of a university counseling center: Knowledge, perceptions and recommendations. *Journal of College Student Personnel, 27,* 413–417.

Boyer, E. L. (1983). *High school, a report on secondary education in America.* New York: Harper and Row.

Brown, D., & Srebalus, D. J. (1973). *Contemporary guidance concepts and practices: An introduction.* Dubuque, IA: William C. Brown.

Brown, M. T., & Chambers, M. (1986). Student and faculty perceptions of counseling centers: What's in a name? *Journal of Counseling Psychology, 33,* 155–158.

Carmichael, K. D. (1993). Counseling the occult-involved student. *The School Counselor, 41,* 5–8.

College Entrance Examination Board. (1986). *Keeping the options open: Recommendations—Final report of the commission on precollege guidance and counseling.* New York: Author.

Crabbs, M. A. (1984). Reduction in force and accountability: Stemming the tide. *Elementary School Guidance and Counseling, 18,* 167–175.

Deslisle, J. R. (1986). Death with honors: Suicide among gifted adolescents. *Journal of Counseling and Development, 64,* 588–590.

Gadwa, K., & Griggs, S. A. (1985). The school dropout: Implications for counselors. *The School Counselor, 33,* 9–17.

Gladding, S. T., & Hageman, M. B. (1984). Reduction in force: Proactive suggestions and creative plodding. *Elementary School Guidance and Counseling, 18,* 163–166.

Hendrick, S. S. (1984). The school counselor and anorexia nervosa. *The School Counselor, 31,* 428–432.

Hendrick, S. S. (1985). The school counselor and bulimia. *The School Counselor, 32,* 275–280.

Heppner, P. P., & Neal, G. W. (1983). Holding up the mirror: Research on the roles and functions of counseling centers in higher education. *The Counseling Psychologist, 11,* 81–98.

Herr, E. L. (1986). The relevant counselor. *The School Counselor, 34,* 7–13.

Ibrahim, F. A., Helms, B. A., & Thompson, D. L. (1983). Counselor role and function: An appraisal by consumers and counselors. *Personnel and Guidance Journal, 61,* 597–601.

Lamb, J., & Deschenses, R. (1974). The unique role of the elementary school counselor. *Elementary School Guidance and Counseling, 8,* 219–223.

Levinson, E. M. (1985). Vocational and career-oriented secondary school programs for the emotionally disturbed. *The School Counselor, 33,* 100–106.

Lutz, E. P., Jacobs, E. E., & Masson, R. L. (1981). Stepfamily counseling: Issues and guidelines. *The School Counselor, 28,* 189–194.

Minard, S. M. (1993). The school counselor's role in confronting child sexual abuse. *The School Counselor, 41,* 9–15.

Partin, R. L. (1993). School counselors' time: Where does it go? *The School Counselor, 40,* 274–281.

Pinkney, J. W., & Jacobs, D. (1985). New counselors and personal interest in the task of career counseling. *Journal of Counseling Psychology, 32,* 307–332.

Satcher, J. (1993). College-bound students with learning disabilities: The role of the counselor. *The School Counselor, 40,* 343–347.

Schmidt, P. (1994, May). Indiana study ignites debate over counselors' role. *Education Week,* 10–11.

Skinner, M. E. (1985). Counseling and special education: An essential relationship. *The School Counselor, 33,* 131–135.

Wellman, M. M. (1984). The school counselor's role in the communication of suicidal ideation by adolescents. *The School Counselor, 32,* 106–109.

Wilcoxen, S. A. (1986). Family counseling practices: Suggested reading guide for school counselors. *The School Counselor, 33,* 272–278.

Chapter 15

Counselors in Community Agencies

Goal of the Chapter

The purpose of this chapter is to overview career options for counselors in community agencies with particular emphasis on community mental health centers.

Chapter Preview

- Typical duties of mental health counselors will be depicted.
- The history and funding of community mental health will be surveyed.
- The early history of the American Mental Health Counselor's Association will be sketched.
- Treatment strategies in community mental health will be described.
- Special attention will be directed toward the outpatient and emergency services in mental health.
- Career opportunities for counselors in vocational rehabilitation, criminal justice, medical settings, and private practice will be described.

Introduction

The purpose of this chapter is to provide an overview of employment options for counselors within the community. At the outset an illustration will be provided of mental health counseling, with issues that confront counselors being highlighted. Historical influences, such as federal funding, will be reviewed, including how such influences helped structure the philosophy and services offered by mental health centers. Particular attention will be paid to the counselor's role in outpatient and emergency services, since by training and orientation these are likely to be areas of specialization. The skills necessary for mental health counseling also have application for other community settings, including the criminal justice system, vocational rehabilitation, private practice, and medical settings such as Health Maintenance Organizations (HMOs).

Working in Mental Health: An Illustration

Brad has worked for three years in western Maryland as a mental health counselor. Prior to that he spent three years working at an inner city crisis center. Street tough since a child, Brad has rarely been surprised by the sometimes zany and difficult challenges he has faced over the past six years. While Brad may have been more adventurous than some, his caseload represents the typical responsibilities of a mental health counselor treating outpatients. Brad works with children, adolescents, and adults in a moderate-sized facility. In a larger center with a larger, more diversified staff, Brad might have had a more specialized set of duties.

Today is going to be a long one. Brad will fill in this evening for a colleague at the first meeting of a new DWI (Driving While Intoxicated) group. While he need only have the group complete forms for the court and self-assessment inventories, show a film on how alcoholism progresses, and lead a brief discussion, he realizes that resistances among the members may be high. Information from the court shows that many of them have a long-term, chronic problem with alcohol abuse.

Brad is able to substitute in the DWI group because he was originally hired at the center as a substance abuse counselor but applied for a vacant mental health position immediately on completion of his probationary period. In his center, general outpatient mental health and substance abuse treatments are administered separately. The more diverse nature of the outpatient service attracted him.

On his way to check his mailbox, Brad notices and greets Brenda, a protective custody worker from Social Services. She is waiting by the elevator while one of her child cases has an appointment. Brenda looks tired. Brad remembers their most recent collaboration: Cindy, sexually abused for years by her uncle, was showing real improvement, but not quite enough to keep her out of trouble in school. When she was finally expelled from school for a lengthy string of minor offenses, she lost her foster care placement and was relocated in a group home seventy miles away. It was a frustrating case; both Brad and Brenda thought they had turned the corner with Cindy, but ended up without enough time to solidify some of the gains that had been made through counseling. She had been able to walk away from fights, get three passing grades last term, and iron out problems with her foster mother's daughter. It wasn't enough. Both Brad and Brenda felt a sense of loss.

Brad's mailbox is full. Nancy, the secretary, has pulled the records he has requested. Behind in his paperwork, Brad needs to complete more than a dozen records by next week when the team from Baltimore arrives for the annual site review. Under the records is a returned MIS form (Management Information System); Brad forgot to write the correct disposition code when he discharged Henry yesterday. The computer needs to know whether his client was discharged because he died, simply quit coming, was arrested, achieved the goals sought in counseling, or any of a number of coded categories. He laughs thinking the computer may have gotten heartburn if it had to decipher that code.

The form reminds him again of Hank; he was one of Brad's first clients at the center. Violent in his struggles with his stepparents, underachieving in school, and without friends, Hank is a child case Brad could discharge, having achieved all stated treatment goals related to the problems listed above. While some of his youthful clients have relatively uncomplicated problems, more have pervasive developmental delays related in part to questionable family circumstances. Even successful counseling does not eliminate all their problems.

On his way to his office Brad passes the waiting room. It is packed. Today one of the part-time psychiatrists will conduct medication checks. The case aides have brought in the partial care (day hospital) clients for this reason. They do not need full hospitalization, but can remain in the community by coming three or so days a week for recreational and supportive therapy. Most of them and their families are well known by the staff after the many years of treating their chronic and severe conditions.

As Brad enters his office the phone rings. James, attending treatment as part of his parole plan, tells Brad he will miss his appointment due to car trouble. In the past James has had difficulty with drug abuse and depression while in prison. It seems that three out of the last five weeks he has had some similar excuse. Brad resolves to discuss the case with the clinical director. Brad's report to the parole officer regarding James' attendance will not be due for another two months, but a decision of the value of seeing him must be made before then. The client waiting list is too long in his opinion. Why not make room for some new clients by discharging some who seem uncommitted to treatment?

The phone rings again; the receptionist indicates that Jason has arrived. Brad originally saw Jason's wife. She wanted to discuss her marital dissatisfaction and growing determination to leave Jason. Both of them were seen conjointly by Brad, but now only Jason remains to work through the emotional aftermath of his wife's departure. He has been doing better the past few weeks.

Before Brad goes to get Jason he looks over the day's schedule. Since James canceled for 10:00 A.M., he might try to get a few signatures on some reports from his supervisor, Dr. Johnson, a paid consultant. Dr. Johnson is in private practice in an adjoining county and is at the center two days each week.

An 11:00 meeting has been scheduled for the Staffing and Assignment Team. He learned yesterday that the team must assign twelve new clients who received intakes the previous week. They also plan to review new grievance procedures for clients, proposed by the state. Barbara comes at 1:00; she has just been released from the general hospital after a four-day stay related to her cyclical depression. At 2:00 Brad sees Martha. He has increased the frequency of her sessions to twice a week, and it seems to be working. His supervisor has helped him to understand her borderline condition; a disorder he had not studied when in graduate school. At first Brad viewed Martha superficially as just a burdensome individual. She was very demanding, challenging what he said more often than most clients. Through supervision he learned that her frequent phone calls, demands for immediate and special treatment, suspiciousness, and continual reports of conflict with family and neighbors were manifestations of the disorder Brad was supposed to treat. He's become more patient and comfortable with Martha, but has been reminded by Dr. Johnson not to take anything for granted in his relationship with her.

Getting away from Martha is often difficult because of her last-minute requests and questions, and at 3:15 Brad must be at the high school to colead a group with the school counselor. The executive director at the center has emphasized the importance of making sure the service contract with the schools is renewed. Several salaries would be at stake if it were not. The group is not going well. Most of the members have been in conflict with teachers, administrators, and other students. They probably would have been expelled if it were not for this cooperative program with the mental health center to keep them in regular classrooms. They are not well prepared for group experiences. The pressure is on to get it going.

Brad's involvements for this day illustrate some of the diverse responsibilities a counselor working in community mental health may encounter. Brad's caseload includes a high percentage of youth with frequent school contacts, but other counselors at the center have a heavier involvement with other client populations. Brad, however, is similar to many mental health counselors; they all get called on to fill many different roles, being more generalists than specialists. To meet such challenges one's professional preparation ought to provide a broad base of personal skills along with an awareness of even larger resources necessary to provide service to the varied clients seeking assistance at a mental health center.

Community Mental Health: Its History and Funding

Bloom (1984) provides a careful review of important events and practices behind the development of the mental health care system in the United States. During the late eighteenth and early nineteenth centuries this country made an effort to improve the treatment given to the chronic mentally ill through the construction of more than 300 state psychiatric hospitals. By the mid-twentieth century this system, built to remedy the inadequate care given to psychiatric patients, had deteriorated badly. The hospitals were in poor physical condition, were very overcrowded, and demonstrated increasingly lower patient recovery rates.

By the 1950s significant advances had taken place in the field of psychopharmacology. New drugs proved effective in controlling psychotic symptoms; antianxiety and antidepression medications were also being developed. Such medications began to speed the rate of recovery in state hospitals; they also enabled many patients, who would otherwise require the protected environment of the hospital, to function in the community. In both Europe and the United States, community-based mental health programs were being developed and evaluated.

In 1946 Congress had passed the National Mental Health Act (P.L. 79-487) that established the National Institute of Mental Health (NIMH). NIMH and other public and private organizations began to develop mental health care recommendations that drew the attention of John F. Kennedy and his administration. Kennedy spoke eloquently before the 88th Congress in favor of restructuring the mental health care system. One month before his death Kennedy signed the Community Mental Health Centers Act (P.L. 88-164), through which considerable funds were made available to build and staff centers.

Under the Johnson administration this legislation was amended and expanded several times. New responsibilities included treatment for substance abuse, expanded child services, rape prevention, and special programs for the elderly. In some respects this expansion taxed the capabilities of the mental health care system beyond the resources that would be available during the Nixon and Ford administrations.

The Carter administration once again energetically promoted mental health care, with particular attention to minority populations. One month before his defeat in the 1980 election, President Carter signed the Mental Health Systems Act (P.L. 96-398). It updated mental health legislation to meet a larger set of needs. However, following Reagan's election, budgetary authorizations for P.L. 96-398 were rescinded in favor of block grants to the states. This legislation, called the Omnibus Budget Reconciliation Act (PL No. 97-35), brought an end to a federally-sponsored mental health care system (VandenBos, 1993). Since that time, funding to mental health centers through the states has continually dwindled.

The content of these federal laws structured much of what exists in community mental health today. Public Law 88-164 divided states into what are called catchment areas, each having a population limit, usually 200,000 residents. The act required each center to offer inpatient, outpatient, and partial care, crisis intervention, and consultation and education. Prevention was viewed as an important part of each center's program. Treatment of the chronic mentally ill, though, remained at the center of the legislation. While community mental health centers were not viewed in these laws as replacements for state mental hospitals, they were to work in tandem with the latter. Bloom (1984) believes that a dual system was actually developed—one being the existing state hospital system, and the other the mental health centers. All the goals of community mental health have not been accomplished, but there has been more mental health care within local communities, with greater attention being paid to short-term services and indirect services to other agencies.

During the last several decades important court decisions have supplemented the influence of mental health legislation. In particular, during the 1950s and 1960s the Warren Court heard cases previously rejected by the Supreme Court. Some of these cases centered on the rights of psychiatric patients. Through them occurred dramatic revisions in commitment procedures, with a dual emphasis on the rights of patients to treatment and to treatment via the least restrictive alternative. The latter led to the process called deinstitutionalization, i.e., releasing back to the community patients who had experienced long-term hospitalization. Also, conscious effort has been made to avoid as much as possible long-term hospitalization as a treatment option. The impact of this was a need to find a cost-effective way to care for mentally ill persons who might otherwise overstress their families or be forced to live on the streets.

Patient advocacy groups ensured that legislative mandates and court decisions favoring the rights of mental health clients were implemented. Today all citizens are less likely to be restrained or secluded except for brief periods of emergency. Mental health clients are guaranteed much greater confidentiality of their records; also they are able to access the information in these records. Current procedures in mental health mandate periodic review of treatment plans along with the right of clients to refuse treatments that they believe to be unnecessary or overly burdensome. These policies represent a dramatic shift away from the historic position that the state automatically knows what is best for its troubled citizens.

The historic influences described have created a mental health care system that serves much of the United States. Knesper, Wheeler, and Pagnucco (1984) surveyed the country and found mental health professionals in public and private practice serving 1,393 counties. They also found that 1,682 counties were without mental health professionals. Underserved areas were more likely to be in the western half of the nation, especially the plains states. Rural sections of the South were also understaffed by such professionals. Such gaps in the system ensure that many troubled individuals do not receive mental health care. Kiesler (1982) notes that in recent years 60 percent of all mental health hospitalizations have occured in general hospitals, with an average stay of 11.6 days. Only 25 percent of the mental health patient days occur in private or state/county psychiatric hospitals. For these patients the average stay is 189 days. Kiesler notes that as of 1978 one-quarter of all inpatient days in hospitals of all kinds were for mental health reasons.

One can still wonder if our mental health care system can really serve all persons in need of treatment. For example, Knitzer (1984) reports that the President's Commission on Mental Health estimates that 5 percent to 15 percent of all children and adolescents (3–9 million children) require some type of mental health service. She notes that as of 1976 only 665,000 children received services from mental health agencies, and only 350,000 more were treated by the schools. Ware, Manning, Duan, Wells, and Newhouse (1984) note that, in spite of lip service to preventive care, the likelihood that mental health care will actually be given is related to the degree of psychological distress experienced by the person in need of service. It seems that at present both clients and the treatment system itself often respond only when mental health problems have become serious.

Mental Health Counseling as a Profession

Since its inception in the 1940s NIMH has included within the category of mental health professions the following: psychiatry, psychology, social work, and nursing. It was only in 1986 that NIMH added mental health counselors as the fifth mental health profession.

The counseling profession, with its emphasis on serving a cross-section of the population, most of whom fall in the "normal" category, has had a different mission from mental health practice, which has tended to emphasize the chronic mentally ill. However, by the mid-1970s more and more counselors became employed in settings other than schools. In particular, there was a need to develop an identity for the master's level counselor working in a variety of agencies and community programs. Weikel (1985) notes that in 1976 formal efforts began to form an association to serve the interests of this group of practitioners. During that year the American Mental Health Counselors Association (AMHCA) was formed. In 1977 its members voted by a narrow margin to join the American Personnel and Guidance Association (APGA). Its priorities became licensure, third-party payments, full parity with other mental health professionals, private practice, and the treatment of special populations in community and private settings. The growth of AMHCA has been rapid. In late 1985 AMHCA became the largest division of the American Counseling Association (ACA) and is currently the second largest division. AMHCA's members come from such diverse backgrounds as psychiatry, nursing, psychology, social work, and the clergy. The record to date indicates that this active and energetic group will effectively influence the mental health care system in the future.

Treatment Philosophies and Strategies in Mental Health

The allied helping professions have an enormous task serving a broad range of clients, whether that practice is within a mental health center, another community agency, or a private practice. Serving diverse clients requires the development of many varied treatments. For example, some clients may be relatively normal persons experiencing mild crises, while others may be suffering from a combination of seriously disabling conditions. Frances, Clarkin, and Perry (1984) use the title "differential therapeutics" to describe an approach to treatment selection that has application to mental health clients. They base treatment selection on (1) the physical setting in which treatment takes place, (2) the format of the treatment, and (3) the theoretical orientation behind the intervention.

Setting

In mental health practice, decisions about how to help a client must often be made quickly, especially for clients in crisis who are possibly dangerous to themselves or others. In some instances the safest treatment may be hospitalization, i.e., inpatient care; in other instances the client may be assisted by partial hospitalization or day hospital care; still others are not in immediate danger and have the resources to benefit from regular outpatient treatment. The decision to hospitalize is often made by a team of mental health professionals, and the actual prescreening for admission is most often done by a psychiatrist. The mental health counselor, however, may be the first contact for a client in need of hospitalization and must be alert to that ultimate setting-related decision.

In mental health practice the selection of setting coincides with the general goals of treatment, whether treatment is seen as a form of acute care, an effort at rehabilitation or prevention, or an attempt to maintain a person with a chronic, possibly deteriorating condition. For example, partial hospitalization is frequently the choice for individuals with chronic, deteriorating conditions.

Treatment Format

Frances, Clarkin, and Perry (1984) note that the next set of decisions after choice of setting has to do with the use of one or more of the following types of therapy: group, family, marital (couples), or individual. These authors conceptualize emotional problems as resulting from one of many different systems, from molecular/cellular systems, through family/community systems, to society in general. The location of the problems via this conceptual framework helps to dictate treatment format.

Decisions regarding format must also take into consideration those factors that enable a client to benefit from such treatments. If those enabling conditions are not present, an alternative treatment may need to be sought. For example, an adolescent client in trouble with the police may be part of a family that is experiencing considerable stress, handling their problems by projecting blame on one another. They may be unable to deal with this or other problems because communication among members is vague and misdirected. It would seem that the client and the entire family unit are good candidates for conjoint family therapy (see Chapter 8). However, within this family the mother manifests extreme agitation along with severe distrust. Because of her personal pathology, the usefulness of family therapy would be reduced. The adolescent might have to be treated individually even though many of the problems are family related.

Treatment Orientation

Various theoretical approaches have differential application across client groups. As indicated in Chapter 3, one client may be more likely to comply with one approach and not another. For example, some clients may find it untenable to consider revealing negative feelings as an avenue to greater psychological strength. They might find an expressive therapy, such as person-centered therapy, too uncomfortable to endure. Other clients may be poor candidates for the more "directive" therapies since they might have little inclination to take suggestions from others, complete homework assignments, or possibly expose themselves to uncomfortable situations in order to practice new behaviors. For these clients, such approaches as reality or behavior therapy may receive considerable resistance.

Other Considerations

Adopting a view of differential treatment that utilizes varying forms of interventions sometimes allows one to consider the combination of several treatments. For example, a client may be in a partial-care program but may also receive an antidepressant medication plus regular counseling. It may be argued that such combinations have additive effects: One ensures immediate safety for the client, another is quick-acting, and another is likely to produce long-lasting gains. The disadvantage of combined treatments are that some may negate others, side effects may develop, and, ultimately the treatment team may never learn what outcomes any individual treatment produced (Frances, et al., 1984). With multiple interventions available in mental health that can be used effectively or misused, the need to collaboratively plan treatment increases in importance. In a well-managed center multidisciplinary client staffing sessions can provide an important training benefit for the counselor-in-training as well as those employed in the setting.

The Outpatient Service

Mental health counselors have been trained primarily to work in the outpatient service of a mental health or other community agency. Prior to assignment to a counselor, outpatient clients usually have completed intake interviews in which data have been gathered about their social history, current complaints, previous treatment history, and current resources. Many outpatient clients also will have seen a psychiatrist for a medical evaluation and the prescription of medication.

When treatment begins the outpatient worker has a written record of the intake, identifying data (including billing information) taken by an office worker, and notes regarding medications. The records of clients with chronic problems will often contain special psychological evaluations, reports sent by psychiatric hospitals, interview notes of previous therapy, and so forth. To this the counselor will need to add, usually within the first two to four interviews, a treatment plan. Such plans include a statement of the client's problems, a diagnosis (DSM-IV), a list of client strengths and weaknesses, short-term and long-term goals, the treatment modality to be used, a list of support services, a prognosis, criteria for discharge, and a plan for follow-up services (Brands, 1978). Notes or interview summaries to be included in the record at later dates should be referenced to this treatment plan, especially to the treatment goals.

A caseload of between fifteen and twenty active clients appears to be manageable for counselors working primarily in outpatient service. The balance of these counselors' schedules will include meetings, time for the completion of paperwork, on-call duty (including walk-in standby), supervision, consultation and education, and special projects.

Over several years the outpatient counselor can expect to be assigned a wide variety of clients, ranging from persons confronting predictable developmental challenges to individuals with life-long histories of adjustment problems. Some clients assigned to outpatient treatment do not have the resources to benefit from such treatment; they are not well enough organized to manage transportation to the center, remember appointments, and other such things. However, their situation does not warrant assignment to another setting. Such clients will be in and out of the center. Other clients with chronic disorders (e.g., cyclical depression), will end treatment when their condition improves but will return at a later date. This cycle may be repeated many times. Thus the counselor is likely to find that an hour may be set aside each week to accommodate the likelihood that old clients will be returning in sufficient numbers.

Counselors may wish to control some of the client assignment process by specializing in serving particular populations (e.g., conduct disordered youth) or by offering special treatments. Specialization provides other advantages, such as (1) recognition to the agency for providing special service, (2) an opportunity for the counselor to devote time to areas of special interest, (3) greater job security by being needed to maintain a special set of services offered by the agency, and (4) clear indications of professional development. In the course of a career the counselor may respecialize several times, broadening expertise with each change.

When clients achieve treatment objectives or for some reason choose to discontinue treatment, the counselor usually documents the end of treatment through a written discharge summary that becomes part of the client's record. If clients remain in the mental health care system for long, clearly their records become rather large. The intent of the paperwork required of mental health professionals is to ensure regular review of client care. In many places state law will specify the types of records that must be kept both to protect client rights and to ensure quality service. Well-managed centers require that every outpatient worker be under supervision regardless of experience level or degree and that treatment plans and discharge summaries be signed by a supervisor.

Centers vary across the country with regard to how the outpatient service may be divided into special units. One center may divide its service between an adult and a children/adolescent unit. Another may separate substance abuse treatment from regular mental health outpatient service. In many cases the funding methods for supporting special treatments may require an administrative separation of different units. Administrators below the executive director of the center who are involved in the management of outpatient services usually include the medical director (chief psychiatrist), the clinical director (usually a licensed psychologist), and directors of special programs (e.g., children services or addictions). A counselor may coordinate yet another smaller unit, say, a school intervention program.

STUDENT LEARNING EXERCISE
Read the following descriptions of counselor activity and indicate whether they are appropriate for a mental health setting. Circle Y for yes or N for no.

1. The counselor has little background in psychopathology and its diagnosis.   Y   N

2. The counselor believes that all individuals can become fully functioning through group counseling.   Y   N

3. The counselor firmly believes that there is seldom, if ever, a valid reason to refer a client to a psychiatrist for medication.   Y   N

4. The counselor enjoys working in a multidisciplinary treatment setting with a wide variety of clients.   Y   N

The Emergency Service

Closely connected with outpatient and other units is the emergency service. When mental health crises arise in the community, mental health professionals coordinate with medical and law enforcement agencies to assist those persons dangerous to themselves or others, or those threatened by a third party. A mental health center usually has at least one person and a backup on call at all times. During office hours that person is free of scheduled appointments; during non-office hours he or she is available through a telephone hotline, through both the center's regular telephone number and the 911 service. Many mental health counselors earn "comp time" (that is, time for which they are compensated with time off) for off-hour emergency duty. This service is very important to a community.

Managing the behavior of people in a state of active crisis mandates the involvement of mental health professionals. Such persons may manifest loss of control, disorganized thinking, acute anxiety, immobilizing fear or panic, escape through substance abuse, and other problematic responses (Everstine & Everstine, 1983). Crisis situations call for quick assessment and assistance. Assessment was treated in Chapter 5.

Treating Assault Victims

Many crisis situations involve victims. They may have been beaten, sexually assaulted, involved in a natural disaster (e.g., tornado or flood), or seriously threatened by some such situation. Prompt attention to these individuals can have the benefit of both relieving a portion of the current pain and also helping to prevent future complications. Many believe that an acute, crisis situation, if left unattended, can leave lasting psychological damage.

Treatment begins with helping the victim to express feelings associated with the situation, be they feelings of guilt, anger, grief, or fear. The counselor then helps the person identify resources within himself or herself along with support from other persons and organizations, including the police and medical professions. Underlying this effort is an emphasis on helping the victim anticipate what is needed and to plan for it. For the person in danger, providing refuge is an essential part of treatment. Although mental health centers are unlikely to operate their own shelters, staff members frequently work in cooperation with agencies that do. For example, a church in a small community may give a battered spouse money for a motel room and meals. In addition, the church will make the arrangements and provide transportation at the request of the mental health center. A larger community may have a "safe house" for the temporary protection of a battered spouse. Even the mental health center staff may not know the location of this house, but can refer their clients to it through the agency that operates it. Often in the case of abuse and neglect of children, social service workers have already intervened, with custody of the child having been transferred to the state. In such cases the child will be presumed to be safe through placement in foster care.

Orzek (1983) discusses some of the complexities of assault cases for females in committed relationships: how the assault affects them, their male partner, and their relationship. Rape produces more than a need for immediate medical attention and support for the victim; after several days have passed the quality of psychological care that follows will influence the prognosis. Orzek warns counselors to pay attention to the client's reaction to the violence of the assault and not just its sexual nature. The woman's male partner at that time may feel very protective, expressing this with physical closeness, but his closeness may be timed too near to the assault. Orzek recommends that sexual activity between the partners be curtailed, if for no other reason than to control the transmission of venereal disease. It is probably better to have the partners agree that sexual contact will be initiated by the female when she is ready. As time passes the female victim may appear outwardly to have healed from the rape, but usually much more psychological healing must follow. If the victim remains in counseling, working through her feelings and issues of trust and dependence are important.

Since the impact of sexual assault leaves such pervasive damage, healing from it is never a simple process. Recovery must integrate memories and feelings of the experience in the ongoing life process of the victim. Also, it is important to understand that power was a key factor in the abuse, and therapy must do something to shift power away from the perpetrator, back to the victim (Herman, 1992). Thus, how the counselor uses power is of key importance. The counselor needs to be highly engaged in the therapy, but not overpowering. It is important to the survivor that the relationship with the therapist be real, clear, clean, and honest (Courtois, 1988).

Processing abuse experiences early in counseling will need to clarify blame, deal with guilt, and explore the victim's own sense of responsibility for what happened. Self-blame can act as a defense against the terror of helplessness and the rage resulting from the abuse (Herman, 1992). Out of this comes a need to mourn losses, clarify self-concept, and reaccept one's body. Often in cases of early abuse development has become impaired, stalling the maturation process. Sometimes it is helpful to think of the client as having a little child inside, stuck and in need of getting back on a growth tract (Briere, 1988).

Suicide

One of the most common situations affecting the emergency service worker is suicide. It is estimated that 1 million people report attempting to kill themselves each year, with 25,000 being successful (Perr, 1979). This makes suicide the tenth leading cause of death, responsible for 1 percent of all fatalities in the United States. In 1987 almost 5,000 young people between the ages of fifteen and twenty-four committed suicide (National Center for Health Statistics, 1989).

The rates of suicide for portions of our population are much higher. For example, suicide is the second or third leading cause of death for people under the age of thirty.

It is likely that persons who make up these statistics will have contacted someone before committing suicide. While most persons committing suicide are depressed and very unhappy, most are not absolutely sure that they want to die (Shneidman, Farberow, & Litman, 1976). Consequently, they almost always cry out to someone else for assistance before actually reaching the point of suicide. Fujimura, Weis, and Cochran (1985) note that this ambivalence provides a major opportunity for the counselor to intervene and help. Many individuals attempt suicide repeatedly and eventually succeed, but many others will abandon suicide as a solution to their problems. The response of the emergency service counselor can promote this change.

The first step for both an intake worker and the emergency service worker—the assessment of suicidal potential—was treated in Chapter 5. The next step is to decide how to treat the crisis if it is deemed as real. Motto (1976) recommends hospitalization when the person (1) is unsure of being able to resist the suicidal impulse, (2) has just made a serious attempt, (3) lacks supportive family and friends, or (4) is under the influence of alcohol or some drug that loosens impulse control. Hospitalization might be avoided if there are suitable persons available to care for the suicidal individual, and intense outpatient contact can be provided to both the persons contemplating suicide and her or his family.

Motto (1976) emphasizes the need for the emergency worker to recognize the client's feelings of alienation and abandonment—viewing the world as rejecting and contemptuous. The presence of these feelings mandates the communication of a desire to understand and accept the individual in an active manner in order to provide quick symptom relief so the life-threatening crisis might end. Such swift and energetic action can convince the suicidal person that something really will be done to improve his or her situation (Fujimura et al., 1985). At times the counselor may try with no avail to get the voluntary cooperation of the individual. In such cases the counselor, in cooperation with other staff members, may file a petition to have the person involuntarily hospitalized. However, if the person does not appear delirious, psychotic, or panic-stricken, and denies suicidal intent, she or he probably will be discharged from the hospital shortly after being transported there by law enforcement personnel.

If emergency service personnel can intervene to prevent a suicide attempt and if they remain in contact, follow-up treatment can be planned and delivered. A therapeutic team that includes the person's family, friends, minister, and physician can develop a more comprehensive approach to changing the situation. Treating the depression is central. Most references (e.g., Motto, 1976) warn the treatment team about the dangerousness of the point when the depression begins to lift; at that time the individual has the energy necessary to commit suicide and may do so if pessimism about the future has not changed. Also, medication, such as a tricyclic antidepressant, may have been prescribed for the individual. Careful monitoring of such medications is required when the client is referred to the outpatient service since these drugs are extremely toxic. Since feelings of alienation are so common among persons contemplating suicide, group therapy may provide another means of support. The group could be one more vehicle to help the individual develop a feeling of inclusion within a social system.

When an individual in crisis does commit suicide, friends and family may need assistance in coping with the complex feelings associated with such a loss. This may also apply to the community personnel who attempted to prevent its occurrence.

Dealing with a crisis can be unsettling to the beginning counselor. One consoling feature of such work is the careful effort made to provide back-up assistance to the on-call counselor. When in doubt, the beginning counselor should use this support. Kahn (1981) offers the following recommendations to a crisis worker:

1. Develop a working relationship with the client.
2. Get the right information from the client. Write it down. Get his or her name and address.
3. Consider both the precipitating factors and the client's personality in assessing the situation.
4. Try to share with the client a view of the situation that might produce more adaptive responses.
5. Explore actual ways the client might approach the problem right away.
6. Work at getting the client to agree on goals that support a new approach to the situation.
7. Arrange for future contacts with the mental health center and other appropriate agencies.

Preparing for a Career in Community Mental Health

Graduates of counselor education programs have excellent backgrounds for careers in mental health. As described earlier in this book, their skills in interviewing, assessment, understanding special populations, and consultation fit directly into their job description.

But as in most community-based programs, the mental health counselor will work hand-in-hand with many other helping professionals and must learn to understand them and relate to their perspectives on client care. Practicum and internship in mental health settings provide an opportunity to gain experience with these different helping professionals. To prepare specifically for this phase of training, the counselor-in-training may be well-advised to:

1. Learn the specific procedures to follow in conducting an intake interview, and become familiar with its elements, such as the mental status examination. These were described briefly in Chapter 6.
2. Intensify your study of psychopathology. Develop an adequate understanding of the format for the diagnosis of mental disorders; this is the basic system used to classify clients undergoing treatment. It is also a way of reporting the types of clients treated.
3. While learning the DSM-IV, recognize that a large percentage of mental health counselors believe that prevention and education are more cost-effective than remedial therapy in achieving long-term success with this nation's mental health problems.
4. Prepare yourself to relate to clients with fewer resources to solve problems than those commonly used by counselors working in educational settings.
5. Practice becoming proficient in writing reports, treatment plans, and progress notes. A great deal of paperwork is involved in mental health counseling. This paperwork is continually reviewed by funding agencies, and thus is very important to administrators in mental health centers.
6. Recognize that there are many governmental laws and regulations affecting mental health care. Be prepared to learn about them when employed as a counselor.

Brooks and Gerstein (1990) also recommend for private practice that mental health counselors become Certified Clinical Mental Health Counselors (CCMHC). This credential through the Academy of Certified Clinical Mental Health Counselors requires submission of transcripts, evidence of clinical supervision, recommendations, and a national examination. Metcalf, Dean, and Britcher (1991) have opposed this position, arguing that CCMHC standards presume a clinical model, and that mental health counselors in large numbers support prevention and education over remediation of psychopathology. Since 1987 the American Counseling Association has been part of a large coalition that has advocated federal legislation that supports preventive programs in mental health (Horner & McElhaney, 1993). Neglecting this emphasis on prevention takes away some of the uniqueness of counseling as a mental health profession.

Counseling in Rehabilitation Settings

Since early in the nineteenth century when special schools and training were begun for deaf, blind, mentally retarded, and physically disabled children, rehabilitation services have emerged with an extensive set of medical, social, and psychological services. Following World War I to the present, numerous pieces of federal legislation have been passed to help fund these services. The most recent legislation was the Americans with Disabilities Act, passed in 1990. It was modeled after the civil rights legislation of the 1960s and is intended to end discrimination of people with disabilities in the workplace and in access to public places. It was estimated that between 1983 and 1985 11.5 percent or 17.4 million Americans outside institutions were partially or totally handicapped (National Institute of Disability and Rehabilitation Research, 1986). The economic impact of this situation has helped mobilize resources toward broad-based rehabilitative treatments.

Rehabilitation counselors play a central role in managing the rehabilitation process. They assess clients for eligibility and study and report their condition to community agencies, making referrals when needed. Counselors provide clients personal and vocational counseling and assist with job placement. Counselors work with clients in groups and with their families.

Most rehabilitation counselors work for governmental agencies, primarily state divisions of vocational rehabilitation. Marinelli (1992) notes that large numbers of rehabilitation counselors also work for the Veterans Administration, state employment services, hospitals and medical centers, correctional facilities, welfare agencies, the Social Security Administration, and workmen's compensation insurance firms. There are also sheltered workshops, independent living centers, colleges and schools, and nonprofit organizations that also employ rehabilitation counselors. Recently, private-for-profit agencies have increased in number, employing many recent graduates of rehabilitation counseling programs, largely through support of these agencies by the insurance industry.

The preparation of rehabilitation counselors has become well defined through the accreditation of training programs by the Council on Rehabilitation Education (Berven & Wright, 1978) and the certification of individual counselors by the Commission on Rehabilitation Counselor Certification. Because of this, persons interested in working primarily with physically and mentally disabled populations are wise to explore training programs holding accreditation and providing eligibility for certification.

A traditional view in rehabilitation has been that employment is therapeutic for most individuals. Job placement and work adjustment become important themes in the rehabilitation process. Counselors typically develop refined skills in vocational evaluation of individuals and in job survey and analysis.

Counseling in Correctional Settings

The American justice system is a massive, complex system involving many different professions with many useful roles for counselors. At each step in the system, from apprehension of suspects to final release of prisoners, counselors can participate with other law enforcement and corrections officials in attempting to ensure the safety of citizens and the rehabilitation of law offenders.

Pretrial Intervention

The prosecution, conviction, and subsequent confinement of law offenders has become such a burdensome and costly process that alternatives have been sought. Diversion programs represent one such alternative; they suspend the criminal justice process in favor of providing counseling and other services for individuals likely to benefit from them. Common offenses treated in such a manner include shoplifting, passing bad checks, property destruction, and battery and disorderly conduct resulting from a temper outburst, often triggered by alcohol (Gotteil & Ghosh, 1983). In such a program a prosecutor may choose to have an assessment of a suspect by a screening panel, mandatory counseling, and some effort at restitution for the damage done.

While this alternative opens opportunities for counselor involvement in treating offenders, Gottheil and Ghosh (1983) note that client resistance to mandatory counseling often exists. In work with juvenile offenders, a court counselor often is responsible for extensive intake work resulting in a written report to the juvenile court judge that strongly influences the final action taken by the court. In such pretrial work the justice system often views the counselor as already beginning the treatment to reduce recidivism by exploring the probable consequences of the current offense and of future ones.

Trial-Related Counselor Involvements

Expert testimony during criminal trials falls usually in the domain of the psychiatrist or licensed psychologist. Doctoral-level counseling psychologists can contribute to this process. The master's level counselor is more likely to function as a social caseworker employed by the court, working much like the mental health counselor when visiting a jail. For juveniles especially, court counselors are likely to maintain contact with the offender following an initial hearing with the judge for the purpose of making presentencing recommendations. Many states have diagnostic centers where juvenile offenders may be placed for a period of time, usually twenty to sixty days, and where they are tested, interviewed, and generally observed by counselors and other correctional staff. Following this placement, juveniles may be put on probation or placed in a group home, a psychiatric facility, or another correctional center.

Correctional Counseling in Prisons and Other Facilities

Prisons and other correctional facilities regularly employ psychiatrists, psychologists, and counselors. These staff members have responsibilities for (1) assessment, (2) treatment, (3) training, (4) consultation, and (5) research (Whitely & Hosford, 1983). In addition to performing these usual duties, the correctional counselor is viewed as a member of the institution's staff and is responsible for protecting that institution and ensuring security throughout. In most prisons there is a clear division between inmates and officers, with fierce loyalty on both sides (Toch, 1978). While at times counselors might be portrayed as intermediaries between inmates and the institution, both sides clearly want counselors identified with the correctional staff. At one time prisons were justified as rehabilitation centers for law offenders; today imprisonment is seen as a punishment for social injury (Geis, 1983). This view of imprisonment maintains the division between inmates and staff.

Problems of prison costs and overcrowding have accelerated the search for alternative forms of incarceration, especially for the nonviolent offender. Community programs such as half-way houses and other supervised living environments often emphasize vocational and interpersonal skill acquisition. Counselors fit well into such programs; however, in recent years there has been a tendency to move away from these types of treatments (Whiteley & Hosford, 1983).

With the demise of the alternatives to incarceration in large prisons, counselors in prisons are usually left with large caseloads. Because of this, group counseling has become a favorite intervention; it fits well with the large caseloads. These groups often address problems with substance abuse, since this problem is widespread among inmate populations (National Institute of Drug Abuse, 1981).

Probation and Parole

Law offenders put on probation or released from prisons on parole often receive counseling from mental health counselors or counselors employed by the courts. Counselor training among parole officers varies from none to advanced degrees. While the mental health counselor is free to give full attention to the person on probation and follow a traditional therapist role, the court counselor has a dual role of both counselor and enforcer of the limits and structure set by the probation/parole plan (Lee & Klopfer, 1978). The latter may call for such noncounseling methods as lecturing, persuading, threatening, and punishing. In addition, since the court counselor must report the activities and progress of his or her caseload back to the court, confidentiality is more limited, and consequently so is the degree of trust between counselor and client. The same is true for correctional counselors working in prisons.

Preparing for a Career in Corrections

The brief overview given of counselor involvement in the criminal justice system identifies some of the problems and challenges one must face when working in such settings. Yet law offenders often have emotional problems that have contributed to their status, and they can benefit from contact with counselors. Besides the differences noted in treating law offenders, similarities between them and other clients also exist.

Page and Shearer (1980) provide a number of recommendations for the training of correctional and court counselors. Learning how to build trust with mistrustful clients, deal with authority games, and generally surviving a harsh physical environment head their recommendations. In addition, counselors need to understand how the criminal justice system works, the types of lifestyles led by offenders, and how to use special confrontational skills. Such work, while potentially rewarding, is not for the faint-hearted.

Pastoral Counseling

There is quite a bit of literature, both pro and con, on the relationship between counseling/psychotherapy and religion. The professional debate notwithstanding, people turn to clergy more often for help with emotional problems than they do to any other group of professionals (Clemens, Corradi, & Wasman, 1978). This is not surprising since more than 90 percent of our population hold some form of religious beliefs (Benson, 1981). These believers turn to their clergy for help with both religious and other problems.

In studying attitudes toward religious and secular counseling, Quackenbos, Privette, and Klentz (1985) showed that laypeople do see religious and secular counseling as different. Thirty-five percent surveyed preferred some form of religious counseling, 79 percent thought religious values were an important topic to be discussed in therapy, and 53 percent stated they would seek counseling at a pastoral center if it were available. The authors conclude that many people want religion to be included in counseling and psychotherapy.

Counselors, however, are often hesitant to discuss spiritual issues with their clients (Loeninger, 1979). Some of the reasons for this suggested by Russo (1984) include:

1. Fear of imposing personal values on clients.
2. Negative attitudes held toward organized religion.
3. Lack of a theoretical model that can aid in the exploration of religious and spiritual issues and values.

Russo (1984) believes that forms of transcendal logic are available that can confront spiritual issues. Apparently more and more counselors are becoming interested in such topics. The Association for Religious and Value Issues in Counseling (ARVIC) has been one of the fastest growing divisions of the American Counseling Association (ACA) with one of the highest percentage of student members (Bartlett, Lee, & Doyle, 1985).

Christian Counseling

One example of pastoral counseling, relevant to a large number of individuals, is Christian counseling. Strong (1980) defines this as a synthesis of psychological procedures for achieving therapeutic change in an interview with the values and realities of faith in Jesus Christ.

Christian thinking holds both the responsibility of the person for self-development and the availability of divine assistance for that development. The secret for the Christian is to become open to the help of God, allowing it to break through the many barriers between God and people. Knowledge of divine assistance is available to the Christian via scripture, especially through the model of Jesus Christ. Prayer and meditation allow God to influence the person's actions that move him or her toward achieving desired changes and growth. By following the tenets of Christianity, the believer can achieve greater adaptation to life challenges and greater emotional health.

Theodore (1984) notes that strong religious convictions are often condemned as being dogmatic and inflexible. He suggests that empirical science can be used, as suggested earlier by Bergin (1980), to test the useful aspects of religion from a mental health viewpoint. These can be compared to the humanistic-atheistic tenets suggested by Ellis (1980).

Christian counseling can be offered at pastoral care centers staffed by clergy and laypersons of interdenominational faiths. Since clergy represent a significant portion of many counselor education programs, many lay therapists and clergy at pastoral care centers receive similar training.

Counseling in Medical Settings

Hospitals, health maintenance organizations (HMOs), private medical practices, and hospice care facilities are medical settings that counseling graduates might consider for employment. These and other facilities and services account for the massive health care system in this country that consumes 11 percent of the gross national product (Starr, 1992). More efforts seem to be underway to reduce the size of this system than to expand it. This will have a negative effect on the future employment of counselors.

More promising has been the trend toward HMOs, which have recently showed an interest in hiring mental health counselors (Cummings, 1986). These are large corporations that offer prepaid health plans. It is estimated that by 1993 more than 50 million persons will be served by these plans, which began in the 1900s. After 1993 a 10 percent annual growth rate is estimated (DeLeon, Uyeda, & Welch, 1985). Since the 1970s and the passage of P.L. 93-222, HMOs have been seen as a major factor in reshaping the American health care system. The emphasis in HMOs is on health maintenance and the treatment of illness, rather than solely the latter. Since hospital costs are lower, HMOs seem to offer more cost-effective health care. HMOs can now offer short-term mental health services (up to twenty visits). Thus, enrollees can come to see counselors at their HMO for "free" (i.e., as part of their prepaid program) rather than pay a fee for services at a mental health center or to a private practitioner.

HMOs vary in their structure. Some HMO corporations own and maintain their own clinics and hospitals; they hire their own staff of medical professionals. Other HMOs are corporations that organize existing hospitals and medical professionals in private practice into a network of medical and related services. Enrollees in the HMO pay nominal copayments above the prepaid cost of the HMO for services within the network. However, services outside the network often are not covered at all. Even many traditional health insurance plans have lists of "preferred providers" that the insuree can go to for treatment and receive maximum coverage. Treatment from practitioners who are not preferred providers may not be covered. Most individuals, either with traditional insurance or part of an HMO, cannot afford too many services outside of the network of providers in their medical plan. Getting into the network is not easy for a provider of mental health services, and one's continued membership as a network provider is never guaranteed.

Besides the increased role of HMOs in providing health services the advent of managed care has strongly influenced the delivery of medical and mental health services. Managed care is a term used to describe ways in which the utilization of health care is regulated (Zimet, 1989). Increasingly, health care plans have the power to deny services considered to be unnecessary or not cost-effective. Preauthorization of treatment is common with health care plans using companies organized specifically to review treatment recommendations from physical and mental health workers. In mental health, authorization has frequently been restricted to short-term therapies, and even brief treatment periods (sometimes as few as six sessions) for serious mental health problems (Applebaum, 1993). More than ever before counselors working in medical settings need to be concerned about the economic implications of their treatments for their clients.

Private Practice

Many counselors working for schools and agencies fantasize about private practice. Appealing is the idea of being one's own boss, having a nicely decorated office, a secretary, and so forth. The reality of a private practice is more than designing an office and offering a counseling service—one operates a business.

This venture includes becoming licensed in many states, paying higher liability insurance rates, becoming a preferred provider for medical plans, providing various treatments, marketing them, and the management of all other services in support of the treatments. Many counselors are not prepared for all these facets of private practice. For this reason many find it wise to join an already established group practice (Foos, Ottens, & Hill, 1991). In this way one can rely on others with more experience in the business side of private practice. In addition one has a chance to join a practice that already is part of a network of preferred providers.

The potential difficulties of private practice has not detracted large numbers of counselors from earning all or part of their income from private practice (Metcalf, et al., 1991). At the time this chapter is being written, it is not clear exactly how changes in the health care system will affect private practice options for counselors. It is likely that networks of private practitioners will remain as an important part of the health care system. Thus, some form of private practice remains as a career option for counselors.

Other Community Settings

Graduates of counselor education programs are employed in many community agencies and programs besides those already discussed. Domestic violence shelters, hospice care, and many service organizations (e.g., Red Cross and YMCA) hire master's level counselors, often within administrative positions. Much of their direct service is provided by volunteers who are managed and trained by the professional counselor. In some cases, but not all, the job description for these employment options may specify a background in counseling or social work. In Chapter 8, additional specialties were discussed for counseling professionals that open additional employment options with chemically dependent clients and the elderly.

Summary

This chapter reviewed numerous employment options for counselors in community agencies and the historic influences affecting the mental health care system in this country. It is a system developed by helping professions other than counseling, with counselors the most recent service providers to join the system. Originally intended to correct some of the deficiencies in the treatment of persons with chronic mental illness, mental health centers have developed a wide variety of services for a diverse population of clients. While mental health counselors may develop unique and special job descriptions, they are primarily trained to work as outpatient therapists and to participate in the emergency service. Because of the seriousness of the problems of certain clients, the mental health counselor will often be part of a treatment team that may include a psychiatrist, a licensed psychologist, and a case worker; together these professionals will provide multiple interventions, including medications, counseling, and environmental control. Since important decisions are often made to protect people's lives, mental health counselors usually develop special skills in diagnosis and crisis intervention.

Related to mental health are many other employment options for counselors in the community. Many of them are less traditional than school or mental health counseling, but each represents a unique set of challenges with varying rewards.

Review Questions

1. Describe the kinds of clients served in community mental health centers.

2. How does the role of the mental health counselor compare to that of a school counselor?

3. What is the relationship between community mental health and historic efforts to care for the chronically mentally ill?

4. What might explain the rapid growth of the American Mental Health Counselors Association (AMHCA)?

5. Describe some of the issues related to outpatient counseling in a mental health center.

6. What are some of the important issues related to the emergency service in mental health?

7. What graduate courses might a counselor-in-training take to prepare for a career in mental health?

8. What are some unique aspects of rehabilitation counseling?

9. Describe how counselors fit into the criminal justice system.

10. Define Christian counseling.

11. What are some of the issues related to working in medical settings? Private practice?

References

Applebaum, P. S. (1993). Legal liability and managed care. *American Psychologist, 48*(3), 251–257.

Bartlett, W. W., Lee, J. L., & Doyle, R. E. (1985). Historical development of the Association of Religious Values and Issues in Counseling. *Journal of Counseling and Development, 63*(7), 448–451.

Benson, J. M. (1981). The polls: A rebirth of religion. *Public Opinion Quarterly, 45*, 576–585.

Bergin, A. E. (1980). Psychotherapy and religious values. *Journal of Consulting and Clinical Psychology, 48*(1), 95–104.

Berven, N. L., & Wright, G. N. (1978). An evaluation model for accreditation. *Counselor Education and Supervision, 17*(2), 188–194.

Bloom, B. L. (1984). *Community mental health: A general introduction,* (2nd ed.). Monterey, CA: Brooks/Cole.

Brands, A. B. (1978). *Individualized treatment planning for psychiatric patients.* Washington, DC: U. S. Department of Health, Education, and Welfare.

Briere, J. (1988). *Therapy for adults molested as children.* Boston: Springer Publishing.

Brooks, D. K., & Gerstein, L. H. (1990). Counselor credentialing and interprofessional collaboration. *Journal of Counseling and Development, 68*(5), 477–484.

Clemens, N., Corradi, R., & Wasman, M. (1978). The parish clergy as a mental health resource. *Journal of Religion and Health, 17,* 227–232.

Courtois, C. (1988). *Healing the incest wound: Adult survivors in therapy.* New York: W. W. Norton.

Cummings, N. A. (1986). The dismantling of our health system: Strategies for the survival of psychological practice. *American Psychologist, 41*(4), 426–431.

DeLeon, P. H., Uyeda, M. K., & Welch, B. L. (1985). Psychology and HMOs: New partnership or new adversary? *American Psychologist, 40*(10), 1122–1124.

Ellis, A. (1980). Psychotherapy and atheistic values. A response to A. E. Bergin's "Psychotherapy and religious values." *Journal of Consulting and Clinical Psychology, 48*(5), 635–639.

Everstine, D. S., & Everstine, L. (1983). *People in crisis: Strategic therapeutic interventions.* New York: Brunner/Mazel.

Foos, J. A., Ottens, A. J., & Hill, L. K. (1991). Managed mental health: A primer for counselors. *Journal of Counseling and Development, 69*(4), 332–336.

Francis, A., Clarkin, J., & Perry, S. (1984). *Differential therapeutics in psychiatry: The art and science of treatment selection.* New York: Brunner/Mazel.

Fujimura, L. E., Weiss, D. M., & Cochran, J. R. (1985). Suicide: Dynamics and implications for counseling. *Journal of Counseling and Development, 63*(10), 612–615.

Geis, G. (1983). Criminal justice and adult offenders: An overview. *The Counseling Psychologist, 11*(2), 11–16.

Goodyear, R. K., & Shaw, M. C. (1984). Introduction to the second special issue on primary prevention. *The Personnel and Guidance Journal, 62*(9), 507–508.

Gotteil, D., & Ghosh, S. A. (1983). Pretrial intervention: Counseling in adult diversion programs. *The Counseling Psychologist, 11*(2), 17–25.

Herman, J. (1992). *Trauma and recovery.* New York: Basic Books.

Horner, J. H., & McElhaney, S. J. (1993). Building fences: Prevention in mental health. *American Counselor, 2*(1), 17–21, 30.

Kahn, M. W. (1981). *Basic methods for mental health practitioners.* Cambridge, MA: Winthrop Publishers.

Kiesler, C. A. (1982). Public and professional myths about mental hospitalization: An empirical reassessment of policy-related beliefs. *American Psychologist, 37*(12), 1323–1339.

Knesper, D. J., Wheeler, J. R., & Pagnucco, D. J. (1984). Mental health services providers' distribution across counties in the United States. *American Psychologist, 39*(12), 1424–1434.

Knitzer, J. (1984). Mental health services to children and adolescents: A national view of public policies. *American Psychologist, 39*(8), 905–911.

Lee, R. E., & Klopfer, C. (1978). Counselors and juvenile delinquents: Toward a comprehensive treatment approach. *Personnel and Guidance Journal, 59*(5), 194–197.

Lewis, J. A., & Lewis, M. D. (1984). Preventive programs in action. *The Personnel and Guidance Journal, 62*(9), 550–553.

Loeninger, R. J. (1979). Therapeutic strategies with "religious" resistances. *Psychotherapy: Theory, Research, and Practice, 16,* 419–427.

Marinelli, R. P. (1992). Rehabilitation services. In M. C. Alkin, (eds.), *Encyclopedia of Educational Research,* (pp. 1085–1090). New York: MacMillan.

Metcalf, H. E., Dean, D. M., & Britcher, J. C. (1991). In response to Brooks and Gerstein: Mental health counseling is more diverse than you imply. *Journal of Counseling and Development, 69*(5), 469–471.

Motto, J. (1976). The recognition and management of the suicidal patient. In F. Flack & S. Draghi, (eds.), *The nature and treatment of depression.* New York: John Wiley and Sons.

National Center for Health Statistics. (1989). *Monthly vital statistics reports.* Vol. 37, no. 13. Public Health Service.

National Institute of Disability and Rehabilitation Research. (1986). Data on disability from the National Health Interview Survey, (1983–1985). In Washington, D.C.: U.S. Government Printing Office.

National Institute of Drug Abuse. (1981). *Drug abuse treatment in prisons.* Washington, D. C.: Department of Health and Human Services.

Norcross, J. C., & Wogan, M. (1983). American psychotherapists in independent practice: Some findings and issues. *Professional Psychology: Research and Practice, 14*(3), 529–539.

Orzek, A. M. (1983). Sexual assault: The female victim, her male partner, and their relationship. *Personnel and Guidance Journal, 62*(3), 143–146.

Page, R. C., & Shearer, R. A. (1980). Some curriculum ideas for training public offender counselors. *Counselor Education and Supervision, 19*(4), 293–300.

Quackenbos, S., Privette, G., & Klentz, B. (1985). Psychotherapy: Sacred or secular. *Journal of Counseling and Development, 63*(5), 290–293.

Russo, T. J. (1984). A model of addressing spiritual issues in counseling. *Counseling and Values, 29*(1), 42–48.

Shneidman, E., Faberow, N., & Litman, R. (1976). *The psychology of suicide,* (2nd ed.). New York: Jason Aronson.

Starr, P. (1992). *The logic of health-care reform.* Knoxville, TN: Grand Rounds Press.

Strong, S. R. (1982). Christian counseling: A synthesis of psychological and Christian concepts. *Personnel and Guidance Journal, 58*(9), 589–592.

Taube, C. A., Burns, B. J., & Kessler, L. (1984). Patients of psychiatrists in office-based practice: 1980. *American Psychologist, 39*(12), 1435–1447.

Theodore, R. M. (1984). Utilization of spiritual values in counseling: An ignored dimension. *Counseling and Values, 28*(4), 162–168.

Toch, H. (1978). *Living in prison.* Glencoe, IL: Free Press.

VandenBos, G. R. (1993). U. S. mental health policy: Proactive evolution in the midst of health care reform. *American Psychologist, 48*(3), 283–290.

Ware, J. E., Manning, W. G., Duan, N., Wells, K. B., & Newhouse, J. P. (1984). Health status and the use of outpatient mental health services. *American Psychologist, 39*(10), 1090–1100.

Weikel, W. J. (1985). The American Mental Health Counselors Association. *Journal of Counseling and Development, 63*(7), 457–460.

Whitely, S. M., & Hosford, R. E. (1983). Counseling in prisons. *The Counseling Psychologist, 11*(2), 27–34.

Zimet, C. N. (1989). The mental health care revolution: Will psychology survive? *American Psychologist, 44*(4), 703–708.

$$C \quad h \quad a \quad p \quad t \quad e \quad r \quad \mathbf{16}$$

Research, Evaluation, and Accountability

Goals of the Chapter

The purposes of this chapter are threefold. The first of these is to address a long-standing issue, the differences between research and evaluation. The second is to provide an overview of the major models of research and to outline some of the strengths and weaknesses of each. The third is to discuss the major approaches to evaluation and to tie these to accountability, an increasing concern of counselors.

Chapter Preview

- Research and evaluation will be distinguished. Some distinctions will also be made between applied and basic research.
- The strengths and weaknesses of some basic research designs will be presented.
- The implications of research for the counseling profession will be discussed, including issues in this area.
- The purposes and processes of program evaluation will be overviewed.
- Accountability as it relates to evaluation will be discussed.

Introduction

At the outset it should be made clear that research and evaluation are *not* two distinctly different processes; in fact they have more commonalities than differences. For many years these similarities tended to confound scholars and practitioners who attempted to differentiate between the two (Drew & Hardman, 1985). However, in the late 1960s and early 1970s, progress toward meaningful differentiation between these two processes was made. Today it is widely accepted that research and evaluation differ in three ways: the purpose for which they are conducted, concern about the generalizability of the findings (external validity), and their relationships to theory. A fourth distinction between research and evaluation that is sometimes made lies in the area of applicability of findings. Evaluation efforts are typically more concerned with generating data that are immediately applicable to the work of the counselor, with research being less concerned with this applicability of findings. However, this distinction does not apply in all cases.

The purpose of evaluation is to provide information that will allow those charged with program management to make decisions regarding the value of an entire program or part of that program (Drew & Hardman, 1985). Some have likened evaluation to the parliamentary move of calling for the question, a move that indicates that it is time to move from discussion of an issue to a vote aimed at determining whether the issue at hand passes or fails (Bardo, Cody, & Bryson, 1978). This analogy is an apt one, but evaluation does not focus just on the end product, that is, whether a program succeeds or fails. It is also aimed at determining what factors contributed to the outcome. Evaluation that focuses on outcome is called "summative" or "product evaluation. " Summative evaluation tries to determine whether those individuals who received the program actually benefited in a meaningful way. Evaluation that focuses on the factors that contribute to outcomes is called "process" or "formative evaluation." Process evaluation tries to identify key variables that have contributed to or retarded the observed outcomes.

Much social science research is initiated to establish cause and effect relationships, although approaches to research do not allow the researcher to draw casual conclusions directly. Researchers are concerned with whether a particular counseling technique or program is effective, but they are more concerned with establishing a causal link between the intervention (A) and the observed outcome (B). Does A produce B? In order to answer this question, all extraneous variables that might produce B, and thus reduce the certainty that A and B are linked causally, must be controlled. Because of the desire to control extraneous variables, research is less likely to be conducted in field settings, such as college counseling centers, because variables that might influence the results cannot be adequately controlled. Evaluation, on the other hand, is always conducted in a field setting. Although evaluators also wish to control extraneous variables and establish causal relationships, projects to be evaluated are in the field.

Evaluation is conducted to fuel the decision-making process. Research is aimed at advancing our knowledge base by determining cause and effect. Researchers are concerned about the generalizability of their findings to other settings and groups. Evaluators are not as concerned about this issue. Generalizability or external validity refers to the extent to which an intervention such as a group counseling program will work in other settings. Will a group treatment program in prison A work in prison B? If the program was established only with the special characteristics of Central Prison in mind, it may not work in Southeastern Prison, but the question being asked in evaluation is, "Should we retain this program in Central Prison?" Researchers attempt to design programs that would be applicable in a number of settings (generalizability). Thus, the researcher attempts to utilize counselors who are typical of counselors in general (i.e., counselors in all prisons), to verify that the inmates being counseled are also representative of other inmates (i.e., in terms of age, race, type of crime committed, etc.), and to be sure that the treatments employed can be utilized in other settings.

As is probably obvious, questions of evaluation grow out of concern for the effectiveness of the technique or program being employed. In applied research, as opposed to basic research, questions may grow out of this same concern. However, in applied research, questions asked may also stem in part from theoretical considerations. This is partially because research, unlike evaluation, is aimed at advancing science, which in addition to explaining *what* works is aimed at explaining *why* things work. Thus a researcher may not simply be concerned with whether a particular technique can increase job interviewing effectiveness in high school students. That researcher may wish to know which techniques drawn from a theoretical perspective such as modeling theory (e.g., written directions, live models, live models plus practice, etc.) produce the most effective learning. While not all research is theory based, much of it is linked to theoretical as well as applied questions.

Some research has little immediate applicability and in fact is not pursued for practical reasons. This research is typically referred to as basic research. Counselors are little concerned about the research that examines the retention rate of nonsense syllables learned under conditions of stress. Nor are they usually interested in knowing about the maze-running habits of rats or the problem-solving skills of great apes. This research becomes relevant only when it is translated into practical application.

The commonalities between research and evaluation outweigh the differences. There are differences between the two but, Posavac and Carey (1985) indicate, evaluation is a process of generating information or facts using research methods. As has already been noted, both research and evaluation are concerned with internal validity—establishing that the program or technique under study produces the observed outcome. Those methods used to control extraneous variables from influencing the outcome are utilized in both processes. These methods involve using no-treatment (control) comparison groups, randomly assigning clients to treatment and control groups, and keeping those who deliver and receive treatments unaware of the research and evaluation design so that they will not inadvertently influence the outcomes of the study.

To illustrate these ideas, let us consider the counselor who is interested in determining whether or not a group counseling intervention enhances occupational choice-making skills. She would begin by identifying a group of students who have deficits in the occupational choice-making areas, perhaps as indicated by the inability to make an occupational choice when asked to do so. She would then design a treatment to remedy this deficiency. Students would then be randomly assigned to the treatment or control (no-treatment) group. Students and counselors leading the groups would be made aware of the general purpose of the groups but not the specific measures to be used in the study to avoid "teaching to the test." After the treatment, the treatment and control groups would be compared, usually by means of a statistical test. This process would be the same whether research or evaluation is involved. Thus while the purposes for which the study was initiated, the selection of counselors and clients to ensure generalizability of results, and the relationship of the research questions to theory may vary, the basic processes involved in research and evaluation are quite similar.

STUDENT LEARNING EXERCISE
Circle to indicate whether the following statements are true or false.

1. Evaluation and research are more similar than they are different. T F
2. Evaluation is more concerned about threats to internal validity, that is, being able to specify that the results are caused by the treatment, than is research. T F
3. Generalizability is an issue related to external validity. T F
4. Evaluators are more concerned about generalizability than are researchers. T F
5. Evaluators use research designs. T F

Research

In the preceding section two types of research were described: applied and basic. This section will briefly describe the various types of applied research approaches, which include approaches in which variables are manipulated (experimental research), relationships explored (correlational research), the status quo described (descriptive research), or development monitored over time (longitudinal research).

Experimental Research

Extensive Designs
Experimental research designs are of two types: extensive and intensive. Extensive design involves the study of groups; intensive design focuses on the individual. Extensive designs are those usually associated with experimental research and typically involve measuring the impact of an experimental manipulation by comparing an experimental group to a control group. A counselor who wishes to determine the impact of an intervention on snake phobics begins by identifying a group of snake phobics, randomly assigning the phobic subjects to two groups (experimental and control), administering the treatment, and then taking a follow-up measure of the phobic behavior and comparing the two groups, usually using some statistical procedure. This classic research design, if properly conducted, allows maximum control of competing hypotheses, and thus fulfills the most basic requirement of experimental research by increasing the researcher's ability to imply cause (treatment) and effect (reduction in snake phobia reactions).

It should be pointed out that there are many other legitimate experimental designs, most of which are described in a classic work by Campbell and Stanley (1963). However, there are also a number of pretenders, that is, research designs that do not allow any semblance of control, that are frequently employed by researchers, and that find their way into the counseling literature. One of these, the one-shot case study, is frequently used and involves only one group (experimental) and one measurement (posttest). This design, if applied to our snake phobia problem, would involve only the selection of the phobic subjects, the administration of the treatment, and a posttest. Since there is no comparison group (control) and no pretest, no real conclusions can be drawn regarding the effectiveness of the *right* treatment.

The one-group, pretest-posttest group (Campbell & Stanley, 1963) design does improve on the one-shot case study approach, but only slightly. Research using this approach identifies subjects using a pretest, follows this by the administration of a treatment and then a posttest. Because a comparison can be made between the pretest and posttest, many naive individuals believe that control has been established. However, without a control group this is not the case. To illustrate, let us assume that during the course of the research on snake phobics, a local television station decided to air a series of spots on its local news regarding the value of snakes, and each night for a week the news team ran a ten-minute segment on snakes. Without a control group the researcher is unable to separate the impact of the television series from his or her treatment and is left to wonder whether extraneous variables or the treatment reduced the intensity of snake phobia.

Extensive designs have been criticized (Goldman, 1978, 1986) because what often occurs is that over the course of treatment some of the subjects get better and some get worse, with the result being that the control and experimental groups are not significantly different with regard to the criterion measure (e.g., intensity of snake phobia). As a result, intensive research designs are increasingly popular.

Intensive Designs

Intensive designs, also called case study or $n = 1$ designs, were developed by behaviorally oriented psychologists and counselors (Tawney & Gast, 1984), but are now used by researchers with a variety of points of view (Anton, 1978). These designs have a number of advantages for counselors because they were developed for use in applied settings, focus on the individual, use the individual as his or her own control, and have a high level of control and thus allow inference of cause and effect. Their one weakness lies in the area of generalizability. Since only one subject is studied at a time it is difficult to argue that the "sample" of subjects adequately represents a broader population. However, even this deficiency can be overcome by repeating the design (replication) (Tawney & Gast, 1984).

Conducting intensive design research begins with making three basic decisions: (1) "What behavior is to be changed?" (2) "How will the target behavior be changed or what will our intervention be?" and (3) "What will be our goal in the behavior change process?" The behavior to be changed (e.g., the ounces of alcohol ingested) is referred to as the dependent variable, and the method for changing it (e.g., drug rehabilitation group) is the independent variable. The goal of the change is the criterion (Tawney & Gast, 1984).

Once the target behavior is identified, a method of measuring the behavior must be determined. As Anton (1978) states, the first principle of single subject research "requires the counselor/researcher to make a series of observations over some period of time" (p. 122). The method of measurement in intensive design research is, typically, systematic observation. However, in many school settings data regarding target behavior can often be determined through existing and ongoing records such as attendance and tardiness reports, grades, proportion of homework handed in, and percentage of work completed correctly.

The units of measurement of the target behavior must also be determined. Those typically used involve a simple count of the target behavior (how often did it occur during a time period), percentage (number of problems completed correctly), rate, number of times a behavior occurs during a time period (calories ingested per day), duration (how long a temper tantrum occurs), latency (how long it takes to respond), and trials to criterion (how many trials before a child learns to add two-digit numbers) (Tawney & Gast, 1984).

Once the units of measure are established, the target behavior must be operationally defined (what is a drunk?; what constitutes name calling?), observers trained, and an observational scheme devised. With regard to the latter, it is usually not possible to observe a subject continuously and thus some form of time sampling procedure is employed. For example, it may be that the subject is observed or only five minutes per hour, with the segments being selected randomly.

Data collection begins with the collection of baseline information regarding the target behavior, which is simply determining the occurrence of the behavior in the units selected under typical circumstances. Determining what is typical is done by simply observing the incidence of the behavior being observed. Once the occurrence stabilizes, the researcher can be relatively certain that a typical pattern for the behavior has been established. Not surprisingly, this is referred to as a "stable baseline." A stable baseline is illustrated in Figure 16.1, and is designated the A phase of data collection.

Note that the rate per half hour fluctuated between nine per period and eight per period during the four observations. A stable baseline cannot be determined with fewer than three observations, but typically more than three are required.

Once a stable baseline is established and the intervention is introduced, the B phase of the research begins. As can be seen in Figure 16.1, the intervention, which in this case was involving the student in individual counseling, produced significant changes in the student.

The design in Figure 16.1 is referred to as the AB design and is the most basic of the intensive research designs. While the AB design is useful for practitioners, it does not fulfill the qualification of greatest concern to researchers—the ability to say with some certainty that the observed change in the B phase is in fact due to

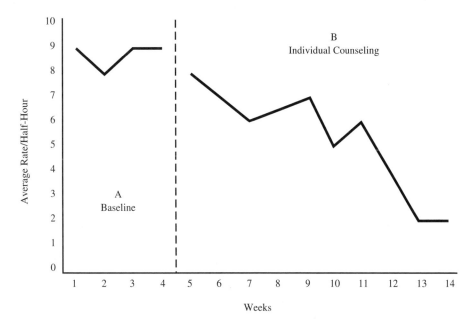

FIGURE 16.1   Incidence of Out-of-Seat Behavior of Fourth-Grade Boy

the intervention. The teacher may have imposed stricter disciplinary standards, or parents, hearing of the child's problem, may have offered a reward for "good behavior." However, there are a number of intensive research designs that meet the criteria established by researchers.

Withdrawal/Reversal Designs

A number of designs fall into this category, but because of space, only the most basic of these, the A-B-A-B and some closely related designs will be discussed. As the letters suggest, the A-B-A-B design begins with baseline (A), the baseline is followed by an intervention (B), the intervention is withdrawn and the baseline reestablished (A), and then the intervention (B) is reintroduced. The logic behind this design is quite simple. If the target behavior returns to baseline once the intervention is withdrawn and then responds to the intervention a second time, it can reasonably be assumed that the target behavior is under the influence of the intervention and thus a reasonable case for cause and effect can be established. Figure 16.2 shows an A-B-A-B design.

A researcher who attained the results observed in Figure 16.2 could be reasonably certain that homework completion was in fact influenced by behavioral contracts offering rewards for completing teacher assignments. This same researcher could establish that this intervention generalizes by replicating this same experiment with a number of deficient students who were failing to complete homework, and so in one sense the A-B-A-B design meets both the need to establish causal relationships and generalizability. The design is also of some use to

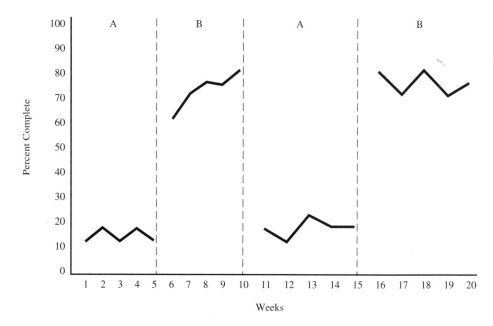

FIGURE 16.2   Percentage of Homework Completed by Eighth-Grade Boy Using Contingency Contracting

practitioners because it allows the substitution of other interventions when the first one fails *or* if the practitioner is simply interested in knowing if one approach to dealing with a problem is superior to another. Therefore, it is possible to have designs in which C represents a second intervention (A-B-A-B-C), where B and C are being compared for effectiveness.

From a scientific point of view the A-B-A-B design gets high marks. From practical and ethical points of view it does not. Practically speaking, behavior, once changed, rarely returns to a baseline condition. Another practical problem with the A-B-A-B design is an ethical one. How does one justify withdrawal of an intervention that is working? It seems, and is, unethical to withdraw an intervention that is helping a client or a subject. These practical problems make the reversal/withdrawal designs all but useless in the applied setting of the counselor. Fortunately, there are alternatives.

Multiple Baseline Design

These designs are conceptualized in much the same way as A-B designs except the design is being carried out simultaneously across three or more data sets. As Tawney and Gast (1984) indicate, a data set may involve three target behaviors under the same condition, the same behavior under three different conditions, or the same behavior for three different people.

Multiple baseline designs require, as do intensive designs, that the target behavior(s) and, if appropriate, target situations be identified and criterion levels (goals) be established. In multiple baseline design in which three different problem behaviors of one individual are to be targeted for one individual in one situation, *independent* behaviors such as spelling, incidence of hitting others, and keeping area around desk free from trash should be selected and base-rated. Then the intervention, perhaps teacher reinforcement, is introduced for behavior one (spelling achievement). Once the goal of the intervention has been attained, the intervention is introduced for behavior two, and so forth. If all three target behaviors respond in the same way, a researcher can say that the observed results can be attributed to the intervention. A similar pattern is followed if the same behavior (incidence of smoking) is to be modified across three situations, or if three individuals with the same problem (binge eating) are to be studied. A multiple baseline design is illustrated in Figure 16.3.

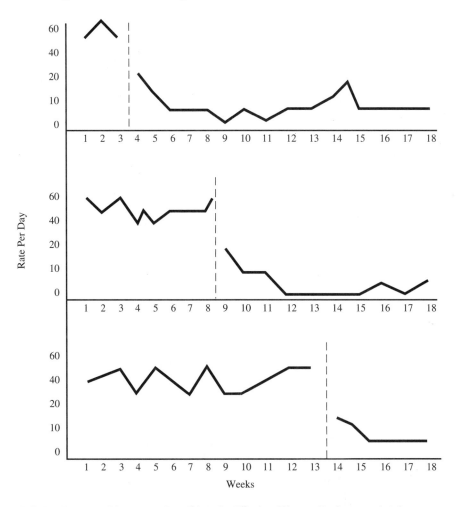

FIGURE 16.3   Cigarette Smoking in Three Clients Before and After Self-Monitoring/Reinforcement Intervention

From a research point of view, the multiple baseline approach has few flaws, particularly if the researcher replicates the design with several individuals in a number of situations. One difficulty with the design is identifying three functionally independent behaviors in an individual. Functionally independent behaviors are those that are not a part of some habit pattern. For example, smoking and drinking are functionally linked for many individuals and would not make good target behaviors. However, since there are alternatives to selecting three or more behaviors in the same individual, this problem does not pose a serious limitation. A more serious concern for the practitioner, and perhaps the researcher, is the monitoring of three behaviors/individuals/situations at the same time (Tawney & Gast, 1984). Observational procedures are time consuming and monitoring three behaviors may be more than can be adequately managed. Finally, just as there was an ethical problem with withdrawing a successful intervention in the withdrawal/reversal designs, a similar problem arises in the multiple baseline design when more than one individual is involved, since a successful treatment is being withheld from a client or subject. Each researcher will have to weigh the relative impact of withholding treatment and make a decision on a case-by-case basis.

Interpreting Intensive Research

The interpretation of extensive research relies primarily on the results of statistical tests. The interpretation of the outcomes of intensive designs is usually done through inspection of the data. This process begins by inspecting baseline data for stability and continues as the researcher collects data. One of the concerns, of course, lies with the extent to which the criterion has been attained. Normally, the expected outcome of this is established using a practical approach such as determining what is "normal" for the individuals being studied. For example, how many times is a typical third grader out of his seat? In other instances the goal may be cessation of smoking or drinking. These goals become important factors in determining whether or not an experiment is judged successful as does the stability of the data line. Just as a stable baseline is important as a prerequisite for determining when to introduce an intervention, a stable treatment data line is necessary before an experiment can be judged successful. If that treatment line is moving back toward the baseline, it may be that the treatment has had only a short-term impact.

Correlational Research

In correlational research we are usually interested not in manipulating variables but merely in establishing relationships between or among them (Cozby, 1981). For example, college admissions officers want to establish the relationship between high school grades and college achievement. Personnel officers are interested in knowing whether tests of clerical speed and accuracy really do relate to functioning as a secretary. These questions and others are answered using correlational research methods. Two of these methods will be discussed briefly here.

Relationships between two variables are examined using an entire family of correlational procedures, the most common of which is the Pearson Product Moment correlation. Like others, this yields a coefficient ranging from +1 to –1 that indicates the degree of relationship among the variables of interest. A coefficient of +1 is a perfect positive correlation and would indicate, as in the case of grades and college achievement, that there is a direct correspondence between high school grades and college achievement; that is, if one gets straight A's in high school, the same thing will occur in college. Negative correlations are just as revealing as positive correlations. The only difference in interpreting negative correlations is the direction of the relationship, since in negative relationships when one variable goes up, another goes down. If there were a –1 relationship between high school grades and college grades, the straight A high school student would be the straight F student in college.

Correlational research gets a bit more difficult to interpret, although the principles are the same, when we are interested in determining the relationship between two or more predictor variables (say high school grades and college entrance examination scores) and a dependent variable (college grades). These relationships are determined using what are called multiple correlation procedures. These procedures are particularly useful in that they allow us to build predictor equations using multiple measures and thus increase our accuracy of predicting such variables as college and job success, likelihood of dropping out of school, and so on.

As indicated at the outset, multiple correlation coefficients are interpreted in the same manner as simple correlations, that is, a +1 correlation between high school grades, Scholastic Aptitude Test scores, family income, and college grade point average are still indicators of a perfect relationship, only this time three variables have to be used to account for college grades.

Perfect relationships are rarely, if ever, attained, and thus we are frequently interpreting correlation coefficients of considerably less than 1.0. There are some straightforward ways of making these interpretations, but generally correlations that exceed .70 are considered to be high, .30–.69 moderate, and less than .30 low. For example, typically, the correlation between Graduate Record Examination scores and success in graduate school falls well below .30, while the relationship between a variety of factors and success as an undergraduate is likely to be much higher. However, even a low correlation may be considered highly valuable in some situations (admission of graduate students) when no other variables are available to suggest who might be successful.

There are a number of limitations in correlational research, but the most important one is that cause-effect relationships cannot be inferred from the correlational data. We know, for example, that there is a high relationship between scores on intelligence tests and grades in school. Does that mean that intelligence causes higher grades, which is the commonly held view? Or is it possible that success in schools results in high intelligence test scores? It is also possible in this IQ-grades relationship that a third variable such as family socioeconomic status is influencing the observed correlation. Therefore, researchers using correlational methods should be cautious not to make causal inferences from their data (Cozby, 1981).

Survey Research

Survey research methods, like those of correlational designs, do not involve manipulating variables. They are utilized to answer two types of questions. The first of these is, "What are the characteristics of a given group, institution, or geographic region?" In answering this question, we may simply want to know the gender and racial and ethnic background of U.S. citizens. We may also want to know how many graduates of Philosophy University took jobs the first year out. At other times, we may wish to describe the attitudes and opinions of voters regarding an issue or issues.

More frequently, survey research in the social sciences is embarked on, not only to describe a given situation, but to make comparisons among different situations. For example, we might wish to know how many juvenile delinquents were produced by towns or cities with various economic conditions.

Survey research studies are conducted using two basic approaches, printed surveys and interviews. As Drew and Hardman (1985) note, regardless of the approach, the most important aspect of survey research is to ask questions that can clearly be understood by the potential respondent. Lack of clarity in the questions, survey instruments that are too long, poor introduction to the research material, and the timing of the arrival of the interviewer or questionnaire are all important factors in determining not only the quality of the responses but also the quantity, that is, the number of actual responses received.

Survey researchers typically begin the process by carefully identifying the goals of the study, determining what types of data are needed to attain those goals, and then drafting questions that will elicit that data. Questionnaires or interview procedures are then field-tested and revised. Once data are received, depending on the purposes of the study, they may be subjected to sophisticated statistical analysis and interpreted much as one would interpret experimental research findings, or the data may be presented matter-of-factly, using percentages and means. In the latter situation, the interpretation is much the same as that resulting from intensive designs; that is, the researcher's judgment comes very much into play.

Longitudinal Research

As the name suggests, longitudinal research involves collecting data on a group of students over a long period of time, perhaps as long as thirty or forty years. Sanborn (1978) believes that the term "longitudinal research" frightens some individuals because of the time involved. He believes that it is most useful to think about this form of research as a method for providing answers to immediate questions, such as how many graduates got jobs. He also suggests that the usual idea that longitudinal research requires expensive, laborious procedures need not be true. In agencies such as schools, colleges and universities, and prisons and rehabilitation agencies, some data are collected routinely over time. In many instances, additional data collection could occur within the usual data collection framework with little difficulty.

Sanborn (1978) indicates that planning longitudinal research studies begins with considering the agency's goals for its clientele. If these goals are not well defined, this would be the first step in the design of the study. Out of these goals, criteria to be assessed in the longitudinal study will emerge. Generally, these are of two types: attitudes, beliefs, or satisfaction, and behavioral or personality change. To illustrate, a longitudinal study might try to determine whether clients at a mental health center were satisfied with the services they received and the degree to which they believe those services have helped them with various adjustment problems. On the other hand, the researchers might look at their personal adjustment (jobs held, marital relationships, etc.). Sanborn suggests that a variety of data sources and types be used in longitudinal research. It is also suggested that using different types of criteria may be worth considering.

Once goals and criteria for judging outcomes are established, counselors should carefully document their activities that relate to the goals, identify sources of data that will relate to the client group, plan for repeated assessments, and analyze data as they are generated.

Longitudinal research studies offer school and college counselors, and others who have client groups, an excellent means of establishing that counseling services have a meaningful impact. One question that must be asked when planning longitudinal research is how long the data collection should continue. Sanborn (1978) suggests that one answer to this can be drawn from how long we expect to make an impact. It is unrealistic to expect a counseling intervention in the elementary school to have a life-long impact, and thus follow-up through high school may be a sufficient period for the study. However, there are also practical matters to consider when planning data collection. A concern about the reasonableness of the data collection period must be addressed.

STUDENT LEARNING EXERCISE
Indicate that a statement is true by circling T or false by circling F

1. The one group, pretest-posttest design is a true experimental group.   T   F
2. Extensive research designs are easy to use in an applied setting.   T   F
3. A baseline in an $n = 1$ design must consist of two observations of the target behavior.   T   F
4. A is the baseline phase in the A-B design.   T   F

5. It is inappropriate to have more than one intervention in an intensive
   design study.   T   F

6. Multiple baseline designs are those that require that at least three baseline
   periods be established prior to intervention.   T   F

7. Correlational designs give indications of relationships, not cause and effect.   T   F

8. Longitudinal designs answer only long-term problems.   T   F

9. A recidivism study in a penal institution would probably employ
   survey techniques.   T   F

10. Process evaluation focuses on variables that influence outcome.   T   F

Research Results and the Counseling Profession

There has been a great deal of controversy regarding the meaning of research to the counseling profession. In 1978, Goldman, writing in the introduction to his edited book on research for counselors, stated that "all authors in this book, to varying extents, agree with the position that much or most of the research published in the counseling field has made little contribution to practice in the field" (p. 3). Goldman (1986) restated this point and reiterated that the reason research has not made a great contribution to the counseling field is not because of research per se, but because of the type of research being done. Goldman (1978, 1986) has recommended that we deemphasize research that focuses on groups, relies on paper and pencil measures, puts too much emphasis on objectification of data, relies heavily on complex statistical methods, and relies too heavily on experimental designs.

The title to one of Krumboltz's (1986) articles clearly denotes that his point of view differs from that of Goldman. The title is "Research is a Very Good Thing." Krumboltz makes the point that literally dozens of techniques now employed by counselors grow out of the traditional scientific tradition. Krumboltz does make the point that research deserves to be criticized and that many research studies are trivial or seriously flawed. He even goes so far as to state, "Most research studies contribute nothing to the field and waste the time of readers, researchers, and editors" (p. 161). Krumboltz also agrees with Goldman that research needs to focus more on individuals, although he does not endorse deemphasizing extensive designs.

Krumboltz's position regarding research seems to be the more prudent one, since many counseling techniques, including the basic interviewing skills taught to most students, almost all of the so-called behavioral and cognitive behavioral techniques, many of the current ideas about groups, and so forth, have come forth from research efforts. The trick, it seems, is to be able to weed through the studies that are being produced and take from them those that produce worthwhile data, not to discard the proverbial baby with the bath water. Lichtenberg's (1986) comment about counselors and research seems relevant here. He wrote, "They [counselors] would be empirical in their practice and accountable for their interventions through awareness of counseling and behavior change procedures showing evidence of effectiveness or promise and of factor mediating or mitigating therapeutic change. Minimally, such practitioners would be good consumers of research" (p. 366).

Evaluation

In the introduction to this chapter, it was suggested that from a technical point of view, evaluation utilizes the methodology of research. The differences between the two processes lie in the basic purposes for which they are conducted, their link to theory, and their concern with generalizability. To reiterate, evaluation originates to inform the decision-making process, is likely to be tied to practical concerns (as opposed to theoretical ones), and is not as concerned about generalization of findings to other settings as is research. In the evaluation process, investigators use extensive and intensive designs, correlational methodology, and survey techniques. This section will deal in more detail with the purposes of research, the models of evaluation that may be utilized to achieve these purposes, and the link between evaluation and accountability.

Purposes of Evaluation

Program evaluators may attempt to answer many questions simultaneously. One of these questions, "What is the need for this program?" is answered by examining the socioeconomic profile of a community, looking at the peculiar needs of a community with regard to the type of program being contemplated, and trying to ascertain what type of program would be most attractive to potential consumers (Posavac & Carey, 1985).

The second type of question that may be answered deals with the processes of the program: "Is the program, as designed and implemented, serving the target population?" (Hughey, Gysbers, & Starr, 1993). To answer this question, a number of subquestions must also be answered, including, "Are sufficient numbers of clients from the target group being attracted to the program?" "How does the workload match that expected when the program was planned?" and "Are there differences among the staff in terms of time and energy spent on the program?" (Posavac & Carey, 1985). Note that the effectiveness of the program does not come up in process evaluation.

Two other questions relate to effectiveness and efficiency. Summative, or outcome, evaluation relates to the gains to the client group in the program, and efficiency issues relate to the cost of the program, particularly the cost per unit of outcome. An individually oriented counseling program might be proven effective, but the costs relative to the gains might be high. A group counseling program might achieve the same ends at a lower cost.

Blocher (1987) identified eight steps in the evaluation process. These are paraphrased below, and a ninth step has been added.

1. Identify the purpose of the evaluation, including the decisions that need to be made.
2. Determine who will make the decisions once the evaluation data are collected.
3. Determine what criteria will be used to make decisions. How will the decision makers decide whether a program is successful or unsuccessful?
4. Determine relevant sources of process and outcome data about the program being evaluated.
5. Design methods for collecting data, including data about comparison groups or programs.
6. Collect the needed data.
7. Analyze the data.
8. Interpret the data and present it to the appropriate individuals.
9. Make decisions about program continuation, revision, etc.

The actual process of evaluation should begin when a program is being planned. Specific goals and objectives make outcome evaluation easier. Job descriptions, role relations, documentation of decision-making processes, clear budget statements, etc., ease process evaluation as well. Clear timelines for goal attainment can also be instrumental in determining when evaluations should be scheduled. Finally, the purposes and questions to be answered will determine the model of evaluation to be employed.

Evaluation and Accountability

Increasingly we live in an age of accountability (Vacc, Rhyne-Winkler, & Poidevant, 1993). Public Law 94-63 requires that mental health centers funded by federal funds document many of their activities and spend no less than 2 percent of their funds on program evaluation (Peterson & Burck, 1982). As Posavac and Carey (1985) state, "No professional is above being held accountable. . . . Increasingly, respect and status have to be earned by performance, not by certification or status" (p. 19).

If counselors are to be accountable they must take the following steps (Hughey, et al., 1993; Vacc, et al., 1993):

- Determine the needs of the clients they serve.
- Establish program objectives based on needs.
- Design interventions to attain objectives.
- Develop outcome measures to determine if needs have been met.

The accountability process can break down at many points. Needs must be carefully determined using systematic needs assessment procedures. Objectives for meeting these needs should be established with administrators and, in the case of school counseling programs, parents. Program interventions that will meet the needs must be carefully designed and delivered. Finally, measures selected must be sensitive enough to determine if target behaviors and other outcomes expected are attained (Vacc, et al., 1993). Accountability also involves the dissemination of the results of the evaluation to the publics of the counseling program including administrators, clients, and governmental groups responsible for funding the program.

STUDENT LEARNING EXERCISE

Indicate that a statement is true by circling T or false by circling F.

1. Research results are embraced generally as a way of selecting the correct counseling technique to use. T F
2. Outcome evaluation is equivalent to summative evaluation. T F
3. Formative evaluation is equivalent to summative evaluation. T F
4. In the best approach to evaluation, outcomes as well as contributing forces would be examined. T F

Summary

Research and evaluation have much in common, but can be distinguished on a number of grounds. Typically, evaluation occurs in the field, while research is likely to occur in a more controlled environment. Research is more concerned with generalizability of results than is evaluation, since the focus of most evaluation efforts is on the worthiness of local programs. However, both research and evaluation are wedded to the scientific tradition in that, if used properly, they can provide counselors with empirical support for their approaches.

The major research designs that counselors employ are extensive, intensive, correlational, longitudinal, and descriptive. Both extensive and intensive designs lend themselves to detecting cause-and-effect relationships if they are carried out properly; the other designs are less useful in this regard. All these designs can be used in evaluation efforts.

There is some debate about the utility of empirical data in the counseling field, with some contending that little of worth has emerged from our research and evaluation and others holding the opposite position. There is little debate, however, about the need to systematically document the value of our programs and to be accountable, however. Recent years have seen the elimination of counseling programs in which counselors have not been accountable.

Review Questions

1. Compare and contrast research and evaluation, paying particular attention to their purposes.

2. Extensive and intensive designs both get high marks from a scientific point of view. Why?

3. Give several examples of the use of correlational research by a practitioner.

4. Give several examples of the use of survey research designs by practitioners.

5. Contrast A-B-A-B designs and multiple baseline intensive designs in terms of their strengths and limitations.

6. Tell how an intensive design could be used as an evaluational device by a counselor.

7. Contrast process and outcome evaluation approaches. What types of evaluation designs lend themselves to each?

8. How can the techniques/designs identified in this chapter be used as the basis for establishing counselor accountability?

References

Anton, J. L. (1978). Studying individual change. In L. Goldman, (ed.), *Research methods for counselors: Practical approaches in field settings,* (pp. 117–154). New York: John Wiley and Sons,

Bardo, H. R., Cody, J. J., & Bryson, S. L. (1978). Evaluation of guidance programs: Call the question. *Personnel and Guidance Journal, 57,* 204–209.

Blocher, D. H. (1987). *The professional counselor.* New York: Macmillan.

Campbell, D. T., & Stanley, J. G. (1963). *Experimental and quasi-experimental designs for research.* Chicago: Rand McNally.

Cozby, P. C. (1981). *Methods in behavioral research,* (2nd ed.). Palo Alto, CA: Mayfield Publishing Company.

Drew, C. J., & Hardman, M. L. (1985). *Designing and conducting behavioral research.* New York: Pergamon.

Goldman, L. (1978). Introduction and point of view. In L. Goldman, (ed.), *Research methods for counselors: Practical approaches in field settings,* (pp. 3–26). New York: John Wiley and Sons.

Goldman, L. (1986). Research and evaluation. In M. D. Lewis, R. L. Hayes, & J. A. Lewis, (eds.), *An introduction to the counseling profession,* (pp. 278–300). Itasca, IL: F. E. Peacock.

Hughey, K. F., Gysbers, N. C., & Starr, M. (1990). Evaluating comprehensive school guidance programs: Assessing the perceptions of students, parents, and teachers. *The School Counselor, 41,* 31–35.

Krumboltz, J. D. (1986). Research is a very good thing. *The Counseling Psychologist, 14,* 152–158.

Lichtenberg, J. W. (1986). Counseling research: Irrelevant or ignored? *Journal of Counseling and Development, 64,* 365–360.

Peterson, G. W., & Burck, H. D. (1982). A competency approach to accountability in human services programs. *Personnel and Guidance Journal, 60,* 491–495.

Posavac, E. J., & Carey, R. G. (1985). *Program evaluation: Methods and case studies.* Englewood Cliffs, NJ: Prentice-Hall.

Sanborn, M. P. (1978). Longitudinal research: Studies in a developmental framework. In L. Goldman, (ed.), *Research methods for counselors: Practical approaches in field settings,* (pp. 203–232). New York: John Wiley and Sons.

Tawney, J. W., & Gast, D. L. (1984). *Single subject research in special education.* Columbus, OH: Charles E. Merrill.

Vacc, N. A., Rhyne-Winkler, M., & Poidevant, J. M. (1993). Evaluation and accountability: Possible implications for a midsize school district. *The School Counselor, 40,* 261–266.

Career Issues for Counselors

Goal of the Chapter

The purpose of this chapter is to look beyond entry into the counseling profession to the promises and pitfalls of a counseling career.

Chapter Preview

- Stages in a counseling career will be portrayed.
- Strategies for growth as a counselor will be proposed.
- Advancement in a counseling career will be outlined.
- Occupational stress or burnout will be described along with other threats to counselors' physical and mental health.
- Strategies for burnout prevention will be discussed.
- Time management, networking, and mentoring will be discussed as specific career advancement strategies.

Introduction

Early in a counselor preparation program the emphasis is on introducing the profession to students with the hope of stimulating interest in its mission. A training program can be looked on as a socialization process in which professional norms are conveyed along with some of the ritual involved in being a member of the professional group.

With a commitment to join the profession follows the need to learn the theories and techniques used. Much information needs to be amassed and synthesized even prior to working with the first "real" client. As this process continues, personal enthusiasm for the work increases, followed by a commitment to continue growth after graduate school.

The first counseling job can be unsettling; most counselors do not feel fully prepared to do the work assigned. Entry-level preparation is useful, since it gets beginners started. However, the development of a competent counselor is an ongoing process. In most cases the full potential of a counselor will not be realized for many years.

Regrettably, all counselors do not meet their potential in the years following entry into the profession. With some the quality of service they offer to clients actually deteriorates. In part this may have been supported unknowingly by the reluctance of counselor educators to forewarn counselors-in-training of the frustrations and disappointments commonly experienced after entry into the profession (Freudenberger & Richelson, 1980).

Again, the reality of being a counselor makes one realize quickly that a caseload of real clients is much more of a challenge than a friend in a counseling class role-playing a client or the internship caseload, which is often carefully selected by a supervisor. Passages in an extended counseling career are not easy. This chapter will attempt to provide an overview of career issues following entry. The processes and pitfalls to being more fully formed as a help-giver will be portrayed.

Phases in a Counselor's Career

Once graduates from an entry-level program become employed, they usually must complete an initial probationary period during which they are scrutinized by the employer and they in turn evaluate the appropriateness of the placement for themselves. The objective of this period is to test the counselor's work identity as she or he attempts to conform to the standards of the employer. Crites (1976) argues that most new employees, no matter how carefully they made their career plans and choices, find that a new job is not quite what they expected; they must make a series of adjustments in order to cope with its demands. All too often beginning employees are on their own as they struggle with the changes and surprises attached to a new job.

Levinson and his associates (1978) note that most younger employees are not immediately accepted as equals by veteran employees. Rather, they are often treated as apprentices, not as peers. It seems that it takes time to earn collegial respect. Thus, beginning a new job as a young adult can be stressful.

Entry-level performance is judged by self and others on a number of dimensions: (1) quality and quantity of work, (2) steadiness of effort, (3) ability to listen and follow instructions, and (4) ability to sustain effort or display stamina. While demonstrating these qualities, a new employee must also maintain interpersonal relationships with coworkers and supervisors (Oetting & Miller, 1977).

Both the formal and informal parts of the probationary period end when a worker is judged to be capable of independent work. With this increased confidence in his or her ability from others, the new counselor is more easily able to assume responsibility for clients without close reliance on the support of supervisors. Still, approval from supervisors and peers must be earned.

When a counselor has been accepted as a peer and trusted by supervisors, he or she enters a period in which career advancement becomes an attainable goal. In order to move toward this goal, the individual must recognize advancement opportunities, their requirements, and how in the future one can obtain one of those positions. One can then begin to work to attain promotions and other changes connected to a career development plan.

Career paths of counselors are rarely steady and direct. Most go through a cycle of periods of energy/achievement, stagnation, and even decreased effectiveness. Super (1984) describes how a worker's emotional involvement in a job tends to increase or decrease at different stages of life. For example, between forty and forty-five (midlife transition) a male's job is of less importance emotionally than at earlier and possibly later times.

As one progresses through different adult stages, entry-level training will become dated, possibly obsolete. Retooling and revitalization will remain as constant needs.

While a small number of counselors may be dismissed early in their careers, more will self-select themselves out of the profession. Still others will wither in the profession, becoming "dead wood"; they emerge as problems to themselves and to the profession.

What It Takes to Survive and Grow as a Counselor

Assuming Responsibility for One's Own Career Development

In chapter 7 a career was defined as an individual's life-long involvement with work. A distinction can be made between "career-oriented" and "job-oriented" counselors. Career-oriented counselors develop a more comprehensive attitude toward their employment than their job-oriented counterparts. The latter are concerned primarily with what is expected of them from others in the present—what they must do to retain employment. They rarely think beyond present issues and problems. They rarely visualize different work roles for themselves. Career-oriented individuals take a broad view of themselves and work, synthesizing the social roles they play within many time dimensions.

Career-oriented counselors are interested in career pathing, that is, the process of planning routes along which their careers will follow; this includes the consideration of important occupational choices, work tasks selected while employed, and self-development activities (Gutteridge, 1976). Most professionals, and particularly counselors, rarely work for an organization that assumes responsibility for employee career pathing; professionals must do this for themselves.

In his discussion of adult development, Gould (1978) identifies the true beginning of adulthood as when one realizes that what a person becomes is entirely up to that individual. Prior to that time individuals believe that powerful parental-like figures know how one should perform; and if one does what he or she is supposed to do, rewards will follow. Thus, people waste much time attempting to conform to imaginary standards and pathways instead of getting down to business and taking control of their own lives.

If a counselor begins to assume responsibility for his or her career development, the chances for success in that career are greater (Scheele, 1979). This responsibility begins with planning. Time is set aside regularly to think about current affairs and the promises and risks for the future.

Planning to Be a Successful Counselor

At first glance occupational success seems to be tied to the process of career advancement. The more successful one becomes, the more one achieves promotions, titles, higher salary, and status. However, Howes' (1981) analysis of operational definitions for success in empirical research identifies job satisfaction as the most often-used index. This makes sense, since satisfaction is a subjective evaluation of experience, one intrinsically tied to a sense of well-being that ultimately becomes more important than impressing others and amassing material wealth.

Anticipating change in the profession and changes for oneself can add to an individual's chances for success, whether success is defined as promotions, wealth, or job satisfaction. Learning about options, present and future, makes sense. This becomes more than simply storing information; it becomes making a commitment to the learning of information-seeking skills that can be applied to one's own personal and professional development.

Developmental changes within an individual are also worth noting. At age thirty one's job will have a personal context entirely different from what it will have at age forty-five or beyond. Anticipating personal passages, as described in Chapter 2, will soften the adjustments required. For example, at age thirty a person is often ready to settle into a permanent position for the first time; at age forty-five a worker may be interested in developing new skills following an intense appraisal of his competitiveness with younger colleagues (Super & Thompson, 1981).

Selecting a Quality Employer

When faced with the anxiety of job-seeking, the counselor-in-training may find it difficult to envision being offered several positions at one time and needing to decide which job offer to accept. Nevertheless this does happen, and the job-seeker must develop a set of criteria to use in evaluating job possibilities (see Table 17.1). Amico (1981) notes that professional growth, not financial gain, is the prime reason for workers to seek job changes. Professional growth may also be an important criterion for one's first job. Starting salary is another important criterion. Most counselors work for public agencies, and these often give annual raises in the form of a percentage of salary increase. Thus, the basis for salary increments over many years is the initial salary accepted.

TABLE 17.1   What to Look for in a Job

Salary
Fringe benefits
Special fringes (e.g., supplemental retirement plan)
Opportunity for advancement
Formal supervision
Supervisory feedback past probation period
Availability of mentors
Adequate support staff (e.g., clerical)
Automated office (e.g., computers, word processors, etc.)
Peer review/feedback
Support for continuing education
Employer respect for personal/family commitments
Pleasant physical environment
Strong financial support of agency/organization
Promotion and retention based on merit
Staff and supervisors free of personal problems
Absence of worker factions/cliques
Conscientious reimbursement of employee business expenses
Access to professional and legal counsel
Job satisfaction of other employees

Good employers do more for workers than offer salary and salary increases. It is wise to judge a prospective employer on his or her record for improving employee productivity and enhancing the quality of the workplace. Since professional competence is developed throughout life, the training and development opportunities offered by the organization are important. Through them personal needs can be satisfied as skills keep pace with changes at the workplace. The best chance of improved effectiveness for the counseling practitioner is achieved through continuous supervision and feedback on the job.

There will be times in the career of a counselor when evidence confirms the inability of one's current employer to contribute substantially to continued professional development. It is then time to move on; the factors described in this section reemerge as criteria in the selection of the next employer.

Doing One's Job Well

Most will agree that the basis for career advancement rests on doing one's current job well. In appraising an employee's suitability for promotion, employers look for potential to fill the role defined in the next position; they rarely encourage or advance an already mediocre employee.

The following profile of the valued employee is based on a synthesis of the personnel management literature. Such an employee (1) is neither too political nor apolitical, (2) demonstrates energy and enthusiasm, (3) is a "team player," (4) is able to meet quotas and deadlines, (5) has no known bad habits that could embarrass the organization (e.g., alcohol abuse, promiscuity, etc.), (6) is even-tempered, (7) makes few mistakes and learns from mistakes made, (8) accepts constructive feedback, (9) can communicate both orally and through written documents, and (10) seems to share the same goals as the organization.

Preserving Mental Health and Job Effectiveness

Research on counselor/therapist mental health, while not extensive, provides a glimpse of the emotional problems faced by members of the allied helping professions. When a counselor seeks the assistance of another therapist, it is usually to (1) work on a relationship difficulty (e.g., poor marriage), or (2) deal with problem emotions (usually depression), or (3) cope with an alcohol or drug problem (Deutsch, 1985). While some of these problems may result from longstanding personal traits, it is believed that the work of counselors makes them susceptible to problems of this sort.

White and Franzoni (1990) administered the MMPI to 180 beginning graduate students in counseling and found higher levels of psychopathology on six of ten scales when their subjects were compared to a normal population. It may very well be the case that a portion of counselors-in-training entered graduate school as a way to treat some of the emotional pain they experience. In addition, many graduate students seem to be persons in transition, in between careers and significant relationships, feeling the strain of these transitions. Important to recognize is the possibility of having personal problems further sensitized by the difficult work of the counseling profession.

Watkins (1983) describes some of the intrapersonal and interpersonal hazards of being a counselor. The counselor's or therapist's role in the community isolates him or her emotionally while paradoxically taking away personal privacy. This difficulty can be compounded by poor boundary management between one's private/personal life and one's professional life. For example, counselors are likely to maintain poor domestic relations (Watkins, 1983) by treating their spouses, friends, and children as they treat their clients. Most of us remember how our friends reacted when we first learned to reflect feelings in a counseling techniques class and tried it on them. In most cases our friends saw this behavior as unauthentic. Most family members and intimate friends do not respond well when the interpretations and procedures designed for clinical use are used on them; they feel manipulated and offended, and such practices are often perceived as an attempt to preserve a subordinate role for the loved one.

Gilbertson, Larson, and Powell (1978) explain such counselor behavior as a result of one's need to accept the identity of a therapist. Switching identities back and forth from counselor to family member can be difficult. Just being a counselor requires great amounts of energy in emphathizing with troubled persons and helping them solve their problems. These difficulties can lead to a form of work-related exhaustion called "burnout."

Coping with Counselor Burnout

Like most forms of occupational stress, burnout is an extremely serious health problem; next to infectious diseases and illness resulting from environmental pollution, work-related stress is viewed as the most serious health hazard facing society today (Kasl, 1978). In addition, since burnout is the single most discussed reason for the deterioration of service from experienced and once effective therapists and counselors, it is a major professional concern as well (Maslach, 1982; Perlman & Hartman, 1982).

Burnout is most often defined as a syndrome, prevalent in the human services professions, in which practitioners manifest a complex set of symptoms—some physiological, others attitudinal and behavioral in nature (Spicuzza & DeVoe, 1982). Freudenberger (1974) believes that burnout is best described as physical and emotional exhaustion. Faced with the demands of their work, human service professionals simply wear out over time, becoming less effective, even inoperative. This form of exhaustion is special in that ordinary rest periods do not relieve the fatigue. A counselor may retire for the day only to awaken the following morning still depleted of energy. The burned-out counselor is different from a lazy one; to "burn out," a person must have been "on fire." Burned-out counselors are often the ones who before burnout sought additional responsibilities and responded to requests for additional service (Freudenberger & Richelson, 1980). It is the deterioration in energy and enthusiasm for the job in the course of a career that marks the presence of burnout.

As this exhaustion progresses, other changes occur. Maslach (1976) reported that the social service workers she interviewed tried to deal with their occupational stress by distancing themselves from their clients. These help-givers increasingly became more negative and cynical in their attitudes, often dehumanizing their clients when discussing them. Maslach also found that burnout was correlated with increased use of alcohol, emotional problems, and suicide. Freudenberger (1974) drew an analogy between these symptoms and what has come to be known as "battle fatigue." Again, the pressures and challenges of the helping professions place such demands on an individual that without some plan to buffer oneself from such pressures, and without a plan to renew and revitalize one's energy, more than likely a dedicated counselor (one who is "on fire") will eventually burn out.

Stressors Affecting the Helping Professions

Factors that produce stress in individuals are called stressors. Stressors that affect counselors and other human service workers include (1) overwork, (2) money issues, (3) job politics, (4) boredom, and (5) lack of control over client outcomes (Forney, Wallace-Schultzman, & Wiggers, 1982). Maher (1980) pinpoints lack of felt control over client outcome as the principal stressor for therapists. He also adds as stressors (1) long working hours, (2) a difficult caseload, (3) poor working relationships, (4) role ambiguity (no clear role description), and (5) role expansion (repeatedly assigned additional duties). Stressors on counselors are summarized in Table 17.2. In general, the longer the list of stressors, the more rapid and intense should be the burnout.

The Stress-Prone Counselor

It can be assumed that all professional help-givers will be exposed to the stressors being discussed, but it is not clear whether or not certain personality characteristics in the worker may make that person more susceptible to burnout. Melendez and DeGuzman (1983) believe that no one trait predisposes a person for rapid burnout. Freudenberger and Richelson (1980) state that naiveté and excessive idealism come closest to predicting burnout. Aloofness and distance from one's family may also be related to burnout (Small, Small, Assure, & Moore, 1969). Maslach (1982) believes that introverted, unassertive, impatient, intolerant, and conventional individuals as well as those lacking self-confidence are the most susceptible to burnout. In general, negative life events (e.g., divorce, problems with children, natural disasters) promote and aggravate burnout (Justice, Gold, & Klein, 1981).

Type A behavior often is associated with individuals most likely to become stressed (Keenan & McBain, 1979). Friedman and Rosenman (1974) characterize Type A behavior as manifesting the following: hard-driving effort, striving for achievement, competitiveness, aggressiveness, haste, impatience, restlessness, alertness, and hurried motor movements. Time consciousness best represents the Type A person. For example, the Type A person is always in a hurry, cannot wait in line, is impatient with the speed at which others respond, likes to work on several tasks at one time, and often interrupts others and finishes for them what they are trying to say.

Arguments have raged for years about the relationship between Type A behavior and coronary heart disease. Type A behavior is supposed to predict susceptibility to coronary heart disease, which in turn is viewed as a stress-related disease. Diamond's review of the literature (1982) suggests that hostility is a major component of Type A personalities. One might conclude that any or all of these

TABLE 17.2   Counselor Stressors

Work-related	Personal
Intense interpersonal contacts	Too idealistic
Insensitive administration at work	Merge work/nonwork (poor boundaries)
Not part of the policy-making process	Poor marriages
Peer isolation	Life too public
Results of work often unknown	Cannot set boundaries
Inadequate feedback/supervision	High expectations
Low salary/economic hardships	
Role ambiguity	
Qualitative work overload	

personality dimensions may make a counselor more stress-prone. Focusing only on the clearly observable, we can say that the stress-prone counselor will work long hours, take little time off, manage a difficult caseload, and maintain poor working relationships with peers (Maher, 1983). Thus, personality characteristics that explain such behavior enter into the effort to control this damaging situation.

Antidotes for Burnout

Reducing burnout among counselors best proceeds with the recognition that this syndrome is a protective mechanism, an attempt to insulate oneself from the physical and emotional damage resulting from occupational stress. It seems wise to begin treating burnout by first reducing contact with the factors causing the stress. Where such stressors cannot be eliminated or reduced (e.g., a caseload of difficult clients), buffers need to be put in place to reduce the impact of those stressors (see Table 17.3).

The most discussed and promising buffer for occupational stress among helping professionals seems to be social support, given by primary partners at home and by colleagues at work (Cooper & Marshall, 1978; Levi, 1978; Kyriacou, 1981; Spicuzza & DeVoe, 1982). Social support means more than merely having someone to talk to; it works best when family and work colleagues recognize the potential for burnout and actively plan to maintain an emotional atmosphere that permits acceptance of work-related strain. Watkins (1983) thinks association with "healthy souls" in particular helps ward off burnout, since interacting with well-adjusted individuals enhances the mental development and well-being of the professional help-giver.

Support at work might take the form of a mutual help group that has a formal structure, has clearly identified members, and meets regularly. Silverman (1980)

TABLE 17.3   Antidotes to Counselor Burnout

Time and boundary management
Detached concern for clients
Work sharing and job rotation
Supervision for professional development
More effective peer/supervisor feedback
See counseling as a job not a "calling"
Cultivate nonwork friendships
Realism about the power of counseling interventions
Written professional development plan
Join a social support/mutual aid group
Treat spouse and children as different from clients
Improve body image
See health as holistic
Preserve privacy better
Cultivate hobbies/take vacations
Reevaluate personal/professional ambitions

describes such groups as providing assistance on a variety of fronts. First, these groups disseminate information that can be used in problem solving. For example, stressors in the workplace can be identified, as can escape routes from them. In addition, such groups might provide material assistance if needed; more often they will make earnest attempts to maintain an emotional climate in which members feel cared for and supported. It is also important for the group to recognize when a colleague is in crisis and to help mobilize aid rapidly to confront problems before they are compounded. For example, a colleague in the midst of a deteriorating marriage often is not asked to talk about his situation. Friends and colleagues are reluctant to interfere in personal business. The person in crisis may begin to drink excessively as his marriage continues to decline. If this negative behavior is not stopped, employment may be jeopardized. A support group hopefully would recognize and treat a problem before it progressed that far.

Just as a support group can prevent burnout, training programs might help reduce the risk of rapid burnout for new helping professionals by providing realistic rather than idealized views of their professions (Savicki & Cooley, 1982). The overall adjustment of most new employees seems best served by realistic job previews (Dugoni & Ilgen, 1981).

Since loss of energy is one of the major symptoms of burnout, the conservation of physical and psychological energy becomes an obvious antidote. Maher's review of important theoretical positions (1983) from Freud to Durkheim supports the notion that humans do not have unlimited energy and stamina. Counselors must make choices regarding situations they should avoid in order to conserve their energy. The conservation of energy includes taking time off from work—"mental health days" and vacations. In addition, social services workers, according to Maher, need to understand what factors in themselves and their lifestyles help create energy. One example might be an investment club in which colleagues pool money for purchasing securities. Seeing the value of investments rise and fall can be entertaining and exciting, that is if they rise more than they fall.

Probably the most commonly recommended antidote to stress, and thus burnout, is the regular incorporation of relaxation into one's lifestyle. Benson (1975) has provided an extremely popular review of various techniques aimed at relieving stress and tension. He offers a simple meditative technique that engages the body's "relaxation response"; Benson says it is biologically opposite of the arousal response, called stress. It is Benson's thesis that contemporary society has erroneously devalued the "relaxation response" and has failed to teach people strategies for relaxing, as earlier civilizations did. The helping professionals need to compensate for this attitude by offering systematic instruction or practice in such techniques as biofeedback, meditation, progressive relaxation, yoga, and so forth.

Keeping Counselors Healthy

It can be argued that reliance on any one strategy or set of techniques to cope with stress will inevitably be fruitless, since stress and subsequent burnout are related to a complex array of lifestyle factors. Ultimate success in coping with stress, especially for those already damaged by it, lies in making lifestyle changes that not only help avoid illness but also promote increased states of wellness.

Wellness has become a popular concept in health promotion. Myers (1992) identifies wellness as the fundamental paradigm that underlies the counseling profession. Wellness goes hand-in-hand with fostering of lifespan development. Wellness has many dimensions, including psychological, spiritual, physical fitness, family and work adjustment, as well as effective leisure time use, and stress management.

It is important for counselors to recognize that stress is not simply a synonym for nervous tension; stress is a biological response, centering on the mobilization of the endocrine system, that is intended to help organisms cope with the challenges and demands of life. It is a form of arousal that can have devastating effects on personal health if not intelligently managed (Selye, 1976). The personal and social cost of allowing individuals to slowly undergo a process of biological destruction, as is the case in imprudent maintenance of stress states, is simply unacceptable.

In recent years periodicals have been filled with articles describing how companies have attempted to keep their employees healthy. The cost of developing managers and technical specialists (e.g., engineers and applied scientists) is simply too great to allow such resources to be squandered by ignoring unhealthy lifestyle habits among these workers. The same is true for people in the social service professions. Thus, stress management becomes equated with lifestyle management, where serious attention is given to habits and behaviors that affect illness, death, health, or wellness. In this regard, Romano (1984) identifies the following as behaviors in need of careful attention: diet, physical exercise, and cigarette smoking.

Succeeding in the Counseling Profession through Proper Nutrition

Vast amounts of material are published each year regarding diet. While many opinions exist to the contrary, there still seems to be an emerging consensus concerning what foods one should eat and what substances one should avoid consuming in order to be healthy (Lapple, 1975; Mahoney & Mahoney, 1976; Pritikin, 1980; Brody, 1983; Haas, 1983).

Basically, a healthy diet is one that:

1. Greatly minimizes the intake of all fat; in particular animal fat.
2. Relies on complex, "slow-burning" carbohydrates (starches) as the principal nutritional base; these include fruits, vegetables, and whole grains.
3. Greatly minimizes the intake of simple carbohydrates (sweets); these include processed foods, principally those that have a high percentage of refined sugar.
4. Restricts the intake of high protein foods below average levels for industrialized nations. This means lowered amounts of all meats and seafood, especially red meats.

5. Pays attention to the kinds of additives or manmade chemicals—in particular those that are known to cause cancer—found especially in processed foods.
6. Minimizes the consumption of alcohol and caffeine.
7. Reduces or eliminates smoking. Breaking the smoking habit can have significant health benefits even if one quits in his or her fifties or sixties (Cooper, 1985).
8. Includes the frequent intake of fluids, especially water.
9. Spreads the eating schedule across the entire day, with an emphasis on smaller, more frequent meals, especially early in the work day.

The benefits of proper nutrition go beyond the delay or avoidance of health problems; increased well-being, both physical and psychological, can result. Such benefits include:

1. Better weight control, which in turn can lead to a more positive body image and greater self-esteem.
2. Increased attractiveness to others, which can result in increased social effectiveness.
3. Greater energy through more efficient oxygen exchange in the cardiovascular system.
4. Fewer digestion problems, which in turn lead to fewer sleep and rest problems.
5. Less risk of sudden death (heart attack) along with increased enjoyment of physical fitness activities.

Succeeding in the Counseling Profession through Increased Physical Fitness
In general, physical fitness is defined according to an individual's endurance (stamina), strength, and flexibility. Also relevant are balance, weight control, and muscular definition (Schwartz, 1982). Of these factors, the most important according to many different experts is cardiovascular endurance. The only real way one can become physically fit is through exercise.

Physically fit employees are more valuable. It is important to understand that physical fitness for workers is different from physical fitness for athletes.

McCullagh (1984) notes that part of the "fitness revolution" that began several decades ago is the emphasis on life-long pursuits that promote physical fitness. Called "lifesports," these include such activities as swimming, racketball, running, bicycling, and other sports that promote cardiovascular fitness while being enjoyable and habitual.

Cardiovascular fitness is developed through what is called aerobic exercise (Cooper, 1970). Aerobic means "living in air." Aerobic exercise is any activity that exercises the heart (raises the heartbeat to 70 percent maximum rate) but is not so strenuous that it causes an oxygen deficit so the participant becomes out of breath. An aerobic exercise regimen is one that exercises the heart in such a way for a minimum of twenty minutes three or four times a week.

Such exercise, while beneficial, is not without risk (see Table 17.4). Every year hundreds of people experience sudden death (heart attack) while exercising; most of these are middle-aged individuals. However, in almost all cases (Cooper, 1985) autopsies confirm that coronary heart disease (usually hardening of the arteries) was present over a long period of time before death. For this reason Cooper (1985) recommends an ECG stress test, particularly for exercisers over age forty.

Career Advancement for Counselors

Research suggests that physical fitness training contributes significantly to one's improved mood, self-concept, and work behavior (Folkins & Sine, 1981). Improved work behavior includes less absenteeism, reduced errors, and improved output. It would seem that career advancement should follow from this state of wellness (see Table 17.5).

TABLE 17.4   Popular Forms of Aerobic Exercise

Type	Advantages	Disadvantages
Aerobic dance	Widely available Fun	Some instructors lack expertise Injuries increase when studio is crowded
Cross-country skiing	Achieves best conditioning Aesthetic and fun	Requires skill Snow and trails often not available Can get lost in woods and bad storms
Cycling	Enjoyable	Dangerous in traffic Equipment often expensive Dependent on dry weather
Indoor exercise (rowing/cycling)	Safe in bad weather Readily available	Boring Can become irregular
Racket/handball	Fun	Encourages Type A personalities Access limited Requires a partner Injuries common; protect eyes
Running/jogging	Very popular Strengthens bones Easy access	Injuries to joints On roads can be dangerous Easy to overdo
Swimming	Safe in a pool Few injuries possible Good while recovering from injuries	Requires skill Does not strengthen bones Infections (eyes/ears)
Walking	Safe Aesthetic/interesting Can provide social contact	Low aerobic effect/must walk fast or longer Requires considerable time

TABLE 17.5 A Holistic Health Plan

Description: This outline represents a summary of the key issues discussed with regard to burnout and healthy lifestyles. Use it in constructing your own health plan.

I. Review of current health habits and important stressors
   A. Habits that are problematic
      1. Use of exercise; general level of activity
      2. Nutritional habits
      3. Smoking
      4. Unhealthy beliefs or personality traits (e.g., Type A)
   B. Stressors in own environment
      1. Complaints I have regarding daily living conditions
      2. Complaints I have regarding my job or schooling
      3. Disappointments in my private life
   C. Summary evaluation of personal health habits
II. My health plan
   A. Improving my physical health to better tolerate stress
      1. My physical fitness plan
      2. How I plan to relax
      3. Improved eating habits
   B. Personality improvement ideas
      1. Restructuring unhealthy ideas and beliefs
      2. Plan to seek counseling or not
      3. A reading plan for personal growth
   C. Controlling stress at work and at school
      1. How I'll avoid stressors listed above (I.B.2)
      2. How to improve relationships with colleagues/supervisors
      3. Getting control of my ambitions
      4. My new self-image as a worker or student
   D. Keeping change rates within limits
      1. Staggering changes to avoid the stress of too much change
   E. Improving my support network at home and with friends
      1. How to become less of a complainer
      2. People I will support more, who can return the support
      3. How I can improve communication with loved ones
   F. My revised philosophy of life
      How my new health can change the way I see meaning in life

Earlier in this chapter, career advancement was touched on when counselor career stages were briefly reviewed. To date there is little data on what happens to counselors after their entry-level training. Two studies (Walton, 1980; Birashk & Kaczhowski, 1984) provided 10- and 13-year follow-ups of master's level counselors who had graduated from National Defense Education Act (NDEA) Training Institutes. While the majority of these graduates accepted school counseling positions on the completion of their degrees, fewer than half remained in counseling positions a decade or so later. A few of these graduates left the counseling profession completely, returning to the classroom or entering some other field with little direct relation to counseling. A number of graduates from both studies completed doctorates in counseling, with most of these accepting university positions as counselor educators. A fair number of these subjects entered administrative positions as guidance directors in school systems or as administrators of counseling-related programs in higher education.

From this data it seems that the career paths followed by counselors are broad in the sense that they "spread out" into related fields, with higher salaries and greater status tied to additional education. This may be the case since career ladders specific to the direct practice of counseling and related interventions are not very long, at least in comparison to other occupations. A mental health center or other agency may have several grades of employment, such as Counselor I and Counselor II. Most practicing counselors who are interested in higher pay, greater status, and more leadership and responsibility, have to leave counseling for the most part and accept administrative positions. Some exceptions to this exist, but they are few in number.

Compare this situation to careers in business administration. Lipsett (1980) has developed career path charts demonstrating the many advancement levels possible for someone with a bachelor's degree in business or accounting. Some of these charts show as many as ten labor grades one could advance through with that degree alone. Another shows six different levels one could be promoted through in just a purchasing department.

Some changes in career direction for counselors probably are a result of personal changes that affect occupational interests and motivation for continued skill development. Stress resulting from comparisons of salary, responsibilities, and skills with other professions may provide additional incentive to leave counseling (Spicuzza & DeVoe, 1982).

Important to remember, however, is the fact that follow-up studies of counselors (Walton, 1980; Birashk & Kaczhowski, 1984) show that graduates from counselor preparation programs are usually satisfied with their training and with the direction their careers take. The chance is good, based on this evidence, that 30 percent to 50 percent of a graduating class of master's level counselors will initially be employed as counselors and remain so for over a decade. The majority of those who seek other positions will advance in terms of salary and status by accepting positions offered to those with further education and work experience. These positions are like entry-level positions; they reflect similar patterns of career interests

TABLE 17.6 Occupations with Worker Trait Codes Similar to Counselors

Occupational Titles	Occupation	Worker Trait Code
Religious	Christian Science Practitioner	129.107–014
	Director of Religious Activities	129.107–018
	Clergy Member	120.007–010
Counseling and Social Work	Director of Counseling	045.107–018
	Psychologist, Clinical	045.107–022

and worker traits or abilities, as described by the U.S. Department of Labor. (See *The Dictionary of Occupational Titles* and *The Guide for Occupational Exploration* for descriptions of the systems of both interests and worker traits.)

Three Strategies for Continued Career Growth

Whether one remains a counselor or moves to another position, three popular strategies can facilitate achieving desired ends. They are effective time management, the development of networks, and the use of mentoring.

Effective Time Management

The concept of time management has been popularized in recent years (e.g., Mackenzie, 1972; Lakein, 1973) as a label for a set of strategies that allow people to be more judicious in how they invest their time.

When people with many different responsibilities say they "never get anything done," what they usually mean is that they never get around to doing really important things. Most overworked people manage to complete many small tasks every day; their discontent often centers on their failure to achieve long-range goals. Part of the reason for this is that important, long-range goals constitute the basis for ultimate self-esteem. So much is at stake in meeting these goals that most become anxious when just thinking about them. To escape this anxiety, people avoid dealing with these big life goals, substituting instead work on immediate, less significant tasks. This process becomes one of the most common forms of procrastination.

Time management strategies help people overcome procrastination. The emphasis in most time management approaches (Mackenzie, 1972; Lakein, 1973) is on goal identification, prioritizing of goals, identification of activities that waste time, and planning work space and time. The emphasis is on not only what one should do, but also what one should avoid doing. When this process works, people find that more time becomes devoted to large, significant life goals. The goals, sometimes overwhelming by their dimension, become more attainable as people learn how to divide them into smaller, more easily achieved parts.

Not all people need to learn better time management methods; many have largely uninvolved lives in which boredom is more of a problem than is overwork. Time management is especially relevant for such workers as full-time homemakers, dual career couples, business managers, and others that have a tendency to take on too many responsibilities.

The Development of Networks

Networking is merely a recent term used to describe the process of making connections with other people, especially those that can be useful in the future. Rawlins and Rawlins (1983) identify a number of benefits resulting from the development of helpful contacts. People who can help us procure needed resources, important information, job leads, opportunities, and feedback can be identified and filed for future reference. Actively networking with others builds participation and self-confidence. Here are some common networking suggestions for beginning counselors:

1. Have a plan on how to file names, addresses, and telephone numbers of people you meet. Select a system (e.g., rolodex or computer file) that can be updated and reorganized easily.
2. Make an effort to get others to know you and remember your name, address, and phone number. Purchase business cards if your employer does not supply them. Use them liberally.
3. Make a special effort to get people to remember you. For example, some professional counselors are rarely without postcards or "speed memos" so that they can easily send a note of appreciation or a request for additional information to someone of potential use in the future.
4. Volunteer to work on committees or groups that will enable you to meet influential people. For example, being a student representative on a college committee may give you access to a dean or vice president from whom most graduate students ordinarily would not get recognition. Scheele (1979) calls this "catapulting" in that one can be projected over barriers that ordinarily block access to important people.
5. Maintain your own identity but remember that psychologically healthy people display a broad wardrobe of behaviors; they are not limited to being just a certain way, regardless of circumstances. Practice acquiring such a wardrobe by forcing yourself into a variety of social situations.

The Use of Mentoring

The recent labeling of an older person as a "mentor"—one who has an impact on the career and personal development of a younger person—seems to have begun with Levinson and his associates (1978). A mentor is not viewed either as a parental figure or as a peer; rather a mentor is seen as an individual roughly one-half generation older than another who teaches, advises, opens doors for, encourages, promotes, cuts red tape for, show the politics and subtleties of the job to, believes in, and thus helps a protegé succeed (Rawlins & Rawlins, 1983).

Having a mentor has been linked to faster promotions and higher pay for the protegé (Roche, 1979). The relationship, however, is mutually beneficial; mentors often get some of the same benefits as protegés. These may include (1) job advancement, (2) creation of a support system, (3) access to system resources, (4) more control over the work environment, (5) development of a reputation, and (6) personal satisfaction (Gerstein, 1985).

Alleman, Cochran, Doverspike, and Newman (1984) note from their review of the mentoring literature that same-sex and opposite-sex mentor-protegé relationships are very similar. Mentors look for potential, not similarity with self, in the protegé. Protegés, though, perceive mentors as like themselves. These same authors note that mentoring in part can become a solution for workers who have reached a plateau (i.e., are not promotable); such employees can contribute much to the organization and to their own meaning by preparing another generation for the work to be done.

Summary

In this chapter, issues related to the career development of counselors were briefly reviewed in order to provide the counselor-in-training with a preview of some of the issues and potential problems that might arise. It is hoped that readers will be better prepared both to avoid the damaging aspects of counseling-related work and to capitalize on opportunities available for advancement. In particular, burnout was treated at length as one of the major threats to quality service in the profession. Strategies for avoiding burnout and other health-related problems were explored.

Review Questions

1. Describe the typical stages in a counseling career.

2. What are some common views regarding success as a counselor?

3. What are some typical mental health problems of counselors?

4. What is burnout? How can it be treated? How can it be minimized?

5. What are the characteristics of the stress-prone counselor?

6. What are some ways to remain healthy as a counselor?

7. What are some advancement strategies for counselors?

References

Alleman, E., Cochran, J., Doverspike, J., & Newman, I. (1984). Enriching mentoring relationships. *Personnel and Guidance Journal, 62*(6), 329–332.

Amico, A. M. (1981). Computerized career information. *Personnel Journal, 60*(8), 632–633.

Benson, H. (1975). *The relaxation response*. New York: Morrow.

Birashk, B., & Kaczhowski, H. (1984). Career patterns of NDEA elementary school counselors. *Vocational Guidance Quarterly, 32*(4), 263–270.

Brody, J. (1983). *Jane Brody's guide to personal health*. New York: Avon.

Brody, J. (1985). *Good food book: Living the high-carbohydrate way*. New York: W. W. Norton.

Cooper, K. H. (1970). *The new aerobics*. New York: Bantam Books.

Cooper, K. H. (1985). *Running without fear: How to reduce the risk of heart attack and sudden death during aerobic exercise*. New York: M. Evans and Company.

Cooper, C. L., & Marshall, J. (1978). Sources of managerial and white collar stress. In C. L. Cooper & R. Payne, (eds.), *Stress at work*, (pp. 81–105). New York: John Wiley and Sons.

Crites, J. O. (1976). A comprehensive model of career development in early adulthood. *Journal of Vocational Behavior, 9*(1), 105–118.

Deutsch, C. (1985). A survey of therapists' personal problems and treatment. *Professional Psychology: Research and Practice, 16*(2), 305–315.

Diamond, E. L. (1982). The role of anger and hostility in essential hypertension and coronary heart disease. *Psychological Bulletin, 92*(2), 410–433.

Dugoni, B. L., & Ilgen, D. R. (1981). Realistic job previews and the adjustment of new employees. *Academy of Management Journal, 24*(3), 579–591.

Folkins, C. H., & Sime, W. E. (1981). Physical fitness training and mental health. *American Psychologist, 36*(4), 373–389.

Forney, D., Wallace-Schultzman, F., & Wiggers, T. T. (1982). Burnout among career development professionals: Preliminary findings and implications. *Personnel and Guidance Journal, 60*(7), 435–439.

Freudenberger, H. J. (1974). Staff burnout. *Journal of Social Issues, 30*(1), 159–165.

Freudenberger, H. J., & Richelson, G. (1980). *Burnout: The high cost of achievement*. Garden City, NY: Doubleday.

Friedman, M., & Rosenman, R. H. (1974). *Type A behavior and your heart*. Greenwich, CN: Fawcett Publications.

Gerstein, M. (1985). Mentoring: An age old practice in a knowledge-based society. *Journal of Counseling and Development, 64*(2), 156–157.

Gilbertson, D., Larson, C., & Powell, T. (1978). Therapist burnout: Perspectives on critical issues. *Social Casework, 59,* 563–565.

Gutteridge, T. G. (1976). *Organizational career development: State of the practice*. Buffalo, NY: SUNY-Buffalo Human Resources Institute.

Haas, R. (1983). *Eat to win*. New York: New American Library.

Howes, N. J. (1981). Characteristics of career success: An additional input to selecting candidates for professional programs. *Journal of Vocational Behavior, 18,* 277–288.

Justice, B., Gold, R. S., & Klein, J. P. (1981). Life events and burnout. *Journal of Psychology, 108,* 219–226.

Kasl, S. V. (1978). Epidemiological contributions to the study of work stress. In C. L. Cooper & R. Payne, (eds.), *Stress at work,* (pp. 3–50). New York: John Wiley and Sons.

Keenan, A., & McBain, G. D. (1979). Effects of Type A behavior, intolerance of ambiguity, and locus of control on the relationship between role stress and work-related outcomes. *Journal of Occupational Psychology, 52,* 277–285.

Kyriacou, C. (1981). Social support and occupational stress among schoolteachers. *Educational Studies, 7,* 55–60.

Lakein, A. (1973). *How to get control of your time and your life*. New York: New American Library.

Lapplé, F. M. (1978). *Diet for a small planet*. New York: Ballantine Books.

Levi, L. (1978). *Quality of the working environment: Protection and promotion of occupational mental health*. (Reports from the Laboratory for Clinical Stress Research. No. 88, 25p.)

Levinson, D. J., Darrow, C. N., Klein, E. B., Levinson, M. H., & McKee, B. (1978). *The seasons of a man's life*. New York: Ballantine Books.

Lipsett, L. (1980). Career path charts as counseling aids. *Vocational Guidance Quarterly, 28*(4), 360–368.

Mackenzie, R. A. (1972). *The time trap*. New York: McGraw-Hill.

Maher, E. L. (1983). Burnout and commitment: A theoretical alternative. *Personnel and Guidance Journal, 61*(7), 390–393.

Mahoney, K., & Mahoney, M. J. (1976). *Permanent weight control*. New York: W. W. Norton.

Maslach, C. (1976). Burnout. *Human Behavior, 5,* 16–22.

Maslach, C. (1982). *Burnout: The cost of caring*. Englewood Cliffs, NJ: Prentice-Hall.

McCullagh, J. C. (1984). *The complete bicycle fitness book*. New York: Warner Books.

Melendez, W. A., & DeGuzman, R. M. (1983). *Burnout: The new academic disease.* Washington, DC: Clearing House on Higher Education.

Morgan, M. A., Hall, D. T., & Martin, A. (1979). Career development strategies in industry: Where are we and where should we be? *Personnel, 56*(2), 13–30.

Myers, J. E. (1992). Wellness, prevention, development: The cornerstone of the profession. *Journal of Counseling and Development, 71*(2), 136–139.

Oetting, E., & Miller, C. D. (1977). Work and the disadvantaged: The work adjustment hierarchy. *Personnel and Guidance Journal, 56*(1), 29–35.

Pearson, J. M. (1982). The transition into a new job: Tasks, problems, and outcomes. *Personnel Journal, 61,* 286–290.

Perlman, B., & Hartman, E. A. (1982). Burnout: Summary and future research. *Human Relations, 35,* 283–305.

Pritikin, N., & McGrady, P. M., Jr. (1979). *The Pritikin program for diet and exercise.* New York: Grosset and Dunlap.

Rawlins, M. E., & Rawlins, L. (1983). Mentoring and networking for helping professionals. *Personnel and Guidance Journal, 62*(2), 116–118.

Roche, G. R. (1979). Much ado about mentors. *Harvard Business Review, 57*(1), 14–16, 20, 24, 26–28.

Romano, J. L. (1984). Stress management and wellness: Reaching beyond the counselor's office. *Personnel and Guidance Journal, 62*(9), 533–537.

Savicki, V., & Cooley, E. J. (1982). Implications of burnout research and theory for counselor educators. *Personnel and Guidance Journal, 60*(7), 415–419.

Scheele, A. M. (1979). *Skills for success: A guide to the top.* New York: Morrow.

Schwartz, L. (1982). *Heavyhands: The ultimate exercise.* Boston: Little, Brown.

Selye, H. (1976). *The stress of life.* New York: McgrawHill.

Silverman, P. R. (1980). *Mutual help groups: Organization and development.* Beverly Hills, CA: Sage Publications.

Small, I., Small, J., Assure, C., & Moore, D. (1969). The fate of the mentally ill physician. *The American Journal of Psychiatry, 125*(10), 1333–1342.

Spicuzza, F. J., & DeVoe, M. W. (1982). Burnout in the helping professions: Mutual aid groups as self-help. *Personnel and Guidance Journal, 61*(2), 95–99.

Super, D. E. (1984). Career and life development. In D. Brown & L. Brooks, (eds.), *Career choice and development.* San Francisco: Jossey-Bass, 192–234.

Super, D. E., & Thompson, A. S. (1981). *Adult career concerns inventory.* New York: Teachers College, Columbia University.

Walton, J. M. (1980). NDEA participants prepared for inner-city counseling: A ten year follow-up. *Counselor Education and Supervision, 20*(1), 50–55.

Watkins, C. E., Jr. (1983). Burnout in counseling practice: Some potential professional and personal hazards of becoming a counselor. *Personnel and Guidance Journal, 61*(5), 304–308.

White, P. E., & Franzoni, J. B. (1990). A multidimensional analysis of the mental health of graduate counselors in training. *Counselor Education and Supervision, 29*(4), 258–267.

Chapter *18*

Issues in the Counseling Profession: Setting Future Directions

Goal of the Chapter

The purpose of this chapter is to present major unresolved issues confronting the counseling profession, and to make recommendations for action.

Chapter Preview

- Eight major unresolved issues will be discussed and recommendations made for addressing them. The issues pertain to:

  a. Professional unity.
  b. The use of technology.
  c. The legal basis for the profession.
  d. Empiricism and counseling practice.
  e. The future of career counseling.
  f. Training requirements.
  g. Acceptance of counselors as allied health professionals.
  h. Impact of the moral majority in school counseling services.

Introduction

What should be quite clear at this juncture is that the counseling profession is in a state of flux. Many important steps have been taken, but much remains to be done. In this chapter, the unresolved issues will be discussed briefly and recommendations will be made as to how the counseling profession should proceed to deal with these issues.

Will There Be a Unified Counseling Profession?

Since 1952 when the American College Personnel Association (ACPA), the National Vocational and Guidance Association (now National Career Development Association, and the National Association of Guidance Supervisors and Counselor Trainers (now Association of Counselor Educators and Supervisors) merged to form the American Personnel and Guidance Association (now American Counseling Association ACA), there has been tension among the groups that comprise the counseling profession. This tension accelerated to some degree when the American Mental Health Association started its own credentialing effort by forming the National Academy of Mental Health Counselors. Some counselors doubted the need for credentialing, but the most pervasive concern was that the Academy was trying to establish an elite group within the counseling profession. It also intensified with the development of the Council for the Accreditation of Counseling and Related Educational Programs (CACREP) because of the fear by many counselor educators that their programs would be unable to meet accreditation standards and thus they would be unable to compete with programs that become accredited. One result of the tension is that ACPA left ACA in 1993. This defection was the result of a host of concerns including the fact that many members of the ACPA felt that because they were administrators and not counselors and thus did not belong in an association that had counseling as its focus. This professional tension continues unabated in spite of the many successful efforts that have been discussed in the earlier sections of this book.

One of the new sources of tension is the name change from American Association of Counseling and Development to American Counseling Association. Some members feel strongly that development, which to some degree is now used euphemistically to mean guidance and other noncounseling activities, should have been retained in the title of the association. ACA still has many members that are noncounselors, but still identify with the profession because of their roles and professional objectives.

A recent change in the membership designation has also raised concerns in many members' minds, particularly in the minds of noncounselors. This change was to designate those members who have degrees as counselors as professional members and those who do not as associate members. Some counselors and noncounselors alike feel this is according nonmembers second-class citizenship within ACA. One result is that NCDA has discussed leaving ACA because it has many noncounselors in its rank.

Other sources of tension include the credentialing effort. Recently, the International Association of Marriage and Family Counselors/Therapists decided to embark on an independent credentialing effort because they did not wish to accede to the National Board for Certified Counselors' requirements for specialty certification. Additionally, arguments about the requirements for licensure continue in many states.

Finally, even though ACA has been in operation since 1952 and has a code of ethics in place, many of the divisions such as the American School Counselors Association still has a separate code of ethics. Some of the divisions such as the Association for Specialists in Group Work has a set of ethical guidelines for group counselors. This situation detracts from the development of a professional image and signals a lack of commitment to a unified set of ethical principles by the these groups. However, the National Board for Certified Counselors, which at this time has a separate set of ethical standards, has committed itself to adopting the ACA ethical guidelines after they have been revised.

Recommendation

Those professionals who identify themselves as counselors must commit themselves to a unified profession. This will mean compromise, and even sacrifice, on the part of some individuals and groups. One of the sacrifices that groups must make are the separate codes of ethics that now exist. No profession tries to abide by several codes of ethics. The other sacrifices will have to be in the area of unified approaches to credentialing and the recognition that ACA is primarily an organization that represents the interests and advancement of counselors.

Will Counselors Take Advantage of Technology to Provide Better Services to Clients?

By their very nature, counselors are people-oriented as opposed to machine- or data-oriented. As a result, many find microprocessors and other technological advances uninviting. However, many of the services offered by counselors can be greatly enhanced by the judicious use of computers. And, perhaps most importantly, the time that counselors have available to spend with clients can be greatly increased if technology is employed properly. As Sampson (1983) put it,

> While aspects of the helping process involving human relationship skills and judgment make good use of human capabilities, other aspects involving data collection, storage and retrieval, statistical computations, actuarial predictions, repetitive instruction, and clerical tasks do not make efficient use of human capabilities and can be better performed by computers (p. 65).

As was pointed out in Chapter 7, computers are being widely employed to assist with the provision of educational and occupational information and with career decision making. In Chapter 6, the application of technology in the administration, scoring, and interpretation of tests was noted. These are but three of the ways computers are enhancing counselors' direct service efforts. Sampson (1983) believes that computers can also be utilized to collect routine data from clients in intake situations, identify appropriate referral sources, provide computer-assisted instruction to clients with information deficits such as child-rearing techniques, provide such intervention as systematic desensitization for phobic clients, and provide biofeedback to aid with problems such as stress control. Sampson also suggests that it may not be outside the realm of possibility of computer programs to provide psychotherapy and that research needs to be conducted on this front as well as on the others already mentioned.

Computers can be readily adapted to perform a wide variety of tasks that now require large amounts of counselors' time in some settings. For example, the scheduling activities performed by many high school and community college counselors can be greatly facilitated by the use of a computer. After a master schedule is developed, students may, with the assistance of an advisor or counselor, construct a schedule and receive a copy of it in minutes. At the same time, the computer keeps track of the availability of spots in each class so that overscheduling will not occur.

Grade point averages can be computed, class ranks determined, transcripts printed and prepared for mailing, personalized letters developed for college admissions offices, and certain tests and inventories administered and scored on the spot. Record keeping of all types can be greatly facilitated with computerized systems. All these activities take extraordinary amounts of time when performed manually.

But the question remains: "Will these resources be embraced by counselors?" At one time, cost was a major barrier to the adoption of technological advances, but inexpensive microprocessors with capacities rivaling very large systems have for the most part removed economic barriers. Certainly the aversion of some counselors to machines has also played a part, as has the concern by some that computers will abridge the human rights of client groups by allowing access to personal data (Ibrahim, 1985) or that they will go awry in performing a routine function such as test administration or test scoring, and thus damage the people involved (Ibrahim, 1985; Sampson & Loesch, 1985). However, one suspects that it is the issue raised by Sampson and Loesch (1985) that provides the greatest barrier to the full utilization of computers and other technological advances: training.

Sampson and Loesch (1985) proposed that the Council for Accreditation of Counseling and Related Education Program Standards (CACREP) be altered to include the following standards:

1. The development of an understanding of the relationship between computers and the services provided by counselors.
2. Supervised experiences that involve students with various types of computer-based activities.

They are not incorporated into the latest CACREP (1994) standards.

While the above purposes are laudable and would, if adopted, prepare counselors trained in CACREP accredited programs to use computers in their work, the fact remains that many counselors are trained in nonaccredited programs, and most counselors who are currently working in the field have inadequate preparation in this area. In-service training programs are being conducted to remedy the deficiencies of the latter group, but the numbers being reached and the impact of these programs is less than optimal.

Recommendations

Given the current situation, it seems that training programs, professional organizations, and agencies that offer counseling services should embark on a massive effort to develop computer skills in counselors. The result can only be a more effective counseling profession.

Will a Legal Basis for Counseling Be Developed?

At the outset, it should be noted that "legal basis" in the current context refers to a set of laws, policies, and regulations that recognize and support the counseling profession. The licensure and registry laws discussed in Chapter 13 are examples of one form of legal basis for a counselor, but there are many others.

In Chapter 14, counselors in educational settings were discussed and mention was made of cutbacks in counseling programs in some states. These cutbacks occurred partially because statutes were not in place that recognized the importance of school counseling and authorized funds for school counseling services. Some states have statutes that not only recognize but require school counseling services, often in the form of authorization statutes that provide monies to local school districts that underwrite counselors' salaries. In these situations, local school boards are less likely to cut back counseling programs because of pressure from local taxpayers.

State statutes are not the only area of concern. Human resource departments often develop personnel classification systems that include social workers and psychologists, but preclude counselors. Insurance companies often have policies that exclude counselors in private practice from receiving payments for the services they render. Accrediting agencies for community colleges may have relatively low standards for the counseling programs, and those that accredit elementary schools may have no standards at all. State boards of education may require that minimal counseling services be offered to high school students before local school districts can receive state support. Federal agencies such as the Veteran's Administration may not recognize counselors as legitimate service providers and do, in fact, preclude from their internship programs students from programs not accredited by the American Psychological Association. Other federal agencies can, and do, discriminate against counselors in a similar way.

Recommendation

The foregoing paragraph has provided some clues regarding what must be accomplished before we can state that a legal basis for the counseling profession has been established. However, what follows is an outline of the needs in this area.

I. Statutory bases
    A. State
        1. All states must pass licensing laws for counselors.
        2. State statutes authorizing monies for schools must include funds for counselors in sufficient amounts to allow schools to develop effective counseling programs.
        3. Third-party payment at the state level must include counselors as mental health services providers.
    B. Federal
        1. Federal legislation regarding the provision of mental health services must include counselors as providers.
        2. Federal legislation pertaining to counselors (e.g., rehabilitation legislation) should recognize credentialed counselors such as certified rehabilitation counselors.
        3. Federal legislation in the future, such as National Health Insurance statutes, must recognize counselors as mental health services providers.
II. Quasi-legal policies and regulations
    A. School counseling
        1. State boards of education must mandate counseling services for students of sufficient quantity and quality to meet students' needs.
        2. Accrediting agencies must require effective counseling programs before accreditation is accorded.
        3. Local school boards must adopt policies that will require that effective counseling programs be offered.
    B. Mental health settings
        1. Federal agencies such as the Veteran's Administration must recognize counselors as legitimate mental health services providers.
        2. State personnel classifications systems must include categories for counselors.
        3. Insurance companies must recognize counselors as legitimate mental health services providers.

The cost, both in terms of money and volunteer time, is staggering. One lobbyist estimated that it would take $10,000 to make an assault on the third-party legislation in one state, even if volunteers did most of the work. In spite of the costs, there is increasing evidence that state and local professional organizations are preparing themselves to deal with developing the legal basis for the counseling profession.

Will There Be an Empirical Basis for the Practices of Counselors?

Throughout the book, the matter of the empirical support for counselors' practices has been raised. Lewis and Hutson (1983) characterize the gap between research data and the effectiveness of counseling as a special concern for counselors. Comas (1986) indicated that research is becoming increasingly important for school counseling programs and outlines a program embarked on by the American School Counselor Association to strengthen the research basis for school counseling. What is obvious is that after a long period of debate about the importance of research to counselors (see Chapter 16), there is a growing consensus that empirical data are needed to support the counseling practice.

One of the very positive aspects of this issue is that many of the practices used by counselors are also used by psychologists, and they, as a group, tend to produce extensive research to support their activities. Counselors can, therefore, draw on an increasingly rich body of literature regarding counseling, consultation, testing, computerized information systems, and so forth. It can also be expected that with the increasing emphasis on the importance of research findings, more research will be produced by counselors themselves.

Even with some very positive trends in the area of research, there are some problems, however. One of these is that many counselors are poorly equipped to read research unless it is extremely rudimentary in nature. Counselors accredited by CACRFP must acquire some preparation in the areas of statistics and research design. Other training programs are under no similar compunction, and many require little or no research preparation.

Research training would be helpful in preparing counselors to generate research and to apply the results of research generated by others. However, strictly speaking, it is not necessary to do or read research to adopt and apply empirically based approaches if the leaders in the field who write books and articles and conduct workshops draw on empirical data for their writings and recommendations.

The problem, as a philosopher might note, is an epistemological one. Epistemology is that branch of philosophy that deals with knowing or, more specifically, what one accepts as knowledge. For some, knowledge must be objectively derived, while for others, subjective data, including their own experiences, are sufficient grounds for knowing that something exists *or* that something works. Many counselors apparently fit into this latter category.

We may be on solid philosophical ground when we argue that our experience is as valid a source of knowledge as is empiricism, but the public of the counseling profession is not likely to accept our experiences as a valid source of data since there is usually a suspicion that the data derived from our experiences about our effectiveness tend to be self-serving.

Even if we could overcome a history of debating the worth of research, the philosophical bias against research data by some, and the deficits in the area of conducting and understanding research that some counselors have, it would still be difficult to develop an empirical basis for the practices of counselors. Group counseling, consultation, classroom guidance, parent education, and individual counseling are all complex activities and, as such, are extremely difficult to research. In most instances, designs must be very complex to accommodate the variables that may influence research outcomes, and, in all instances, numerous replications and extensions of an original research design are required to verify that a technique or approach works. The settings in which counseling activities occur makes it quite difficult to implement complex designs and to go through the extensive replications that will be necessary.

As was pointed out in Chapter 16, there are viable options to traditional research designs, such as those in which single subjects are studied. In the short run, and perhaps in the long run as well, individual counselors may have to validate their own practices using these alternatives because the likelihood of developing an empirically based set of practices seems slight, at least in the near future.

Recommendation

The beginning point for establishing an empirical basis for counseling practice is the development of an awareness of research findings of the counselor's practice. We know that there is widespread empirical support for the treatment of phobias and the development of certain social skills such as assertiveness (Rimm & Cunningham, 1985). There is also limited empirical support for most approaches to counseling. Counselors must be made aware of this support in training programs and through the publication of research review articles in professional journals.

Counselor education programs also need to develop basic research skills in counselor trainees. This is a recommendation not for extensive research and statistic training but for the development of fundamental statistical knowledge and a rudimentary understanding of research design, particularly intensive designs that can easily be taught to and applied by practicing counselors.

The current trend among journal editorial boards to require authors to discuss the practical implications of their findings should be continued and strengthened.

Will Counselors Move from a Focus on Career Planning and Counseling to One on Life-Career Planning and Counseling?

In Chapter 2, an overview of some of the major theories of life development were presented. In Chapter 7, mention was made of theories of career development that exist as a subset of theories that focus on the career choice and adjustment process. Also introduced in Chapter 3 were the concepts of life career planning and counseling in which the individual is viewed holistically and all life roles are considered potentially important sources of life satisfaction. There is considerable evidence that this holistic approach is gaining acceptance, but whether it can overcome a history of counselors' focusing primarily on the career as a source of life satisfaction remains to be seen.

As noted above, one of the major barriers to adopting a stance favoring a holistic consideration of the individual is history. Some (e.g., Super, 1990, Tiedeman & Miller-Tiedeman, 1990) have advocated a more holistic approach. However, trait and factor thinking still dominates the career counseling field (Srebalus, Marinelli, & Messing, 1982), and it is probably true that an updated version of trait and factor thinking (Holland, 1985) dominates much of the research and thinking in the area of career choice and testing. This theoretical perspective provides little in the way of assistance in conceptualizing life career planning and counseling. There are strong counter trends, such as an increasing emphasis on a systems perspective that views the individual as being, to some degree, interdependent with the people in his or her environment (Okun, 1984), and research that demonstrates that life roles interact to create or attenuate stress (Zunker, 1986).

It is also important to note that career development theorists such as Super (1990) have set the stage for an approach to life career planning by altering theoretical perspectives and by developing some practical tools such as the Life Career Rainbow to help clients conceptualize their various life roles.

A number of tasks will probably have to be completed before counselors will embrace life career counseling over career counseling. Human development and career development theories still need integration.

More importantly, counselors need to be provided with tools that will enable them to engage in life career planning and counseling. Currently, there are numerous interest inventories, occupational aptitude tests, computer programs, and so forth that can be used with client groups to facilitate career planning. In addition, the Department of Labor turns out reams of labor force information, ranging from job descriptions to trends in a given occupational field. There are few instruments and very little other information that would support counselors in their life career counseling efforts.

Recommendation

The counseling profession should increasingly emphasize life career planning as opposed to planning educational, career, or marital/family roles separately. The major implication of this is that current theories need to be reconsidered and refocused on all life roles and that new tools (e.g., inventories) need to be developed to assist counselors in this endeavor.

Will the Training Requirements of Counselors Continue to Escalate?

Twenty years ago, few programs required more than thirty semester hours of graduate courses in their counselor preparation programs. As indicated in Chapter 13, the current recommendation is that a program consist of no less than forty-eight semester hours (CACREP, 1994), and there is increasing pressure to increase this to sixty hours plus internship experiences to make counselor training commensurate with that of master's degree level psychologists and social workers who have completed a master's in social work.

It should also be obvious from much of the material that was presented throughout the book that counselors are under great pressure to provide computerized services, to conduct research, and to provide services to a variety of groups including some (e.g., drug abusers) that would require specialized training.

The counterpressure regarding the length of the training program comes from those who contend that there is little support for lengthening training programs beyond the point that would guarantee minimum competencies, that many counselors, particularly those in schools, are not paid well enough to justify a lengthy training program, and that counselors such as those in employment offices perform a relatively limited set of functions that can be learned in a shorter training program.

One underlying issue that pervades the training issue is the fear among some counselor educators that student enrollment will decline if programs are lengthened and their programs will be threatened. It is interesting to note that many programs that have lengthened their training programs have seen demand go up. However, this may not be true in all cases.

Length of training and quality of training, while related, are not necessarily highly correlated. Some argue that before lengthening programs, every effort should be made to increase the quality of offerings. While there is validity to the argument that quality should be stressed, there is also validity to the argument that in programs training individuals to work with diverse populations, a lengthy program is required.

A number of factors will ultimately play a role in determining the length of training programs for counselors. One of those will be that the general public, legislators, insurance companies, and other professional groups seem to have accepted the mentality that longer is better. On the other hand, counselor preparation programs may have difficulty attracting and preparing enough counselors for some settings, particularly school counseling. Informal reports indicate that some training programs have a great deal of difficulty attracting school counseling candidates, and the escalating demand for those professionals in some sections of the country may bring pressure to keep training programs relatively short.

Recommendation

The counseling profession must do what the other helping professions have not done, namely document the relationship between length of the training period and counselor effectiveness, particularly if it intends to resist the trend toward longer training programs. In the pursuit of this documentation, the overall goal must be to develop guidelines for educating counselors who can most effectively serve the public.

Recommendation

In spite of pressure to pursue remedial activities, the counseling profession should continue to emphasize preventive approaches and should redouble its efforts to gain support for these activities.

Will Counselors Be Fully Accepted as Mental Health Practitioners?

As noted in Chapters 1 and 13, counselors have begun to flex their professional muscles and demand legal recognition, third-party payments, equal employment opportunities, and so forth. These moves have not gone unnoticed and, in fact, have resulted in opposition from other mental health professionals. In some instances, the opposition from a single group has led to enhanced relationships among counselors and other groups of mental health workers. For example, social workers and counselors in Texas and Ohio worked together to achieve certain legislative goals.

Drawing on the somewhat stormy historical relationship of psychology and psychiatry to predict the future, one could readily conclude that relationships among the various mental health groups are likely to be adversarial as counselors make increasing demands. One could also draw on this same history to predict that if counselors are diligent and persist in their efforts, they will eventually win most of these battles.

There is a more peaceful scenario than the one depicted above. It was mentioned earlier that in some states professional group coalitions have been formed to advance the causes of all the groups concerned. It may well be that increased communication among various professional organizations can reduce tension in some instances and eliminate it in others. At this point, it is unclear whether all groups of mental health professions are willing to engage in these types of discussions, but what is clear is that discussions aimed at finding a common ground have not often been tried.

Recommendation

The counseling profession should take the lead in trying to develop collaborative working relationships with other mental health practitioners such as psychologists and social workers. The focus of these activities should be to find common concerns and to develop joint approaches to solving these problems. Should collaborative approaches fail, counselors must be prepared to assert themselves in the legislative arena, in the courts, and through direct lobbying with those agencies that regulate mental health services.

Summary

The counseling profession has made tremendous strides during the last decade, but there is much work to be done. A part of this work involves introspection on the part of the profession. Ultimately, a profession exists for only one purpose, to serve the public. Our introspection should dwell on our ability as a profession to adequately serve.

In addition to self-analysis, the counseling profession must continue to assert itself with other professional groups, with governmental agencies, and with the public at large. Counselors as individuals are often reluctant to advertise their strengths, but as a profession in a competitive environment, we cannot have the same inclination. The continued recognition and advancement of the profession rests on the ability of counselors to continue to make the difficult decisions regarding internal control and also the adeptness with which counselors present themselves to the public.

Review Questions

1. What theories run through the issues listed in this chapter?

2. What concerns may groups such as psychologists have about increased recognition for counselors? How can these concerns be combatted?

3. Outline the arguments that the "moral majority" might lodge *against* school counselors.

4. Discuss the pros and cons of lengthening the training programs. Speculate about future trends in this area.

5. Corporate and mental health counselors have many similar issues confronting them. Briefly outline these issues and talk about ways of resolving them.

6. Is empirical evidence the only basis for practice? If not, list others and defend them.

References

CACREP (1994). *Accreditation standards and procedures manual.* Alexandria, VA: Author.

Comas, R. E. (1986). Research becomes increasingly vital to school counseling programs. *The ASCA Counselor, 24,* 15.

Holland, J. L. (1985). *Making vocational choices: A theory of careers,* (2nd ed.). Englewood Cliffs, NJ: Prentice-Hall.

Ibrahim, F. A. (1985). Human rights and ethical issues in the use of advanced technology. *Journal of Counseling and Development, 64,* 134–135.

Lewis, W. A., & Hutson, S. P. (1983). The gap between research and practice in the question of counseling effectiveness. *Personnel and Guidance Journal, 61,* 532–535.

Okun, B. F. (1984). *Working with adults: Individual, family, and career development.* Monterey, CA: Brooks/Cole.

Rimm, D. C., & Cunningham, H. M. (1985). Behavior therapies. In S. J. Lynn & D. Garske, (eds.), *Contemporary psychotherapies: Models and methods,* (pp. 220–221). Columbus, OH: Charles E. Merrill.

Sampson, J. P., Jr. (1983). An integrated approach to computer applications in counseling psychology. *The Counseling Psychologist, 11,* 65–74.

Sampson, J. P., Jr., & Loesch, L. C. (1985). Computer preparation standards for counselors and human development specialists. *Journal of Counseling and Development, 64,* 31–34.

Srebalus, D. J., Marinelli, R. P., & Messing, J. L. (1982). *Career development: Concepts and procedures.* Monterey, CA: Brooks/Cole.

Super, D. E. (1990). Career and life development. In D. Brown & L. Brooks, (eds.), *Career choice and development: Applying contemporary theories to practice,* (2nd ed.), (pp. 197–261). San Francisco: Jossey-Bass.

Tiedeman, D. R., & Miller-Tiedeman, A. (1990). Career decision making: An individualistic perspective. In D. Brown & L. Brooks, (eds.), *Career choice and development: Applying contemporary theory to practice,* (2nd ed.), (pp. 308–330). San Francisco: Jossey-Bass.

Zunker, V. G. (1986). *Career counseling: Applied concepts of life planning,* (2nd ed.). Monterey, CA: Brooks/Cole.

Education, Experience, and Examination Requirements of Credentialed Counselors as Dictated by State Statutes

Acronyms: CMHCE = Clinical Mental Health Counselors Examination (used by the National Board for Certi-fied Counselors [NBCC] for certification of Certified Clinical Mental Health Counselors [CCMHCs])

CCMHC = Certified Clinical Mental Health Counselor

CRCE = Certified Rehabilitation Counselor Examination (used by Commission on Rehabilitation Counselor Certification [CRCC])

NCE = National Counselor Examination (used by NBCC)

NCCCE = National Career Counselor Examination (used by NBCC for certification as a National Certified Career Counselor)

State	Title(s)	Minimum Education Requirements	Experience Requirements	Examination Requirements
Alabama Board of Examiners in Counseling P. O. Box 550397 Birmingham, AL 35255 205/933–8100 205/933–6700 (FAX)	Licensed Professional Counselor (LPC)	*Effective 9/1/94:* Master's degree from a CACREP or CORE accredited program or the substantial equivalent as defined in regulations.	3 years supervised F/T experience, 1 year of which may be obtained prior to granting of master's. May subtract 1 year of experience for every 15 graduate semester hours beyond master's (up to 2 years).	NCE

State	Title(s)	Minimum Education Requirements	Experience Requirements	Examination Requirements
			In addition to current requirements effective 9/1/94: F/T requirements may be modified for part-time work but must be completed within six years. Supervised experiences must include: (a) minimum of 3,000 hours of professional counseling service including 2,250 hours of face-to-face counseling and 750 hours related to counseling services in a clinical supervisory setting, (b) 150 hours of individual, face-to-face supervision by an LPC.	
Arizona Counselor Credentialing Committee of the Board of Behavioral Examiners 1645 W. Jefferson, 4th Floor Phoenix, AZ 85007 602/542–1882 602/542–1830 (FAX)	Certified Professional Counselor (CPC)	Master's degree in counseling that includes 48 graduate semester hours and a supervised practicum.	2 years F/T postmaster's experience or equivalent (3,200 hours.), including 1 year under supervision of a CPC (or CPC eligible). May use a doctoral-clinical internship to satisfy the requirement for 1 year of supervised experience.	NCE, CRCE, or CMHCE
Arkansas Board of Examiners in Counseling Southern Arkansas University P. O. Box 1396 Magnolia, AR 71753 501/235–4052 or 234–1842	Licensed Professional Counselor	Graduate degree with a minimum of 48 semester hours.	3 years post-master's F/T supervised experience. One year of experience may be gained for each 30 semester hours earned beyond master's (up to 2 years).	NCE, audio- or video-tape sample and oral interview.
California Board of Behavioral Science Examiners 400 R Street, Suite 3150 Sacramento, CA 95814–6240 916/445–4933: recorded info. 916/322–4910	Licensed Marriage, Family and Child Counselor	Master's degree with a minimum of 48 semester hours, 12 units of M&F therapy, 6 units of practicum.	2 years and 3,000 hours experience with 1 hour of direct supervision each week.	Written state prepared exam and oral exam.

State	Title(s)	Minimum Education Requirements	Experience Requirements	Examination Requirements
Colorado Board of Licensed Professional Counselor Examiners 1560 Broadway, Suite 1340 Denver, CO 80202 303/894–7766 303/894–7790 (FAX)	Licensed Professional Counselor	Master's degree with 48 semester hours, or doctorate with 96 hours, and 700 hours. practicum and/or internship from a program offering a F/T graduate course of study in counseling.	2 years post-master's practice or 1 year post-doctoral practice under board approved supervision.	NCE
Delaware Board of Professional Counselors of Mental Health P. O. Box 1401 Margaret O'Neill Bldg. Dover, DE 19903 302/739–4522 302/739–2711 (FAX)	Licensed Professional Counselor of Mental Health	Graduate degree. Must also be certified by NBCC (including as a CCMHC) or other acceptable certifying agency (therefore must meet their requirements).	3 years. (4,200 hrs.) F/T clinical experience within a 5-year period with minimum of 100 hours. of supervision; 1 year. may be obtained prior to completion of master's. May substitute 30 graduate semester hours. or more beyond master's degree for 1 year of required experience but must have no less than 2 years of post-master's experience.	NCE or CMHCE
District of Columbia DC Board of Professional Counselors Room LL-202, 605 G St., NW Washington, DC 20001 202/727–7454	Licensed Professional Counselor	60 graduate semester hours including a master's degree in counseling. Regulations have not been written yet regarding specific coursework requirements.	2 years post-master's supervised experience. Regulations are to be written.	To be determined.
Florida Board of Clinical Social Workers, M&F Therapists, and Mental Health Counselors Florida Dept. of Professional Regulation 1940 N. Monroe Street Tallahassee, FL 32399–0753 904/487–2520 904/921–2569 (FAX)	Licensed Mental Health Counselor	Master's degree including a supervised practicum, internship, or field experience.	3 years of clinical experience. 2 years must be supervised post-master's.	NCE

State	Title(s)	Minimum Education Requirements	Experience Requirements	Examination Requirements
Georgia Composite Board of Professional Counselors, Social Workers, and M&F Therapists 166 Pryor Street, SW Atlanta, GA 30303 404/656–3933	Licensed Professional Counselor	Master's degree or higher with a supervised practicum or a specialist degree in a program that is primarily counseling.	4 years post-master's experience with 1 year of supervision. Up to 1 year may have been in an approved practicum placement. If doctoral degree is earned, 1 year of supervised internship is required.	NCE
Idaho Idaho State Counselor Licensure Board Bureau of Occupational Licenses 1109 Main Street, Suite 220 Boise, ID 83702–5642 208/334–3233 208/334–3945 (FAX)	Licensed Professional Counselor	Graduate degree, 60 semester hours including a 6-hour advanced practicum.	1,000 hours of experience with supervision by an LPC.	NCE
Illinois Dept. of Counselor Education Northeastern Illinois University 5500 North St. Louis Avenue Chicago, IL 60625–4699 312/794–2970	Licensed Professional Counselor	Master's or doctoral degree in counseling, rehabilitation counseling, psychology, or related field from degree program approved by the Department of Professional Regulation; or baccalaureate from an approved program and the equivalent of 5 years of full-time supervised experience.	If applicant has a master's degree, no specific requirements are noted in the statute as to supervised experience. If someone holds a baccalaureate degree, one must document the equivalent of 5 years of full-time supervised experience. Regulations are not final yet.	To be determined.
	Licensed Clinical Professional Counselor	Master's or doctoral degree in counseling, rehabilitation counseling, psychology or related field from a program approved by the Department of Professional Regulation.	2 years (or equivalent) of full-time supervised experience as a clinical professional counselor. Regulations are not final yet.	To be determined.
Iowa Board of Behavioral Sciences Examiners 2507 University Memorial, 307 Des Moines, IA 50311 515/242–5937 515/281–4958 (FAX)	Licensed Mental Health Counselor	Master's degree in counseling with at least 45 semester hours.	2 years post-graduate, supervised clinical experience.	NCE or CMHCE

State	Title(s)	Minimum Education Requirements	Experience Requirements	Examination Requirements
Kansas Behavioral Sciences Regulatory Board Landon Office Bldg, Rm. 651-S 900 SW Jackson Topeka, KS 66612–1263 913/296–3240 913/296–3112 (FAX)	Registered Professional Counselor	60 semester hours as part of a graduate degree in counseling including 45 hours distributed among the CACREP core courses (or the equivalent).	3 years F/T post-graduate supervised experience. May subtract 1 year of experience for each 30 graduate semester hours beyond the 60 credits required for registration. Must have at least 1 year of post-graduate experience.	NCE
Louisiana Licensed Professional Counselors Board of Examiners 4664 Jamestown Ave., Suite 125 Baton Rouge, LA 70808–3218 504/922–1499 504/922–2160 (FAX)	Licensed Professional Counselor	Graduate degree from a regionally accredited institution with 48 semester hours including coursework in 7 of 9 specified areas, with a supervised mental health counseling practicum and internship.	2 years and 3,000 hours post-master's experience supervised by qualified LPC. 500 hours of supervised experience may be gained for each 30 graduate semester hours beyond master's. Must have no less than 2,000 hours of supervised post-master's experience.	NCE or oral
Maine Board of Counseling Professionals State House Station N-35 Augusta, ME 04333 207/582–8723	Licensed Professional Counselor	Master's in counseling or allied mental health field with a minimum core curriculum, a practicum, and 600-hour internship.	2 years post-master's experience with a minimum of 2,000 hours of supervised experience.	NCE
	Licensed Clinical Professional Counselor	Master's in counseling or allied mental health field including at least 45 semester hours, practicum and 1,200-hour internship.	2 years post-master's experience to include at least 3,000 hours of supervised clinical experience. Minimum of 100 hours of personal supervision.	CMHCE & NCE
Maryland Board of Examiners of Professional Counselors Metro Executive Ctr, 3rd Floor 4201 Patterson Avenue Baltimore, MD 21215–2299 410/764–4732	Certified Professional Counselor	Master's degree with 60 semester hours (or doctorate with 90 semester hours) including coursework in 9 specified areas.	3 years supervised experience, 2 years must be post-master's. If doctorate is earned, must have 2 years of experience, 1 of which is post-doctorate.	NCE

State	Title(s)	Minimum Education Requirements	Experience Requirements	Examination Requirements
Massachusetts Board of Allied Mental Health & Human Service Professionals 100 Cambridge St., 15th Floor Boston, MA 02202 617/727–1716	Licensed Mental Health Counselor	Minimum of 48 graduate credit hours and a master's degree in relevant field (rehabilitation or mental health counseling), from an institution meeting national standards for granting a master's degree with a major in rehabilitation, mental health or marriage and family counseling.	2 years post-master's supervised clinical experience including not less than 200 hours of supervision, 100 of which must be individual with an approved clinician who has a master's degree or higher and experience in specialty area. Ask for regulations for details on supervisors.	Written; accepts CMHCE. If person is a CCMHC can be automatically licensed provided s/he has 200 hours of supervision.
Michigan Board of Professional Counselors P. O. Box 30018 Lansing, MI 48909 517/335–0918 (applications) 517/373–3596	Licensed Professional Counselor	Master's or doctoral degree in counseling or student personnel including specific coursework areas approved by the board.	2,000 hours post-master's counseling experience in no less than a 2-year period under the supervision of a LPC. No less than 100 hours (of the 2,000) must be accrued in the immediate physical presence of the supervisor.	NCE or CRCE
Mississippi Board of Examiners for LPCs P. O. Drawer 6239 Mississippi State, MS 39762–6239 601/325–8182	Licensed Professional Counselor	Master's degree, 60 semester hours and courses reflecting the CACREP core curriculum or equivalent.	2 years and 3,500 hours of supervised experience (1,167 of these must be direct counseling) 1,750 of which must be post-master's. Minimum of 100 hours of supervision (1 hour per week); 50 hours may be group supervision.	NCE
Missouri Missouri Committee for Professional Counselors P. O. Box 162 Jefferson City, MO 65102 314/751–0018	Licensed Professional Counselor	Master's degree in counseling with 45 semester hours reflecting CACREP core curriculum; doctorate; or specialist's degree with a major in counseling.	3,000 hours post-master's exp. in 24 to 48 months with 1 hour/week of face-to-face individual supervision (no less than 48 weeks per year). May substitute 30 graduate semester hours post-master's study for 1,000 of the 3,000 hours of required experience.	NCE

State	Title(s)	Minimum Education Requirements	Experience Requirements	Examination Requirements
Montana Board of Social Work Examiners & Professional Counselors Arcade Bldg., Lower Level 111 North Jackson P. O. Box 200513 Helena, MT 59620–0513 406/444–4285	Licensed Professional Counselor, Licensed Clinical Professional Counselor, or Licensed Clinical Counselor (requirements are the same for all)	Advanced degree, 90 quarter hours or 60 semester hours including an advanced counseling practicum.	2 years and 2,000 hours of supervised experience; 50 percent must be post-master's. Supervision by LPC or licensed allied mental health professional.	NCE or CMHCE
Nebraska Board of Examiners in Professional Counseling Bureau of Examining Boards 301 Centennial Mall South P. O. Box 95007 402/471–2115 402/471–0383 (FAX)	Certified Professional Counselor (CPC)	Master's from CACREP-approved school or a counseling program from a regionally accredited institution, or meets course requirements as stated by board.	3 years F/T post-master's experience. Master's internship may count for 1 year of experience 30 graduate semester hours beyond master's may be substituted for 1 year of required experience (up to 2 years)	NCE or equivalent
	CPC Licensed Professional Counselor — 9/1/94: must be a licensed Mental Health Practitioner and certified as a professional counselor	Master's from an approved educational program to be determined by the board.	3 years F/T post-master's experience. Master's with an internship may count for 1 year if internship meets board approval. 30 graduate semester hours related to professional counseling beyond master's may be substituted for 1 year of experience. In no case may the applicant have less than 1 year F/T experience.	To be determined.
	Licensed Mental Health Practitioner (effective 9/1/94)	Master's that was primarily therapeutic mental health in content including a practicum or internship with a minimum of 300 clock hours direct client contact under the supervision of a qualified supervisor.	3,000 hours post-master's supervised experience in mental health practice accumulated during the 5 years immediately preceding application for licensure. Must include a minimum of 1 hour/week face-to-face supervision with a qualified supervisor. Hours shall include 1,500 hours direct client contact.	To be determined.

State	Title(s)	Minimum Education Requirements	Experience Requirements	Examination Requirements
New Hampshire NH Board of Examiners of Psychology & Mental Health Practice 105 Pleasant St., #457 Concord, NH 03301 603/226–2599	Certified Mental Health Counselor	Master's or doctorate in counseling from a program that meets NBCC guidelines (or guidelines for the CCMHC). After 7/1/95, master's must be at least a 2–year program with minimum of 60 graduate semester hours.	3,000 hours paid, post-master's supervised clinical work in no less than 2 years and no more than 5 years. 100 hours of face-to-face supervision provided by a nationally or state certified mental health professional.	NCE or CMHCE
New Jersey 37 Elm St., Room 10 Westfield, NJ 07090 908/232–3638	Licensed Professional Counselor	Minimum of 60 graduate semester hours in a planned educational program that includes a master's degree or doctorate in counseling from a regionally accredited institution; 45 of the 60 hours are to be distributed in at least 8 of 9 core coursework areas. Further requirements will be stipulated in rules and regulations.	3 years F/T supervised counseling experience in a professional counseling setting, 1 year of which may be obtained prior to the granting of the master's degree. 1 year of the experience may be eliminated by substituting 30 graduate semester hours beyond the master's degree. In no case may an applicant have less than 1 year of post-master's supervised work experience. Further requirements to be stipulated in rules and regulations.	NCE
New Mexico P. O. Box 25101 Santa Fe, NM 87504 505/827–7197 505/527–7095 (FAX)	Professional Mental Health Counselor	Master's degree. Regulations are not final yet.	1,000 client contact hours of professional post-graduate experience with a minimum of 100 hours of supervision. Regulations are not final yet.	To be determined.
	Professional Clinical Mental Health Counselor	Master's degree with a minimum of 60 graduate hours. Regulations are not final.	2 years post-graduate professional clinical counseling including 3,000 client contact hours with a minimum of 100 hours of supervision. Regulations are not final yet.	To be determined.
North Carolina NC Board of Licensed Professional Counselors P. O. Box 12023 Raleigh, NC 27605	Licensed Professional Counselor	Master's degree in counseling including a minimum of 48 semester hours or a graduate degree in a related field supplemented with courses the board determines to be equivalent.	No less than 2 years of master's or post-master's counseling experience, or both, in a professional setting including a minimum of 2,000 hours of supervised professional practice. Regulations have not been written yet.	To be determined.

State	Title(s)	Minimum Education Requirements	Experience Requirements	Examination Requirements
North Dakota Board of Counselor Examiners P. O. Box 2735 Bismarck, ND 58502 701/224–8234	Licensed Professional Counselor	Master's degree in counseling.	2 years of supervision by LPC as a Licensed Associate Counselor.	NCE
Ohio Counselor & Social Worker Board 77 South High St., 16th Floor Columbus, OH 43266–0340 614/466–0912	Licensed Professional Counselor	Master's or doctoral degree in counseling with 60 quarter hours or 40 semester hours. Course content specified by law.	3 years supervised experience of which 2 years must be paid post-master's. If doctorate is earned, must have 2 years of supervised experience, 1 of which is paid post-doctorate.	NCE or other as approved by board (within 1 year prior to application).
	Licensed Professional Clinical Counselor (LPCC)	Master's or doctoral degree in counseling with 60 semester or 90 quarter hours. Course content specified by law.	3 years supervised experience of which 2 years must be paid post-master's. If doctorate is earned, must have 2 years of supervised experience, 1 of which is paid post-doctorate.	CMHCE for LPCC or other test approved by the board.
Oklahoma Licensed Professional Counselors Licensed M&F Therapists 1000 NE 10th Street Oklahoma City, OK 73117–1299 405/271–6030 405/271–5493 (FAX)	Licensed Professional Counselor	Master's degree in mental health counseling, community psychology, psychology, guidance or rehabilitation with a minimum of 45 semester hours.	3 years or 3,000 hours F/T post-application experience supervised by an LPC. Up to 2 years of required experience may be gained at a rate of 1 year for each 30 graduate semester hours beyond master's.	NCE
Oregon Board Administrator Board of Licensed Professional Counselors and Therapists 796 Winter Street, NE Salem, OR 97310 503/378–5499	Licensed Professional Counselor	Graduate degree, 48 semester hours in a CACREP approved program or the equivalent.	3 years F/T supervised experience (2,400 client-contact hours). 1 year (up to 800 hours) may be obtained prior to granting of master's degree; 120 hours of supervision, 60 of which must be individual.	NCE, CRCE, CMHCE or other as approved by the board.
Rhode Island Boards of Mental Health Counselors & M&F Therapists Division of Professional Regulation 3 Capitol Hill Cannon Bldg., Room 104 Providence, RI 02908–5097 401/277–2827 401/277–1272 (FAX)	Certified Counselor in Mental Health	Certification as a CCMHC or; graduate degree in counseling/therapy and a minimum of 12 semester hours of supervised practicum and 1 calendar year of supervised internship consisting of 20 hours per week in mental health counseling.	2 years and 2,000 hours direct client contact post-master's and 100 hours of post-master's supervision.	CCMHC certification or state exam (CMHCE).

State	Title(s)	Minimum Education Requirements	Experience Requirements	Examination Requirements
South Carolina Executive Secretary Board of Examiners in Counseling P. O. Box 7965 Columbia, SC 29202 803/734–1765 803/734–0362 (FAX)	Licensed Professional Counselor	Master's degree in counseling or the substantial equivalent (a master's degree in a counseling-related field and additional graduate coursework equal to the coursework required in a master's degree program in counseling).	2 years F/T post-master's experience with 1,500 hours of direct clinical contact with clients and 150 hours of supervision provided by a board-licensed professional counselor supervisor, at least 100 of which must be individual supervision.	NCE
South Dakota South Dakota Board of Counselor Examiners P. O. Box 1115 Pierre, SD 57501 605/224–6281 605/224–6060 (FAX)	Licensed Professional Counselor	Master's degree or higher, 48 semester hours with a supervised counseling practicum.	1,800 hours of supervised F/T experience, 50 percent of which must be post-master's.	NCE or CMHCE
Tennessee State Board of Professional Counselors & M&F Therapists 283 Plus Park Blvd. Nashville, TN 37247–1010 615/367–6280 615/367–6210 (FAX)	Licensed Professional Counselor (law amended in 1991: regulations printed 7/92 —no longer certifies professional counselors)	60 graduate semester hours including a master's degree and 500-hour practicum or internship (300 hours of which must be completed in a mental health or community agency setting).	2 years post-degree experience.	NCE and oral.
Texas Board of Examiners of Professional Counselors 1100 W. 49th Street Austin, TX 78756–3183 512/834–6658 512/834–6677 (FAX)	Licensed Professional Counselor	Graduate degree with 45 semester hours including a 300-hour practicum.	2 years or 2,000 hours of post-master's supervised experience.	State developed written exam.
Utah 801/524–4278	Licensed Professional Counselor	To be determined.	To be determined.	To be determined.
Vermont CCMHC Advisory Board Office of Professional Regulation 109 State Street Montpelier, VT 05609–1106 1–800–439–8683 (in Vermont) 802/828–2390 802/828–2496 (FAX)	Certified Clinical Mental Health Counselor	Master's degree including a supervised practicum.	2 years of post-master's experience including 3,000 hours of practice in clinical mental health counseling and a minimum of 100 hours of face-to-face supervision.	CMHCE

State	Title(s)	Minimum Education Requirements	Experience Requirements	Examination Requirements
Virginia Board of Professional Counselors Dept. of Health Professions 6606 W. Broad St., 4th Floor Richmond, VA 23230–1717 804/662–9912 804/662–9943 (FAX)	Licensed Professional Counselor	60 semester hours or 90 quarter hours of graduate study in counseling to include a graduate degree in counseling or a related field.	4,000 hours post-graduate supervised experience with 200 hours (at least 1 hour per week) of face-to-face supervision. Up to 100 hours may be group supervision. Post-graduate degree practicum or internship may count for up to 2,000 hours of required experience.	State developed written exam.
Washington Dept. of Health Professional Licensing Services Division P. O. Box 47869 Olympia, WA 98504–7869 206/753–6936 206/586–7774 (FAX)	Certified Mental Health Counselor	Master's degree or higher, or completion of 30 graduate semester hours, and a postgraduate supervised mental health counseling practicum.	2 years post-master's supervised experience with 100 hours of face-to-face supervision.	NCE or CMHCE
West Virginia Board of Examiners in Counseling P. O. Box 6492 Charlestown, WV 25362 304/345–3852	Licensed Professional Counselor	Master's degree.	2 years professional supervised experience, 1 year of which must be post-master's (1 year post-doctorate).	NCE or CRCE
Wisconsin Social Work, M&F Therapy, & Professional Counselors Dept. of Regulations & Licensing 1400 E. Washington Ave. P. O. Box 8935 Madison, WI 53708 608/267–7212 608/267–0644 (FAX)	Certified Professional Counselor	Master's degree in counseling. Contact the board for more specific coursework requirements.	2,000 hours of post-master's supervised experience to be further delineated in regulations (contact the board for details).	To be determined.
Wyoming Mental Health Professions Licensing Board 2301 Central Avenue Barrett Bldg., 3rd Floor Cheyenne, WY 82002 307/777–7788 307/777–6005	Licensed Professional Counselor	Master's degree.	3,000 hours post-master's supervised clinical experience including 100 hours of face-to-face supervision.	NCE

Proposed Revision to the American Counseling Association Code of Ethics and Standards of Practice

ACA Proposed Standards of Practice and Ethical Standards

Proposed Standards of Practice

All members of the American Counseling Association (ACA) are required to adhere to the *Standards of Practice* and the *Code of Ethics. Standards of Practice* are minimal behavioral statements of the *Code of Ethics.*

Section A: The Counseling Relationship

Standard of Practice One (SP-1): Nondiscrimination

Counselors respect diversity and must not discriminate against clients because of age, color, culture, disability, ethnic group, gender, race, religion, sexual orientation, or socioeconomic status. (See A.2.a.)

Date Issued: June 30, 1994

Source: ACA (1994), *Counseling Today, 37,* 20–28. Reprinted by permission.

Standards of Practice Two (SP-2): Disclosure to Clients
Counselors must adequately inform clients regarding the counseling process and counseling relationship at or before the time it begins. (See A.3.a.)

Standards of Practice Three (SP-3): Disclosure of Supervision
Counselors must inform clients if supervisors will have access to confidential information during the counseling relationship. (See A.3.d.)

Standard of Practice Four (SP-4): Dual Relationships
Counselors must make every effort to avoid dual relationships with clients that could impair their professional judgment or increase the risk of harm to the client. When a dual relationship cannot be avoided, counselors must take appropriate steps to ensure that judgment is not impaired and that no exploitation occurs. (See A.6.a. and A.6.b.)

Standard of Practice Five (SP-5): Sexual Intimacies with Clients
Counselors must not engage in any type of sexual intimacies with current and former clients. (See A.7.a. and A.7.b.)

Standard of Practice Six (SP-6): Protecting Clients During Group Work
Counselors must take steps to protect clients from physical or psychological trauma resulting from interactions during group work. (See A.9.b.)

Standard of Practice Seven (SP-7): Advance Understanding of Fees
Counselors must explain to clients, prior to their entering the counseling relationship, financial arrangements related to professional services. (See A.11.a–d. and A.12.c.)

Standard of Practice Eight (SP-8): Termination
Counselors must assist in making appropriate arrangements for the continuation of treatment of clients, when necessary, following termination. (See A.12.a.)

Standards of Practice Nine (SP-9): Inability to Assist Clients
Counselors must avoid entering or immediately terminate a counseling relationship if a determination is made they are unable to be of professional assistance to a client. (See A.12.b)

Section B: Confidentiality

Standard of Practice Ten (SP-10): Confidentiality Requirement
Counselors must keep information related to counseling services confidential unless disclosure is in the best interest of clients, is required for the welfare of others,

is in response to obligations to society, or is required by law. When disclosure is required, only information that is essential is revealed. (See B.1.a–f.)

Standard of Practice Eleven (SP-11): Confidentiality Requirement for Subordinates

Counselors must take measures to ensure that privacy and confidentiality of clients are maintained by subordinants. (See B.1.g.)

Standard of Practice Twelve (SP-12): Confidentiality in Group Work

Counselors must clearly communicate to group members that confidentiality cannot be guaranteed in group work. (See B.2.a.)

Standard of Practice Thirteen (SP-13): Confidentiality in Family Counseling

Counselors must not disclose information about one family member in counseling to another family member without prior consent. (See B.2.b.)

Standard of Practice Fourteen (SP-14): Confidentiality of Records

Counselors must maintain appropriate confidentiality in creating, storing, accessing, transferring, and disposing of counseling records. (See B.4.b.)

Standard of Practice Fifteen (SP-15): Permission to Record or Observe

Counselors must obtain consent from clients in order to electronically record or observe sessions. (See B.4.c.)

Standard of Practice Sixteen (SP-16): Disclosure or Transfer of Records

Counselors must obtain client consent to disclose or transfer records to third parties, unless exceptions listed in SP-10 exist. (See B.4.e.)

Standard of Practice Seventeen (SP-17): Data Disguise Required

Counselors must disguise the identity of the client when using data for training, research, or publication. (See B.5.a.)

Section C: Professional Responsibility

Standard of Practice Eighteen (SP-18): Boundaries of Competence

Counselors must practice only within the boundaries of their competence. (See C.2.a.)

Standard of Practice Nineteen (SP-19): Continuing Education

Counselors must engage in continuing education to maintain their professional competence. (See C.2.f.)

Standard of Practice Twenty (SP-20): Impairment of Professionals
Counselors must refrain from offering professional services when their personal problems or conflicts are likely to lead to harm to a client or others. (See C.2.g.)

Standard of Practice Twenty-one (SP-21): Accurate Advertising
Counselors must accurately represent their credentials and services when advertising. (See C.3.a.)

Standard of Practice Twenty-two (SP-22): Recruiting Through Employment
Counselors must not use their place of employment or institutional affiliation to recruit clients for their private practices. (See C.3.d.)

Standard of Practice Twenty-three (SP-23): Credentials Claimed
Counselors must claim or imply only professional credentials possessed and must correct any known misrepresentations of their credentials by others. (See C.4.a.)

Standard of Practice Twenty-four (SP-24): Sexual Harassment
Counselors must not engage in sexual harassment. (See C.5.b.)

Standard of Practice Twenty-five (SP-25): Unjustified Gains
Counselors must not use their professional positions to seek or receive unjustified personal gains, sexual favors, unfair advantage, or unearned goods or services. (See C.5.e.)

Standard of Practice Twenty-six (SP-26): Clients Served by Others
Counselors must inform other mental health professionals serving the same client that a counseling relationship between the counselor and client exist. (See C.6.c.)

Standard of Practice Twenty-seven (SP-27): Negative Employment Conditions
Counselors must alert their employers to conditions that may be potentially disruptive or damaging to their professional responsibilities or that may limit their effectiveness. (See D.1.c.)

Standard of Practice Twenty-eight (SP-28): Personnel Selection
and Assignment
Counselors must select competent staff and must assign responsibilities compatible with staff skills and experiences. (See D.1.h.)

Standard of Practice Twenty-nine (SP-29): Sexual Relationships
with Subordinates
Counselors must not engage in sexual relationships with individuals over whom they have supervisory, evaluative, or instructional control or authority. (See D.1.k.)

Section D: Relationships with Other Professionals

Standard of Practice Thirty (SP-30): Accepting Fees from Agency Clients

Counselors must not accept fees or other remuneration for consultation with persons entitled to such services through the counselor's employing agency or institution. (See D.3.a.)

Standard of Practice Thirty-one (SP-31): Referral Fees

Counselors must not accept referral fees without fully disclosing this fact to clients. (See D.3.b.)

Section E: Evaluation, Assessment, and Interpretation

Standard of Practice Thirty-two (SP-32): Limits of Competence

Counselors must perform only testing and assessment services for which they are competent. Counselors must not allow the use of psychological assessment techniques by unqualified persons under their authority. (See E.2.a.)

Standard of Practice Thirty-three (SP-33): Appropriate Use of Assessment Instruments

Counselors must use assessment instruments in the manner for which they were intended. (See E.2.b.)

Standard of Practice Thirty-four (SP-34): Assessment Explanations to Clients

Counselors must provide explanations to clients prior to assessment about the nature and purpose of testing and the specific uses of results. (See E.3.a.)

Standard of Practice Thirty-five (SP-35): Recipients of Test Results

Counselors must ensure that accurate and appropriate interpretations accompany any release of testing and assessment information. (See E.3.b.)

Standard of Practice Thirty-six (SP-36): Obsolete Tests and Outdated Test Results

Counselors must not base their assessment or intervention decisions or recommendations on data or test results that are obsolete or outdated for the current purpose. (See E.11.)

Standard of Practice Thirty-seven (SP-37): Sexual Relationships with Students or Supervisees

Counselors must not engage in sexual relationships with students or supervisees. (See F.1.c.)

Standard of Practice Thirty-eight (SP-38): Credit for Contributions to Research
Counselors must give credit to students or supervisees for their contributions to research and scholarly projects. (See F.1.d.)

Section F: Teaching, Training, and Supervision

Standard of Practice Thirty-nine (SP-39): Supervision Preparation
Counselors who offer clinical supervision services must be trained and prepared in supervision methods and techniques. (See F.1.f.)

Standard of Practice Forty (SP-40): Evaluation Information
Counselors must clearly state to students and supervisees in advance of training, the levels of competency expected, appraisal methods, and timing of evaluations. Counselors must provide students and supervisees with periodic performance appraisal and evaluation feedback throughout the training program. (See F.2.c.)

Standard of Practice Forty-one (SP-41): Peer Relationships in Training
Counselors must make every effort to ensure that the rights of peers are not violated when students and supervisees are assigned to lead counseling groups or provide clinical supervision. (See F.2.e.)

Standard of Practice Forty-two (SP-42): Limitations of Students and Supervisees
Counselors must assist students and supervisees in securing remedial assistance when needed, and must dismiss from the training program students and supervisees who are unable to provide competent service. (See F.3.a.)

Standard of Practice Forty-three (SP-43): Self-growth Experiences
Counselors who conduct experiences for students or supervisees that include self-growth or self-disclosure must inform participants of counselors' ethical obligations to the profession and must not grade participants based on their performance. (See F.3.b.)

Standard of Practice Forty-four (SP-44): Standards for Students and Supervisees
Students and supervisees preparing to become counselors must adhere to the Code of Ethics and Standards of Practice of counselors. (See F.3.e.)

Standard of Practice Forty-five (SP-45): Precautions to Avoid Injury in Research
Counselors must avoid causing physical, social, or psychological harm or injury to subjects in research. (See G.1.c.)

Section G: Research and Publication

Standard of Practice Forty-six (SP-46): Confidentiality of Research Information
Counselors must keep confidential information obtained about research participants. (See G.2.d.)

Standard of Practice Forty-seven (SP-47): Information Affecting Research Outcome
Counselors must report all variables and conditions known to the investigator that may have affected research data or outcomes. (See G.3.a.)

Standard of Practice Forty-eight (SP-48): Accurate Research Results
Counselors must not distort or misrepresent research data, engage in fraudulent research, or intentionally bias research results. (See G.3.b.)

Standard of Practice Forty-nine (SP-49): Publications Contributors
Counselors must give appropriate credit to those who have contributed to research. (See G.4.a. and G.4.b.)

Section H: Resolving Ethical Issues

Standard of Practice Fifty (SP-50): Ethical Behavior Expected
Counselors must take appropriate action when they possess information that raises doubts as to whether counselors or other mental health professionals are acting in an ethical manner. (See H.2.a.)

Standard of Practice Fifty-one (SP-51): Frivolous Complaints
Counselors must not initiate, participate in, or encourage the filing of ethics complaints that are frivolous or intended to harm a mental health professionals rather than to protect clients or the public. (See H.2.f.)

Standard of Practice Fifty-two (SP-52): Cooperation with Ethics Committees
Counselors must cooperate with investigations, proceedings, and requirements of the ACA Ethics Committee or ethics committees of other duly constituted associations or boards having jurisdiction over those charged with a violation. (See H.3.)

Ethical Standards

Section A: The Counseling Relationship

A.1. Client Welfare
a. **Primary Obligation.** The primary obligation of Professional Counselors is to respect the integrity and promote the welfare of clients.

b. **Positive Growth and Development.** Professional counselors encourage positive client growth and development, and avoid fostering dependent counseling relationships.

c. **Family Involvement.** Professional counselors recognize that families are usually an important factor in clients' lives and strive to enlist family understanding and involvement as a positive resource, when appropriate.

d. **Counseling Plans.** Professional counselors and their clients work jointly in devising an integrated, individualized counseling plan that offers reasonable promise of success and is consistent with the abilities and circumstances of clients. Professional counselors regularly monitor counseling plans to ensure their continued viability and effectiveness, remembering that clients have the right to make choices. (See A.3.b.)

e. **Employment Counseling.** Professional counselors work with their clients in considering employment in jobs and circumstances that are consistent with the clients' overall abilities, vocational limitations, physical restrictions, general temperament, interest and aptitude patterns, social skills, education, general qualifications, and other relevant characteristics and needs. Professional counselors will neither place nor participate in placing clients in positions that will result in damaging the interest and welfare of clients, employers, or the public.

A.2. Respecting Diversity

a. **Nondiscrimination.** Professional counselors do not condone or engage in discrimination based on age, color, culture, disability, ethnic group, gender, race, religion, sexual orientation, or socioeconomic status. (See C.5.a., C.5.b., and D.1. i.)

b. **Respecting Differences.** Professional counselors who counsel clients from backgrounds different from their own respect these differences and gain knowledge, personal awareness, and sensitivity pertinent to the client populations served and incorporate culturally relevant practices into their work. (See F.2.h.)

A.3. Client Rights

a. **Informed Consent.** At or before the time that the counseling relationship is entered, professional counselors inform clients of the purposes, goals, techniques, rules of the purposes, goals, techniques, rules of procedure, limitations, and potential dangers of services to be performed and other information that may affect the ongoing counseling relationship. Professional counselors ensure that clients understand the implications of any diagnosis assigned, the intended use of tests and reports, fees, and billing arrangements. Clients have the right to expect confidentiality, to have explained to them any limitations to confidentiality, to obtain information about their case record and have this information explained clearly, to participate in the ongoing treatment plan, and to refuse any recommended services and to be advised of the consequences of such action. (See E.5 and G.2.)

b. **Freedom of Choice.** Professional counselors promote the freedom of clients to choose whether to enter into a counseling relationship and to determine which professional will provide those services. Restrictions that limit choices of clients are fully explained. (See A.1.d.)

c. **Inability to Give Consent.** When counseling minors or persons unable to give consent, professional counselors act in these clients' best interests. (See B.3.)

d. **Disclosure of Supervision.** At the beginning of counseling relationships, professional counselors inform clients if supervisors will have access to confidential information during the counseling relationship.

A.4. Clients Served by Others

If a client is receiving services from another mental health professional, professional counselors inform the professional persons already involved in order to avoid confusion and conflict for the client. (See C.6.c.)

A.5. Personal Needs and Values

a. **Personal Needs.** In the counseling relationship, professional counselors are aware of the intimacy of the relationship, maintain respect for clients and avoid engaging in activities that seek to meet their personal needs at the expense of clients.

b. **Personal Values.** Professional counselors are aware of their own values, attitudes, beliefs, and behaviors and how these apply in a diverse society, and take care to avoid imposing their values on clients. (See C.5.a.)

A.6. Dual Relationships

a. **Avoid When Possible.** Professional counselors are aware of their influential position with respect to clients, and they avoid exploiting the trust and dependency of clients. Professional counselors make every effort to avoid dual relationships with clients that could impair professional judgment or increase the risk of harm to clients. (Examples of such relationships include, but are not limited to, social, financial, business, or close personal relationships with clients.) When a dual relationship cannot be avoided, professional counselors take appropriate professional precautions (such as informed consent, consultation, supervision, and documentation) to ensure that judgment is not impaired and no exploitation occurs. (See F.1.b.)

b. **Superior/Subordinate Relationships.** When professional counselors have superior or subordinate relationships of an administrative, supervisory, or evaluative nature, they do not accept superiors or subordinates as counseling clients.

A.7. Sexual Intimacies with Clients

a. **Current Clients.** Professional counselors do not have any type of sexual intimacies with clients. Professional counselors do not provide counseling services to persons with whom they have had a sexual relationship.

b. **Former Clients.** When professional services have included personal counseling, professional counselors do not engage in sexual intimacies with former clients because sexual intimacies are so frequently harmful to former clients and because such intimacies undermine public confidence in the counseling profession.

A.8. Multiple Clients

When professional counselors agree to provide counseling services to two or more persons who have a relationship (such as husband and wife, or parents and children), professional counselors attempt to clarify at the outset which person or persons are clients and the nature of the relationships professional counselors will have with each involved person. If it becomes apparent that professional counselors may be called on to perform potentially conflicting roles, they attempt to clarify, adjust, or withdraw from roles appropriately. (See B.2. and B.4.c.)

A.9. Group Counseling

a. **Screening.** Professional counselors screen prospective group participants and maintain an awareness of group participants' suitability throughout the life of the group.

b. **Protecting Clients.** In a group setting, professional counselors take reasonable precautions to protect clients from physical or psychological trauma resulting from interactions within the group.

c. **Follow-up Assistance.** When engaged in short-term treatment or training groups, professional counselors ensure there is professional assistance available during and immediately following the group experience.

A.10. Experimental Methods of Treatment

All experimental methods of treatment must be clearly indicated to prospective recipients prior to their involvement. Professional counselors utilize safety measures when using experimental methods. (See G.1.c.)

A.11. Fees and Bartering (See D.3.a. and D.3.b.)

a. **Advance Understanding.** Financial arrangements related to professional services are clearly understood by clients prior to entering the counseling relationship. (See A.12.c.)

b. **Establishing Fees.** In establishing fees for professional counseling services, professional counselors consider the financial status of clients and locality. In the event that the established fee structure is inappropriate for a client, assistance is provided in finding comparable services of acceptable cost. (See A.11.d., D.3.a., and D.3.b.)

c. **Bartering Discouraged.** Professional counselors ordinarily refrain from accepting goods or services from clients in return for counseling services because such arrangements create inherent potential for conflicts, exploitation, and distortion of the professional relationship. Professional counselors may participate in bartering only if the relationship is not exploitative, if the client requests it, and if such arrangements are an accepted practice among professionals in the local community. (See A.6.a.)

d. **Pro Bono Service.** Professional counselors contribute to society by devoting a portion of their professional activity to services for which there is little or no financial return (pro bono).

A.12. Termination And Referral

a. **Abandonment.** Professional counselors do not abandon or neglect clients in treatment. Professional counselors assist in making appropriate arrangements for the continuation of treatment, if appropriate, following termination.

b. **Inability to Assist Clients.** If professional counselors determine an inability to be of professional assistance to clients, they should either avoid initiating the counseling relationship or immediately terminate that relationship. In either event, professional counselors are knowledgeable about referral resources and suggest appropriate alternatives. If clients decline the suggested referral, professional counselors are not obligated to continue the relationship.

c. **Appropriate Termination.** Professional counselors terminate a counseling relationship, securing client agreement when possible, when it is reasonably clear that the client is no longer benefiting, when the services are no longer required, when counseling no longer serves the client's needs or interests, or when clients do not pay fees charged by professional counselors. (See C.2.g.)

A.13. Computer Technology

a. **Use of Computers.** When computer applications are used as a component of counseling services. Professional counselors must ensure that: (1) the client is intellectually, emotionally, and physically capable of using the computer application; (2) the computer application is appropriate for the needs of the client; (3) the client understands the purpose and operation of the computer application; and (4) a follow-up of client use of a computer application is provided to correct possible misconceptions, discover inappropriate use, and assess subsequent needs.

b. **Explanation of Limitations.** In view of common misconceptions related to the perceived inherent validity of computer-generated data and narrative reports. Professional counselors must ensure that the clients are provided information as a part of the counseling relationship that adequately explains the limitations of computer technology.

c. **Access to Computer Applications.** Professional counselors ensure that all client applications used to support counseling services and that the content of these applications does not discriminate against any client populations. (See A.2.a.)

Section B: Confidentiality

B.1. Right to Privacy

a. **Respect of Privacy.** Professional counselors respect their clients' right to privacy in counseling relationships. Professional counselors take appropriate steps to protect the privacy of their clients and avoid unnecessary disclosures of confidential information. (See B.6.a.)

b. **Client Waiver.** The right to privacy belongs to clients and may be waived.

c. **Exceptions.** The general requirement that professional counselors keep information confidential does not apply when the best interests of clients, welfare of others, obligations to society, or legal requirements demand that confidential information be revealed. Professional counselors consult with other mental health professionals when they are unsure of whether an exception to confidentiality exists.

d. **Legally Required Disclosure.** Before confidential information is disclosed over the client's objection because of legal requirements, professional counselors request to the court that the disclosure not be required and explain why disclosures are harmful to clients. Steps are taken to limit the extent of the unwanted disclosure. (See B.1.c.)

e. **Minimal Disclosure.** When circumstances require the disclosure of confidential information, only information that is essential is revealed. To the extent possible, clients are informed before confidential information is disclosed.

f. **Explanation of Limitations.** At the beginning of the counseling relationship, professional counselors discuss with clients the relevant limitations of confidentiality and the foreseeable uses of information generated through counseling services. (See G.2.a.)

g. **Subordinants.** Professional counselors ensure that privacy and confidentiality of clients are maintained by subordinants including employees, supervisees, clerical assistants, and volunteers. (See B.1.a.)

B.2. Groups and Families

a. **Group Counseling.** In group counseling, professional counselors define confidentiality clearly, explain its importance, and discuss the difficulties related to confidentiality involved in group counseling. The fact that confidentiality cannot be guaranteed is clearly communicated to group members.

b. **Family Counseling.** In family counseling, information from one family member cannot be disclosed to another member without permission. The privacy rights of each family member must be protected to the extent possible. (See A.8. and B.4.c.)

B.3. Minor or Incompetent Clients

When counseling clients who are minors or individuals who are unable to give voluntary, informed consent, parents or guardians may be included in the counseling process, as appropriate. At the same time, the counselor must assure the client proper confidentiality. The best interest of the client is the guiding principle. (See A.3.c.)

B.4. Records

a. **Requirement of Records.** Professional counselors maintain records that are necessary to render professional counseling services to their clients. Professional counselors have no ethical obligations to maintain unnecessary counseling records, or to keep records in a specified format or for a particular length of time, except as may be required by laws, regulations, or agency procedures.

b. **Confidentiality.** Professional counselors maintain appropriate confidentiality in creating, storing, accessing, transferring, and disposing of counseling records that are written, taped, computerized, or in any medium. (See B.1.a.)

c. **Client Access.** Professional counselors recognize that counseling records are kept for the benefit of clients and therefore provide access to records and copies of records when reasonably requested by competent clients. In situations involving multiple clients, access to records is limited to those parts of records that do not include confidential information related to another client. (See A.8., B.1.a., and B.2.b.)

d. **Disclosure or Transfer.** Professional counselors obtain the permission of clients to disclose or transfer records to third parties unless exceptions to confidentiality listed in Section B.1. exist.

B.5. Research

a. **Data Disguise Required.** Use of data derived from counseling relationships for purposes of professional counselors' training, research, or publication is confined to content that can be disguised to ensure the anonymity of the individuals involved. (See B.1.g. and G.3.d.)

b. **Agreement for Identification.** Identification of the client in a presentation or publication is possible only when the client has reviewed the material or read the report and agreed to its presentation or publication. (See G.3.d.)

c. **Permission to Record or Observe.** Professional counselors obtain permission from clients in order to electronically record or observe sessions. (See A.3.a., A.3.c., and A.3.d.)

B.6. Consultation (See E.2.)

a. **Concern for Client Privacy.** Information obtained in a consulting relationship is discussed for professional purposes only with persons clearly concerned with the case. Written and oral reports present data germane to the purposes of the consultation, and every effort is made to protect client identity and avoid undue invasion of privacy.

b. **Cooperating Agencies.** Professional counselors ensure there are defined policies and practices in other agencies serving clients that effectively protect the confidentiality of information.

Section C: Professional Responsibility

C.1. Standards Knowledge

Professional counselors have a responsibility to read, understand, and follow these *Standards of Practice* and *Ethical Standards*.

C.2. Professional Competence

a. **Boundaries of Competence.** Professional counselors practice only within the boundaries of their competence, based on their education, training, supervised experience, and appropriate professional experience.

b. **New Specialty Areas of Practice.** Professional counselors practice in specialty areas new to them only after appropriate education, training, and supervised experience. When developing skills in new specialty areas, members take reasonable steps to ensure the competence of their work and to protect others from harm.

c. **Qualified for Employment.** Professional counselors accept employment only for positions for which they are qualified by education, training, supervised experience, and appropriate professional experience. Professional counselors hire for professional counseling positions only individuals who are qualified and competent.

d. **Monitor Effectiveness.** Professional counselors continually monitor their effectiveness as professionals and take steps to improve when necessary.

e. **Ethical Issues Consultation.** Professional counselors consult with other professionals when they have questions regarding their ethical obligations or professional practice. (See H.2.a.)

f. **Continuing Education.** Professional counselors recognize the need for continuing education to maintain a reasonable level of awareness of current scientific and professional information in their fields of activity. They take steps to maintain competence in the skills they use and are open to new procedures.

g. **Impairment.** Professional counselors refrain from offering professional services when their personal problems or conflicts are likely to lead to harm to a client or others. Professional counselors are alert to the signs of impairment and seek assistance for problems. If necessary, because of impairment, professional counselors limit, suspend, or terminate their professional responsibilities. (See A.12.c.)

C.3. Advertising and Soliciting Clients

a. **Accurate Advertising.** Professional counselors advertise their services in an accurate manner that is not false, misleading, partial, out of context, inaccurate, deceptive, misleading, or fraudulent.

b. **Testimonials.** Professional counselors who use testimonials do not solicit them from counseling clients or other persons who, because of their particular circumstances, are vulnerable to undue influence.

c. **Statements by Others.** Professional counselors make reasonable efforts to ensure that statements by others made about them or the profession of counseling are accurate.

d. **Recruiting through Employment.** Professional counselors do not use their place of employment or institutional affiliation to recruit or gain clients for their private practices. (See C.5.e.)

e. **Products and Training Advertisements.** Professional counselors ensure that advertisements related to counseling-related products they have developed, or training events they are conducting are accurate and disclose adequate information for consumers to make informed choices.

f. **Promoting to Those Served.** Professional counselors do not use counseling, teaching, training, or supervision relationships to promote products they have developed or training events they are conducting in a manner that is deceptive or would exert undue influence on individuals who are vulnerable. Professors may adopt as texts, books they have authored.

C.4. Credentials

a. **Credentials Claimed.** Professional counselors claim or imply only professional credentials possessed and are responsible for correcting any misrepresentations of their credentials by others. Professional credentials include appropriate graduate degrees, accreditation of graduate programs, national voluntary certifications, government-issued certifications or licenses, ACA professional membership, or any other credential that might indicate to the public specialized knowledge or expertise in professional counseling.

b. **ACA Professional Membership.** ACA professional members may announce to the public their membership status. Regular members may not announce their ACA membership in a manner that might imply they are credentialed professional counselors.

c. **Credential Guidelines.** Professional counselors follow the guidelines for use of credentials that have been established by the entities that issue the credentials.

d. **Misrepresentation of Credentials.** Professional counselors do not attribute to credentials they hold more than the credentials represent, and do not imply that professional counselors who do not hold specific credentials are not qualified because they do not hold the credentials.

e. **Graduate Degrees.** Professional counselors who hold a graduate degree in counseling or a closely related field from a college or university that was accredited when the degree was awarded by one of the recognized regional accrediting bodies, may announce to the public such degrees in relation to their practice or status as a professional counselor. The possession of a graduate degree or degrees in other than counseling or a closely related field, or from other than a college or university that was accredited when the degree was awarded by one of the recognized regional accrediting bodies, may not be announced to the public in relation to the practice or status of members as professional counselors.

f. **Doctoral Degrees from Other Fields.** Professional counselors who hold a master's degree in counseling or a closely related field, but hold a doctoral degree from other than counseling or a closely related field do not use the term, "Dr." in their practice and do not announce to the public in relation to their practice or status as a professional counselor that they hold a doctorate.

g. **Doctoral Degrees from Nonaccredited Universities.** Professional counselors who hold a master's degree in counseling or a closely related field, and hold a doctorate in any field (including counseling) from a university that was not accredited by one of the recognized regional accrediting bodies when the doctorate degree was awarded do not use the term, "Dr." in their practice, and do not announce to the public in relation to their practice or status as a professional counselor that they hold a doctorate.

C.5. Public Responsibility

a. **Discrimination.** Professional counselors do not discriminate against clients, students, or supervisees in a manner that has a negative impact based on their age, color, culture, disability, ethnic group, gender, race, religion, sexual orientation, or socioeconomic status. (See A.2.a.)

b. **Sexual Harassment.** Professional counselors do not engage in sexual harassment. Sexual harassment is defined as sexual solicitation, physical advances, or verbal or nonverbal conduct that is sexual in nature, that occurs in connection with professional activities or roles, and that either: (1) is unwelcome, is offensive, or creates a hostile workplace environment, and professional counselors know or are told this; or (2) is sufficiently severe or intense to be abusive to a reasonable person in the context. Sexual harassment can consist of a single intense or severe act or of multiple persistent or pervasive acts.

c. **Reports to Third Parties.** Professional counselors are accurate, honest, and unbiased in reporting their professional activities and judgments to appropriate third parties including courts, health insurance companies, those who receive evaluation, reports, and others. (See B.1.g. and D.3.b.)

d. **Media Presentations.** When professional counselors provide advice or comment by means of public lectures, demonstrations, radio or television programs, prerecorded tapes, printed articles, mailed material, or other media, they take reasonable precautions to ensure that (1) the statements are based on appropriate professional counseling literature and practice; (2) the statements are otherwise consistent with these *Standards of Practice* and *Ethical Standards;* and (3) the recipients of the information are not encouraged to infer that a professional counseling relationship has been established. (See C.6.b.)

e. **Unjustified Gains.** Professional counselors refrain from using their professional positions to seek or receive unjustified personal gains, sexual favors, unfair advantage, or unearned goods or services.

C.6. Responsibility to Other Professionals

a. **Different Approaches.** Professional counselors are respectful of approaches to professional counseling that differ from their own. Professional counselors know and take into account the traditions and practices of other professional groups with which they work.

b. **Personal Public Statements.** Professional counselors are careful to clarify when making public statements when they are speaking from their personal perspectives that they are not speaking on behalf of all professional counselors or for the profession of counseling. (See C.5.d.)

c. **Clients Served by Others.** Professional counselors inform other mental health professionals serving the same client that a counseling relationship between the professional counselor and client exists and strive to establish positive and collaborative relationships with the other mental health professionals. (See A.4.)

Section D: Relationships with Other Professionals

D.1. Relationships With Employers And Employees

a. **Role Definition.** Professional counselors define and describe the parameters and levels of their professional role.

b. **Agreements.** Professional counselors establish interpersonal relations and working agreements with supervisors and subordinates regarding counseling or clinical relationships, confidentiality, distinction between public and private material, maintenance and dissemination of recorded information, workload, and accountability. Working agreements in each instance are specified and made known to those concerned.

c. **Negative Conditions.** Professional counselors provide a positive environment for clients. Professional counselors alert their employers to conditions that may be potentially disruptive or damaging to their professional responsibilities or that may limit their effectiveness.

d. **Evaluation.** Professional counselors submit regularly to professional review and evaluation.

e. **In-service.** Professional counselors are responsible for in-service development of self and staff.

f. **Goals.** Professional counselors inform their staff of goals and programs.

g. **Practices.** Professional counselors provide personnel and agency practices that guarantee and enhance the rights and welfare of each employee and recipient of agency services. Professional counselors strive to maintain the highest levels of professional services.

h. **Personnel Selection.** Professional counselors select competent staff and assign responsibilities compatible with their skills and experiences. Professional counselors maintain personnel who provide competent service to clients.

i. **Discrimination.** Professional counselors, as either employers or employees, do not engage in or condone practices that are inhumane, illegal, or unjustifiable (e.g., considerations based on age, color, culture, disability, ethnic group, gender, race, religion, sexual orientation, or socioeconomic status) in hiring, promotion, or training. (See A.2.a.)

j. **Professional Conduct.** Professional counselors have a responsibility both to the individual who is served and to the institution within which the service is performed to maintain high standards of professional conduct.

k. **Sexual Relationships.** Professional counselors do not engage in sexual relationships with individuals over whom they have supervisory, evaluative, or instructional control or authority.

l. **Employer Policies.** The acceptance of employment in an institution implies that professional counselors are in agreement with the general policies and principles of the institution. Professional counselors strive to reach agreement with employers as to acceptable standards of conduct that allow for changes in institutional policy conducive to the positive growth and development of clients.

D.2. Consultation (See B.6.)

a. **Consultation as an Option.** Professional counselors may choose to consult with any other professionally competent person about a client. In choosing a consultant, professional counselors avoid placing the consultant in a conflict of interest situation that would preclude the consultant being a proper party to the professional counselor's efforts to help the client. Should professional counselors be engaged in a work setting that compromises this consultation standard, they consult with other professionals whenever possible to consider justifiable alternatives.

b. **Consultant Competency.** Professional counselors are reasonably certain that they or the organization represented possess the necessary competencies and resources for giving the kind of current or future consulting services needed and that appropriate referral resources are available.

c. **Understanding with Client.** Professional counselors develop with their clients a clear understanding for a consultation including problem definition, goals for change, and predicted consequences of interventions selected.

d. **Consultant Goals.** The consulting relationship is one in which client adaptability and growth toward self-direction are encouraged and cultivated. Professional counselors maintain this role consistently and do not become a decision maker for the client or create a future dependency on the consultant. (See A.1.b.)

D.3. Fees for Referral

a. **Accepting Fees from Agency Clients.** Professional counselors refuse a private fee or other remuneration for rendering services to persons who are entitled to such services through the professional counselor's employing institution or agency. The policies of a particular agency may make explicit provisions for private practice with agency clients by members of its staff. In such instances, the clients must be apprised of other options open to them should they seek private counseling services. (See A.11.a., A.12.b., and C.3.d.)

b. **Sharing Fees.** Professional counselors do not split fees or engage in fee sharing arrangements with other professionals for recruiting clients for them and do not accept fees for referring clients to other professionals. (See A.11.)

D.4. Subcontractor Arrangements

When professional counselors work as subcontractors for counseling services for a third party, they have a duty to inform clients of the limits of confidentiality that the organization may place on professional counselors in providing counseling services to clients. The limits of such confidentiality ordinarily are discussed as part of the intake session. (See B.1.e. and B.1.f.)

Section E: Evaluation, Assessment, and Interpretation

E.1. General

a. **Appraisal Techniques.** The primary purpose of educational and psychological testing is to provide descriptive measures that are objective and interpretable in either comparative or absolute terms. Professional counselors recognize the need to interpret the statements in this section as applying to the whole range of appraisal techniques including test and nontest data. Test results constitute only one of a variety of pertinent sources of information for counseling decisions.

b. **Client Welfare.** In the development, publication, and utilization of educational and psychological assessment techniques, professional counselors promote the welfare and best interests of the client. They guard against the misuse of assessment results and interpretations and take reasonable steps to prevent others from misusing the information these techniques provide. They respect the client's right to know the results, the interpretations made, and the bases for their conclusions and recommendations.

E.2. Competence to Use and Interpret Tests

a. **Limits of Competence.** In providing testing and assessment services, professional counselors recognize the limits of their competence and perform only those functions for which they have been trained. They are familiar with reliability, validity, related standardization, error of measurement, and proper application and uses of the techniques they use. Professional counselors using computer-based test interpretations must be trained in the construct being measured and the specific instrument being used prior to using this type of computer application. Professional counselors do not allow the use of psychological assessment techniques by unqualified persons under their authority.

b. **Appropriate Use.** Professional counselors are responsible for the appropriate application, scoring, interpretation, and use of assessment instruments, whether they score and interpret such tests themselves or use computerized or other services.

c. **Decisions Based on Results.** Professional counselors responsible for decisions involving individuals or policies that are based on assessment results have a thorough understanding of educational and psychological measurement, including validation criteria, test research, and guidelines for test development and use.

d. **Accurate Information.** When making statements to the public about assessment instruments or techniques, professional counselors provide accurate information and avoid false claims or misconceptions. Special efforts are often required to avoid unwarranted connotations of such terms as IQ and grade equivalent scores. (See C.5.d.)

E.3. Informed Consent

a. **Explanations to Clients.** Prior to assessment, professional counselors provide explanations about the nature and purposes of testing, and the specific use of results in language the client (or other legally authorized person on behalf of the client) can understand, unless an explicit exception to this right has been agreed on in advance. Regardless of whether scoring and interpretation are completed by professional counselors, by assistants, by computer or other outside services, professional counselors take responsible steps to ensure that appropriate explanations are given to the client.

b. **Recipients of Results.** The examinee's welfare, explicit understanding, and prior agreement are the factors used when determining the recipients of the test results. Professional counselors see that appropriate interpretations accompany any release of individual or group test results. (See B.1.a. and C.5.d.)

E.4. Release of Information to Competent Professionals

a. **Misuse of Results.** Professional counselors refrain from misusing assessment results, including test results, and interpretations, and take reasonable steps to prevent the misuse of such by others. Assessment results are released only to persons qualified to use such information. (See C.5.d.)

b. **Release of Raw Data.** Raw psychological data (e.g., protocols, counseling or interview notes, or questionnaires) in which the user is identified are ordinarily released only with the written consent of the user or the user's legal representative, and are released only to persons recognized by professional counselors as competent to interpret the data. (See B.1.a.)

E.5. Proper Diagnosis of Mental Disorders

When using assessment techniques (including personal interview of the individual when appropriate) to make decisions about client care (e.g., locus of treatment, type of treatment, and recommended follow-up), professional counselors take special care to provide proper diagnoses of mental disorders. (See A.3.a. and C.5.d.)

E.6. Test Selection

In selecting tests for use in a given situation or with a particular client, professional counselors consider carefully the specific validity, reliability, psychometric limitations, and appropriateness of the tests.

E.7. Conditions of Test Administration

a. **Administration Conditions.** Tests must be administered under the same conditions that were established in their standardization. When tests are not administered under standard conditions or when unusual behavior or irregularities occur during the testing session, those conditions must be noted and the results designated as invalid or of questionable validity.

　　b. **Computer Administration.** In situations where a computer or other electronic methods are used for test administration, professional counselors are responsible for ensuring that administration programs function properly to provide clients with accurate results. (See A.13.b.)

　　c. **Unsupervised Test-taking.** Unsupervised test-taking, such as the use of tests through the mail, is not allowed. However, the use of instruments that are designed or standardized to be self-administered and self-scored is appropriate.

　　d. **Disclosure of Favorable Conditions.** Conditions that produce most favorable test results must be made known to the examinee.

E.8. *Diversity in Testing*

Professional counselors must proceed with caution when selecting assessment techniques, making evaluations, and interpreting the performance of special populations or other persons who are not represented in the norm group on which an instrument was standardized. They recognize the effects of age, color, culture, disability, ethnic group, gender, race, religion, sexual orientation, and socioeconomic status on test administration and interpretation so that results may be placed in proper perspective with other relevant factors. (See A.2.a.)

E.9. *Test Scoring and Interpretation*

　　a. **Reporting Reservations.** In reporting assessment results, professional counselors indicate any reservations that exist regarding validity or reliability because of the circumstances of the assessment or the inappropriateness of the norms for the person tested.

　　b. **Research Instruments.** Professional counselors are cautious when interpreting the results of research instruments possessing insufficient technical data. The specific purposes for the use of such instruments are stated explicitly to examinees.

　　c. **Testing Services.** Professional counselors who provide test scoring and test interpretation services to support the assessment process ensure the validity of such interpretations. They accurately describe the purpose, norms, validity, reliability, and applications of the procedures and any special qualifications applicable to their use. The public offering of an automated test interpretation service is considered a professional-to-professional consultation. The formal responsibility of the consultant is to the consultee, but the ultimate and overriding responsibility is to the client.

E.10. *Test Security*

Because prior coaching or dissemination of test materials can invalidate test results, professional counselors make reasonable efforts to maintain the integrity and security of tests and other assessment techniques consistent with the law and contractual obligations. Professional counselors do not appropriate, reproduce, or modify published tests or parts thereof without acknowledgment and permission from the publisher.

E.11. Obsolete Tests and Outdated Test Results
Professional counselors do not base their assessment or intervention decisions or recommendations on data or test results that are obsolete or outdated for the current purpose. Every effort is made to prevent the misuse of obsolete measures and test data by others. Periodic review of testing material is conducted to prevent client stereotyping.

E.12. Test Construction
In the development, publication, and utilization of educational and psychological assessment techniques, professional counselors use established scientific procedures, relevant standards, and current professional knowledge for test design.

Section F: Teaching, Training, and Supervision

F.1. Counselor Educators and Trainers
a. **Educators as Teachers and Practitioners.** Professional counselors who are responsible for developing, implementing, and supervising educational programs are skilled as teachers and practitioners. Professional counselors conduct counselor education and training programs in an ethical manner and serve as role models for professional behavior.

b. **Dual Relationships with Students and Supervisees.** In order to avoid harmful dual relationships between professional counselors and their students or supervisees, professional counselors are aware of the differential in power that exists and the student's or supervisee's possible incomprehension of that power differential. Professional counselors explain to students and supervisees the potential for the relationship to become exploitative. Professional counselors clearly define and maintain ethical, professional, and social relationship boundaries with their students and supervisees.

c. **Sexual Relationships.** Professional counselors do not engage in sexual relationships with students or supervisees and do not subject them to sexual harassment. (See A.6. and C.5.b.)

d. **Contributions to Research.** Professional counselors give credit through coauthorship or acknowledgment to students or supervisees for their contributions to scholarly and research projects. (See G.4.c.)

e. **Close Relatives.** Professional counselors do not accept close relatives as students or supervisees.

f. **Professional Knowledge.** Professional counselors serving as counselor educators or trainers are knowledgeable regarding the ethical, legal, and regulatory aspects of the profession, are skilled in applying that knowledge, and make students and supervisees aware of their responsibilities.

g. **Supervision Preparation.** Professional counselors who offer clinical supervision services are adequately prepared in supervision methods and techniques.

h. **Responsibility for Services to Clients.** Professional counselors who supervise the counseling services of others take reasonable measures to ensure that counseling services provided to clients are professional.

i. **Endorsement.** Professional counselors do not endorse students or supervisees for certification, licensure, employment, or completion of an academic or training program if professional counselors believe students or supervisees are not qualified for the endorsement. Professional counselors take reasonable steps to assist students or supervisees who are not qualified for an endorsement to become qualified.

F.2. *Counselor Education and Training Programs*

a. **Orientation.** Prior to accepting students, professional counselors orient them to the counselor education or training program's expectations, including but not limited to the following: (1) the type and level of skill acquisition required for successful completion of the training; (2) subject matter to be covered; (3) basis for evaluation; (4) training components that encourage self-growth or self-disclosure as part of the training process; (5) the type of supervision settings and requirements of the sites for required clinical field experiences; (6) student and supervisee evaluation and dismissal policies and procedures; and (7) up-to-date employment prospects for graduates.

b. **Integration of Study and Practice.** Professional counselors establish counselor education and training programs that integrate academic study and supervised practice.

c. **Evaluation.** The levels of competency expected, appraisal methods, and timing of evaluations for both the didactic and experimental components are clearly stated to students and supervisees in advance of the training by professional counselors. Professional counselors provide students and supervisees with periodic performance appraisal and evaluation feedback throughout a training program.

d. **Teaching Ethics.** Professional counselors make students and supervisees aware of the ethical responsibilities and standards of the profession and the students' and supervisees' ethical responsibilities to the profession. (See C.1. and F.3.e.)

e. **Peer Relationships.** When students or supervisees are assigned to lead counseling groups or provide clinical supervision for their peers, professional counselors ensure that students and supervisees placed in these roles do not have personal or adverse relationships with peers and that they understand they have the same ethical obligations as counselor educators, trainers, and supervisors. Professional counselors ensure that the rights of peers are not compromised when students or supervisees are assigned to lead counseling groups or provide clinical supervision.

f. **Varied Theoretical Positions.** Professional counselors present varied theoretical positions so that students and supervisees may make comparisons and have an opportunity to develop their own positions. Professional counselors provide information concerning the scientific basis of professional practice. (See C.6.a.)

g. **Field Placements.** Professional counselors develop clear policies within their training program regarding field placement and other clinical experiences. Professional counselors provide clearly stated roles and responsibilities for the student or supervisee, the site supervisor, and the program supervisor. They ensure that site supervisors are qualified to provide supervision and are informed of their professional and ethical responsibilities in this role. Professional counselors avoid dual relationships as site supervisor and evaluator in the student's or supervisee's training program. Professional counselors do not accept any form of professional services, fees, commissions, reimbursement, or remuneration from a site for a student or supervisee placement.

h. **Diversity in Programs.** Professional counselors are responsive to their institution's and program's recruitment and retention needs for training program administrators, faculty, and students with diverse backgrounds and special needs. (See A.2.a.)

F.3. Students and Supervisees

a. **Limitations.** Professional counselors, through continual evaluation and appraisal, are aware of the academic and personal limitations of students and supervisees that might impede future performance. Professional counselors assist limited students and supervisees in securing remedial assistance and dismiss from a training program students and supervisees who are unable to provide competent service. Professional counselors seek professional consultation and document the reasoning for their professional judgment to refer students and supervisees for assistance or to dismiss students and supervisees. Professional counselors ensure that students and supervisees have recourse to address decisions made to require them to seek assistance or to dismiss them.

b. **Self-growth Experiences.** Professional counselors use professional judgment when designing training experiences conducted by the professional counselors themselves that require student and supervisee self-growth or self-disclosure. Safeguards are provided to ensure that students and supervisees are aware of the ramifications their self-disclosure may have upon professional counselors whose primary role as teacher, trainer, or supervisor requires acting on ethical obligations to the profession. Students and supervisees are assured that the evaluation process for training will focus on the competencies required by the training and not on their performance as group members. (See A.6.)

c. **Counseling for Students and Supervisees.** If students or supervisees request counseling, professional counselors provide them with acceptable alternatives that do not require professional counselors to serve as a counselor to students or supervisees over whom they hold administrative, teaching, or evaluative roles. (See A.6.b.)

   d. **Clients of Students and Supervisees.** Professional counselors assure that the clients at field placements are aware of the services rendered and the qualifications of the students and supervisees rendering those services. Clients receive professional disclosure information and are informed of the limits of confidentiality. Client permission is obtained in order for the students and supervisees to use any information concerning the counseling relationship in the training process. (See B.1.e.)

   e. **Standards for Students and Supervisees.** Students and supervisees preparing to become professional counselors follow the *Standards of Practice* and *Ethical Standards* of professional counselors. Students and supervisees have the same obligations to clients as those required of professional counselors. (See H.1.)

Section G: Research and Publication

G.1. Research Responsibilities

   a. **Use of Human Subjects.** Professional counselors plan, design, conduct, and report research in a manner consistent with pertinent ethical principles, federal and state laws, host institutional regulations, and scientific standards governing research with human subjects.

   b. **Deviation from Standard Practices.** To the extent that a research problem suggests a deviation from standard acceptable practices, professional counselors seek consultation and observe stringent safeguards to protect the rights of research participants. (See B.6.)

   c. **Precautions to Avoid Injury.** Professional counselors who conduct research with human subjects are responsible for the subjects' welfare throughout the experiment and take reasonable precautions to avoid causing injurious psychological, physical, or social effects to their subjects.

   d. **Principal Researcher Responsibility.** The ultimate responsibility for ethical research practice lies with the principal researcher although others involved in the research activities share ethical obligation and full responsibility for their own actions.

   e. **Minimum Interference.** In conducting research, professional counselors limit the degree of interference with the participants' milieu to the minimum warranted by the appropriate research design.

   f. **Diversity.** Professional counselors are sensitive to diversity research issues with special populations and seek consultation when appropriate. (See A.2.a. and B.6.)

G.2. Informed Consent

   a. **Topics Generated.** In obtaining informed consent for research, professional counselors use language that is understandable to research participants and include the following: (1) a fair explanation of the purpose and procedures to be followed; (2) identification of any procedures that are experimental; (3) a description of the attendant discomforts and risks; (4) a description of the benefits or changes in individuals or organizations that might be reasonably expected; (5) a disclosure of appropriate alternative procedures that would be advantageous for subjects; (6) an offer to answer any inquiries concerning the procedures; (7) a description of any limitations on confidentiality; and (8) instruction that subjects are free to withdraw their consent and to discontinue participation in the project at any time. (See B.1.f.)

b. **Deception.** Professional counselors do not conduct research involving deception unless alternative procedures are not feasible and the prospective value of the research justifies the deception. When the methodological requirements of a study necessitate concealment or deception, the investigator is required to ensure the participants' understanding of the reasons for this action as soon as possible.

c. **Voluntary Participation.** Participation in research must be voluntary and without any imposed penalty for refusal to participate. Involuntary participation is appropriate only when it can be demonstrated that participation will have no harmful effects on subjects and is essential to the investigation.

d. **Confidentiality of Information.** Information obtained about research participants during the course of an investigation is confidential. When the possibility exists that others may obtain access to such information, ethical research practice requires that the possibility, together with the plans for protecting confidentiality, be explained to participants as a part of the procedure for obtaining informed consent. (See B.1.e.)

e. **Those Incapable of Giving Informed Consent.** When a person is legally incapable of giving informed consent, professional counselors provide an appropriate explanation, obtain agreement to participate and obtain appropriate consent from a legally authorized person.

f. **Commitments to Participants.** Professional counselors take reasonable measures to honor all commitments to research participants.

g. **Explanations after Data Collection.** After the data are collected, professional counselors provide participants with a full clarification of the nature of the study to remove any misconceptions that may have arisen. Where scientific or human values justify delaying or withholding information, professional counselors take reasonable measures to avoid causing harm.

h. **Undesirable Consequences for Participants.** Where research procedures may result in undesirable consequences for the participant, professional counselors detect and remove or correct these consequences, including where relevant, long-term after effects are possible.

i. **Agreement to Cooperate.** Professional counselors who agree to cooperate with another individual in research or publication incur an obligation to cooperate as promised in terms of punctuality of performance and with full regard to the completeness and accuracy of the information required.

j. **Informed Consent for Agencies.** In the pursuit of research, professional counselors give sponsoring agencies, institutions, and publication channels the same respect and opportunity for giving informed consent that they accord to individual research participants. They are aware of their obligation to future research workers and ensure that host institutions are given feedback information and proper acknowledgment.

G.3. Reporting Results

a. **Information Affecting Outcome.** When reporting research results, professional counselors explicitly mention all variables and conditions known to the investigator that may have affected the outcome of a study or the interpretation of data.

b. **Accurate Results.** Professional counselors plan, conduct, and report research in a manner that minimizes the possibility that results will be misleading. Professional counselors conduct and report research studies accurately. They provide thorough discussions of the limitations of their data and alternative hypotheses. Professional counselors do not engage in fraudulent research, distort data, misrepresent data, or deliberately bias their results.

c. **Obligation to Report Unfavorable Results.** Professional counselors communicate to other professional counselors the results of any research judged to be of professional value. Results that reflect unfavorably on institutions, programs, services, prevailing opinions, or vested interests are not withheld.

d. **Identity of Subjects.** Professional counselors who supply data, aid in the research of another person, report research results, or make original data available, must take due care to disguise the identity of respective subjects in the absence of specific authorization from the subjects to do otherwise. (See B.1.g. and B.5.a.)

e. **Replication Studies.** Professional counselors are obligated to make available sufficient original research data to qualified professionals who may wish to replicate the study.

G.4. Publication

a. **Recognition of Others.** When conducting and reporting research, professional counselors are familiar with and give recognition to previous work on the topic, observe copyright laws, and give full credit to those to whom credit is due. (See G.4.c.)

b. **Contributors.** Professional counselors give credit through joint authorship, acknowledgment, footnote statements, or other appropriate means to those who have contributed significantly to research or concepts in accordance with such contributions. The principal contributor is listed first and minor technical or professional contributions are acknowledged in notes or introductory statements.

c. **Student Research.** For an article that is substantially based on a student's dissertation or thesis, the student is listed as the principal author. (See F.1.d.)

d. **Duplicate Submission.** Professional counselors submit manuscripts for consideration to only one journal at a time if journals require that procedure. In addition, manuscripts that are published in whole or in substantial part in another journal or published work are not submitted for publication without acknowledgment and permission from the previous publication.

e. **Professional Review.** Professional counselors who review material submitted for publication, grant, or other research or scholarly purposes respect the confidentiality and proprietary rights of those who submitted it.

Section H: Resolving Ethical Issues

H.1. Knowledge of Standards
Professional counselors are familiar with these *Standards of Practice* and *Ethical Standards,* and other applicable ethics codes. Lack of knowledge or misunderstanding of an ethical responsibility is not a defense when charged with unethical conduct. (See F.3.e.)

H.2. Suspected Violations
a. **Ethical Behavior Expected.** Professional counselors expect professional associates to adhere to ethical standards. When professional counselors possess information that raises doubts as to whether a mental health professional is acting in an ethical manner, they must take appropriate actions.

b. **Consultation.** When uncertain as to whether a particular situation or course of action would violate ethical standards, professional counselors consult with other Professional counselors who are knowledgeable about ethics, with colleagues, with applicable ethics committees, or with appropriate authorities. (See C.2.e.)

c. **Organization Conflicts.** If the demands of an organization with which professional counselors are affiliated pose a conflict with ethical standards, professional counselors work toward change within the organization to allow full adherence to ethical standards.

d. **Informal Resolution.** When professional counselors have reasons to believe that another mental health professional is violating an ethical standard, if appropriate or feasible, they attempt to first resolve the issue informally by bringing it to the attention of the other mental health professional if such action does not violate confidentiality rights that may be involved.

e. **Reporting Suspected Violations.** When an informal resolution is not appropriate or feasible, professional counselors take further action such as reporting the suspected ethical violation to state or national ethics committees or to state licensing boards, unless this action conflicts with confidentiality rights that cannot be resolved. ACA members must report suspected violations of the ACA *Standards of Practice* and *Ethical Standards* to the ACA Ethics Committee.

f. **Frivolous Complaints.** Professional counselors do not initiate, participate in, or encourage the filing of ethics complaints that are frivolous or intend to harm a mental health professional rather than to protect clients or the public.

H.3. Cooperation with Ethics Committees

Professional counselors assist in the process of enforcing ethical standards. Professional counselors cooperate with investigations, proceedings, and requirements of the ACA Ethics Committee or ethics committees of other duly constituted associations or boards having jurisdiction over those charged with a violation.

Author Index

Subject Index

i